THE

SOUL OF THE WAR

BY

PHILIP GIBBS

POPULAR EDITION

LONDON
WILLIAM HEINEMANN

CONTENTS

CHAPTER I

THE FOREBODING

1

WHAT man may lay bare the soul of England as it was stirred during those days of July when suddenly, without any previous warning, loud enough to reach the ears of the mass of people, there came the menace of a great, bloody war, threatening all that had seemed so safe and so certain in our daily life ? England suffered in those summer days a shock which thrilled to its heart and brain with an enormous emotion such as a man who has been careless of truth and virtue experiences at a " Revivalist " meeting or at a Catholic mission when some passionate preacher breaks the hard crust of his carelessness and convinces him that death and the judgment are very near, and that all the rottenness of his being will be tested in the furnace of a spiritual agony. He goes back to his home feeling a changed man in a changed world: The very ticking of the clock on the mantelpiece of his sitting-room speaks to him with a portentous voice, like the thunder-strokes of fate. Death is coming closer to him at every tick. His little home, his household goods, the daily routine of his toil for the worldly rewards of life, his paltry jealousies of next-door neighbours are dwarfed to insignificance. They no longer matter, for the judgment of God is at hand. The smugness of his self-complacency, his life-long hypocrisy in the shirking of truth, are broken up. He feels naked, and afraid, clinging only to the hope that he may yet have time to build up a new character, to acquire new spiritual strength, and to do some of the things he has left undone—if only he had his time over again !—before the enemy comes to grips with him in a final bout.

1   A

That, with less simplicity and self-consciousness, was the spirit of England in those few swift days which followed the Austrian ultimatum to Serbia, and Germany's challenge to France and Russia. At least in some such way one might express the mentality of the governing, official, political, and so-called intellectual classes of the nation who could read between the lines of diplomatic dispatches, and saw, clearly enough, the shadow of Death creeping across the fields of Europe and heard the muffled beating of his drum.

Some of our public men and politicians must have spent tortured days and nights in those last days of July. They, too, like the sinner at the mission service, must have seen the judgment of God approaching them. Of what avail now were their worldly ambitions and their jealousies ? They too had been smug in their self-complacency, hypocrites, shirkers of truth and stirrers up of strife, careless of consequences. If only they could have their time over again ! Great God ! was this war with Germany an unavoidable horror, or, if the worst came, was there still time to cleanse the nation of its rottenness, to close up its divisions and to be ready for the frightful conflict ?

2

All things were changed in England in a day or two. The things that had mattered no longer mattered. The Arming of Ulster and the Nationalists, Votes for Women, Easier Divorce, the Craze for Night Clubs—had any of these questions any meaning now ? A truce was called by the men who had been inflaming the people's passion to the point of civil war. The differences of political parties seemed futile and idiotic now that the nation itself might be put to the uttermost test of endurance by the greatest military power in Europe. In fear, as well as with a nobler desire to rise out of the slough of the old folly of life, the leaders of the nation abandoned their feuds. Out of the past voices called to them. Their blood thrilled to old sentiments and old traditions which had seemed to belong to the lumber-room of history, with the moth-eaten garments of their ancestors. There were no longer Liberals or Conservatives or Socialists, but only Englishmen, Scotsmen, Irishmen and Welshmen, with the old instincts of race and with the old fighting qualities which in the past they had used against each other. Before the common menace they closed up their ranks.

3

Yet there was no blood-lust in England, during those days of July. None of the old Jingo spirit which had inflamed great crowds before the Boer War was visible now or found expression. Among people of thoughtfulness there was a kind of dazed incredibility that this war would really happen, and at the back of this unbelief a tragic foreboding and a kind of shame—a foreboding that secret forces were at work for war, utterly beyond the control of European democracies who desired to live in peace, and a shame that civilization itself, all the ideals and intellectual activities and democratic progress of modern Europe, would be thrust back into the primitive barbarities of war, with its wholesale, senseless slaughter, its bayonet slashings and disembowellings—" heroic charges " as they are called by the journalists—and its gospel of hatred. So humanity was still beastlike, as twenty centuries ago, and the message of Christianity was still unheard ? Socialistic theories, Hague conventions, the progress of intelligence in modern democracy had failed utterly, and once again, if this war came upon the world, not by the will of simple peoples, but by the international intrigues of European diplomats, the pride of a military caste and the greed of political tradesmen, the fields of Europe would be drenched with the blood of our best manhood and Death would make an unnatural harvesting. Could nothing stop this bloody business ?

4

I think the Middle Classes in England—the plain men and women who do not belong to intellectual cliques or professional politics—were stupefied by the swift development of the international " situation," as it was called in the news-

papers, before the actual declarations of war which followed
with a series of thunder-claps heralding a universal tempest.
Was it true then that Germany had a deadly enmity against
us, and warlike ambitions which would make a shambles of
Europe ?   Or was it still only newspaper talk, to provide
sensations for the breakfast table ?   How could they tell,
these plain, ignorant men who had always wanted straight-
forward facts ?   For years the newspaper press of England
had been divided over Germany's ambitions, precisely as,
according to their political colour, they had been divided over
Tariff Reform or Home Rule for Ireland.   The Liberal Press
had jeered at the hair-raising fears of the Conservative Press,
and the latter had answered the jeers by more ferocious attacks
upon German diplomacy and by more determined efforts to
make bad blood between the two nations.   The Liberal
Press had dwelt lovingly upon the brotherly sentiment of the
German people for their English cousins.   The Conservative
Press had searched out the inflammatory speeches of the
war lords and the junker politicians.   It had seemed to the
man in the street a controversy as remote from the actual
interests of his own life—as remote from the suburban garden
in which he grew his roses or from the golf links on which
he spent his Saturday afternoons as a discussion on the
canals of Mars.   Now and again, in moments of political excitement, he had taken sides and adopted newspaper phrases
as his own, declaring with an enormous gravity which he did
not really feel that " The German Fleet was a deliberate
menace to our naval supremacy," or joining in the chorus of
" We want eight and we won't wait," or expressing his utter
contempt for " all this militarism," and his belief in the
" international solidarity " of the new democracy.   But there
never entered his inmost convictions that the day might come
during his own lifetime when he—a citizen of Suburbia—
might have to fight for his own hearthside and suffer the
intolerable horrors of war while the roses in his garden were
trampled down in mud and blood, and while his own house
came clattering down like a pack of cards—the family photographs, the children's toys, the piano which he had bought on

the hire system, all the household gods which he worshipped, mixed up in a heap of ruin—as afterwards at Scarborough and Hartlepool, Ipswich, and Southend.

If such a thing were possible, why had the nation been duped by its Government ? Why had we been lulled into a false sense of security without a plain statement of facts which would have taught us to prepare for the great ordeal ? The Government ought to have known and told the truth. If this war came the manhood of the nation would be unready and untrained. We should have to scramble an army together, when perhaps it would be too late.

The middle classes of England tried to comfort themselves even at the eleventh hour by incredulity.

" Impossible ! " they cried. " The thing is unbelievable. It is only a newspaper scare ! "

But as the hours passed the shadow of war crept closer, and touched the soul of Europe.

5

In Fleet Street, which is connected with the wires of the world, there was a feverish activity. Walls and tables were placarded with maps. Photographs, gazetteers, time tables, cablegrams littered the rooms of editors and news editors. There was a procession of literary adventurers up the steps of those buildings in the Street of Adventure—all those men who get lost somewhere between one war and another and come out with claims of ancient service on the battlefields of Europe when the smell of blood is scented from afar ; and scores of new men of sporting instincts and jaunty confidence, eager to be " in the middle of things," willing to go out on any terms so long as they could see " a bit of fun," ready to take all risks. Special correspondents, press photographers, the youngest reporters on the staff, sub-editors emerging from little dark rooms with a new excitement in eyes that had grown tired with proof correcting, passed each other on the stairs and asked for their Chance. It was a chance of seeing the greatest drama in life with real properties, real corpses, real blood, real horrors with a devilish thrill in them. It was not to be missed by any self-respecting journalist to whom all life is a stage play which he describes and criticises from a free seat in the front of the house.

Yet in those newspaper offices in Fleet Street there was no real certainty. Even the foreign editors who are supposed to have an inside knowledge of international politics were not definite in their assertions. Interminable discussions took place over their maps and cablegrams. " War is certain." " There will be no war as far as England is concerned." " Sir Edward Grey will arrange an international conference." " Germany is bluffing. She will climb down at the eleventh hour. How can she risk a war with France, Russia, and England ? " " England will stand out." " But our honour ? What about our understanding with France ? "

There was a profound ignorance at the back of all these opinions, assertions, discussions. Fleet Street, in spite of the dogmatism of its leading articles, did not know the truth and had never searched for it with a sincerity which would lead now to a certain conviction. All its thousands of articles on the subject of our relations with Germany had been but a clash of individual opinions coloured by the traditional policy of each paper, by the prejudice of the writers and by the influence of party interests. The brain of Fleet· Street was but a more intense and a more vibrant counterpart of the national psychology, which in these hours of enormous crisis was bewildered by doubt and, in spite of all its activity, incredulous of the tremendous possibility that in a few days England might be engaged in the greatest war since the Napoleonic era, fighting for her life.

6

On my own lips there was the same incredulity when I said good-bye. It was on July 29, and England had not yet picked up the gauntlet which Germany had flung into the face of European peace.

" I shall be back in a few days. Armageddon is still a long way off. The idea of it is too ridiculous and too damnable ! "

I lay awake on the night before I left England with the credentials of a war correspondent on a roving commission, and there came into my head a vision of the hideous thing which was being hatched in the council chambers of Europe, even as the little clock ticked on my bedroom mantelpiece. I thrust back this vision of blood by old arguments, old phrases which had become the rag-tags of political writers.

War with Germany ? A war in which half the nations of Europe would be flung against each other in a deadly struggle—millions against millions of men belonging to the peoples of the highest civilization ? No, it was inconceivable and impossible. Why should England make war upon Germany or Germany upon England ? We were alike in blood and character, bound to each other by a thousand ties of tradition and knowledge and trade and friendship. All the best intellect of Germany was friendly to us. . . .

7

In Hamburg two years ago I had listened to speeches about all that, obviously sincere, emotional in their protestations of racial comradeship. That young poet who had become my friend, who had taken me home to his house in the country and whose beautiful wife had plucked roses for me in her garden, and said in her pretty English, " I send my best love with them to England "—was he a liar when he spoke fine and stirring words about the German admiration for English literature and life, and when—it was late in the evening and we had drunk some wine—he passed his arm through mine and said, " If ever there were to be a war between our two countries I and all my friends in Hamburg would weep at the crime and the tragedy."

On that trip to Hamburg we were banqueted like kings, we English journalists, and the tables were garlanded with flowers in our honour, and a thousand compliments were paid to us with the friendliest courtesy. Were they all liars, these smiling Germans who had clinked glasses with us ?

Only a few weeks before this black shadow of war had loomed up with its deadly menace a great party of German.

editors had returned our visit and once again I had listened
to speeches about the blood-brotherhood of the two nations,
a little bored by the stale phrases, but glad to sit between
these friendly Germans whom I had met in their own country.
We clinked glasses again, sang " God Save the King " and
the " Wacht am Rhein," compared the character of German
and English literature, of German and English women, clasped
hands, and said, " Auf wiedersehen ! "   Were we all liars in
that room, and did any of the men there know that when
words of friendship were on their lips there was hatred in
their hearts and in each country a stealthy preparation for
great massacres of men ?   Did any of those German editors
hear afar off the thunderstrokes of the Krupp guns which
even then were being tested for the war with France and
England ?   I believe now that some of them must have
known. . . .

8

Perhaps I ought to have known, too, remembering the
tour which I had made in Germany two years before.

It was after the Agadir incident, and I had been sent to
Germany by my newspaper on a dovelike mission of peace,
to gather sentiments of good will to England fr m prominent
public men who might desire out of their intellectual friendship to us to pour oil on the troubled waters which had been
profoundly stirred by our challenge to Germany's foreign
policy.   I had a sheaf of introductions, which I presented in
Berlin and Leipzig, Frankfort and Düsseldorf, and other
German towns.

The first man to whom I addressed myself with amiable
intent was a distinguished democrat who knew half the
members of the House of Commons and could slap Liberal
politicians on the back with more familiarity than I should
dare to show.   He had spent both time and trouble in
organizing friendly visits between the working men and
municipalities of both countries.   But he was a little
restrained and awkward in his manners when I handed him
my letter of introduction.   Presently he left the room for a

few minutes and I saw on his desk a German newspaper with a leading article signed by his name. I read it and ,was amazed to find that it was a violent attack upon England, demanding unforgetfulness and unforgiveness of the affront which we had put upon Germany in the Morocco crisis. When the man came back I ventured to question him about this article, and he declared that his old friendship for England had undergone a change. He could give me no expression of good will.

I could get no expression of good will from any public man in Germany. I remember an angry interview with an ecclesiastic in Berlin, a personal friend of the Kaiser, though for many years an ardent admirer of England.

He paced up and down the room with noiseless footsteps on a soft carpet.

" It is no time for bland words ! " he said. " England has insulted us. Such acts are not to be tolerated by a great nation like ours. There is only one answer to them, and it is the answer of the sword ! "

I ventured to speak of Christian influences which should hold men back from the brutality of war.

" Surely the Church must always preach the gospel of peace ? Otherwise it is false to the spirit of Christ."

He believed that I intended to insult him, and in a little while he rang the bell for my dismissal.

Even Edward Bernstein, the great leader of the Social Democrats, could give me no consoling words for my paper.

" The spirit of nationality," he said—and I have a note of his words—" is stronger than abstract ideals. Let England make no mistake. If war were declared to-morrow the Social Democrats would march as one man in defence of the Fatherland. . . . And you must admit that England, or rather the English Foreign Office, has put rather a severe strain upon our pride and patience ! "

My mission was a failure. I came back without any expressions of good will from public men and with an uneasy sense of dangerous fires smouldering beneath the political life of Germany—fires of hate not easily quenched by friendly or sentimental articles in the English Liberal Press. And yet among the ordinary people in railway trains and restaurants, beer-halls and hotels, I had found no hostility to me as an Englishman. Rather they had gone out of their way to be friendly. Some of the university students of Leipzig had taken me to a public dance, expressed their admiration for English sports, and asked my opinion about the merits of various English boxers of whom I had to confess great ignorance. They were good friendly fellows and I liked them. In various towns of Germany I found myself admiring the cheerful, bustling *gemuthlichkeit* of the people, the splendid organization of their civic life, their industry and national spirit. Walking among them sometimes, I used to ponder over the possibility of that *unvermeidliche krieg*— that " unavoidable war " which was being discussed in all the newspapers. Did these people want war with England or with anyone ? The laughter of the clerks and shop-girls swarming down the Friedrichstrasse, the peaceful enjoyment of the middle-class crowds of husbands and wives, lovers and sweethearts, steaming in the heat of brilliantly lighted beer-halls seemed to make my question preposterous. The spirit of the German people was essentially peaceful and democratic. Surely the weight of all this middle-class common sense would save them from any criminal adventures proposed by a military caste rattling its sabre on state occasions ? So I came back with a conflict of ideas. . . .

9

A little bald-headed man came into London about two years ago, and his arrival was noted in a newspaper paragraph. It appeared that he was a great statistician. He had been appointed by the Governments of Canada and the United States jointly to prepare a " statistical survey of Europe," whatever that may mean. I was sent down to call upon him somewhere in the Temple, and I was to get him to talk about his statistics.

But after my introduction he shut the door carefully and,

with an air of anxious inquiry through his gold-rimmed spectacles, asked a strange question :

" Are you an honest young man and a good patriot ? "

I could produce no credentials for honesty or patriotism, but hoped that I might not fail in either.

" I suppose you have come to talk to me about my statistics," he said.

I admitted that this was my mission.

" They are unimportant," he said, " compared with what I have to tell you. I am going to talk to you about Germany. The English people ought to know what I have learnt during a year's experience in that country, where I have lived all the time in the company of public officials. Sir, it seems to me that the English people do not know that the entire genius of intellectual Germany is directed to a war against England. It dominates their thoughts and dreams, and the whole activity of their national intelligence."

For an hour the little bald-headed man spoke to me of all he had heard and learnt of Germany's enmity to England during twelve months in official circles. He desired to give this information to an English newspaper of standing and authority. He thought the English people had a right to know.

I went back to my office more disturbed than I cared to admit even to myself. There had been a kind of terror in the voice of the little man who had found time for other interests besides his " statistical survey of Europe." It seemed that he believed himself in the possession of an enormous and terrible secret threatening the destiny of our Empire. Yet nobody would believe him when he told it, however fervently. My editor would not believe him, and none of his words were published, in my paper or any other. But sometimes I used to remember him and wonder whether perhaps in all such warnings that came to us there were not a horrible truth which one day, when brutally revealed, would make a mockery of all those men in England who pooh-poohed the peril, and of the idealists who believed that friendly relations with Germany could be secured by

friendly words.   Meanwhile the Foreign Office did not reveal
its secrets or give any clear guidance to the people as to perils
or policy—to the people who would pay in blood for ignorance.

10

When I stood on the deck of the Channel boat in Dover
Harbour looking back on England, whose white cliffs gleamed
faintly through the darkness, a sense of tragic certainty
came to me that a summons of war would come to England,
asking for her manhood.   Perhaps it would come to-night.
The second mate of the boat came to the side of the steamer
and stared across the inky waters, on which there were
shifting pathways of white radiance, as the searchlights of
distant warships swept the sea.

" God ! " he said, in a low voice.

" Do you think it will come to-night ? " I asked, in the
same tone of voice.   We spoke as though our words were
dangerous.

" It's likely.   The German fleet won't wait for any
declaration, I should say, if they thought they could catch
us napping. . . . But they won't.   I fancy we're ready for
them—here, anyhow ! "

He jerked his thumb at some dark masses looming through
the darkness in the harbour, caught here and there by a
glint of metal reflected in the water.   They were cruisers
and submarines nosing towards the harbour mouth.

" There's a crowd of 'em ! " said the second mate, " and
they stretch across the Channel. . . . The Reserve men
have been called out—taken off the trams in Dover to-night.
But the public has not yet woken up to the meaning of it."

He stared out to sea again, and it was some minutes
before he spoke again.

" Queer, isn't it ?   They'll all sleep in their beds to-night
as though nothing out of the way were happening.   And
yet, in a few hours, maybe, there'll be Hell !   That's what
it's going to be—Hell and damnation, if I know anything
about war ! "

" What's that ? " I asked, pointing to the harbour bar.

From each side of the harbour two searchlights made a straight beam of light, and in the glare of it there passed along the surface of the sea, as it seemed, a golden serpent with shining scales.

"Sea-gulls," said the mate. "Scared, I expect, by all these lights. They know something's in the wind. Perhaps they can smell—blood!"

He spoke with a laugh, but it had a strange sound.

11

In the saloon were about a dozen men, drinking at the bar. They were noisy and had already drunk too much. By their accent it was easy to guess that they came from Manchester, and by their knapsacks, which contained all their baggage, it was obvious that they were on a short trip to Paris. A man from Cook's promised them a "good time!" There were plenty of pretty girls in Paris. They slapped him on the back and called him "old chap!"

A quiet gentleman seated opposite to me on a leather lounge—I met him afterwards at the British Embassy in Paris—caught my eye and smiled.

"They don't seem to worry about the international situation. Perhaps it will be easier to get to Paris than to get back again!"

"And now drinks all round, lads!" said one of the trippers.

On deck there were voices singing. It was the hymn of the Marseillaise. I went up towards the sound and found a party of young Frenchmen standing aft, waving farewells to England, as the syren hooted, above a rattle of chains and the crash of the gangway which dropped to the quayside. They had been called back to their country to defend its soil and, unlike the Englishmen drinking themselves fuddled, were intoxicated by a patriotic excitement.

"Vive l'Angleterre!"

An answer came back from the quayside:

"Vive la France!"

It was to this shout that we warped away from the jetty

and made for the open sea. A yacht with white sails all agleam as it crossed the bar of a searchlight so that it seemed like a fairy ship in the vision of a dream, crept into the harbour and then fluttered into the darkness below the Admiralty pier.

"That's a queer kind of craft to meet to-night!" I said to the second mate. "What is she doing?"

"I'd like to know. She's got a German skipper and crew. Spies all of them, I guess. But nobody seems to bother."

There were spies watching our own boat as we went across the Channel, but they were on English vessels. Searchlights from many warships turned their rays upon us, staring at us from stem to stern, following us with a far-flung vigilance, transmuting the base metal of our funnel and brasswork into shining silver and burnished gold. As I stared back into the blinding rays I felt that the eyes of the warships could look into my very soul, and I walked to the other side of the boat as though abashed by this scrutiny. I looked back to the shore, with its winking lights and looming cliffs, and wished I could see by some kind of searchlight into the soul of England on this night of fate. Beyond the cliffs of Dover, in the profound darkness of the night, England seemed asleep. Did not her people hear the beating of Death's war drums across the fields of Europe, growing louder and louder, so that on a cross-Channel boat I heard it booming in my ears, louder than the wind?

CHAPTER II

MOBILIZATION

1

THE thunderbolt came out of a blue sky and in the midst of a brilliant sunshine which gleamed blindingly above the white houses of Paris and flung back shadows from the poplars across the long straight roads between the fields of France. The children were playing as usual in the gardens of the Tuileries, and their white-capped nurses were sewing and chatting in the shade of the scorched trees. The old bird man was still calling " Viens ! Viens ! " to the sparrows who came to perch on his shoulders and peck at the bread between his lips, and Punch was still performing his antique drama in the Petit Guignol to laughing audiences of boys and girls. The *bâteaux mouches* on the Seine were carrying heavy loads of pleasure-seekers to Sèvres and other riverside haunts. In the Pavilion Bleu at St. Cloud elegant little ladies of the demi-monde sipped rose-tinted ices and said for a thousand times : " Ciel, comme il fait chaud ! " and slapped the hands of beaky-nosed young men with white slips beneath their waistcoats and shiny boots and other symbols of a high civilization. Americans in Panama hats sauntered down the Rue de Rivoli, staring in the shop windows at the latest studies of nude women, and at night went in pursuit of adventure to Montmartre, where the orchestras at the Bal Tabarin were still fiddling mad tangoes in a competition of shrieking melody and where troops of painted ladies in the Folies Bergères still paraded in the *promenoir* with languorous eyes, through wafts of sickly scent. The little tables were all along the pavements of the boulevards and the *terrasses* were crowded with all

15

those bourgeois Frenchmen and their women who do not move out of Paris even in the dogdays, but prefer the scenery of their familiar streets to that of Dieppe and Le Touquet. It was the same old Paris—crowded with Cook's tourists and full of the melody of life as it is played by the hoot of motor horns, the clang of steam trams, the shrill-voiced camelots shouting " La Presse ! La Presse ! " and of the light laughter of women.

Then suddenly the thunderbolt fell with its signal of war, and in a few days Paris was changed as though by some wizard's spell. Most of the children vanished from the Tuileries gardens with their white-capped nurses, and the sparrows searched in vain for their bird man. Punch gave a final squawk of dismay and disappeared when the theatre of the Petit Guignol was packed up to make way for a more tragic drama. A hush fell upon Montmartre, and the musicians in its orchestras packed up their instruments and scurried with scared faces—to Berlin, Vienna, and Budapesth. No more boats went up to Sèvres and St. Cloud with crowds of pleasure-seekers. The Seine was very quiet beneath its bridges, and in the Pavilion Bleu no dainty creatures sat sipping rose-tinted ices or slapped the hands of the beaky-nosed boys who used to pay for them. The women were hiding in their rooms, asking God—even before the war they used to ask God funny questions—how they were going to live now that their lovers had gone away to fight, leaving them with nothing but the memory of a last kiss wet with tears. It was not enough to live on for many days.

2

During the last days of July and the first days of August Paris was stunned by the shock of this menace, which was approaching swiftly and terribly. War ! But why ? Why, in the name of God, should France be forced into a war for which she was not prepared, for which she had no desire, because Austria had issued an ultimatum to Servia, demanding the punishment of a nation of cut-throats for the murder of an unnecessary Archduke ?   Germany was behind the business, Germany was forcing the pace, exasperating Russia, presenting a grim face to France and rattling the sword in its scabbard so that it resounded through Europe.   Well, let her rattle, so long as France could keep out of the whole affair and preserve that peace in which she had built up prosperity since the nightmare of 1870 !

L'année terrible!   There were many people in France who remembered that tragic year, and now, after forty-four years, the memory came back, and they shuddered.   They had seen the horrors of war and knew the meaning of it—its waste of life, its sacrifice of splendid young manhood, its wanton cruelties, its torture of women, its misery and destruction.   France had been brought to her knees then and had suffered the last humiliations which may be inflicted upon a proud nation.   But she had recovered miraculously, and gradually even her desire for revenge, the passionate hope that one day she might take vengeance for all those indignities and cruelties, had cooled down and died.   Not even for vengeance was war worth while.   Not even to recover the lost provinces was it worth the lives of all those thousands of young men who must give their blood as the price of victory.   Alsace and Lorraine were only romantic memories, kept alive by a few idealists and hotheads, who once a year went to the statue in the Place de la Concorde and deposited wreaths and made enthusiastic speeches which rang false, and pledged their allegiance to the lost provinces—" Quand même ! "   There was a good deal of *blague* in these annual ceremonies, laughed at by Frenchmen of common sense.   Alsace and Lorraine had been Germanized.   A Frenchman would find few people there to speak his own tongue.   The old ties of sentiment had worn very thin, and there was not a party in France who would have dared to advocate a war with Germany for the sake of this territory.   Such a policy would have been a crime against France itself, who had abandoned the spirit of vengeance, and had only one ambition—to pursue its ideals and its business in peace.

B

3

There was no wild outbreak of Jingo fever, no demon-strations of blood-lust against Germany in Paris or any town of France, on that first day of August, when the people waited for the fateful decision which, if it were for war, would call every able-bodied man to the colours and arrest all the activities of a nation's normal life, and demand a dreadful sacrifice in blood and tears. There was only a sense of stupefaction which seemed to numb the intelligence of men so that they could not reason with any show of logic, or speak of this menace without incoherence, but thrust back the awful possibility with one word, uttered passionately and repeated a thousand times a day : *" Incroyable ! "*

4

This word was dinned in my ears. I caught the sound of it as I walked along the boulevards. It would come like a refrain at the end of sentences spoken by little groups of men and women sitting outside the cafés and reading every issue of those innumerable newspapers which flung out editions at every hour. It was the answer I had from men of whom I tried to get a clue to the secret movements of diplomacy, and an answer to that question of war or peace. *" C'est incroyable ! "* They found it hard to believe—they would not believe—that without any provocation from France, without any challenge, Germany would deliberately, force this war upon the Triple Entente and make a bloody shambles of European civilization. Beneath this incredulity, this stupefaction, there was among most of the Frenchmen whom I personally encountered a secret dread that France was unready for the great ordeal of war and that its out-break would find her divided by political parties, inefficient in organization, corrupt in some of her Government depart-ments. The Socialists and Syndicalists who had fought against the three years' service might refuse to march. Only a few months before a deputy had hinted at grave scandals in the provisioning and equipment of the army.

The history of 1870, with its awful revelations of disorganiza-
tion and unreadiness was remembered now and lay heavy
upon the hearts of those educated Frenchmen who, standing
outside the political arena, distrust all politicians, having
but little faith in their honesty or their ability.   Who could
tell whether France—the new France she had been called—
would rise above her old weaknesses and confront the peril
of this war with a strong, pure, and undivided spirit ?

5

On August 1 there was a run on one of the banks.   I
passed its doors and saw them besieged by thousands of
middle-class men and women drawn up in a long queue
waiting very quietly—with a strange quietude for any crowd
in Paris—to withdraw the savings of a lifetime or the capital
of their business houses.   There were similar crowds outside other banks, and on the faces of these people there
was a look of brooding fear, as though all that they had
fought and struggled for, the reward of all their petty
economies and meannesses, and shifts and tricks, and denials
of self-indulgences and starvings of soul might be suddenly
snatched from them and leave them beggared.   A shudder
went through one such crowd when a young man came to
speak to them from the steps of the bank.   It was a kind
of shuddering sigh, followed by loud murmurings, and here
and there angry protests.   The cashiers had been withdrawn from their desks and cheques could not be paid.

" We are ruined already ! " said a woman.   " This war
will take all our money !   Oh, my God ! "

She made her way through the crowd with a fixed white
face and burning eyes.

6

It was strange how in a day all gold disappeared from
Paris.   I could not see the glint of it anywhere, unless I
drew it from my own purse.   Even silver was very scarce
and everybody was trying to cash notes, which were refused
by the shopkeepers.   When I put one of them down on a

table at the Café Tourtel the waiter shook his head and said,
" La petite monnaie, s'il vous plaît ! " At another place
where I put down a gold piece the waiter seized it as though
it were a rare and wonderful thing, and then gave me all my
change in paper, made up of new five franc notes issued by
the Government. In the evening an official notice was
posted on the walls prohibiting the export of grain and flour.
People stared at it and said, " That means war ! " Another
sign of coming events, more impressive to the imagination
of the Parisian, was the sudden dwindling in size of the
evening newspapers. They were reduced to two sheets, and
in some cases to a single broadside, owing to the possibility of
a famine in paper if war broke out and cut off the supplies of
Paris while the railways were being used for the mobilization
of troops.

7

The city was very quiet and outwardly as calm as on any
day in August. But beneath this normal appearance of
things there was a growing anxiety and people's nerves were
so on edge that any sudden sound would make a man start on
his chair on the *terrasse* outside the café restaurant. Paris
was afraid of itself. What uproar or riot or criminal demonstration might not burst suddenly into this tranquillity ?
There were evil elements lurking in the low quarters. Apaches
and anarchists might be inflamed with the madness of blood
which excites men in time of war. The socialists and syndicalists might refuse to fight, and fight in maintaining their
refusal. Some political crime might set all those smouldering
passions on fire and make a hell in the streets. So people
waited and watched the crowds and listened to the pulse-beat
of Paris.

The sharp staccato of revolver shots heard in the rue
Montmartre on the night of July 31 caused a shudder to
pass through the city, as though they were the signal for a
criminal plot which might destroy France by dividing it while
the enemy was on the frontier.

I did not hear those shots but only the newspaper reports

which followed them almost as loudly in the soul of Paris. And yet it was only the accidental meeting of a friend which diverted my attention of dining in the Croissant Restaurant in which the crime took place at the very hour when I should have been there. Some years before in Paris, when France was in the throes of a railway strike which developed almost to the verge of revolution, I had often gone to the Croissant at two, three or four in the morning, because it had police privileges to keep open all night for the comfort of journalists. Other night birds had found this roost—ladies who sleep by day, and some of the queer adventurers of the city which never goes to bed. One night I had come into the midst of a strange company—the inner circle of Parisian anarchists who were celebrating a victory over French law. Their white faces had eyes like live coals. They thrust long thin fingers through shaggy hair and spoke passionate orations nose to nose. Their sluttish women shrieked with mirth and gave their kisses to the leader of the gang, who had the face of Christ as painted by Ary Scheffer.

It was in this interesting place, on the very velvet cushions where I used to sit to watch the company, that Jaurés was killed on the eve of the war. The veteran orator of French socialism, the man who could stir the passions of the mob— as I had seen more than once—so that at his bidding they would declare war against all the powers of Government, was struck down as he sat with his back to an open window divided from the street by a thin curtain. The young assassin—a patriot he called himself—had been excited to an hysteria of hate for a man who had tried to weaken the military power of France by opposing the measure for a three years' service. It was the madness of war which had touched his brain, and although Jaurés had called upon the Socialists of France to march as one man in defence of " La Patrie," this young neurasthenic made him the first victim of that enormous sacrifice of blood which has since recked up to God. Jaurés, an honest man, perhaps, in spite of all his theatrical appeals to mob passion—honest at least in his desire to make life more tolerable for the sweated workers of

France—was mortally wounded by those shots through the window blind, and the crimson cushions of his seat were dyed with deeper stains.

8

For twenty-four hours France was scared by the murder. It seemed possible that the crime might let loose a tide of passion among the followers of the Socialist leader. Placards were hastily posted on the walls by the military governor of Paris professing abhorrence of the assassination of a great Frenchman, promising a just punishment of the crime, and calling upon the people to remain calm in this great national crisis which would decide the destiny of France.

The appeal was not challenged. By a strange irony of fate the death of Jaurés strengthened the Government which he had attacked throughout his life, and the dead body of the man of strife became, on its way to the grave, the symbol of a united France, of obedience to its laws, and of a martial fervour which in the old days of rebellion he had ridiculed and denounced. On a gusty day I saw the Red Flag of revolutionary socialism fluttering across the Place de la Concorde in front of the coffin containing the corpse of its leader. Blood red, flag after flag streamed past, all aglow in the brilliant sunshine, and behind walked the representatives of every party in the State, including all those who had denounced Jaurés in life as a traitor, a revolutionist, and the most evil influence in France. For the first time in history the aristocrats and the monarchists, the Conservative Republicans and the Clericals walked in procession behind the blood-red rag.

9

Part of the active army of France was already on the frontiers. Before the first whisper of war had reached the ears of the people, large bodies of troops had been sent to the frontier towns to strengthen the already existing garrisons. But the main army of the nation was pursuing the ordinary pursuits of civil life. To resist the might of Germany, the greatest military Power in Europe, already approaching the frontiers in vast masses of men and machines, France would have to call out all her manhood which had been trained in military service.

Aux armes, citoyens !
Formez vos bataillons !

The call to arms came without any loud clamour of bugles or orations. Unlike the scenes in the early days of 1870, there were no street processions of civil enthusiasts. No painted beauty of the stage waved the tricolour to the shout of " À Berlin ! " No mob orators jumped upon the café tables to wave their arms in defiance of the foe and to prophesy swift victories.

The quietness of Paris was astounding, and the first mobilization orders were issued with no more publicity than attends the delivery of a trade circular through the halfpenny post. Yet in hundreds of thousands of houses through France and in all the blocks and tenements of Paris there was a drama of tragic quietude when the cards were delivered to young men in civilian clothes, men who sat at table with old mothers or young wives, or in lowly rooms with some dream to keep them company, or with little women who had spoilt the dream, or fostered it, or with comrades who had gone on great adventures with them between the Quartier Latin and the Mountain of Montmartre.

" *It has come !* "

10

Fate had come with that little card summoning each man to join his depot, and tapped him on the shoulder with just a finger touch. It was no more than that—a touch on the shoulder. Yet I know that for many of those young men it seemed a blow between the eyes, and, to some of them, a strangle-grip as icy cold as though Death's fingers were already closing round their throats.

I seem to hear the silence in those rooms when for a moment or two young men stared at the cards and the formal words on them, and when, for just that time, all that life and death, means, came before their souls. Was this the summons, Death itself? Somewhere on the German side was a little steel bullet or a bit of shell waiting for the Frenchman to whom it was destined. How long would it have to wait to find its billet? Perhaps only a day or two—a question of hours, slipping away now towards eternity as the clock ticked on. . . . From the old mother, or the young wife, from the little woman whose emotions and quarrels, greediness or self-denial, had seemed all that mattered in life, all that life meant to a young man of twenty-five or so, there came perhaps a cry, a name spoken with grief, or no word at all but the inarticulate expression of foreboding, terror, and a woman's anguish.

" Jean ! . . . Mon petit ! . . . O, mon pauvre petit ! "

" C'est pour la patrie . . . mon devoir . . . je reviendrai bientôt. . . . Courage, ma femme ! "

Courage ! How many million times was the word spoken that night of mobilization by women who saw the sudden pallor of their men, by men who heard the cry of their women ? I heard it in the streets, spoken quite brutally sometimes, by men afraid of breaking down, and with a passionate tenderness by other men, sure of their own strength but pitiful for those whose spirit fainted at the spectre of death which stood quite close.

II

In the days that followed the Second of August I saw the whole meaning of mobilization in France—the call of a nation to arms—from Paris to the Eastern frontier, and the drama of it all stirs me now as I write, though many months have passed since then and I have seen more awful things on the harvest fields of death. More awful, but not more pitiful. For even in the sunshine of that August, before blood had been spilt and the brooding spectre of war had settled drearily over Europe, there was a poignant tragedy beneath the gallantry and the beauty of that squadron of cavalry that I had seen riding out of their barrack gates to entrain for the front. The men and the horses were superb—clean-limbed,

finely trained, exquisite in their pride of life. As they came
out into the streets of Paris the men put on the little touch
of swagger which belongs to the Frenchman when the public
gaze is on him. Even the horses tossed their heads and
seemed to realize the homage of the populace. Hundreds of
women were in the crowd, waving handkerchiefs, springing
forward out of their line to throw bunches of flowers to those
cavaliers, who caught them and fastened them to *képi* and
jacket. The officers—young dandies of the Chasseurs—
carried great bouquets already and kissed the petals in
homage to all the womanhood of France whose love they
symbolized. There were no tears in that crowd, though the
wives and sweethearts of many of the young men must have
stood on the kerbstone to watch them pass. At those
moments, in the sunshine, even the sting of parting was forgotten in the enthusiasm and pride which rose up to those
splendid ranks of cavalry who were on their way to fight for
France and to uphold the story of their old traditions. I
could see no tears then but my own, for I confess that suddenly
to my eyes there came a mist of tears and I was seized with
an emotion that made me shudder icily in the glare of the
day. For beyond the pageantry of the cavalcade I saw the
fields of war, with many of those men and horses lying
mangled under the hot sun of August. I smelt the stench of
blood, for I had been in the muck and misery of war before
and had seen the death carts coming back from the battlefield and the convoys of wounded crawling down the rutty
roads—from Adrianople—with men, who had been strong and
fine, now shattered, twisted and made hideous by pain. The
flowers carried by those cavalry officers seemed to me like
funeral wreaths upon men who were doomed to die, and the
women who sprang out of the crowds with posies for their men
were offering the garlands of death.

12

In the streets of Paris in those first days of the war I saw
many scenes of farewell. All day long one saw them, so
that at last one watched them without emotion, because the

pathos of them became monotonous. It was curious how men said good-bye, often, to their wives and children and comrades at a street corner, or in the middle of the boulevards. A hundred times or more I saw one of these conscript soldiers who had put on his uniform again after years of civilian life, turn suddenly to the woman trudging by his side or to a group of people standing round him and say: " Alors, il faut dire ' Adieu ' et ' Au revoir ' ! " One might imagine that he was going on a week-end visit and would be back again in Paris on Monday next. It was only by the long-drawn kiss upon the lips of the woman who raised a dead white face to him and by the abruptness with which the man broke away and walked off hurriedly until he was lost in the passing crowds that one might know that this was as likely as not the last parting between a man and a woman who had known love together and that each of them had seen the vision of death which would divide them on this side of the grave. The stoicism of the Frenchwomen was wonderful. They made no moan or plaint. They gave their men to " La Patrie " with the resignation of religious women who offer their hearts to God. Some spiritual fervour, which in France permeates the sentiment of patriotism, giving a beauty to that tradition of nationality which, without such a spirit, is the low and ignorant hatred of other peoples, strengthened and uplifted them.

13

Sometimes when I watched these scenes I raged against the villainy of a civilization which still permits these people to be sent like sheep to the slaughter. Great God ! These poor wretches of the working quarters in Paris, these young peasants from the fields, these underpaid clerks from city offices had had no voice in the declaration of war. What could they know about international politics ? Why should they be the pawns of the political chessboard, played without any regard for human life by diplomats and war lords and high financiers ? These poor weedy little men .with the sallow faces of the clerical class, in uniforms which hung loose

round their undeveloped frames, why should they be caught
in the trap of this horrible machine called " War " and let loose
like a lot of mice against the hounds of death ? These
peasants with slouching shoulders and loose limbs and clumsy
feet, who had been bringing in the harvest of France, after
their tilling and sowing and reaping, why should they be
marched off into tempests of shells which would hack off
their strong arms and drench unfertile fields with their blood ?
They had had to go, leaving all the things that had given a
meaning and purpose to their days, as though God had commanded them, instead of groups of politicians among the
nations of Europe, damnably careless of human life. How
long will this fetish of international intrigue be tolerated by
civilized democracies which have no hatred against each other,
until it is inflamed by their leaders and then, in war itself, by
the old savageries of primitive nature ?

14

I went down to the East frontier on the first day of
mobilization. It was in the evening when I went to take
the train from the Gare de l'Est. The station was filled with
a seething crowd of civilians and soldiers, struggling to get
to the booking-offices, vainly seeking information as to the
times of departure to distant towns of France. The railway
officials were bewildered and could give no certain information. The line was under military control. Many trains had
been suppressed and the others had no fixed time-table. I
could only guess at the purpose animating the individuals in
these crowds. Many of them, perhaps, were provincials,
caught in Paris by the declaration of war and desperately
anxious to get back to their homes before the lines were
utterly choked by troop trains. Others belonged to neutral
countries and were trying to escape across the frontier before
the gates were closed. One of the " neutrals " spoke to me—
in German, which was a dangerous tongue in Paris. He was
a Swiss who had come to Paris on business for a few days,
leaving his wife in a village near Basle. It was of his wife
that he kept talking.

" Ach, mein armes Weib !   Sie hat Angst für mich."

I pitied this little man in a shoddy suit and limp straw hat who had tears in his eyes and no courage to make inquiries of station officials because he spoke no word of French.   I asked on his behalf and after jostling for half an hour in the crowd and speaking to a dozen porters who shrugged their shoulders and said, " Je n'en sais rien ! " came back with the certain and doleful news that the last train had left that night for Basle.   The little Swiss was standing between his packages with his back to the wall, searching for me with anxious eyes, and when I gave him the bad news tears trickled down his face.

" Was kann ich thun ?   Mein armes Weib hat Angst für mich."

There was nothing he could do that night, however anxious his poor wife might be, but I did not have any further conversation with him, for my bad German had already attracted the notice of the people standing near, and they were glowering at me suspiciously, as though I were a spy.

15

It was an hour later that I found a train leaving for Nancy, though even then I was assured by railway officials that there was no such train.   I had faith, however, in a young French officer who pledged his word to me that I should get to Nancy if I took my place in the carriage before which he stood.   He was going as far as Toul himself.

I could see by the crimson velvet round his *képi* that he was an army doctor, and by the look of sadness in his eyes that he was not glad to leave the beautiful woman by his side who clasped his arm.   They spoke to me in English.

" This war will be horrible ! " said the lady.   " It is so senseless and so unnecessary.   Why should Germany want to fight us ?   There has been no quarrel between us and we wanted to live in peace."

The young officer made a sudden gesture of disgust.

" It is a crime against humanity—a stupid, wanton crime ! "

Then he asked a question earnestly and waited for my answer with obvious anxiety :

" Will England join in ? "

I said " Yes ! " with an air of absolute conviction, though on that night England had not yet given her decision. During the last twenty-four hours I had been asked this question a score of times. The people of Paris were getting impatient of England's silence. Englishmen in Paris were getting very anxious. . If England did not keep her unwritten pledge to France, it would be dangerous and a shameful thing to be an Englishman in Paris. Some of my friends were already beginning to feel their throats with nervous fingers.

" I think so too ! " said the officer, when he heard my answer. " England will be dishonoured otherwise ! "

16

The platform was now thronged with young men, many of them being officers in a variety of brand-new uniforms, but most of them still in civilian clothes as they had left their workshops or their homes to obey the mobilization orders to join their military depots. The young medical officer who had been speaking to me withdrew himself from his wife's arm to answer some questions addressed to him by an old colonel in his own branch of service. The lady turned to me and spoke in a curiously intimate way, as though we were old friends.

" Have you begun to realize what it means ? I feel that I ought to weep because my husband is leaving me. . . . We have two little children. . . But there are no tears higher than my heart. It seems as though he were just going away for a week-end—and yet he may never come back to us. Perhaps to-morrow I shall weep."

She did not weep even when the train was signalled to start and when the man put his arms about her and held her in a long embrace, whispering down to her. Nor did I see any tears in other women's eyes as they waved farewell. It was only the pallor of their faces which showed some hidden agony.

17

Before the train started the carriage in which I had taken my seat was crowded with young men who, excepting one cavalry officer in the corner, seemed to belong to the poorest classes of Paris. In the corner opposite the dragoon was a boy of eighteen or so in the working clothes of a *terrassier* or labourer. No one had come to see him off to the war, and he was stupefied with drink. Several times he staggered up and vomited out of the window with an awful violence of nausea, and then fell back with his head lolling sideways on the cushions of the first-class carriage. None of the other men—except the cavalry officer, who drew in his legs slightly—took the slightest interest in this poor wretch—a handsome lad with square-cut features and fair tousled hair, who had tried to get courage out of absinthe before leaving for the war.

18

In the corner opposite my own seat was a thin pallid young man, also a little drunk, but with an excited brain in which a multitude of strange and tragic thoughts chased each other. He recognized me as an Englishman at once, and with a shout of " Camarade ! " shook hands with me not once but scores of times during the first part of our journey.

He entered upon a monologue that seemed interminable, his voice rising into a shrill excitement and then sinking into a hoarse whisper. He belonged to the " apache " type, and had come out of one of those foul lairs which lie hidden behind the white beauty of Paris—yet he spoke with a terrible eloquence which kept me fascinated. I remember some of his words, though I cannot give them his white heat of passion, nor the infinite pathos of his self-pity.

" I have left a wife behind, the woman who loves me and sees something more in me than vileness. Shall I tell you how I left her, Monsieur ? Dying—in a hospital at Charenton. I shall never see her again. I shall never again take her thin white face in my dirty hands and say, ' You and I have tasted

the goodness of life, my little one, while we have starved
together ! ' For life is good, Monsieur, but in a little while
I shall be dead in one place and my woman in another.
That is certain. I left a child behind me—a little girl.
What will happen to her when I am killed ? I left her with
the concierge, who promised to take care of her—not for
money, you understand, because I had none to give. My
little girl will never see me again, and I shall never see her
grow into a woman. Because I am going to be killed.
Perhaps in a day or two there will be no more life for me.
This hand of mine—you see I can grasp things with it, move
it this way and that, shake hands with you—camarade !—
salute the spirit of France with it—*comme ça* ! But to-
morrow or the next day it will be quite still. A dead thing—
like my dead body. It is queer. Here I sit talking to you
alive. But to-morrow or the next day my corpse will lie
out on the battlefield, like a bit of earth. I can see that corpse
of mine, with its white face and staring eyes. Ugh ! it is
a dirty sight—a man's corpse. Here in my heart something
tells me that I shall be killed quite soon, perhaps at the first
shot. But do you know I shall not be sorry to die. . . .
I shall be glad, Monsieur ! And why glad, you ask ? Because I love France and hate the Germans who have put this
war on to us. I am going to fight—I, a Socialist and a
syndicalist—so that we shall make an end of war, so that
the little ones of France shall sleep in peace, and the women
go without fear. This war will have to be the last war.
It is a war of Justice against Injustice. When they have
finished this time the people will have no more of it. We
who go out to die shall be remembered because we gave the
world peace. That will be our reward, though we shall know
nothing of it but lie rotting in the earth—dead ! It is sad
that to-morrow, or the next day, I shall be dead. I see my
corpse there——."

He saw his corpse again, and wept a little at the sight of
it.

A neurotic type—a poor weed of life who had been
reared in the dark lairs of civilization. Yet I had no con-

tempt for him as he gibbered with self-pity. The tragedy of the future of civilization was in the soul of that pallid, sharp-featured, ill-nourished man who had lived in misery within the glitter of a rich city and who .was now being taken to his death—I feel sure he died in the trenches even though no bullet may have reached him—at the command of great powers who knew nothing of this poor ant. What did his individual life matter ? . . . I stared into the soul of a soldier of France and wondered at the things I saw in it —at the spiritual faith which made a patriot of that apache.

19

There was a change of company in the carriage, the democrats being turned into a third-class carriage to make way for half a dozen officers of various grades and branches. I had new types to study and was surprised by the calmness and quietude of these men—mostly of middle age—who had just left their homes for active service. They showed no signs of excitement but chatted about the prospects of the war as though it were an abstract problem. The attitude of England was questioned and again I was called upon to speak as the representative of my country and to assure Frenchmen of our friendship and co-operation. They seemed satisfied with my statements and expressed their belief that the British Fleet would make short work of the enemy at sea.

One of the officers took no part in the conversation. He was a handsome man of about forty years of age, in the uniform of an infantry regiment, and he sat in the corner of the carriage, stroking his brown moustache in a thoughtful way. He had a fine gravity of face and once or twice when his eyes turned my way I saw an immense sadness in them.

20

As our train passed through France on its way to Nancy, we heard and saw the tumult of a nation arming itself for war and pouring down to its frontiers to meet the enemy. All through the night, as we passed through towns and villages and under railway bridges, the song of the Marseillaise rose up to the carriage windows and then wailed away like a sad plaint as our engine shrieked and raced on. At the sound of the national hymn one of the officers in my carriage always opened his eyes and lifted his head, which had been drooping forward on his chest, and listened with a look of puzzled surprise, as though he could not realize even yet that France was at war and that he was on his way to the front. But the other officers slept; and the silent man, whose quiet dignity and sadness had impressed me, smiled a little in his sleep now and then and murmured a word or two, among which I seemed to hear a woman's name.

In the dawn and pallid sunlight of the morning I saw the soldiers of France assembling. They came across the bridges with glinting rifles, and the blue coats and red trousers of the infantry made them look in the distance like tin soldiers from a children's playbox. But there were battalions of them close to the railway lines, waiting at level crossings, and with stacked arms on the platforms, so that I could look into their eyes and watch their faces. They were fine young men, with a certain hardness and keenness of profile which promised well for France. There was no shouting among them, no patriotic demonstrations, no excitability. They stood waiting for their trains in a quiet, patient way, chatting among themselves, smiling, smoking cigarettes, like soldiers on their way to sham fights in the ordinary summer manœuvres. The town and village folk, who crowded about them and leaned over the gates at the level crossings to watch our train, were more demonstrative. They waved hands to us and cried out " Bonne chance ! " and the boys and girls chanted the Marseillaise again in shrill voices. At every station where we halted, and we never let one of them go by without a stop, some of the girls came along the platform with baskets of fruit, of which they made free gifts to our trainload of men. Sometimes they took payment in kisses, quite simply and without any bashfulness, lifting their faces to the lips of bronzed young men who thrust their *képis* back and leaned out of the carriage windows.

C

"Come back safe and sound, my little one," said a girl.
·" Fight well for France ! "

"I do not hope to come back," said a soldier, "but I
·shall die fighting."

21

The fields were swept with the golden light of the sun,
and the heavy foliage of the trees sang through every note of
green.   The white roads of France stretched away straight
between the fields and the hills, with endless lines of poplars
as their sentinels, and in clouds of greyish dust rising like
smoke the regiments marched with a steady tramp.   Gun
carriages moved slowly down the roads in a glare of sun
which sparkled upon the steel tubes of the field artillery and
made a silver bar of every wheel-spoke.   I heard the creak
of the wheels and the rattle of the limber and the shouts of
the drivers to their teams ; and I thrilled a little every
time we passed one of these batteries because I knew that in
a day or two these machines, which were being carried along
the highways of France, would be wreathed with smoke
denser than the dust about them now, while they vomited
forth shells at the unseen enemy whose guns would answer
with the roar of death.

Guns and men, horses and wagons, interminable convoys
of munitions, great armies on the march, trainloads of soldiers
on all the branch lines, soldiers bivouacked in the roadways
and in market places, long processions of young civilians
carrying bundles to military depots where they would change
their clothes and all their way of life—these pictures of
preparation for war flashed through the carriage windows
into my brain, mile after mile, through the country of France,
until sometimes I closed my eyes to shut out the glare and
glitter of this kaleidoscope, the blood-red colour of all those
French trousers tramping through the dust, the lurid blue
of all those soldiers' overcoats, the sparkle of all those gun-
wheels.   ·What does it all mean, this surging tide of armed
men ?   What would it mean in a day or two, when another
tide of men had swept up against it, with a roar of conflict,

striving to overwhelm this France and to swamp over its barriers in waves of blood ? How senseless it seemed that those mild-eyed fellows outside my carriage windows, chatting with the girls while we waited for the signals to fall, should be on their way to kill other mild-eyed men, who perhaps away in Germany were kissing other girls, for gifts of fruit and flowers.

22

It was at this station near Toul that I heard the first words of hatred. They were in a conversation between two French soldiers who had come with us from Paris. They had heard that some Germans had already been taken prisoners across the frontier, and they were angry that the men were still alive

" Prisoners ? Pah ! Name of a dog ! I will tell you what I would do with German prisoners ! "

It was nothing nice that that man wanted to do with German prisoners. He indulged in long and elaborate details as to the way in which he would wreath their bowels about his bayonet and tear out their organs with his knife. The other man had more imagination. He devised more ingenious modes of torture so that the Germans should not die too soon.

I watched the men as they spoke. They had the faces of murderers, with bloodshot eyes and coarse features, swollen with drink and vice. There was a life of cruelty in the lines about their mouths, and in their husky laughter. Their hands twitched and their muscles gave convulsive jerks, as they worked themselves into a fever of blood-lust. In the French Revolution it was such men as these who leered up at the guillotine and laughed when the heads of patrician women fell into the basket, and who did the bloody work of the September massacre. The breed had not died out in France, and war had brought it forth from its lairs again.

23

These men were not typical of the soldiers of France. In the headquarters at Nancy, where I was kept waiting for some time in one of the guard-rooms before being received by the commandant, I chatted with many of the men and found them fine fellows of a good, clean, cheery type. When they heard that I was a war correspondent, they plied me with greetings and questions. "You are an English journalist ? You want to come with us ? That is good ! Every Englishman is a comrade and we will give you some fine things to write about ! "

They showed me their rifles and their field kit, asked me to feel the weight of their knapsacks, and laughed when I said that I should faint with such a burden. In each black sack the French soldier carried—in addition to the legendary bâton of a field-marshal—a complete change of underclothing, a second pair of boots, provisions for two days, consisting of desiccated soup, chocolate and other groceries, and a woollen night-cap. Then there were his tin water-bottle, or *bidon* (filled with wine at the beginning of the war), his cartridge belt, rifle, military overcoat strapped about his shoulders, and various other impedimenta.

"It's not a luxury, this life of ours," said a tall fellow with a fair moustache belonging to the famous 20th Regiment of the line, which was the first to enter Nancy after the German occupation of the town in 1870.

He pointed to the rows of straw beds on which some of his comrades lay asleep, and to the entire lack of comfort in the whitewashed room.

"Some of you English gentlemen," he said, "would hardly like to lie down here side by side with the peasants from their farms, smelling of their barns. But in France it is different. We have aristocrats still, but some of them have to shake down with the poorest comrades and know no distinction of rank now that all wear the same old uniform."

It seemed to me a bad uniform for modern warfare— the red trousers and blue coat and the little *képi* made

famous in many great battle pictures—but the soldier told
me they could not fight with the same spirit if they wore
any other clothes than those which belong to the glorious
traditions of France.

24

When I was taken to Colonel Duchesne, second-in-com-
mand to General Foch, he gave me a smiling greeting, though
I was a trespasser in the war zone, and he wanted to know
what I thought of his " boys," what was my opinion of the
mobilization, and what were my impressions of the way
in which France had responded to the call. I answered
with sincerity, and when I spoke of the astonishing way in
which all classes seemed to have united in defence of the
nation, Colonel Duchesne had a sudden mist of tears in his
eyes which he did not try to hide.

" It is sublime ! All politics have been banished. We
are one people, with one ideal and one purpose—La France ! "

Then he came to the business of my visit—to obtain a
permit to march with the French troops.

" It is very difficult," said the Colonel. " General Foch
would do all he could for you—he loves the English—but no
French correspondents are allowed on the frontier, and we
can hardly make a distinction in your favour. Still, I will
put your appeal before the general. The answer shall be
sent to your hotel."

25

It was while waiting for this reply that I was able to
explore Nancy and to see the scenes of mobilization. The
town was under martial law. Its food-supplies were under
strict supervision by the commandant. Every motor-car
and cart had been commandeered for the use of the army,
and every able-bodied citizen had been called to the colours.
I was the only guest in the Grand Hotel and the manager
and his wife attended to my wants themselves. They were
astounded to see me in the town.

" You are the only foreigner left," they said, " except

those who are under armed guard, waiting to be taken to the Swiss frontier.   Look ! there go the last of them ! "

Through the glass windows of the hotel door I saw about two hundred men marching away from the square surrounded by soldiers with fixed bayonets. They carried bundles and seemed to droop under the burden of them already. But I fancy their hearts were heaviest, and I could see that these young men—waiters and hairdressers and tradesmen mostly of Swiss nationality—were unwilling victims of this tragedy of war which had suddenly thrust them out of their business and smashed their small ambitions and booted them out of a country which had given them a friendly welcome. On the other side of the fixed bayonets were some women who wept as they called out " Adieu ! " to their fair-haired fellows. One of them held up a new-born baby between the guards as she ran alongside, so that its little wrinkled face touched the cheek of a young man who had a look of agony in his eyes.

That night I heard the shrill notes of bugle calls and going to my bedroom window listened to the clatter of horses' hoofs and saw the dim forms of cavalry and guns going through the darkness—towards the enemy. No sound of firing rattled my window panes. It still seemed very quiet —over there to the East. Yet before the dawn came a German avalanche of men and guns might be sweeping across the frontier, and if I stayed a day or two in the open town of Nancy I might see the spiked helmets of the enemy glinting down the streets. The town was not to be defended, I was told, if the French troops had to fall back from the frontier to the fortresses of Belfort and Toul.

A woman's voice was singing outside in the courtyard when I awakened next day. How strange that any woman should sing in an undefended town confronted by such a peril. But none of the girls about the streets had any fear in their eyes. German frightfulness had not yet scared them with its nameless horrors.

26

I did not stay in Nancy. It was only the French War Office in Paris who could give permission for a correspondent to join the troops. This unfortified town has never echoed in the war to the tramp of German feet, and its women's courage has not been dismayed by the worst horrors. But since those days of August 1914, many women's faces have blanched at the sight of blood—streams of blood sopping the stretchers in which the wounded have been carried back from the frontier, which seemed so quiet when I listened at the open window. Those soldiers I talked to in the general headquarters—how many of them are now alive ? They were the men who fought in Alsace and Lorraine, when whole battalions were decimated under a withering shell-fire beyond the endurance of human courage, and who marched forward to victories, and backward in retreats, and forward again over the dead bodies of their comrades and corrupting heaps of German dead, in an ebb and flow of warfare which made the fields and the woods one great stench of horror, from which there came back madmen and maimed creatures, and young men, lucky with slight wounds, who told the tale of things they had seen as though they had escaped from hell. I met some of them afterwards and turned sick and faint as I listened to their stories ; and afterwards on the western side of the French front, three hundred miles from Nancy, I came upon the dragoons of Belfort who had ridden past me in the sunshine of those August days. Then they had been very fine to see in their clean uniforms and on their glossy horses, garlanded with flowers. At the second meeting they were stained and war-worn, and their horses limped with drooping heads, and they rode as men who have seen many comrades fall and have been familiar with the ways of death. They were fine to see again, those dirty, tired, grim-faced men. But it was a different kind of beauty which sent a queer thrill through me as I watched them pass.

CHAPTER III

THE SECRET WAR

1

IT was the most astounding thing in modern history, the secrecy behind which great armies were moving and fighting. To a civilization accustomed to the rapid and detailed accounts of news, there was something stupefying in the veil of silence which enshrouded the operations of the legions which were being hurled against each other along the frontiers. By one swift stroke of the military censorship journalism was throttled. All its lines of communication were cut, suddenly, as when, in my office, I spoke from Paris to England, and found myself with a half-finished sentence before a telephone which would no longer "march," as they say across the Channel. Pains and penalties were threatened against any newspaper which should dare to publish a word of military information beyond the official communiqués issued in order to hide the truth. Only by a careful study of maps from day to day and a microscopic reading between the lines could one grope one's way to any kind of clear fact which would reveal something more than the vague optimism, the patriotic fervour, of those early dispatches issued from the Ministry of War. Now and again a name would creep into these communiqués which after a glance at the map would give one a cold thrill of anxiety and doubt. Was it possible that the enemy had reached that point ? If so, then its progress was phenomenal and menacing. But M. le Marquis de Messimy, War Minister of France, was delightfully cheerful. He assured the nation day after day that their heroic army was making rapid progress. He omitted to say in what direction. He gave no details of these continual victories. He did not publish lists of casualties. It seemed, at first, as though the war were bloodless.

2

One picture of Paris, in those first days of August, comes to my mind now. In a great room to the right of the steps of the War Office a number of men in civilian clothes sit in gilded chairs with a strained look of expectancy, as though awaiting some message of fate. They have interesting faces. My fingers itch to make a sketch of them, but only Steinlen could draw these Parisian types who seem to belong to some literary or Bohemian coterie. What can they be doing at the Ministry of War ? They smoke cigarettes incessantly, talk in whispers *tête-à-tête*, or stare up at the steel casques and cuirasses on the walls, or at the great glass candelabra above their heads as though they can only keep their patience in check by gazing fixedly at some immovable object. Among the gilded chairs and beneath the Empire mirrors which reflect the light there are three iron bedsteads with straw mattresses, and now and again a man gets up from one of these straight-backed chairs and lies at full length on one of the beds. But a minute later he rises silently again and listens intently, nervously, to the sound of footsteps coming sharply across the polished boards. It seems to be the coming of the messenger for whom all these men have been waiting. They spring to their feet and crowd round a table as a gentleman comes in with a bundle of papers from which he gives a sheet to every outstretched hand. The Parisian journalists have received the latest bulletin of war. They read it silently, devouring with their eyes those few lines of typewritten words. Here is the message of fate. Those slips of paper will tell them whether it goes well or ill with France. One of them speaks to his neighbour :

" Tout va bien ! "

Yes, all goes well, according to the official bulletin, but there is not much news on that slip of paper, not enough for men greedy for every scrap of news. Perhaps the next dispatch will contain a longer story. They must come again, these journalists of France, to smoke more cigarettes, to stare at the steel armour, to bridle their impatience with clenched hands. This little scene at the Ministry of War is played four times a day, and there is a tremendous drama behind the quietude of those waiting men, whose duty it is to tell France and the world what another day of war has done for the flag.

3

Another little scene comes to my mind as I grope back to those first days of war. At the Ministry of Foreign Affairs, on the Quai d'Orsay, there is more quietude. It is difficult to realise that this house has been the scene of a world-drama within the last few days, and that in one of its reception-rooms a German gentleman spoke a few quiet words, before asking for some papers, which hurled millions of men against each other in a deadly struggle involving all that we mean by civilization. I went to that house and waited for a while in an ante-chamber where the third Napoleon once paced up and down before a war which ended disastrously for France. Presently a footman came through the velvet curtains and said, " Monsieur le Président vous attend." I was taken into another room, a little cabinet overlooking a garden, cool and green under old trees through which the sunlight filtered. A stone goddess smiled at me through the open windows. I saw her out of the corner of my eye as I bowed to M. Doumergue, Minister of Foreign Affairs, and, for a time, Prime Minister of France. For some reason my imagination was touched by that garden of peace where a Greek goddess smiled in the green twilight.

But M. Doumergue was smiling, too, with that expression of *tout va bien* which masked the anxiety of every statesman who had seen behind the veil. After a few preliminary words he spoke of the progress of the war and of its significance to the world.

" Civilization itself," he said, " depends upon the success of our arms. For years Germany has played the part of a bully, basing her policy upon brute force, and thrusting her sword before the eyes of men. She was swollen-headed with her military pride. She preached the gospel of the swashbuckler. And now, after the declaration of this war, which was none of our seeking, how are they behaving, these Germans ? Like barbarians. They have treated our Ambassador with infamous discourtesy. They have behaved with incredible insolence and boorishness to our Consuls. The barbaric nature of the enemy is revealed in a way which will never be forgotten. Fortunately, we have European civilization on our side. All the cultured races sympathize with us. They know that Europe would be lost if the German Empire, with its policy of blood and iron, with its military caste and tyranny, should become more dominant and stride across the frontiers of civilized States. But of the ultimate issue of this war there can be no doubt. With Great Britain fighting side by side with France, with Russia attacking on the Eastern front, what hopes can Germany nourish now ? The war may be a long struggle ; it may lead to many desperate battles ; but in the end the enemy must be doomed. Where is her boasted organization ? Already our prisoners tell us that they were starving when they fought. It seems as though these critics of French military organization were demoralized at the outset. *Ils ont bluffé tout le temps !* I can assure you that we are full of confidence, and perfectly satisfied with the way in which the war is progressing."

4

This Minister of France was " perfectly satisfied." His optimism cheered me, though all his words had not told me the things I wanted to know, nor lifted the corner of that veil which hid the smoke and flash of guns. But the French had taken prisoners and somewhere or other masses of men were fighting and dying. . . . As I came back from the Quai d'Orsay and a stroll in the Champs Elysées through the golden twilight of a splendid day, when the lamps of Paris began to gleam like stars through the shimmering haze and the soft foliage of the most beautiful highway in the world, there came a clatter of hoofs and the music of soldiers' harness. It was a squadron of the Garde Republicaine riding on the last patrol of the day round the ramparts of Paris. I watched them gallop through the Arc de Triomphe, their black *crinières* streaming backwards like smoke from their helmets. They rode towards the setting sun, a crimson bar across the blue of the sky, and when I walked back slowly to the heart of Paris the boulevards were already quiet, and in the velvety darkness which overtook me there was peace and order. Only the silence of the streets told me that France was at war.

5

Obviously it was hopeless to stay in Paris waiting for official permission to follow the armies as a correspondent and to penetrate more deeply into the heart of that mystery which was fogged more deeply by the words that came forth every day from the Ministry of War. The officials were very polite and took great trouble to soothe the excited emotions of would-be war correspondents. " In a few days, gentlemen, if all continues to go well." They desired our photographs, in duplicate, a medical certificate of health, recommendations as to our mental and moral qualities, formal applications and informal interviews. But meanwhile the war was being fought and we were seeing nothing.

News of great victory came to Paris when the bulletins announced the advance of French troops in Alsace and the capture of Mulhouse and Altkirch. Instantly there were joyous scenes in the streets. Boulevards, which had been strangely quiet, became thronged with men and women called out from the twilight of their rooms by this burst of sunlight, as it seemed. The news held the magic thrill of an Alsace restored to France. . . . It was long afterwards that Paris heard strange and evil rumours of reverses down there, of a regiment which flung down its rifles and fled under a tempest of shells, of officers shot by their own guns, of a general cashiered for grievous errors.

From Liège there came more news. The imagination of Paris, deprived of all sustenance as regards its own troops, fed greedily upon the banquet of blood which had been given to it by the gallant Belgians. In messages coming irregularly through the days and nights, three or four lines at a time, it was possible to grasp the main facts of that heroic stand against the German legions. We were able to perceive from afar the raking fire of the forts around the city, which swept the ground so that the most famous regiments of the German army were mowed down as they advanced with desperate courage.

" If Liège holds out the German troops are in a hopeless position." These words were repeated along the boulevards of Paris, and because Liège held out so long the spirit of Paris was exalted.

But, as a journalist out to see things, I was depressed. It was useless to wait in Paris while the days were slipping by and history was being made. Official permission was delayed, by fair and courteous words. I decided to go in search of the war without permission and to get somehow or other behind the scenes of its secrecy. So my adventures began, and in a little while my eyes became seared with the sight of tragedy and my soul filled with the enormous woe of war.

6

It was a strange kind of melodrama that experience in the first two months of the war. Looking back upon it now, it has just the effect of a prolonged nightmare stimulated by hasheesh or bang—fantastic, full of confused dreams, changing kaleidoscopically from one scene to another, with vivid clear-cut pictures, intensely imagined, between gulfs of dim twilight memories, full of shadow figures, faces seen a little while and then lost, conversations begun abruptly and then ended raggedly, poignant emotions lasting for brief moments and merging into others as strong but of a different quality, gusts of laughter rising between moods of horrible depression, tears sometimes welling from the heart and then choked back by a brutal touch of farce, beauty and ugliness in sudden clashing contrasts, the sorrow of a nation, the fear-of a great people, the misery of women and children, the intolerable anguish of multitudes of individuals each with a separate agony, making a dark background to this too real dream from which there was no awakening.

I was always travelling during those eight or nine weeks of history—for the most time I had two companions with me—dear fellows whose comradeship was a fine personal pleasure, in spite of all the pain into which we plunged. Together we journeyed continually and prodigiously, covering thousands of miles during those weeks, in all sorts of directions, by all sorts of ways, in troop trains and cattle trucks, in motor-cars and taxi-cabs, and on Shanks's nag. There were no couriers in those days between France and England, and to get our dispatches home we often had to take them across the Channel, using most desperate endeavours to reach a port of France in time for the next boat home and staying in Fleet Street only a few hours before hurrying back to Dover or Folkestone in order to plunge again into the fever of invaded France. Later Paris was our goal, and we would struggle back to it along lines choked with munitions of war or completely held for the transport of great masses of troops, arriving, at night as a rule, weary for lack of sleep, dirty from the filth of cattle trucks crowded with unwashed men and women, hungry after meagre rations of biscuits and cheese, mentally and physically exhausted; so that one such night I had to be carried upstairs to my room, so weak that I could not drag one leg after the other nor lift a hand from the coverlet. On another day one of my companions—the Strategist—sat back, rather quiet, in a taxi-cab which panted in a wheezy way along the interminably straight roads of France, through villages from which all their people had fled under the shadow of a great fear which followed them, until when the worn-out vehicle could go no further, but halted helplessly on a lonely highway remote as it seemed from any habitation, my friend confessed that he was weak even as a new-born babe and could not walk a hundred yards to save his life. Yet he is a strong man who had never been in a doctor's hands since childhood.

His weakness, the twist of pain about his mouth, the weariness in his eyes, scared us then. The Philosopher, who had not yet begun to feel in his bones the heat of the old tropical fever which afterwards made him toss at nights and call out strange words, shook his head and spoke with the enormous gravity which gives an air of prophecy and awful wisdom to a man whose sense of humour and ironic wit have often twisted me into painful knots of mirth. But there was no glint of humour in the Philosopher's eyes when he stared at the greyness of the Strategist.

"The pace has been too hot," he said. "We seem to forget that there's a limit to the strain we can put on the human machine. It's not only the physical fatigue. It's the continual output of nervous energy. All this misery, all that damn thing over there "—he waved his paw at the darkening hills beyond which was a great hostile army— "the sight of all these refugees spilt out of their cities and homes as though a great hand had tipped up the earth, is beginning to tell on us, my lads. We are spending our reserve force, and we are just about whacked ! "

Yet we went on, mixed up always in refugee rushes, in masses of troops moving forward to the front or backwards in retreat, getting brief glimpses of the real happenings behind the screen of secrecy, meeting the men who could tell us the hidden truth, and more than once escaping, by the nick of time only, from a death-trap into which we had tumbled unwittingly, not knowing the whereabouts of the enemy, nor his way of advance.

7

In the early days of the war, the first stampede which overwhelmed us had a touch of comedy unless one's imagina tion were shocked by the panic of great crowds, in which always and for whatever cause there is something degrading to the dignity of human nature. It was the panic rush of the world's tourists suddenly trapped by war in the pleasure haunts of Europe. They had come out to France, Switzerland, Italy and Egypt with well-lined purses, for the most part, and with the absolute conviction not disturbed by any shadow of doubt, that their ways would be made smooth by Cook's guides, hotel managers, British and American consuls, and foreigners of all classes eager to bow before them, to show them the sights, to carry their baggage, to lick, if need be, their boots. They had money, they belonged to the modern aristocracy of the well-to-do. Was not Europe their garden of pleasure, providing for them, in return for the price of a season ticket, old monuments, famous pictures, sunsets over Swiss mountains, historic buildings starred by Baedeker, peculiar customs of aborigines, haunts of vice to be viewed with a sense of virtue, and good hotels in which there was a tendency to over-eat?

The pleasure of these rich Americans and comfortable English tourists was suddenly destroyed by the thunderbolt of war. They were startled to find that strong laws were hastily enacted against them and put in force with extraordinary brutality. Massed under the name of *étrangers* —they had always looked upon the natives as the only foreigners—they were ordered to leave certain countries and certain cities within twenty-four hours, otherwise they would be interned in concentration camps under armed guards for the duration of the war. But to leave these countries and cities they had to be provided with a passport —hardly an American among them had such a document— and with a *laisser-passer* to be obtained from the police and countersigned by military authorities, after strict interrogation.

The comedy began on the first day of mobilization, and developed into real tragedy as the days slipped by. For although at first there was something a little ludicrous in the plight of the well-to-do, brought down with a crash to the level of the masses and loaded with paper money which was as worthless as Turkish bonds, so that the millionaire was for the time being no richer than the beggar, pity stirred in one at the sight of real suffering and anguish of mind.

Outside the *commissariats de police* in Paris and provincial towns of France, like Dijon and Lyons, and in the ports of Calais, Boulogne and Dieppe, there were great crowds of these tourists lined up in queue and waiting wearily through the hours until their turn should come to be measured with their backs to the wall and to be scrutinized by police officers, sullen after a prolonged stream of entreaty and expostulation, for the colour of their eyes and hair, the shape of their noses and chins, and the "distinctive marks" of their physical beauty or ugliness.

" I guess I'll never come to this Europe again ! " said an American lady who had been waiting for five hours in a side street in Paris for this ordeal. " It's a cruel shame to treat American citizens as though they were thieves and rogues. I wonder the President of the United States don't make a protest about it. Are people here so ignorant they don't even know the name of Josiah K. Schultz, of Boston, Massachusetts ? "

The commissary's clerk inside the building was quite unmoved by the name of Josiah K. Schultz, of Boston, Massachusetts. It held no magic for him, and he seemed to think that the lady-wife of that distinguished man might be a German spy with American papers. He kept her waiting, deliberately, though she had waited for five hours in the street outside.

8

The railway time-tables ceased to have a meaning after the first hour of mobilization. Bradshaw became a lie and civil passengers were only allowed on the rare trains which ran without notice at any hour of the day or night, at the discretion of military officers, according to the temporary freedom of the line from troop trains and supply trains. Those tourist crowds suffered intolerable things, which I shared with them, though I was a different kind of traveller. I remember one such scene at Dijon, typical of many others. Because only one train was starting on that day to the capital, and the time of it was utterly unknown to the railway officials, three or four hundred people had to wait hour after hour, for half a night, penned up in a waiting-room, which

D

became foul with the breath and heat of so many people. In vain did they appeal to be let out on to the platform where there would be more air and space. A sentry with fixed bayonet stood with his back to them and barred the way Old ladies sat down in despair on their baggage, wedged between legs straddled across their bags. A delicate woman near me swooned in the stifling atmosphere. I had watched her grow whiter and whiter and heard the faintness of her sighs, so that when she swayed I grasped her by the arm and held her up until her husband relieved me of her weight. A Frenchwoman had a baby at her breast. It cried with an unceasing wail. Other babies were crying; and young girls, with sensitive nerves, were exasperated by this wailing misery and the sickening smell which pervaded this closed room.

9

When the train came in, the door was opened and there was a wild rush for the carriages, without the English watchword of "women and children first." Thrust on one side by sharp elbows, I and my two friends struggled at last into the corridor, and for nineteen hours sat there on the sharp edges of our upturned trunks, fixed rigidly between the bodies of other travellers. To the left of us was a French peasant, a big, quiet man, with a bovine gift of patience and utterly taciturn. After the first five minutes I suspected that somewhere concealed about his person was a ripe cheese. There was a real terror in the malodorous vapours which exhaled from him. In a stealthy way they crept down the length of the corridor, so that other people, far away, flung open windows and thrust out heads, in spite of the night air with a bite of frost in it. I dozed uneasily with horrid dreams as I sat on three inches of hard box, with my head jogging sideways. Always I was conscious of the evil smell about me, but when the peasant was still I was able to suffer it, because of sheer weariness, which deadened my senses. It was when he moved, disturbing invisible layers of air, that I awakened horribly. . . .

10

For the nice people of the world whom fate had pampered, there was a cruelty in this mode of travel. Hunger, with its sharp tooth, assailed some of them for the first time. We stopped at wayside stations—still more often between the stations—but American millionaires and English aristocrats were stupefied to find that not all their money could buy a sandwich. Most of the buffets had been cleaned out by the army passing to the front. Thirst, intolerable and choking, was a greater pain in those hot dog-days and in those tedious interminable journeys.

Yet it is only fair to say that on the whole those tourists chased across the Continent by the advancing spectre of war, behaved with pluck and patience. Some of them had suffered grievous loss. From Bâle and Geneva to Paris and Boulogne the railways were littered with their abandoned luggage, too bulky to be loaded into overcrowded trains. On the roads of France were broken-down motor-cars which had cost large sums of money in New York and London. But because war's stupendous evil makes all other things seem trivial, and the gifts of liberty and life are more precious than wealth or luxury, so these rich folk in misfortune fraternized cheerfully in the discussion of their strange adventures and shared the last drop of hot tea in a Thermos flask with the generous instincts of shipwrecked people dividing their rations on a desert isle.

11

This flight of the pleasure-seekers was the first revelation of the way in which war would hurt the non-combatant and sacrifice his business or his comfort to its supreme purpose. Fame was merely foolishness when caught in the trap of martial law. I saw a man of European reputation flourish his card before railway officials, to be thrust back by the butt end of a rifle. No money could buy a seat in a railway carriage already crowded to suffocation. No threat to write a letter to the *Times* would avail an old-fashioned Englishman when his train was shunted for hours on to a side line to make way for troop trains, passing, passing, through the day and night. Nations were at war, and whatever stood in the way of the war's machine would be trampled underfoot or thrust on one side with brutal indifference. Their fame did not matter nor their struggles to escape from a closing net. Neither the beauty of women nor the weakness of children nor the importance of the world's great somebodies mattered a jot. Nothing mattered except fighting-men, and guns, and food for guns and men.

12

The French soldiers who were being sent towards the unknown front—not knowing their own destination and forbidden to ask—had recovered from the shock of the sudden call to the colours and the tragedy of their hurried partings from wives, and sweethearts, and old mothers, who are always dearest to Frenchmen's hearts. The thrill of a nation's excitement brought a sparkle to their eyes and a flush to their cheeks. The inherent gaiety of the French race rose triumphant above the gloom and doubt which had preceded the declaration of war. Would they never tire of singing the Marseillaise ? Would all this laughter which came in gusts through the open doors of cattle trucks and the windows of third-class carriages change into the moan of the wounded at their journey's end ? It was hard to look forward to that inevitable fate as I watched them pass. They had tied flowers to the handles of their trains and twisted garlands round the bars. There were posies in their *képis*, and bouquets were pinned by the plump hands of peasant girls to the jackets of the soldiers of the line, gunners, cuirassiers, dragoons, and *fusiliers marins*. Between the chorus of the Marseillaise came snatches of songs learnt in the cabarets of Montmartre and the cafés chantants of provincial towns. They swarmed like bees—in blue coats and red trousers—upon those enormous troop trains which passed through Gournai and Pontoise, Rouen and Amiens. Rows of them, grinning down under peaks at freakish angles, dangled their legs over as they squatted on the roofs of the wooden trucks. They hung on to the iron ladders of the guards' vans. Sometimes six of them would be installed on the ledge behind the funnel of the engine, with their russet faces to the wind. In the argot of Paris slums, or in the dialects of seaport towns, they hurled chaff at comrades waiting on the platforms with stacked arms, and made outrageous love to girls who ran by the side of their trains with laughing eyes and saucy tongues and a last farewell of " Bonne chance, mes petits ! Bonne chance et toujours la victoire ! " At every wayside halt artists were at work with white chalk drawing grotesque faces on the carriage doors below which they scrawled inscriptions referring to the death of " William," and banquets in Berlin, and invitations for free trips to the Rhine. In exchange for a few English cigarettes, too few for such trainloads, they gave me ovations of enthusiasm, as though I stood for England.

" Vive l'Angleterre ! Vos soldats, ou sont ils, camarade ? "

Where were the English soldiers ? It was always that question which sprang to their lips. But for a little while I could not answer. It was strange. There was no news of the crossing of the Expeditionary Force to France. In the French and English newspapers no word was said about any British soldiers on French soil. Was there some unaccountable delay, or were we fulfilling our bond privately, a great drama being played behind the scenes, like the secret war ?

18

Then just for a moment the veil was lifted and Lord Kitchener allowed the British people to know that their soldiers had landed on the other side. Even then we who knew more than that were not allowed to mention the places to which they had gone. Never mind. They were here. We heard quite suddenly the familiar accents of English Tommies in provincial towns of France, and came unexpectedly upon khaki-clad battalions marching and singing along the country roads. For the first time there rang out in France the foolish ballad which has become by a queer freak the war song of the British Army : " It's a long way to Tipperary," learnt with comical accent by French peasants and French girls, who, in those early days, in the first fine thrill of enthusiasm, sang it emotionally as though it were a hymn, holding all their love for England, all their hope of England's help, all their admiration of these clean-shaven boys going to war in France in a sporting spirit as though it were a great game.   I went back to Paris for a day when General French arrived, and even now in remembrance I hear those shouts of " Vive l'Angleterre ! " which followed the motor-car in which our General made his triumphant progress.   The shopgirls of Paris threw flowers from the windows as the car passed.   Dense crowds of citizens thronged the narrow street of the Faubourg St. Honoré, and waited patiently for hours outside the Embassy to catch one glimpse of the strong, stern, thoughtful face of the man who had come with his legions to assist France in the great hour of need. They talked to each other about the inflexibility of his character, about the massive jaw which, they said, would bite off Germany's head.   They cheered in the English manner, with a " Heep ! heep ! hooray ! "—when they caught sight for the first time of the khaki uniforms of English officers on the steps of the Ministry of War.   The arrival of English troops here was red wine to the hearts of the French people. It seemed to them the great guarantee of victory.   " With England marching side by side with us," they said, " we shall soon be in Berlin ! "

14

A train-load of Royal Engineers came into one of the stations where I happened to be waiting (my memory of those days is filled with weary hours on station platforms). It was the first time I was able to talk to British Tommies in France, and to shake their hands, and to shout out " Good luck ! " to them.   It was curious how strong my emotion was at seeing those laughing fellows and hearing the cockney accent of their tongues.   They looked so fine and clean. Some of them were making their toilet in the cattle trucks brushing their hair as though for a picnic party, shaving before little mirrors tacked up on the planks. Others, crowding at the open doorways of the trucks, shouted with laughter at the French soldiers and peasants, who grabbed at their hands and jabbered enthusiastic words of welcome.

" Funny lingo, Bill ! " said one of the men. " Can't make out a bit of it. But they mean well, I guess ! "

It was impossible to doubt that they meant well, these soldiers of France greeting their comrades of England. One man behaved like a buffoon, or as though he had lost his wits. Grasping the hand of a young engineer he danced round him, shouting " Camarade ! camarade ! " in a joyous sing-song which was ridiculous, and yet touching in its simplicity and faith. It was no wonder, I thought, that the French people believed in victory now that the British had come. A Jingo pride took possession of me. These Tommies of ours were the finest soldiers in the world ! They went to war with glad hearts. They didn't care a damn for old Von Kluck and all his hordes. They would fight like heroes, these clean-limbed chaps, who looked upon war as a great game. Further along the train my two friends, the Philosopher and the Strategist, were in deep conversation with different groups. I heard gusts of laughter from the truck-load of men looking down on the Philosopher. He had discovered a man from Wapping, I think, and was talking in the accent of Stratford-atte-Bow to boys from that familiar district of his youth. The Strategist had met the engineers in many camps in England. They were surprised at his knowledge of their business. And what were we doing out here ? Newspaper correspondents ? Ah, there would be things to write about ! When the train passed out, with waving hands from every carriage, with laughing faces caught already by the sun of France, with farewell shouts of " Good luck, boys ! " and " Bonne chance, camarades ! " three Englishmen turned away silently and could not speak for a minute or two. Why did the Philosopher blink his eyes in such a funny way, as though they smarted at specks of dust ? And why did the Strategist look so grave all of a sudden, as he stood staring after the train, with his cap in his hand, so that the sunlight gleamed on his silver-grey hair ?

15

So the British Army had come to France, and a strange chapter was being written in the history of the world, contrasting amazingly with former chronicles. English battalions bivouacked by old French houses which had looked down upon scenes of revolution in 1789, and in the shadow of its churches which rang for French victories or tolled for French defeats when Napoleon's generals were fighting English regiments exactly one hundred years ago. In seaport villages and towns which smell of tar and nets and absinthe and stale wine I saw horses stabled in every inn-yard ; streets were littered with straw, and English soldiers sauntered about within certain strict boundaries, studying picture post-cards and giving the " glad eye " to any little French girl who peeped at them through barred windows. Only officers of high rank knew where they were bound. The men, devoid of all curiosity, were satisfied with the general knowledge that they were " on the continong," and well on the way to " have a smack at the Germans." There was the rattle and rumble of English guns down country highways. Long lines of khaki-clad men, like a writhing brown snake when seen from afar, moved slowly along winding roads, through cornfields where the harvest was cut and stacked, or down long avenues of poplars, interminably straight, or through quaint old towns and villages with whitewashed houses and overhanging gables, and high stone steps leading to barns and dormer-chambers. Some of those little provincial towns have hardly changed since D'Artagnan and his Musketeers rode on their way to great adventures in the days of Richelieu and Mazarin. And the spirit of D'Artagnan was still bred in them, in the France of Poincaré, for they are the dwelling-places of young men in the cuirassiers and the chasseurs who had been chasing Uhlans through the passes of the Vosges, capturing outposts even though the odds were seven to one.

The English officers and men will never have to complain

of their welcome in France. It was overwhelming—even a little intoxicating to young soldiers. As they marched through the towns peasant girls ran along the ranks with great bouquets of wild flowers, which they thrust into the soldiers' arms. In every market square where the regiments halted for a rest there was free wine for any thirsty throat, and soldier boys from Scotland or England had their brown hands kissed by girls who were eager for hero worship and had fallen in love with these clean-shaven lads and their smiling grey eyes. In those early days there seemed no evil in the worship of the women nor in the hearts of the men who marched to the song of " Tipperary." Every man in khaki could claim a hero's homage for himself on any road in France, at any street corner of an old French town. It was some time before the romance wore off, and the realities of human nature, where good is mixed with evil and blackguardism marches in the same regiment with clean-hearted men, destroyed some of the illusions of the French and demanded an iron discipline from military police and made poor peasant girls repent of their abandonment in the first ecstasy of their joyous welcome.

16

Not yet did the brutalities of the war spoil the picture painted in khaki tones upon the green background of the French countryside. From my notebook I transcribe one of the word pictures which I wrote at the time. It is touched with the emotion of those days, and is true to the facts which followed :

" The weather has been magnificent. It has been no hardship to sleep out in the roads and fields at night. A harvest moon floods the country with silver light and glints upon the stacked bayonets of this British Army in France when the men lie down beneath their coats, with their haversacks as pillows. Each sleeping figure is touched softly by those silver rays while the sentries pace up and down upon the outskirts of the camp. Some of the days have been intensely hot, but the British Tommy unfastens his coat and leaves his shirt open at the chest, and with the sun bronzing his face to a deeper, richer tint, marches on, singing a cockney ballad as though he were on the road to Weybridge or Woking. They are young fellows, many of them—beardless boys who have not yet been hard-bitten by a long campaign and have not received their baptism of fire. Before they have been many days in the fields of France they will not look so fresh and smart. Those grey eyes of theirs will be haunted by the memory of battlefields at night, when the stretcher-bearers are searching for the wounded who lie among the dead. Not yet do these boys know the real meaning of war. But they belong to the same breed of men who a hundred years ago fought with Wellington in the Peninsula. There is no possible need to doubt that they will maintain the old traditions of their regiments and add new records to their colours. Before this war is finished these soldiers of ours, who are singing on their way, in dapper suits of khaki, will be all tattered and torn, with straw tied round their feet, with stubby beards on their chins, with the grime of gunpowder and dust and grease and mud and blood upon their hands and faces. They will have lost the freshness of their youth : but those who remain will have gained—can we doubt it ?—the reward of stubborn courage and unfailing valour."

17

Not many days after these words were written, I came upon a scene which fulfilled them, too quickly. At a French junction there was a shout of command in English, and I saw a body of men in khaki, with Red Cross armlets, run across a platform to an incoming train from the north, with stretchers and drinking bottles. A party of English soldiers had arrived from a battle at a place called Mons. With French passengers from another train, I was kept back by soldiers with fixed bayonets, but through the hedge of steel I saw a number of " Tommies " with bandaged heads and limbs descending from the troop train. Some of them hung limp between their nurses. Their faces, so fresh when

I had first seen them on the way out, had become grey and muddy, and were streaked with blood. Their khaki uniforms were torn and cut. One poor boy moaned pitiably as they carried him away on a stretcher. They were the first fruits of this unnatural harvesting, lopped and maimed by a cruel reaper. I stared at them with a kind of sickness, more agonized than afterwards when I saw more frightful things. It came as a queer, silly shock to me then to realize that in this secret war for which I was searching men were really being smashed and killed, and that out of the mystery of it, out of the distant terror from which great multitudes were fleeing, out of the black shadow creeping across the sunlit hills of France, where the enemy, whom no fugitives had seen, was advancing like a moving tide, there should come these English boys, crippled and broken, from an unknown battle. I was able to speak to one of them, wounded only in the hand, but there was no time for more than a question or two and an answer which hardly gave me definite knowledge.

" We got it in the neck ! " said the sergeant of the R.F.A. He repeated the words as if they held all truth.

" We got it in the neck ! "

" Where ? " I asked.

He waved his wounded hand northwards, and said : " Mons."

" Do you mean we were beaten ? In retreat ? "

He shrugged his shoulders.

" We gave 'em what for. Oh, yes, they had to pay right enough. But they were too much for us. Came on like lice . . . swarming. . . . Couldn't kill enough. . . . Then we got it in the neck. . . . Lost a good few men. . . . Gord, I've never seen such work ! South Africa ? No more than child's play to this 'ere game ! "

He gave a queer kind of grin, with no mirth in his eyes, and went away with the other wounded men.

Mons ? It was the first I had heard of a battle there And our men were having a hard time. The enemy were too much for us. Was it a retreat ? Perhaps a rout ?

18

The Philosopher answered these unspoken questions.

" You always get the gloomy view from wounded men. I dare say it's not an easy thing to stop those blighters, but I've faith in the justice of God. The Great Power ain't going to let Prussian militarism win out. It's going to be smashed because of its essential rottenness. It's all right, laddie ! "

The Strategist was studying his map, and working out military possibilities.

" Mons. I expect our next line of defence will be Le Cateau and Cambrai. If we're hard pressed we shall hear something about St. Quentin, too. It's quite on the cards we shall have to fall back, but I hope to Heaven in good order and with sound lines of communication."

" It's frightful ! " I said. " We are seeing nothing of all this. Nothing ! . . . If only we could get near it ! "

19

It was some time before we heard the guns, but not long before we saw the effects of war, in blood, anguish, and tears.

The French newspapers, telling little of the truth, giving barely one single fact to a page full of heroic sentiment, had not let us guess that, beyond the frontiers of France, the enemy was doing frightful damage, with a rapidity and ruthlessness which, after the check at Liège, was a tremendous menace to the Allied armies. I understood these things better, in a stark nakedness of truth, when I found myself caught in the tumult of a nation in flight.

I have already touched upon one tide of panic—the stampede of the pleasure-seekers. That was a mere jest' lacking all but the touch of cruelty which gives a spice to so many of life's witticisms ; but the second tide, overflowing in wave after wave of human misery, reached great heights of tragedy which submerged all common griefs. From that day in August until many months of war had passed I was seldom out of sight of this ruin of Belgium

I went into the heart of it, into the welter of blood and wreckage, and stood, expecting death, in the very process of its deadly torture. Week after week, month after month, I walked and talked with Belgian fugitives, and drifted in that stream of exiled people, and watched them in the far places of their flight, where they were encamped in settled hopelessness, asking nothing of the fate which had dealt them such foul blows, expecting nothing. But I still remember my first impressions of war's cruelty to that simple people who had desired to live in peace and had no quarrel with any Power. It was in a kind of stupor that I saw the vanguard of this nation in retreat, a legion of poor old women whose white hairs were wild in this whirl of human derelicts, whose decent black clothes were rumpled and torn and fouled in the struggle for life ; with Flemish mothers clasping babies at their breasts and fierce-eyed as wild animals because of the terror in their hearts for those tiny buds of life ; with small children scared out of the divine security of childhood by this abandonment of homes which had seemed the world to them, and terrorized by an unknown horror which lurked in the name of Germany ; with men of all classes and all ages, intellectuals and peasants, stout bourgeois, whose overload of flesh was a burden to their flight, thin students whose book-tired eyes were filled with a dazed bewilderment, men of former wealth and dignity reduced to beggary and humiliation ; with school-girls whose innocence of life's realities was suddenly thrust face to face with things ugly and obscene, and cruel as hell.

20

I think it is impossible to convey to those who did not see this exodus of the Belgian people the meaning and misery of it. Even in the midst of it I had a strange idea at first that it was only a fantasy and that such things do not happen. Afterwards I became so used to it all that I came to think the world must always have been like this, with people always in flight, families and crowds of families drifting about aimlessly, from town to town, getting into

trains just because they started somewhere for somewhere
else, sitting for hours on bundles which contained all their
worldly goods saved from the wreckage of ancient homes,
losing their children on the roadside, and not fretting very
much, and finding other children, whom they adopted as
their own ; never washing on that wandering, so that
delicate women who had once been perfumed with fine
scents were dirty as gipsies and unashamed of draggled
dresses and dirty hands ; eating when they found a meal
of charity, sleeping in railway sidings, coalsheds, and derelict
trains shunted on to grass-covered lines ; careless as pariah
dogs of what the future held in store now that they had lost
all things in the past.

21

On the railway sidings near Calais there was one sight
that revealed the defeat of a nation more even than these
crowds of refugees. Hundreds of Belgian engines had been
rushed over the frontier to France to escape from being
used in the enemy's service. These derelict things stood
there in long rows with a dismal look of lifelessness and
abandonment, and as I looked at them I knew that though
the remnants of the Belgian army might be fighting in its
last ditch and holding out at Antwerp against the siege guns
of the Germans, there could be no hope of prolonged resistance
against overwhelming armies. These engines, which should
have been used for Belgian transport, for men and food
and guns, were out of action, and dead symbols of a nation's
ruin.

22

For the first time I saw Belgian soldiers in France, and
although they were in small number compared with the
great army of retreat which, after the fall of Antwerp, I saw
marching into Dunkirk, their weariness and listlessness told
a tale of woe. At first sight there was something comical
in the aspect of these top-hatted soldiers. They reminded
me of battalions of London cabbies who had ravaged the

dustbins for discarded "toppers." Their double-breasted coats had just the cut of those of the ancient jehus who used to sit aloft on decrepit " growlers." Other bodies of Belgian soldiers wore ludicrous little *képis* with immense eye-shades, mostly broken or hanging limp in a dejected way. In times of peace I should have laughed at the look of them. But now there was nothing humorous about these haggard, dirty men from Ghent who had borne the first shock of the German attack. They. seemed stupefied for lack of sleep, or dazed after the noise of battle. I asked some of them where they were going, but they shook their heads and answered gloomily :

"We don't know. We know nothing, except that our Belgium is destroyed. What is the news ? "

23

There was no news—beyond what one could glean from the incoherent tales of Belgian refugees. The French newspapers still contained vague and cheerful bulletins about their own military situation, and filled the rest of their meagre space with eloquent praise of *les braves petits Belges*. The war was still hidden behind impenetrable walls of silence. Gradually, however, as I dodged about the western side of France, from the middle to the end of August, it became clear to me, and to my two friends, the Philosopher and the Strategist, who each in his way of wisdom confirmed my worst suspicions, that the situation for both the French and the British armies was enormously grave. In spite of the difficulty of approaching the war zone—at that time there was no certain knowledge as to the line of front—we were seeing things which could not be concealed by any censorship. We saw, too clearly for any doubt, that the war zone was approaching us, steadily and rapidly. The shadow of its looming terror crept across the fields of France, though they lay all golden in the sunlight of the harvest month.

24

After the struggling tides of fugitive tourists, and over-lapping the waves of Belgian refugees, there came new streams of panic-stricken people, and this time they were French. They came from the northern towns—Lille, Roubaix, Tourcoing, Armentières, and from scores of villages further south which had seemed utterly safe and aloof from hostile armies which, with faith in official communiqués issued by the French Ministry of War, we believed to be still checked beyond the French frontier in Belgium. Lille? Was Lille threatened by the Kaiser's troops? It had been evacuated? No, that could not be true, unless treachery had been at work, Lille could hold out, surely, at least as long as Liège! Had we not read long articles by the military experts of the French Press describing the strength of that town and the impregnable position of its forts? Yet here were refugees from Lille who had heard the roar of German guns, and brought incredible stories of French troops in retreat, and spoke the name of a French general with bitter scorn, and the old cry of "*Nous sommes trahis!*"

The refugees from the north were in as pitiable a state as those who had preceded them from Belgium. More pitiable, because when they reached such ports as Calais or Boulogne or Havre, the hotels and lodging-houses were overcrowded from attic to cellars, the buffets had been swept clear of food, and committees of relief were already distracted with the overwhelming needs of a Belgian invasion.

25

I remember a day and night in Boulogne. The narrow streets—evil with odours brought forth by a hot sun, were filled with surging crowds which became denser as new trains arrived from Calais and Dunkirk and junctions on northern lines. The people carried with them the salvage of their homes, wrapped up in blankets, sheets, towels and bits of ragged paper. Parcels of grotesque shapes, containing copper pots, frying pans, clocks, crockery and all kinds of domestic utensils or treasured ornaments, bulged on the pavements and quaysides, where whole families sat encamped. Stalwart mothers of Normandy and Picardy trudged through the streets with children clinging to their skirts, with babies in their arms and with big French loaves—the commissariat of these journeys of despair—cuddled to their bosoms with the babes. Old grandfathers and grandmothers, who looked as though they had never left their native villages before, came hand in hand, with shaking heads and watery eyes, bewildered by all this turmoil of humanity which had been thrust out, like themselves, from its familiar ways of life. Well-to-do bourgeois, hot, with frayed nerves, exhausted by an excess of emotion and fatigue, searched for lodgings, anywhere and at any price, jostled by armies of peasants, shaggy-haired, in clumping sabots, with bundles on their backs, who were wandering on the same quest for the sake of the women and children dragging wearily in their wake. I heard a woman cry out words of surrender : " Je n'en peux plus ! " She was spent and could go no further, but halted suddenly, dumped down her bundles and her babies and, leaning against a sun-baked wall, thrust the back of a rough hand across her forehead, with a moan of spiritual pain.

" Dieu ! . . . C'est trop ! c'est trop ! "

All day long these scenes went on, until I could bear them no longer, but went indoors to the room which made me feel a selfish monster because I shared it with only two friends. Boulogne became quiet in the darkness. Perhaps by some miracle all those homeless ones had found a shelter. . . . I awakened out of a drowsy sleep to hear the tramp of innumerable feet. A new army of fugitives had come into the town. I heard voices murmuring below my window, arguing, pleading. There was a banging at doors down the street.

" C'est impossible ! Il n'y a pas de place ! Il y a une foule qui dort en plein air. Voyez ! voyez ! "

The night porter slammed his own door in a rage. Perhaps there was pity in his heart as well as rage, but what can a man do when people demand admittance to an hotel where there are already six people in the bathroom and sixty on the floor of the salon, and stiff bodies wrapped in blankets, like corpses in eternal sleep, lying about in the corridors ?

" There are crowds of people sleeping in the open air," he said, and when I leaned out of the window, staring into the darkness of the night and breathing in the cool air which had an autumn touch, I saw dimly on the pavement below huddled figures in the doorways and under the shelter of the eaves. A baby wailed with a thin cry. A woman's voice whimpered just below my window, and a man spoke to her.

" C'est la guerre ! "

The words came up to me as though to answer the question in my own mind as to why such things should be.

" C'est la guerre ! "

Yes, it was war; with its brutality against women and children, its horrible stupidity, its senseless overthrow of all life's decencies, and comforts, and security. The non-combatants were not to be spared, though they had not asked for war, and hated it.

CHAPTER IV

THE WAY OF RETREAT

1

OMINOUS things were happening behind the screen. Good God ! was France to see another *année terrible,* a second edition of 1870, with the same old tale of unreadiness, corruption in high quarters, breakdown of organization, and national humiliation after irreparable disasters ?

The very vagueness of the official communiqués and their word-jugglings to give a rose colour to black shadows advancing rapidly over the spirit of France suggested horrible uncertainties to those who were groping in search of plain truth. But not all the severity of the censorship, with its strangle-grip upon the truth-tellers, could hide certain frightful facts. All these refugees pouring down from the north could not be silenced, though none of their tales appeared in print. They came with the news that Lille was invested, that the German tide was rolling upon Armentières, Roubaix, Tourcoing and Cambrai, that the French and English were in hard retreat. The enemy's cavalry was spreading out in a great fan, with outposts of Uhlans riding into villages where old French peasants had not dreamed of being near the line of battle until, raising their heads from potato fields or staring across the stacked corn, they had seen the pointed casques and the flash of the sun on German carbines.

There were refugees who had seen the beginning of battles, taking flight before the end of them. I met some from Le Cateau, who had stared speechlessly at familiar hills over which came without warning great forces of foreign soldiers. The English had come first, in clouds of dust which powdered their uniforms and whitened their sun-baked faces. They seemed in desperate hurry and scratched up mounds of loose earth, like children building sand castles, and jumped down into wayside ditches which they used as cover, and lay on their stomachs in the beetroot fields. They were cheerful enough, and laughed as they littered the countryside with beef tins, and smoked cigarettes incessantly, as they lay scorched under the glare of the sun, with their rifles handy. Their guns were swung round with their muzzles nosing towards the rising ground from which these English soldiers had come. It seemed as though they were playing games of make believe, for the fun of the thing. The French peasants had stood round grinning at these English boys who could not understand a word of French, but chattered cheerfully all the time in their own strange language. War seemed very far away. The birds were singing in a shrill chorus. Golden flowerlets spangled the green slopes. The sun lay warm upon the hillside, and painted black shadows beneath the full foliage of the trees. It was the harvest peace which these peasants had known all the years of their lives. Then suddenly the click of rifle bolts, a rapid change in the attitude of the English soldier boys, who stared northwards where the downs rose and fell in soft billows, made the French peasants gaze in that direction, shading their eyes from the hot sun. What was that grey shadow moving ? What were those little glints and flashes in the greyness of it ? What were all those thousands of little ant-like things crawling forward over the slopes ? Thousands and scores of thousands of— men, and horses and guns !

"Les Anglais ?   Toujours les Anglais ? "

An English officer laughed, in a queer way, without any mirth in his eyes.

"Les Allemands, mon vieux.   Messieurs les Boches ! "

"L'enemi ?   Non—pas possible ! "

It only seemed possible that it was the enemy when from that army of ants on the hillsides there came forth little puffs of white smoke, and little stabbing flames, and when, quite soon, some of those English boys lay in a huddled way

over their rifles, with their sunburned faces on the warm
earth. The harvest peace was broken by the roar of guns
and the rip of bullets. Into the blue of the sky rose clouds
of greenish smoke. Pieces of jagged steel, like flying scythes,
sliced the trees on the roadside. The beetroot fields spurted
up earth, and great holes were being dug by unseen ploughs.
. . . Then, across the distant slopes behind the smoke
clouds and the burst of flame came, and came, a countless
army, moving down towards those British soldiers.

So the peasants had fled with a great fear.

2

There was an extraordinary quietude in some of the
port towns of northern France. At first I could not understand the meaning of it when I went from Calais to Boulogne,
and then to Havre. In Calais I saw small bodies of troops
moving out of the town early in the morning, so that afterwards there was not a soldier to be seen about the streets.
In Boulogne the same thing happened, quietly, and without
any bugle calls or demonstrations. Not only had all the
soldiers gone, but they were followed by the police, whom I
saw marching away in battalions, each man carrying a little
bundle, like the refugees who carried all their worldly goods
with them, wrapped in a blanket or a pocket-handkerchief,
according to the haste of their flight. Down on the quay
there were no custom-house officers to inspect the baggage
of the few travellers who had come across the Channel and
now landed on the deserted siding, bewildered because there
were no porters to clamour for their trunks and no *douane*
to utter the familiar ritual of " Avez-vous quelquè-chose à
declarer ? Tabac ? Cigarettes ? . . ." For the first time
in living memory, perhaps in the history of the port, the
Douane of Boulogne had abandoned its office. What did it
all mean ? Why were the streets so deserted as though the
town had been stricken with the plague ?

There was a look of plague in the faces of the few fisher-
men and harbour folk who stood in groups at the street
corners. There was a haggard fear in their eyes and they

talked in low voices, as though discussing some doom that had come upon them. Even the houses had a plaguy aspect, with shuttered windows and barred doors. The town, which had resounded to the tramp of British regiments and to the tune of " Tipperary," these streets through which had surged a tide of fugitives, with wave after wave of struggling crowds, had become a silent place, with only a few shadows creeping through the darkness of that evening in war, and whispering a fear.

The truth came to me as a shock. The ports of France had been abandoned. They lay open to the enemy, and if any Uhlans came riding in, or a German officer in a motor-car with three soldiers to represent an army, Calais and Boulogne would be surrendered without a shot.

Looking back upon those days the thing seems inconceivable. Months afterwards the enemy tried to fight its way to Calais and failed after desperate attacks which cost the lives of thousands of German soldiers and a stubborn defence which, more than once, was almost pierced and broken. " The Fight for Calais " is a chapter of history which for the Germans is written in blood. It is amazing to remember that in the last days of August Calais was offered as a free gift, with Boulogne and Dieppe to follow, if they cared to come for them.

Even Havre was to be abandoned as the British base. It was only a little while since enormous stores had been dumped here for the provisioning and equipment of our Expeditionary Force. Now I saw a great packing up. " K." had issued an amazing order which made certain young gentlemen of the A.S.C. whistle between their teeth and say rather quietly : " Ye gods ! things must be looking a bit blue up there." The new base was to be much further south, at St. Nazaire, to which the last tin of bully beef or Maconochie was to be consigned, without delay. Yes, things were looking very " blue," just then.

3

One may afford now to write about mistakes, even the mistakes of our French Allies, who have redeemed them all by a national heroism beyond the highest words of praise, and by a fine struggle for efficiency and organization which were lamentably lacking in the early days of the war. Knowing now the frightful blunders committed at the outset, and the hair's-breadth escape from tremendous tragedy, the miracle of the sudden awakening which enabled France to shake off her lethargy and her vanity, and to make a tiger's pounce upon an enemy which had almost brought her to her knees is one of the splendid things in the world's history which wipe out all rankling criticism.

Yet then, before the transformation, the days were full of torture for those who knew something of the truth. By what fatal microbe of folly had the French generals been tempted towards that adventure in Alsace ? Sentiment, overwhelming common sense, had sent the finest troops in France to the frontiers of the "lost provinces," so that Paris might have its day of ecstasy round the statue of Quand-Même. While the Germans were smashing their way through Belgium, checked only a little while at Liège and giving a clear warning of the road by which they would come to France, the French active army was massed in the east from Luxembourg to Nancy and wasting the strength which should have been used to bar the northern roads, in pressing forward to Mulhouse and Altkirch. It gave Georges Scott the subject of a beautiful allegory in *L'Illustration*— that French soldier clasping the Alsatian girl rescued from the German grip. It gave Parisian journalists, gagged about all other aspects of the war zone, a chance of heroic writing, filled with the emotion of old heartaches now changed to joy. Only the indiscretion of a deputy hinted for a moment at a bad reverse at Mulhouse, when a regiment recruited from the South, broke and fled under the fire of German guns because they were unsupported by their own artillery. "Two generals have been cashiered." " Some of the officers have been shot." Tragic rumours leaked into Paris, spoiling the dream of an irresistible advance.

So far, however, neither Paris nor the French public as a whole had any inkling of graver things than this. They did not know—how could they know anything of this secret war?—that on all parts of the front the French armies were falling back before the German invasion which bore down upon them in five great columns of overwhelming strength; and that on the extreme left, nearest to Paris, the French army was miserably weak, made up for the most part of old Territorials who were never meant to be in the first line of defence, and of African regiments who had never seen shell-fire, so that the main German attack could only be held back by a little British army which had just set foot on the soil of France.

Everywhere, from east to west, the French were yielding before the terrific onslaught of the German legions, who came on in close formation, reckless of their losses, but always advancing, over the bodies of their dead, with masses of light artillery against which the French gunners, with all their skill and courage, could not hold ground. By a series of strange adventures, which took me into the vortex of the French retreat, into the midst of confused movements of troops rushed up to various points of menace and into the tide of wounded which came streaming back from the fighting lines, I was able to write the first account which gave any clear idea of the general situation—sharing this chance with the Philosopher and the Strategist who were my fellow travellers—and, by good luck again, the censor was kind to me in England. French officers and soldiers with bandaged heads and limbs told me their stories, while their wounds were still wet, and while their clothes still reeked of the smoke of battle. Women who had fled with empty hands from little châteaux on the hillsides of France, with empty hearts too because they had no hope for husbands still fighting in the inferno, described to me the scenes which still made them pant like wild animals caught after a chase. And with my own eyes I saw the unforgettable drama of the

French army in retreat, blowing up bridges on its way, shifting to new lines of defence, awaiting with its guns ready for a new stage of the enemy's advance.

Out of a wild confusion of impressions, the tumult of these scenes, the inevitable contradictions and inconsistencies and imaginings of men and women drunk with the excitement of this time, I sorted out some clear threads of fact and with the aid of the Strategist, who spread out his maps on wayside banks, blotting out the wild flowers, or on the marble-topped tables outside fly-blown estaminets in village streets, tracked out the line of the German advance and saw the peril of the French.

From one of my dispatches I transcribe a narrative which records one of the most bloody battles in the first phase of the war. Written to the jolt of a troop train, in which wounded men hugged their bandaged hands, it tells how five thousand Frenchmen did their best to check a German army corps.

4

August 29

It was nearly a fortnight ago that the Germans concentrated their heaviest forces upon Namur, and began to press southwards and over the Meuse Valley. After the battle of Dinant the French army, among whom, at this point, were the 2nd and the 7th Corps, were heavily outnumbered at the time, and had to fall back gradually in order to gain time for reinforcements to come up to their support. The French artillery was up on the wooded heights above the river, and swept the German regiments with a storm of fire as they advanced. On the right bank the French infantry was entrenched, supported by field guns and mitrailleuses, and did very deadly work before leaping from the trenches which they occupied and taking up position in new trenches further back, which they held with great tenacity. In justice to the Germans, it must be said that they were heroic in their courage. They were reckless of their lives, and the valley of the Meuse was choked with their corpses. The river itself was strewn with dead bodies of men and horses, and literally ran red with blood. The most tremendous fighting took place for the possession of the bridges, but the French engineers blew them up one after the other as they retired southwards. No fewer than thirty-three bridges were destroyed in this way before they could be seized by the German advance guard. The fighting was extended for a considerable distance on either side of the Meuse, and many engagements took place between the French and German cavalry and regiments working away from the main armies.

There was, for instance, a memorable encounter at Merville which is one of the most heroic episodes of the war. Five thousand French soldiers of all arms, with quick-firers, engaged twenty thousand German infantry. In spite of being outnumbered in this way, the French dash and " bite," as they call it, was so splendid that they beat back the enemy from point to point in a fight lasting for twelve hours, inflicting a tremendous punishment, and suffering very few losses on their own side. A German officer captured in this engagement expressed his unbounded admiration for the valour of the French troops, which he described as " superb." It was only for fear of getting too far out of touch with the main forces that the gallant five thousand desisted from their irresistible attack, and retired, with a large number of German helmets as trophies of their victorious action. Nevertheless, in accordance with the general plan which had been decided upon by the French generals in view of the superior numbers pressing upon them, the French troops retreated and the Germans succeeded in forcing their way steadily down the Meuse as far as Mézières, divided by a bridge from Charleville on the other side of the river. This is in the neighbourhood of Sedan, and in the hollow or *trou* as it is called which led to the great disaster of 1870, when the French army was caught in a trap, and threatened with annihilation by the Germans, who had taken possession of the surrounding heights. There was to be no repetition of that tragedy. The French were determined that this time the position would be reversed.

On Monday, August 24, the town of Charleville was evacuated, most of its civilians were sent away to join the wanderers who had had to leave their homes, and the French troops took up magnificent positions commanding the town and the three bridges dividing it from Mézières. Mitrailleuses were hidden in the abandoned houses, and as a disagreeable shock to any German who might escape their fire was a number of the enemy's guns—no fewer than ninety-five of them—which had been captured and disabled by the French troops in the series of battles down the river from Namur. The German outposts reached Charleville on Tuesday, August 25. They were allowed to ride quietly across the bridges into the apparently deserted town. Then suddenly their line of retreat was cut off. The three bridges were blown up by contact mines, and the mitrailleuses hidden in the houses were played on to the German cavalry across the streets, killing them in a frightful slaughter. It was for a little while a sheer massacre in that town of white houses with pretty gardens where flowers were blooming under the brilliant sunshine of a glorious summer day. But the Germans fought with extraordinary tenacity, regardless of the heaped bodies of their comrades, and utterly reckless of their own lives. They, too, had brought quick-firers across the bridges and, taking cover behind some of the houses, trained their guns upon those from which the French gunners were firing their last shots. There was no way of escape for those heroic men who voluntarily sacrificed themselves in the service of their country, and it is probable that every man died, because at such a time the Germans are not in the habit of giving quarter. When the main German advance came down the valley the French artillery on the heights raked them with a terrific fire in which they suffered heavy losses, the forefront of the column being mowed down. But under this storm of fire they proceeded with incredible coolness to their pontoon bridges across the river, and although hundreds of men died on the banks they succeeded in their endeavour while their guns searched the hills with shells and forced the French gunners to retire from their positions. The occupation of Charleville was a German victory, but it was also a German graveyard.

After this historic episode in what had been an unending battle, the main body of the French troops withdrew before the Germans, who were now pouring down the valley, and retired to new ground.

5

Meanwhile, on the western side of the battle line, the French army was holding a crescent from Abbeville, round the south of Amiens, and the situation was not a happy one in view of the rapid advance of the enemy under General Von Kluck, before whom the British troops were already in continual battle.

I shall not soon forget a dreadful night near Amiens, when I saw beaten and broken men coming back from the firing lines, and the death-carts passing down the roads. The whole day had been exciting and unnerving. The roads along which I had passed were filled with soldiers marching towards an enemy which was rapidly drawing close upon them, for whom they seemed but ill-prepared—and by civilians stampeding with wild rumours that the Uhlans were close upon them.

They were not very far wrong. At Picquigny, they were less than four miles distant—a small patrol of outposts belonging to the squadrons which were sweeping out in a fan through the northern towns and villages of France.

As I passed, French Territorials were hastily digging trenches close to the railway line. Reports came from stations further along that the line might be cut at any moment. A train crowded with French and Belgian fugitives had come to a dead halt. The children were playing on the banks—with that divine carelessness and innocence which made one's heart ache for them in this beastly business of war—and their fathers and mothers, whose worldly goods had been packed into baskets and brown paper parcels—the poor relics of all that had been theirs—wondered whether after all their sufferings and struggles they would reach the town of Amiens and find safety there.

It was obvious to me that there was a thrill of uneasiness in the military machine operating in the district. Troops were being hurried up in a north-westerly direction. A regiment of Algerians came swinging along the road. The sight of the Turcos put some heart into the fugitives. Those brown faces were laughing like children at the prospect of a fight. They waved their hands with the curious Arab gesture of salute, and shuffled along merrily with their rifles slung behind their backs. Military motor-cars carrying little parties of French officers swept down the roads, and then there were no more battalions but only stragglers, and hurrying fugitives driving along in farmers' carts, packed with household goods, in two-wheeled gigs, overburdened with women and children, riding on bicycles, with parcels tied to the saddles, or trudging wearily and anxiously along, away from the fear where the blood-red sun was setting over France. It was pitiful to see the children clinging to the women's skirts along that road of panic, and pitiful but fine, to see the courage of those women. Then night fell and darkness came across the fields of France, and through the darkness many grim shadows of war, looming up against one's soul.

There was *une affaire des patrouilles*—what the British soldier calls a " scrap "—along the road at Albert, between Amiens and Cambrai. A party of German Uhlans, spreading out from a strong force at Cambrai itself, had been engaged by the French Territorials, and after some sharp fighting had retired, leaving several dead horses in the dust and a few huddled forms from which the French soldiers had taken burnished helmets and trophies to their women folk.

That was on Friday night of August 28. The real fighting was taking place fifteen kilometres further along the road, at a place called Bapeaume. All day on Friday there was very heavy fighting here on the left centre, and a victory was announced by the French Ministry of War.

I did not see the victory. I saw only the retreat of some of the French forces engaged in the battle.

It was a few minutes before midnight on that Friday, when they came back along the road to Amiens, crawling back slowly in a long, dismal trail, with ambulance wagons laden with dead and dying, with hay-carts piled high with saddles and accoutrements upon which there lay, immobile, like men already dead, spent and exhausted soldiers. They passed through crowds of silent people—the citizens of Amiens—who only whispered as they stared at this procession in the darkness. A cuirassier with his head bent upon his chest stumbled forward, leading a horse too weak and tired to bear him. There were many other men leading their poor beasts in this way ; and infantry soldiers, some of them with bandaged heads, clung on to the backs of the carts and wagons, and seemed to be asleep as they shuffled by. The light from the roadside lamps gleamed upon blanched faces and glazed eyes—flashed now and then into the caverns of canvas-covered carts where twisted, bandaged men lay huddled on the straw. Not a groan came from those carts. There was no shout of " Vive la France ! " from the crowd of citizens who are not silent as a rule when their soldiers pass.

Every one knew it was a retreat, and the knowledge was colder than the mist of night. The carts, carrying the quick and the dead, rumbled by in a long convoy, the drooping heads of the soldiers turned neither to the right nor to the left for any greeting with old friends; there was a hugger-mugger of uniforms on provision carts and ambulances. It was a part of the wreckage and wastage of the war, and to the onlooker, exaggerating unconsciously the importance of the things close at hand and visible, it seemed terrible in its significance, and an ominous reminder of 1870, when through Amiens there came the dismal tramp of beaten men. Really this was the inevitable part of a serious battle, and not necessarily the retreat from a great disaster.

I turned away from it, rather sick at heart. It is not a pleasant thing to see men walking like living corpses, or as though drugged with fatigue. It is heartrending to see poor beasts stumbling forward at every step at the very last gasp of their strength until they fall never to rise again.

But more pitiful even than this drift back from Bapeaume were the scenes which followed immediately as I turned back into the town. Thousands of boys had been called out to the colours, and had been brought up from the country to be sent forward to the second lines of defence. They were the reservists of the 1914 class, and many of them were shouting and singing, though here and there a white-faced boy tried to hide his tears as women from the crowd ran to embrace him. The Marseillaise, the hymn of faith, rang out a little raggedly, but bravely all the same. The lads— " poor children " they were called by a white-haired man who watched them—were keeping up the valour of their hearts by noisy demonstrations ; but having seen the death-carts pass through the darkness between lines of silent and dejected onlookers, I could not bear to look into the faces of those little ones of France who were following their fathers to the guns. Once again I had to turn away to blot out the pictures of war in the velvety darkness of the night.

Early next morning there was a thrill of anxiety in Amiens itself. Reports had come through that the railway line had been cut between Boulogne and Abbeville. There had been mysterious movements of regiments from the town barracks. They had moved out of Amiens, and there was a strange quietude in the streets, hardly a man in uniform to be seen in places which had been filled with soldiers the day before. I think only a few people realized the actual significance of all this. Only a few—the friends of officers or the friends of officers' friends—had heard that Amiens itself was to be evacuated.

To these people it seemed incredible and horrible—an admission that France was being beaten to her knees. How could they believe the theory of an optimist among them that it was a part of a great plan to secure the safety of France ? How could they realize that the town itself would be saved from possible bombardment by this withdrawal of the troops to positions which would draw the Germans into the open ? They only knew that they were undefended, and presently they found that the civilian trains were being suspended, and that there would be no way of escape. It was in the last train that by a stroke of luck I escaped from Amiens. Shortly afterwards the tunnel leading to the junction was blown up by the French engineers, and the beautiful city of Amiens was cut off from all communication with the outer world.

It was on the last train that I realized to the full of its bitterness the brutality of war as it bludgeons the heart of the non-combatant. In the carriage with me were French ladies and children who had been hunted about the country in the endeavour to escape the zone of military operations. Their husbands were fighting for France, and they could not tell whether they were alive or dead. They had been without any solid food for several days, and the nerves of those poor women were tried to the uttermost, not by any fear for their own sakes, but for the sake of the little ones who were all they could save from the wreckage of their lives, all yet enough if they could save them to the end. One lady whose house had been burnt by the Germans had walked over twenty miles with a small boy and girl.

For a little while, when she told me her story she wept passionately, yet only for a few minutes. For the sake of her handsome boy, who had a hero's courage, and for the tiny girl who clung to her, she resisted this breakdown and conquered herself.

" That is the real meaning of war, almost the worst tragedy of it " (so I wrote at the time). " The soldier suffers less than the women and the non-combatants. His agony perhaps is sharper, but the wound of the spirit is hardest to bear."

So it seemed to me then, before I had seen greater ghastliness. I was surprised also by the cheerfulness of some of our wounded soldiers. They were the " light cases," and had the pluck to laugh at their pain. Yet even they had had a dreadful time. It is almost true to say that the only rest they had was when they were carried into the ambulance cart or the field-hospital. The incessant marching, forwards and backwards, to new positions in the blazing sun was more awful to bear than the actual fighting under the hideous fire of the German guns. They were kept on the move constantly, except for the briefest lulls—when officers and men dropped, like brown leaves from autumn trees, on each side of the road, so utterly exhausted that they were almost senseless, and had to be dragged up out of their short sleep when once again they tramped on to a new line, to scratch up a few earthworks, to fire a few rounds before the bugle sounded the cease fire and another strategical retirement.

6

On September 2 the Germans had reached Creil and Senlis—staining their honour in these two places by unnecessary cruelty—and were no further than thirty miles from Paris, so that the shock of their guns might be heard as vague vibrations in the capital.

To the population of Paris, and to all civilians in France, it seemed a stupendous disaster, this rapid incredible advance of that great military machine of death which nothing, so far, had been able to stop—not even the unflinching courage and the utter recklessness of life with which the Allies flung themselves against it. Yet with an optimism which I could hardly justify, I, who had seen the soldiers of France, was still confident that, so far from all being lost, there was hope of victory which might turn the German advance.

I had seen the superb courage of French regiments rushing up to support their left wing, and the magnificent confidence of men who after the horrors of the battlefields, and with the full consciousness that they were always retiring, still said : "We shall win. We are leading the enemy to its destruction. In a little while they will be in a death-trap from which there is no escape for them."

" This spirit," I wrote in my dispatch, " must win in the end. It is impossible that it should be beaten in the long run. And the splendour of this French courage, in the face of what looks like defeat, is equalled at least by the calm and dogged assurance of our English troops."

F

They repeated the same words to me over and over again—those wounded men, those outposts at points of peril, those battalions who went marching on to another fight, without sleep, without rest, knowing the foe they had to meet.

" We are all right.   You can call it a retreat if you like. But we are retreating in good order and keeping our end up."

Retiring in good order !   It had been more than that. They had retired before a million of men swarming across the country like a vast ant-heap on the move, with a valour that had gained for the British and French forces a deathless glory.   Such a thing has never been done before in the history of warfare.   It would have seemed incredible and impossible to military experts, who know the meaning of such fighting, and the frightful difficulty of keeping an army together in such circumstances.

7

When I escaped from Amiens before the tunnel was broken up and the Germans entered into possession of the town—on August 28—the front of the allied armies was in a crescent from Abbeville by the wooded heights south of Amiens, and thence in an irregular line to the south of Mézières.   The British forces under Sir John French were on the left centre, supporting the heavy thrust forward of the German right wing.

On Saturday afternoon fighting was resumed along the whole line.   The German vanguard had by this time been supported by fresh army corps, which had been brought from Belgium.   At least a million men were on the move, pressing upon the allied forces with a ferocity of attack which has never been equalled.   Their cavalry swept across a great tract of country, squadron by squadron, like the mounted hordes of Attila, but armed with the deadly weapons of modern warfare.   Their artillery was in enormous numbers, and their columns advanced under the cover of it, not like an army but rather like a moving nation.   It did not move, however, with equal pressure at all parts of the line. It formed itself into a battering ram with a pointed end, and this point was thrust at the heart of the English wing with its base at St. Quentin, and advanced divisions at Péronne and Ham. It was impossible to resist this onslaught. If the British forces had stood against it they would have been crushed and broken. Our gunners were magnificent, and shelled the advancing German columns so that the dead lay heaped up along the way which was leading down to Paris. But, as one of them told me, " It made no manner of difference. As soon as we had smashed one lot another followed, column after column, and by sheer weight of numbers we could do nothing to check them."

The railway was destroyed and the bridges blown up on the main line from Amiens to Paris, and on the branch lines from Dieppe. After this precaution the British forces fell back, fighting all the time, as far as Compiègne. The line of the Allies was now in the shape of a V, the Germans thrusting their main attack deep into the angle.

General d'Amade, the most popular of French generals owing to his exploits in Morocco, had established his staff at Aumale, holding the extreme left of the allied armies. Some of his reserves held the hills running east and west at Beauvais, and they were in touch with Sir John French's cavalry along the road to Amiens.

This position remained until Monday, or rather had completed itself by that date, the retirement of the troops being maintained with masterly skill and without any undue haste.

Meanwhile the French troops were sustaining a terrific attack on their centre by the German left centre, which culminated at Guise, on the River Oise, to the north-east of St. Quentin, where the river, which runs between beautiful meadows, was choked with corpses and red with blood.

From an eye-witness of this great battle who escaped with a slight wound—an officer of an infantry regiment—I learned that the German onslaught had been repelled by the work of the French gunners, followed by a series of bayonet and cavalry charges.

"The Germans," he said, "had the élite of their army engaged against us, including the 10th Army Corps and the Imperial Guard.   But the heroism of our troops was sublime. Every man knew that the safety of France depended upon him, and was ready to sacrifice his life, if need be, with a joyful enthusiasm.   They not only resisted the enemy't attack but took the offensive, and, in spite of their over-powering numbers, gave them a tremendous punishment. They had to recoil before our guns, which swept their ranks, and their columns were broken and routed.   Hundreds of them were bayoneted, and hundreds more hurled into the river, while the whole front of battle was outlined by the dead and dying men whom they had to abandon.   Certainly their losses were enormous, and when I felt the German retreat was in full swing, and for the time being we could claim a real victory."   Nevertheless the inevitable happened.   Owing to the vast reserves the enemy brought up fresh divisions, and the French were compelled to fall back upon Laon and La Fère.

On Tuesday the German skirmishers with light artillery were coming southwards to Beauvais, and the sound of their field guns greeted my ears in this town, which I shall always remember with unpleasant recollections, in spite of its old-world beauty and the loveliness of the scene in which it is set.

Beauvais lies directly between Amiens and Paris, and it seemed to me that it was the right place to be in order to get into touch with the French army barring the way to the capital.   As a matter of fact it seemed to be the wrong place from all points of view.

8

I might have suspected that something was wrong by the strange look on the face of a friendly French peasant whom I met at Gournay.   He had described to me in a very vivid way the disposition of the French troops on the neigh-bouring hills who had disappeared in the undulation below the sky-line, but when I mentioned that I was on the way to

Beauvais he suddenly raised his head and looked at me in a queer, startled way which puzzled me. I remember that look when I began to approach the town. Down the road came small parties of peasants with fear in their eyes. Some of them were in farm carts, and they shouted to tired horses and put them to a stumbling gallop. Women with blanched faces, carrying children in their arms, trudged along the dusty highway, and it was clear that these people were afraid of something behind them—something in the direction of Beauvais. There were not many of them, and when they had passed the countryside was strangely and uncannily quiet. There was only the sound of singing birds above the fields which were flooded with the golden light of the setting sun.

Then I came into the town. An intense silence brooded there, among the narrow little streets below the old Norman church—a white jewel on the rising ground beyond. Almost every house was shuttered, with blind eyes, but here and there I looked through an open window into deserted rooms. No human face returned my gaze. It was an abandoned town, emptied of all its people, who had fled with fear in their eyes like those peasants along the roadway.

But presently I saw a human form. It was the figure of a French dragoon, with his carbine slung behind his back. He was standing by the side of a number of gunpowder bags. A little further away were groups of soldiers at work by two bridges—one over a stream and one over a road. They were working very calmly, and I could see what they were doing. They were mining the bridges to blow them up at a given signal. As I went further I saw that the streets were strewn with broken bottles and littered with wire entanglements, very artfully and carefully made.

It was a queer experience. It was obvious that there was a very grim business being done in Beauvais, and that the soldiers were waiting for something to happen. At the railway station I quickly learnt the truth. The Germans were only a few miles away in great force. At any moment they might come down, smashing everything in their way, and killing every human being along that road. The station-master, a brave old type, and one or two porters, had determined to stay on to the last. " Nous sommes ici," he said, as though the Germans would have to reckon with him. But he was emphatic in his request for me to leave Beauvais if another train could be got away, which was very uncertain. As a matter of fact, after a *mauvais quart d'heure*, I was put into a train which had been shunted into a siding and left Beauvais with the sound of the German guns in my ears.

Sitting in darkness and shaken like peas in a pod because of defective brakes, we skirted the German army, and by a twist in the line almost ran into the enemy's country; but we rushed through the night, and the engine-driver laughed and put his oily hand up to the salute when I stepped out to the platform of an unknown station.

" The Germans won't have us for dinner after all," he said. " It was a little risky all the same ! "

9

The station was Creil, the headquarters, at that time, of the British forces. It was crowded with French soldiers, and they were soon telling me their experience of the hard fighting in which they had been engaged.

They were dirty, unshaven, dusty from head to foot, scorched by the heat of the August sun, in tattered uniforms, and broken boots. But they were beautiful men for all their dirt ; and the laughing courage, the quiet confidence, the un-bragging simplicity with which they assured me that the Germans would soon be caught in a death-trap and sent to their destruction, filled me with an admiration which I cannot express in words. All the odds were against them ; they had fought the hardest of all actions along the way of retreat ; they knew and told me that the enemy were fighting at Senlis, within ten miles of the Parisian fortifications, but they had an absolute faith in the ultimate success of their allied arms.

One of the French soldiers gave me his diary to read. In

spite of his dirty uniform, his brown unwashed hands and the blond unkempt beard which disguised fine features and a delicate mouth, it was clear to see that he was a man of good breeding and education.

"It may amuse you," he said. "You see, I have been busy as a destroyer."

It was a record of the blowing up of bridges, and the words had been scribbled into a small note-book on the way of retreat. In its brevity this narrative of a sergeant of sappers is more eloquent than long descriptions in polished prose. One passage in it seemed to me almost incredible ; the lines which tell of a German aviator who took a tiny child with him on his mission of death. But a man like this, whose steel-blue eyes looked into mine with such fine frankness, would not put a lie into his note-book, and I believed him. I reproduce the document now as I copied it away from the gaze of a French officer who suspected this breach of regulations :

August 25. Started for St. Quentin and arrived in evening. Our section set out again next morning for a point twelve kilometres behind, at Montescourt-Lezeroulles, in order to mine a bridge. We worked all the night and returned to St. Quentin, where we did reconnaissance work.

August 27. Germans signalled and station of St. Quentin evacuated. We were directed to maintain order among the crowd who wished to go away. It was a very sad spectacle, all the women and children weeping and not enough trains to save them.

At last we go away, and destroy line and station of Essigny-le-Grand and at Montescourt, where we destroy bridge already mined.

Arrive in afternoon at Tergnier. Sleep there, and set out on afternoon of 28th for Chauny and Noyon.

August 29 (morning). We receive order to go back to Tergnier, the Germans having succeeded in piercing British lines. We pass Montescourt, and arrive Jussy, where the bridge of the canal being blown up, we hold up Germans momentarily. Coming from Tergnier, we were ordered to destroy bridges and stations of the line, which is main line to Paris.

Work in the evening to sound of cannon. It is pitiable to see the miserable people on the road with their boxes and children.

In the afternoon set out for Chauny, in direction of Compiègne, where we arrive in the evening. All along the line were scattered the poor people. We have twelve on our wagon, and let them eat our food. We had our own provisions, and we gave them to these people.

August 30 (*Sunday*). Stationed at Compiègne awaiting orders. One hears more clearly the sound of the cannon. After the news this morning I write a line. It appears that the Germans have been destroyed at St. Quentin.

To-day we have assisted at a duel between a biplane and an aeroplane. I had nearest me the German aeroplane, which fell in the English lines. The officer in charge with it had with him a child of six years old, who was also a German. They were only wounded.

After St. Quentin were with the English troops under the orders of the English Headquarters Staff.

The rumours which tell of German defeats must be false, because the English troops retire, and we evacuate Longuart, where we destroy the station and the railway lines.

<h3 style="text-align:center">10</h3>

The retreat of the British army—it is amazing to think that there were only 45,000 men who had tried to stem the German avalanche—was developing into a run. Only some wild fluke of chance (the pious patriot sees God's hand at work, while the cynic sees only the inefficiency of the German Staff) saved it from becoming a bloody rout. It is too soon even now to write the details of it. Only when scores of officers have written their reminiscences shall we have the full story of those last days of August, when a little army which was exhausted after many battles staggered hard away from the menace of enormous odds seeking to envelop it. It was called a " retirement in good order." It was hardly that when the Commander-in-Chief had to make a hurried flight with a mounted escort, when the Adjutant-General's department, busy in the château of a French village, suddenly awakened to the knowledge that it had been forgotten and left behind (I heard a personal story of the escape that followed the awakening), and when companies, battalions, and regiments lost touch with each other, were bewildered in dark woods and unknown roads, and were shelled unexpectedly by an enemy of whose whereabouts they had now no definite knowledge. The German net of iron was drawing tighter. In a few hours it might close round and make escape impossible. General Allenby's division of cavalry

had a gallop for life, when the outposts came in with reports
of a great encircling movement of German horse, so that
there was not a moment to lose if a great disaster were to be
averted.   It was Allenby himself who led his retreat at the
head of his division by the side of a French guide carrying
a lantern.   For twenty miles our cavalry urged on their
tired horses through the night, and along the sides of the
roads came a struggling mass of automobiles, motor-cycles,
and motor-wagons, carrying engineers, telegraphists and
men of the Army Service Corps.   Ambulances crammed
with wounded who had been picked up hurriedly from the
churches and barns which had been used as hospitals, joined
the stampede, and for many poor lads whose heads had been
broken by the German shells and whose flesh was on fire
with frightful wounds, this night-ride was a highway of torture
which ended in eternal rest.   All the way the cavalry and
the convoys were followed by the enemy, and there were
moments when it seemed inevitable that the strength of
the horses would give out and that the retreating force
would be surrounded.   But as we know now, the enemy was
exhausted also.   Their pursuit was a chase by blown horses
and puffed men.   They called a halt and breathed heavily,
at the very time when a last gallop and a hard fight would
have given them their prize—the flower of the British army.

On that last stage of the retreat we lost less men than
any text-book of war would have given as a credible number
in such conditions.   Many who were wounded as they
tramped through woods splintered by bursting shells and
ripped with bullets, bandaged themselves as best they could
and limped on, or were carried by loyal comrades who would
not leave a pal in the lurch.   Others who lost their way or
lay down in sheer exhaustion, cursing the Germans and not
caring if they came, straggled back later—weeks later—
by devious routes to Rouen or Paris, after a wandering life in
French villages, where the peasants fed them and nursed
them so that they were in no hurry to leave.   It was the
time when the temptation to desert seized men with a devilish
attraction.   They had escaped from such hells at Charleroi

and Cambrai and Le Cateau. Boys who had never heard
the roar of guns before except in mimic warfare had crouched
and cowered beneath a tempest of shells, waiting, terrified,
for death. Death had not touched them. By some miracle
they had dodged it, with dead men horribly mutilated on
either side of them, so that blood had slopped about their
feet and they had jerked back from shapeless masses of
flesh—of men or horses —sick with the stench of it, cold with
the horror of it. Was it any wonder that some of these
young men who had laughed on the way to Waterloo Station,
and held their heads high in the admiring gaze of London
crowds, sure of their own heroism, slunk now in the backyards of French farmhouses, hid behind hedges when men in
khaki passed, and told wild, incoherent tales, when cornered`
at last by some cold-eyed officer in some town of France
to which they had blundered ? It was the coward's chance,
and I for one can hardly bring myself to blame the poor
devil I met one day in Rouen, stuttering out lies to save his
skin, or the two gunners, disguised in civil clothes, who
begged from me near Amiens, or any of the half-starved
stragglers who had "lost" their regiments and did not go
to find them. Some of them were shot and deserved their
fate, according to the rules of war and the stern justice of
men who know no fear. But in this war there are not many
men who have not known moments of cold terror, when all
their pride of manhood oozed away and left them cowards,
sick with horror at all the frightfulness. Out of such knowledge pity comes.

It was pity and a sense of impending tragedy which took
hold of me in Creil and on the way to Paris when I was
confronted with the confusion of the British retreat, and,
what seemed its inevitable consequences, the siege and fall
of the French capital.

11

I reached Paris in the middle of the night on September 2
and saw extraordinary scenes. It had become known during
the day that German outposts had reached Senlis and

Chantilly, and that Paris was no longer the seat of Government. Quietly and without a word of warning the French Ministry had stolen away, after a Cabinet meeting at which there had been both rage and tears, and after a frantic packing up of papers in Government offices. This abandonment came as a paralysing shock to the citizens of Paris and was an outward and visible sign that the worst thing might happen—a new siege of Paris, with greater guns than those which girdled it in the terrible year.

A rumour had come that the people were to be given five days' notice to leave their houses within the zone of fortifications, and to add to the menace of impending horrors an aeroplane had dropped bombs upon the Gare de l'Est that afternoon. There was a wild rush to get away from the capital, and the railway stations were great camps of fugitives, in which the richest and the poorest citizens were mingled, with their women and children. The tragedy deepened when it was heard that most of the lines to the coast had been cut and that the only remaining line to Dieppe would probably be destroyed during the next few hours. From the crowds which had been waiting all day for a chance to get to the *guichets* in the rear of other and greater crowds, there rose a murmur which seemed to me like a great sigh from stricken hearts. There were many old men and women there who knew what a siege of Paris meant. To younger people they told the tale of it now—the old familiar tale—with shaking heads and trembling forefingers. "Starvation!" "We ate rats, if we were lucky." "They would not hesitate to smash up Notre Dame." "It is not for my sake I would go. But the little ones! Those poor innocents!"

They did not make much noise in those crowds. There was no loud sound of panic. No woman's voice shrieked or wailed above the murmurs of voices. There was no fighting for the station platforms barred against them all. A few women wept quietly, mopping their eyes. Perhaps they wept for sheer weariness after sitting encamped for hours on their baggage. Most of the men had a haggard

look and kept repeating the stale old word, " Incroyable ! "
in a dazed and dismal way. Sadness as well as fear was
revealed in the spirit of those fugitives, a sadness that Paris,
Paris the beautiful, should be in danger of destruction, and
that all her hopes of victory had ended in this defeat.

Among all these civilians were soldiers of many regiments
and of two nations—Turcos and Zouaves, chasseurs and
infantry, regulars and Highland British. Many of these
were wounded and lay on the floor among the crying babies
and weary-eyed women. Many of them were drinking and
drunk. They clinked glasses and pledged each other in
French and English and broadest Scotch, with a " Hell to
the Kaiser ! " and " à bas Guillaume ! " A Tommy with the
accent of the Fulham Road stood on a chair, steadying
himself by a firm grasp on the shoulder of a French *dragon*,
and made an incoherent speech in which he reviled the
French troops as dirty dogs who ran away like mongrels,
vowed that he would never have left England for such a
bloody game if he had known the rights of it, and hoped
Kitchener would break his blooming neck down the area of
Buckingham Palace. The French soldier greeted these
sentiments with a " Bravo, mon vieux ! " not understanding
a word of them, and the drunkard swayed and fell across
the marble-topped table, amid a crash of broken glass.

" Serve him damn well right ! " said a sergeant to whom I
had been talking. Like many other English soldiers here
who had been fighting for ten days in retreat, he had kept
his head, and his heart.

" We've been at it night and day," he said. " The only
rest from fighting was when we were marching with the
beggars after us."

He spoke of the German army as " a blighted nation on
the move."

" You can't mow that down. We kill 'em and kill 'em,
and still they come on. They seem to have an endless line
of fresh men. Directly we check 'em in one attack a fresh
attack develops. It's impossible to hold up such a mass
of men. Can't be done, nohow ! "

This man, severely wounded, was so much master of himself, so strong in common sense that he was able to get the right perspective about the general situation.

"It's not right to say we've met with disaster," he remarked. "Truth's truth. We've suffered pretty badly—perhaps twelve per cent. of a battalion knocked out. But what's that? You've got to expect it nowadays. 'Taint a picnic. Besides, what if a battalion *was* cut up—wiped clean out, if you like? That don't mean defeat. While one regiment suffered another got off light."

And by the words of that sergeant of the Essex Regiment I was helped to see the truth of what had happened. He took the same view as many officers and men to whom I had spoken, and by weighing up the evidence, in the light of all that I had seen and heard, and with the assistance of my friend the Philosopher—whose wisdom shone bright after a glass of Dubonnet and the arsenic pill which lifted him out of the gulfs of the black devil doubt to heights of splendid optimism based upon unerring logic—I was able to send a dispatch to England which cheered it after a day of anguish.

12

Because I also was eager to reach the coast—not to escape from the advancing Germans, for I had determined that I would do desperate things to get back for the siege of Paris, if history had to be written that way—but because I must find a boat to carry a dispatch across the Channel, I waited with the crowd of fugitives, struggled with them for a seat in the train which left at dawn and endured another of those journeys when discomfort mocked at sleep, until sheer exhaustion made one doze for a minute of unconsciousness from which one awakened with a cricked neck and cramped limbs, to a reality of tragic things.

We went by a tortuous route, round Paris towards the west, and at every station the carriages were besieged by people trying to escape.

"Pour l'amour de Dieu, laissez-moi entrer!"

" J'ai trois enfants, messieurs ! Ayez un peu de pitié ! "

" 'Cré nom de Dieu, c'est le dernier train ! Et j'ai peur pour les petits. Nous sommes tous dans le même cas, n'est-ce-pas ? "

But entreaties, piteous words, the exhibition of frightened children and wailing babes could not make a place in carriages already packed to bursting-point. It was impossible to get one more human being inside.

" C'est impossible ! C'est absolument impossible ! Regardez ! On ne peut pas faire plus de place, Madame ! "

I was tempted sometimes to yield up my place. It seemed a coward thing to sit there jammed between two peasants while a white-faced woman with a child in her arms begged for a little pity and—a little room. But I had a message for the English people. They, too, were in anguish because the enemy had come so close to Paris in pursuit of a little army which seemed to have been wiped out behind the screen of secrecy through which only vague and awful rumours came. I sat still, shamefaced, scribbling my message hour after hour, not daring to look in the face of those women who turned away in a kind of sullen sadness after their pitiful entreaties.

Enormous herds of cattle were being driven into Paris. For miles the roads were thronged with them, and down other roads away from Paris families were trekking to far fields, with their household goods piled into bullock carts, pony carts, and wheelbarrows.

At Pontoise there was another shock, for people whose nerves were frayed by fright. Two batteries of artillery were stationed by the line, and a regiment of infantry was hiding in the hollows of the grass slopes. Out of a nightmare dream not more fantastic than my waking hours so that there seemed no dividing line between illusion and reality, I opened my eyes to see those faces in the grass, bronzed bearded faces with anxious eyes, below a hedge of rifle barrels slanted towards the north. The Philosopher had jerked out of slumber into a wakefulness like mine. He rubbed his eyes and then sat bolt upright, with a tense searching look, as though trying to pierce to the truth of things by a violence of staring.

" It doesn't look good," he said.   " Those chaps in the grass seem to expect something—something nasty ! "

The Strategist had a map on his knees. which overlapped his fellow passenger's on either side.

" If the beggars cut the line here it closes the way of escape from Paris.   It would be good business from their point of view."

I was sorry my message to the English people might never be read by them.   Perhaps after all they would get on very well without it, and my paper would appoint another correspondent to succeed a man swallowed up somewhere inside the German lines.   It would be a queer adventure.   I conjured up an imaginary conversation in bad German with an officer in a pointed casque.   Undoubtedly he would have the best of the argument.   There would be a little white wall, perhaps. . . .

One of the enemy's aeroplanes flew above our heads, circled round and then disappeared.   It dropped no bombs and was satisfied with its reconnaissance.   The whistle of the train shrieked out, and there was a cheer from the French gunners as we went away to safety, leaving them behind at the post of peril.

After all my message went to Fleet Street and filled a number of columns, read over the coffee cups by a number of English families, who said perhaps : " I wonder if he really knows anything, or if it is all made up.   Those newspaper men . . ."

Those newspaper men did not get much rest in their quest for truth, not caring much, if the truth may be told, for what the English public chose to think or not to think, but eager to see more of the great drama and to plunge again into its amazing vortex.

Almost before the fugitives who had come with us had found time to smell the sea we were back again along the road to Paris, fretful to be there before it was closed by a hostile army and a ring of fire.   •

13

There are people who say that Paris showed no sign of panic when the Germans were at their gates. . . . "The calmness with which Paris awaits the siege is amazing," wrote one of my confrères, and he added this phrase : "There is no sign of panic." He was right if by panic one meant a noisy fear, of crowds rushing wildly about tearing out handfuls of their hair, and shrieking in a delirium of terror. No, there was no clamour of despair in Paris when the enemy came close to its gates. But if by panic one may mean a great fear spreading rapidly among great multitudes of people, infectious as a fell disease so that men ordinarily brave felt gripped with a sudden chill at the heart, and searched desperately for a way of escape from the advancing peril, then Paris was panic-stricken.

I have written many words about the courage of Paris, courage as fine and noble as anything in history, and in a later chapter of this book I hope to reveal the strength as well as the weakness in the soul of Paris. But if there is any truth in my pen it must describe that exodus by one and a half millions of people who, under the impulse of a great fear—what else was it ?—fled by any means and any road from the capital which they love better than any city in the world because their homes are there and their pride and all that has given beauty to their ideals.

In those few days before the menace passed the railway stations were stormed and stormed again, throughout the day and night, by enormous crowds such as I had seen on that night of September 2. Because so many bridges had been blown up and so many lines cut on the way to Calais and Boulogne, in order to hamper the enemy's advance, and because what had remained were being used for the transport of troops, it was utterly impossible to provide trains for these people. Southwards the way was easier, though from that direction also regiments of French soldiers were being rushed up to the danger zone. The railway officials under the pressure of this tremendous strain, did their best to hurl out the population of Paris, somehow and anyhow.   For military reasons the need was urgent.   The less mouths to feed the better in a besieged city.   So when all the passenger trains had been used, cattle trucks were put together and into them, thanking God, tumbled fine ladies of France, careless of the filth which stained their silk frocks, and rich Americans who had travelled far to Paris for the sake of safety, who offered great bribes to any man who would yield his place between wooden boards for a way out again, and bourgeois families who had shut up shops from the Rue de la Paix to the Place Pigalle, heedless for once of loss or ruin, but desperate to get beyond the range of German shells and the horrors of a beleaguered city.

There were tragic individuals in these crowds.   I could only guess at some of their stories as they were written in lines of pain about the eyes and mouths of poor old spinsters such as Balzac met hiding their misery in backstairs flats of Paris tenements—they came blinking out into the fierce sunlight of the Paris streets like captive creatures let loose by an earthquake—and of young students who had eschewed delight and lived laborious days for knowledge and art which had been overthrown by war's brutality.   All classes and types of life in Paris were mixed up in this retreat, and among them were men I knew, so that I needed no guesswork for their stories.   For weeks some of them had been working under nervous pressure, keeping " a stiff upper lip " as it is called to all rumours of impending tragedy.   But the contagion of fear had caught them in a secret way, and suddenly their nerves had snapped, and they too had abandoned courage and ideals of duty, slinking, as though afraid of daylight, to stations more closely sieged than Paris would be. Pitiful wrecks of men, and victims of this ruthless war in which the non-combatants have suffered even more sometimes than the fighting men.   The neuroticism of the age was exaggerated by writing men—we have seen the spirit of the old blood strong and keen—but neurasthenia is not a myth, and God knows it was found out and made a torture to many men and women in the city of Paris, when the Great Fear

came—closing in with a narrowing circle until it seemed to
clutch at the throats of those miserable beings.

There were thousands and hundreds of thousands of people
who would not wait for the trains.   Along the southern road
which goes down to Tours there were sixty unbroken miles of
them.   They went in every kind of vehicle—taxi-cabs for
which rich people had paid fabulous prices, motor-cars which
had escaped the military requisition, farmers' carts laden with
several families and piles of household goods, shop carts
drawn by horses already tired to the point of death, because
of the weight of the people who had crowded behind, pony
traps, governess carts, and innumerable cycles.

But for the most part the people were on foot, and they
trudged along, bravely at first, quite gay, some of them, on the
first stage of the march ; mothers carrying their babies,
fathers hoisting children to their shoulders, families stepping
out together.   They were of all classes, rank and fortune being
annihilated by this common tragedy.   Elegant women, whose
beauty is known in the Paris salons, whose frivolity perhaps
in the past was the main purpose of their lives, were now on a
level with the peasant mothers of the French suburbs, and
with the midenettes of Montmartre—and their courage did
not fail them so quickly.

It was a tragic road.   At every mile of it there were
people who had fainted on the wayside, and poor old people
who could go no further but sat down on the banks below the
hedges weeping silently or bidding the younger ones go forward and leave them to their fate.

Young women who had stepped out so jauntily at first
were footsore and lame, so that they limped along with lines
of pain about their lips and eyes.   Many of the taxi-cabs,
bought at great prices, and many of the motor-cars had
broken down and had been abandoned by their owners, who
had decided to walk.

Farmers' carts had jolted into ditches and had lost their
wheels.   Wheelbarrows, too heavy to trundle, had been tilted
up, with all their household goods spilt into the roadway,
and the children had been carried further, until at last dark-

ness came, and their only shelter was a haystack in a field under the harvest moon.

I entered Paris again from the south-west, after crossing the Seine where it makes a loop to the north-west beyond the forts of St. Germain and St. Denis. The way seemed open to the enemy. Always obsessed with the idea that the Germans would come from the east—the almost fatal error of the French General Staff, Paris had been girdled with forts on that side, from those of Ecouen and Montmorency by the distant ramparts of Chelles and Champigny to those of Sucy and Villeneuve—the outer lines of a triple cordon. But on the western side there was next to nothing, and it was a sign to me of the utter unreadiness of France that now at the eleventh hour when I passed thousands of men were digging trenches in the roads and fields with frantic haste, and throwing up earthworks along the banks of the Seine. Great God! that such work should not have been done weeks before and not left like this to a day when the enemy's guns were rumbling through Creil and smashing back the allied armies in retreat!

It was a pitiful thing to see the deserted houses of the Paris suburbs. It was as though a plague had killed every human being save those who had fled in frantic haste. Those little villas on the riverside, so coquette in their prettiness, built as love nests and summer-houses, were all shuttered and silent Roses were blowing in their gardens, full-blown because no woman's hand had been to pick them, and spilling their petals on the garden paths. The creeper was crimsoning on the walls and the grass plots were like velvet carpeting, so soft and deeply green. But there were signs of disorder, of some hurried transmigration. Packing-cases littered the trim lawns and cardboard boxes had been flung about. In one small bower I saw a child's perambulator, where two wax dolls sat staring up at the abandoned house. Their faces had become blotchy in the dew of night, and their little *maman* with her pigtail had left them to their fate. In another garden a woman's parasol and flower-trimmed hat lay on a rustic seat with an open book beside them. I imagined a lady of France called suddenly away from an old romance of false sentiment by the visit of grim reality—the first sound of the enemy's guns, faint but terrible to startled ears.

" Les Allemands sont tout près ! "

Some harsh voice had broken into the quietude of the garden on the Seine, and the open book, with the sunshade and the hat, had been forgotten in the flight.

Yet there was one human figure here on the banks of the Seine reassuring in this solitude which was haunted by the shadow of fear. It was a fisherman. A middle-aged man with a straw hat on the back of his head and a big pair of spectacles on the end of his nose, he held out his long rod with a steady hand and waited for a bite, in an attitude of supreme indifference to Germans, guns, hatred, tears and all the miserable stupidities of people who do not fish. He was at peace with the world on this day of splendour, with a golden sun and a blue sky, and black shadows flung across the water from the tree trunks. He stood there, a simple fisherman, as a protest against the failure of civilization and the cowardice in the hearts of men. I lifted my hat to him.

Close to Paris, too, in little market gardens and poor plots of land, women stooped over their cabbages, and old men tended the fruits of the earth. On one patch a peasant girl stood with her hands on her hips staring at her fowls, which were struggling and clucking for the grain she had flung down to them. There was a smile about her lips. She seemed absorbed in the contemplation of the feathered crowd. Did she know the Germans were coming to Paris ? If so, she was not afraid.

How quiet it was in the great city ! How strangely and deadly quiet ! The heels of my two companions, and my own, made a click-clack down the pavements, as though we were walking through silent halls. Could this be Paris—this city of shuttered shops and barred windows and deserted avenues ? There were no treasures displayed in the Rue de la Paix. Not a diamond glinted behind the window panes. Indeed, there were no windows visible, but only iron sheeting, drawn down like the lids of dead men's eyes.

In the Avenue de l'Opéra no Teutonic tout approached us with the old familiar words, " Want a guide, sir ? "   " Lovely ladies, sir ! "   The lovely ladies had gone.   The guides had gone.   Life had gone out of Paris.

It was early in the morning, and we were faint for lack of sleep and food.

" My kingdom for a carriage," said the Philosopher, in a voice that seemed to come from the virgin forests of the Madeira in which he had once lost hold of all familiar things in life, as now in Paris.

A very old cab crawled into view, with a knock-kneed horse which staggered aimlessly about the empty streets, and with an old *cocher* who looked about him as though doubtful as to his whereabouts in this deserted city.

He started violently when we hailed him, and stared at us as nightmare creatures in a bad dream after an absinthe orgy.   I had to repeat an address three times before he understood.

" Hôtel St. James. . . . Écoutez donc, mon vieux ! "

He clacked his whip with an awakening to life.

" Allez ! " he shouted to his bag of bones.

Our arrival at the Hotel St. James was a sensation, not without alarm.   I believe the concierge and his wife believed the Germans had come when they heard the outrageous noise of our horse's hoofs thundering into the awful silence of their courtyard.   The manager, and the assistant manager, and the head waiter, and the head waiter's wife, and the chambermaid, and the cook, greeted us with the surprise of people who behold an apparition.

" The hotel has shut up.   Everybody has fled !   We are quite alone here ! "

I was glad to have added a little item of history to that old mansion where the Duc de Noailles lived, where Lafayette was married, and where Marie Antoinette saw old ghost faces—the dead faces of laughing girls—when she passed on her way to the scaffold.   It was a queer incident in its story when three English journalists opened it after the great flight from Paris.

Early that morning, after a snatch of sleep, we three friends walked up the Avenue des Champs Élysées and back again from the Arc de Triomphe. The autumn foliage was beginning to fall, and so wonderfully quiet was the scene that almost one might have heard a leaf rustle to the ground. Not a child scampered under the trees or chased a comrade round the Petit Guignol. No women with twinkling needles sat on the stone seats. No black-haired student fondled the hand of a pretty *couturière*. No honest bourgeois with a fat stomach walked slowly along the pathway meditating upon the mystery of life which made some men millionaires. Not a single carriage nor any kind of vehicle, except one solitary bicycle, came down the road where on normal days there is a crowd of light-wheeled traffic.

The Philosopher was silent, thinking tremendous things, with his sallow face transfigured by some spiritual emotion. It was when we passed the Palais des Beaux-Arts that he stood still and raised two fingers to the blue sky, like a priest blessing a kneeling multitude.

"Thanks be to the Great Power!" he said, with the solemn piety of an infidel who knows God only as the spirit is revealed on lonely waters and above uprising seas, and in the life of flowers and beasts, and in the rare pity of men.

We did not laugh at him. Only those who have known Paris and loved her beauty can understand the thrill that came to us on that morning in September when we had expected to hear the roar of great guns around her, and to see the beginning of a ghastly destruction. Paris was still safe! By some kind of miracle the enemy had not yet touched her beauty nor tramped into her streets. How sharp and clear were all the buildings under that cloudless sky! Spears of light flashed from the brazen-winged horses above Alexander's bridge, and the dome of the Invalides was a golden crown above a snow-white palace. The Seine poured in a burnished stream beneath all the bridges and far away beyond the houses and the island trees, and all the picture of Paris etched by a master-hand through long centuries of time the towers of Notre Dame were faintly pencilled in the blue screen of sky. Oh, fair dream-city, in which the highest passions of the spirit have found a dwelling-place—with the rankest weeds of vice—in which so many human hearts have suffered and strived and starved for beauty's sake, in which always there have lived laughter and agony and tears, where Liberty was cherished as well as murdered, and where Love has redeemed a thousand crimes, I, though an Englishman, found tears in my eyes because on that day of history your beauty was still unspoilt.

CHAPTER V

THE TURN OF THE TIDE

1

THE Germans were baulked of Paris. Even now, looking back on those days, I sometimes wonder why they made that sudden swerve to the south-east, missing their great objective. It was for Paris that they had fought their way westwards and southwards through an incessant battlefield from Mons and Charleroi to St. Quentin and Amiens, and down to Creil and Compiègne, flinging away human-life as though it were but rubbish for the death-pits. The prize of Paris—Paris the great and beautiful—seemed to be within their grasp, and the news of its fall would come as a thunderstroke of fate to the French and British peoples, reverberating eastwards to Russia as a dread proof of German power.

As I have said, all the north-west corner of France was denuded of troops, with the exception of some poor Territorials, ill-trained and ill-equipped, and never meant to withstand the crush of Imperial troops advancing in hordes with masses of artillery, so that they fled like panic-stricken sheep. The forts of Paris on the western side would not have held out for half a day against the German guns. All that feverish activity of trench work was but a pitiable exhibition of an unprepared defence. The enemy would have swept over them like a rolling tide. The little British army was still holding together, but it had lost heavily and was winded after its rapid retreat. The army of Paris was waiting to fight and would have fought to the death, but without support from other army corps still a day's journey distant, its peril would have been great, and if the enemy's

104

right wing had been hurled with full force against it at the critical moment it might have been crushed and annihilated. Von Kluck had twenty-four hours in his favour. If he had been swift to use them before Joffre could have hurried up his regiments to the rescue, German boots might have tramped down through the Place de la République to the Place de la Concorde, and German horses might have been stabled in the Palais des Beaux-Arts. I am sure of that, because I saw the beginning of demoralization, the first signs of an enormous tragedy, creeping closer to an expectant city. In spite of the optimism of French officers and men, an optimism as strong as religious faith, I believe now, searching back to facts, that it was not justified by the military situation. It was justified only by the miracle that followed faith. Von Kluck does not seem to have known that the French army was in desperate need of those twenty-four hours which he gave them by his hesitation. If he had come straight on for Paris with the same rapidity as his men had marched in earlier stages and with the same resolve to smash through regardless of cost, the city would have been his and France would have reeled under the blow. The psychological effect of the capital being in the enemy's hands would have been worth more to them at this stage of the war than the annihilation of an army corps. It would have been a moral debacle for the French people, who had been buoyed up with false news and false hopes until their Government had fled to Bordeaux, realizing the gravity of the peril. The Terrible Year would have seemed no worse than this swift invasion of Paris, and the temperament of the nation, in spite of the renewal of its youth, had not changed enough to resist this calamity with utter stoicism. I know the arguments of the strategists, who point out that Von Kluck could not afford to undertake the risk of entering Paris while an undefeated army remained on his flank. They are obvious arguments, thoroughly sound to men who play for safety, but all records of great captains of war prove that at a decisive moment they abandon the safe and obvious game for a master-stroke of audacity, counting the risks and taking them, and striking terror into the hearts of their enemy by the very shock of their contempt for caution. Von Kluck could have entered and held Paris with twenty thousand men. That seems to me beyond dispute by anyone who knows the facts. With the mass of men at his disposal he could have driven a wedge between Paris and the French armies of the left and centre, and any attempt on their part to pierce his line and cut his communications would have been hampered by the deadly peril of finding themselves outflanked by the German centre swinging down from the north in a western curve, with its point directed also upon Paris. The whole aspect of the war would have been changed, and there would have been great strategical movements perilous to both sides, instead of the siege war of the trenches in which both sides played for safety and established for many months a position bordering upon stalemate.

The psychological effect upon the German army if Paris had been taken would have been great in moral value to them as in moral loss to the French. Their spirits would have been exalted as much as the French spirits would have drooped, and even in modern war victory is secured as much by temperamental qualities as by shell-fire and big guns.

The Headquarters Staff of the German army decided otherwise. Scared by the possibility of having their left wing smashed back to the west between Paris and the sea, with their communications cut, they swung round steadily to the south-east and drove their famous wedge-like formation southwards, with the purpose of dividing the allied forces of the West from the French centre. The exact position then was this : Their own right struck down to the south-east of Paris, through Château Thierry to La Ferté-sous-Jouarre and beyond ; and another strong column forced the French to evacuate Rheims and fall back in a south-westerly direction. It was not without skill, this sudden change of plan, and it is clear that the German Staff believed it possible to defeat the French centre and left centre and then to come back with a smashing blow against the army of Paris and the " contemptible " British. But two great factors in the case were overlooked. One was the value of time, and the other was the sudden revival in the spirit of the French army now that Paris might still be saved. They gave time—no more than that precious twenty-four hours—to General Joffre and his advisers to repair by one supreme and splendid effort all the grievous errors of the war's first chapter. While they were hesitating and changing their line of front, a new and tremendous activity was taking place on the French side, and Joffre, by a real stroke of genius which proves him to be a great general in spite of the first mistakes, for which he was perhaps not responsible, prepared a blow which was to strike his enemy shrewdly.

2

I had the great fortune of seeing something of that rush to the rescue which gave hope that perhaps, after all, the tragedy which had seemed so inevitable—the capture of the world's finest city—might not be fulfilled.

This great movement was directed from the west, the south, and the east, and continued without pause by day and night.

In stations about Paris I saw regiment after regiment entraining—men from the southern provinces speaking the patois of the south, men from the eastern departments whom I had seen a month before, at the beginning of the war, at Châlons, and Epernay and Nancy, and men from the southwest and centre of France in the garrisons along the Loire.

They were all in splendid spirits, strangely undaunted by the rapidity of the German advance. " Fear nothing, my little one," said a dirty unshaven gentleman with the laughing eyes of d'Artagnan, " we shall bite their heads off. These brutal ' Boches ' are going to put themselves in a veritable death-trap. We shall have them at last."

The railway carriages were garlanded with flowers of the fields. The men wore posies in their *képis*. In white chalk they had scrawled legends upon the cattle-trucks in which they travelled. " À mort Guillaume ! " " Vive la Gloire ! " " Les Français ne se rendent jamais ! " Many of them had fought at Longwy and along the heights of the Vosges. The youngest of them had bristling beards. Their blue coats with the turned-back flaps were war-worn and flaked with the dust of long marches. Their red trousers were sloppy and stained.

But they had not forgotten how to laugh, and the gallantry of their spirits was good to see. A friend of mine was not ashamed to say that he had tears at least as high as his throat when he stood among them and clasped some of those brown hands. There was a thrill not to be recaptured in the emotion of those early days of war. Afterwards the monotony of it all sat heavily upon one's soul.

They were very proud, those French soldiers, of fighting side by side with their old foes the British, now after long centuries of strife, from Edward the Black Prince to Wellington, their brothers-in-arms upon the battlefields ; and because I am English they offered me their cigarettes and made me one of them.

In modern war it is only masses of men that matter, moved by a common obedience at the dictation of mysterious far-off powers, and I thanked Heaven that masses of men were on the move, rapidly, in vast numbers, and in the right direction—to support the French lines which had fallen back from Amiens a few hours before I left that town, whom I had followed in their retirement back and back, with the British always strengthening their left, but retiring with them almost to the outskirts of Paris itself.

Only this could save Paris—the rapid strengthening of the Allied front by enormous reserves strong enough to hold back the arrow-shaped battering-ram of the enemy's right.

All our British reserves had been rushed up to the front from Havre and Rouen. There was only one deduction to be drawn from this great swift movement. The French and British lines had been supported by every available battalion to save Paris from its menace of destruction, to meet the weight of the enemy's metal by a force strong enough to resist its mass.

3

One of the most dramatic incidents of the war was the transport of the army of Paris to the fighting line—in taxi-cabs. There were 2000 of these cabs in Paris, and on this day of September 1 they disappeared as though the earth had swallowed them, just as the earth had swallowed one of them not long before when the floods had sapped the streets. A sudden order from General Galliéni, the Military Governor of Paris, had been issued to each driver, who immediately ignored the upraised hands of would-be passengers and the shouts of people desperate to get to one of the railway stations with household goods and a hope of escape. At the depots the drivers knew that upon the strength of their tyres and the power of their engines depended the safety of Paris and perhaps the life of France. It was an extraordinary incident in the history of modern war. Five soldiers were loaded into each cab, four inside and one next to the driver, with their rifles and kit crammed in between them. In one journey twenty thousand men were taken on the road to Meaux. It was a triumph of mobility, and when in future the Parisian is tempted to curse those red vehicles which dash about the streets to the danger of all pedestrians who forget that death has to be dodged by never-failing vigilance, his righteous wrath will be softened, perhaps, by the remembrance that these were the chariots of General Manoury's army before the battle of Meaux, which turned the tide of war and flung back the enemy in retreat.

4

It will be to the lasting credit of General Joffre and the French Staff that after six weeks of disorder owing to the unreadiness of their army and their grievous errors in the disposition of the available troops, they recovered themselves in a supreme effort and by a brilliant stroke of strategy took the enemy completely by surprise and dealt him a staggering blow. The German Headquarters Staff—the brains of the greatest military machine in Europe—sublimely arrogant in their belief that they had an exclusive knowledge of the whole science of war and that the allied armies were poor blunderers without intelligence and without organization, utterly incapable of resisting the military genius of the German race, found themselves foiled and out-manœuvred at the very moment when the prize of victory seemed to be within their grasp.

For the first time since the beginning of their advance into French territory they were confronted with something like equal numbers, and they were brought to a halt at once. This arrest, shocking to their self-confidence, was found to be more than a mere check easily overpowered by bringing up more battalions. General von Kluck realized that the French had gathered together a formidable mass of men ready to be flung upon his right flank. Their guns were already beginning to open fire with frightful effect upon his advanced columns. The pressure of French regiments marching steadily and swiftly from the south-east and south-west after weeks of retirement, was forcing in his outposts, chasing back his cavalry and revealing a strong and resolute offensive. On September 4 and 5 there was heavy fighting on the German left and centre, to the south of the Marne and the west of the Ourcq. While General von Kluck was endeavouring to resist the thrust of the French and British troops who were massing their guns with great strength on his right, General . von Bülow's left wing, with the Saxon army and the Prince of Würtemberg's army, made desperate attempts to break the French centre by violent attacks to the north of Sezanne and Vitry-le-François. For two days the Germans tested the full measure of the strength opposed to them, but failed in smashing through any part of the French line, so that the Allies, successful in holding their ground against the full weight of the enemy, gained time for the supports to reach them and then developed a complete and general attack.

Von Kluck found that his troops were yielding. The French *mordant* was too much for Prussians as well as

Saxons, who in many villages of France and in the hollows of the downs were heavily punished by the Anglo-French artillery, and routed by bayonet charges thrust home with incredible ferocity.   The German Headquarters Staff, receiving these reports from all parts of the line, must have had many moral shocks, undermining their pride and racking their nerves.   Perhaps one day we shall read the history of those councils of war between the German generals, when men who had been confident of victory began to be haunted by doubt, hiding their fears even from themselves until they were forced to a gloomy recognition of grave perils.   Some of these men must have wept and others cursed, while Von Kluck decided to play again for safety, and issued an order for retreat.   Retreat !   What would the Emperor say in Berlin where he waited for the prize of Paris and heard that it had slipped from his grasp ?   How could they explain the meaning of that retreat to the people at home, expecting loot from the Louvre and souvenirs from Paris shops ?

Some of the officers thought these things—I have read their letters—but General von Kluck must have had only one dominating and absorbing thought, more important even than an Emperor's anger.   " Gott im Himmel, shall I get this army back to a stronger line or shall I risk all on a fight in the open, against those French and British guns and almost equal odds ? "   The failure of the German centre was the gravest disaster, and threatened von Kluck with the menace of an enveloping movement by the Allied troops which might lead to his destruction, with the flower of the Imperial troops. Away back there on the Aisne were impregnable positions tempting to hard-pressed men.   Leaving nothing to chance, the Germans had prepared them already in case of retreat, though it had not been dreamed of then as more than a fantastic possibility.   The fortune of war itself as well as cautious judgment pointed back to the Aisne for safety.   The allied armies were closing up, increasing in strength of men and guns as the hours passed.   In a day or two it might be too late to reach the strongholds of the hills. . . .

5

So the retreat of the German right wing which had cut like a knife through northern France until its edge was blunted by a wall of steel, began on September 5 and increased in momentum as the allied troops followed hard upon the enemy's heels. The great mass of the German left swung backwards in a steady and orderly way, not losing many men and not demoralized by this amazing turn in Fortune's wheel. "It is frightfully disappointing," wrote a German officer whose letter was found afterwards on his dead body. "We believed that we should enter Paris in triumph and to turn away from it is a bitter thing for the men. But I trust our chiefs and I know that it is only a strategical retirement. Paris will still be ours."

Truly it was a strategical retirement and not a "rout," as it was called by the English Press Bureau. But all retire‑ments are costly when the enemy follows close, and the rearguard of Von Kluck's army was in a terrible plight and suffered heavy losses. The French light artillery opened fire in a running pursuit, advancing their guns from position to position with very brief halts, during which the famous *soixante-quinze* flung out shells upon bodies of troops at close range—so that they fell like wheat cut to pieces in a hailstorm. The British gunners were pushing forward, less impetuously but with a steady persistence, to the west of the River Ourcq, and after all their hardships, losses, and fatigues, the men who had been tired of retreating were heartened now that their turn had come to give chase.

Episodes that seem as incredible as a boy's romance of war took place in those first days of September when the German right rolled back in a retreating tide. On one of those days an English regiment marched along a dusty road for miles with another body of men tramping at the same pace on a parallel road, in the same white dust which cloaked their uniforms—not of English khaki, but made in Germany. Hundreds of German soldiers, exhausted by this forced march in the heat, without food or water, fell out, took to the cover of woods, and remained there for weeks, in parties of six or eight, making their way to lonely farmhouses where they demanded food with rifles levelled at frightened peasants, taking pot-shots at English soldiers who had fallen out in the same way, and hiding in thickets until they were hunted out by *battues* of soldiers long after the first great battle of the Marne. It was the time for strange adventures when even civilians wandering in the wake of battle found themselves covered by the weapons of men who cared nothing for human life, whether it was their own or another's, and when small battalions of French or English, led by daring officers, fought separate battles in isolated villages, held by small bodies of the enemy, cut off from the main army but savagely determined to fight to the death.

Out of the experiences of those few days many curious chapters of history will be written by regimental officers and men. I have heard scores of stories of that kind, told while the thrill of them still flushed the cheeks of the narrators, and when the wounds they had gained in these fields of France were still stabbed with red-hot needles of pain, so that a man's laughter would be checked by a quivering sigh and his lips parched by a great thirst.

6

Because of its vivid interest and its fine candour, I will give one such story. It was told to me by a young officer of Zouaves who had been in the thickest of the fighting to the east of Paris. He had come out of action with a piece of shell in his left arm, and his uniform was splashed with the blood of his wound. I wish I could write it in his soldierly French words—so simple and direct, yet emotional at times with the eloquence of a man who speaks of the horrors which have scorched his eyes and of the fear that for a little while robbed him of all courage and of the great tragedy of this beastly business of war which puts truth upon the lips of men.

I wish also I could convey to my readers' minds the portrait of that young man with his candid brown eyes,

H

his little black moustache, his black stubble of beard, as I saw him in the rags and tatters of his Zouave dress, concealed a little beneath 'his long grey-blue cape of a German Uhlan, whom he had killed with his sword.

When he described his experience he puffed at a long German pipe which he had found in the pocket of the cape, and laughed now and then at this trophy, of which he was immensely proud.

"For four days previous to Monday, September 7," he said, "we were engaged in clearing out the German ' boches ' from all the villages on the left bank of the Ourcq, which they had occupied in order to protect the flank of their right wing.

"Unfortunately for us the English heavy artillery, which would have smashed the beggars to bits, had not yet come up to help us, although we expected them with some anxiety, as the big business events began as soon as we drove the outposts back to their main lines.

"However, we were quite equal to the preliminary task, and heartened by the news of the ammunition convoy which had been turned into a very pretty firework display by ' Soixante-dix Pau.' My Zouaves—as you see I belong to the First Division, which has a reputation to keep up—n'est-ce pas ?—were in splendid form.

"They were just like athletes who want to be first off the mark, or rather perhaps I should say like bloodhounds on the scent.

"Still, just to encourage them a little, don't you know, I pulled out my revolver, showed it to my little ones, and said very gently that the first man who hesitated to advance under the fire of the German guns would be a dead man before he took a step to the rear. (In every regiment there are one or two men who want encouraging in thi , way.) Of course, they all laughed at me. They wanted to get near those German guns, and nearer still to the gunners. That was before they knew the exact meaning of shell-fire. Well, they did good things, those Zouaves of mine. But it wasn't pleasant work. We fought from village to village, very close fighting, so that sometimes we could look into our enemy's eyes. The Moroccans were with us, the native troops, unlike my boys who are Frenchmen, and they were like demons with their bayonet work.

" Several of the villages were set on fire by the Germans before they retired from them, and soon great columns of smoke with pillars of flame and clouds of flying sparks rose up into the blue sky, and made a picture of hell there. For really it was hell on earth.

" Our gunners were shelling the Germans from pillar to post, as it were, and strewing the ground with their dead. It was across and among these dead bodies that we infantry had to charge. They lay about in heaps, masses of bleeding flesh. It made me sick, even in the excitement of it all. . . .

" The enemy's quickfirers were marvellous I am bound to say we did not get it all our own way. They always manœuvre them in the same style, and very clever it is. First of all they mask them with infantry. Then when the French charge they reveal them and put us to the test under the most withering fire. It is almost impossible to stand against it, and in this case we had to retire after each rush for about 250 metres.

" Then quick as lightning the Germans got their mitrailleuses across the ground which we had yielded to them, and waited for us to come on again ; when they repeated the same operation.

" I can tell you it was pretty trying to the nerves, but my Zouaves were very steady in spite of fairly heavy losses.

" In a village named Penchard there was some very sharp fighting, and some of our artillery were posted hereabouts. Presently a German aeroplane came overhead circling round in reconnaissance. But it was out for more than that. Suddenly it began to drop bombs, and whether by design or otherwise—they have no manners, these fellows—they exploded in the middle of a field hospital. One of my friends, a young doctor, was wounded in the left arm by a bullet from one of these bombs, though I don't know what other casualties there were. But the inevitable happened. Shortly after the disappearance of the aeroplane the German shells searched the position, and found it with unpleasant accuracy. It is always the same. The German aeroplanes are really wonderful in the way they search out the positions of our guns. We always know that within half an hour of an observation by aeroplane the shells will begin to fall above the gunners unless they have altered their position. It was so in this fighting round Meaux yesterday.

"For some days this rat-hunting among the villages on the left bank of the Ourcq went on all the time, and we were not very happy. The truth was that we had no water for ourselves, and were four days thirsty. It was really terrible, for the heat was terrific during the day, and some of us were almost mad with thirst. Our tongues were blistered and swollen, our eyes had a silly kind of look in them, and at night we had horrid dreams. It was, I assure you, an intolerable agony.

"But we did our best for the horses. I have said we were four days without drink. That was because we used our last water for the poor beasts. A gentleman has to do that—you will agree?—and the French soldier is not a barbarian. Even then the horses had to go without a drop of water for two days, and I'm not ashamed to say that I wept salt tears to see the sufferings of those poor innocent creatures, who did not understand the meaning of all this bloody business and who wondered at our cruelty.

"The nights were dreadful. All around us were burning villages, the dear hamlets of France, and at every faint puff of wind the sparks floated about them like falling stars. But other fires were burning. Under the cover of the darkness the Germans had collected their dead and had piled them into great heaps and had covered them with straw and paraffin. Then they had set a torch to these funeral pyres.

"Carrion crows were about in the dawn that followed. Not many of them, but they came flopping about the dead bodies, and the living, with hungry beaks. One of my own comrades lay very badly wounded, and when he wakened out of his unconsciousness one of these beastly birds was sitting on his chest waiting for him to die. That is war!

" Yet there are other things in war. Fine and splendid things. It was magnificent to see your English gunners come up. They were rather late in the field. They did not appear until midday on September 7, when the big battle was going on, and when we were doing our best to push back the German right wing. They came up just as if they were on the parade ground, marvellously cool, very chic fellows, superb in their manner of handling their guns. It was heavy artillery, and we badly wanted it. And nothing could budge your men, though the German shell-fire was very hot.

" That is the way with your British gunners. They are different from the French, who are always best when they are moving forward, but do not like to stay in one position. But when your men have taken up their ground, nothing can move them. Nothing on earth !

" And yet the German shells were terrifying. I confess to you that there were times when my nerves were absolutely gone. I crouched down with my men—we were in open formation—and ducked my head at the sound of the bursting ' obus ' and trembled in every limb as though I had a fit of ague. God rebuked me for the bombast with which I had spoken to my men.

" One hears the zip-zip of the bullets, the boom of the great guns, the tang of our sharp French artillery, and in all this infernal experience of noise and stench, the screams of dying horses and men joined with the fury of the gun-fire, and rose shrill above it. No man may boast of his courage. Dear God, there were moments when I was a coward with all of them !

" But one gets used to it, as to all things. My ague did not last long. Soon I was cheering and shouting again. We cleared the enemy out of the village of Bregy, and that was where I fell wounded in the arm pretty badly, by a bit of shell. I bled like a stuck pig, as you can see, but when I came to myself again a brother officer told me that things were going on well, and that we had rolled back the German right. That was better than a bandage to me. I felt very well again, in spite of my weakness

" It is the beginning of the end. The Germans are on

the run. They are exhausted and demoralized. Their pride has been broken. They are short of ammunition. They know that their plans have failed. Now that we have them on the move nothing will save them. This war is going to finish quicker than people thought. I believe that in a few days the enemy will be broken, and that we shall have nothing more to do than kill them as they fight back in retreat."

That is the story without any re-touching of my own, of the young lieutenant of Zouaves whom I met after the battle of Meaux, with the blood still splashed upon his uniform.

It is a human story, giving the experience of only one individual in a great battle, but clearly enough there emerges from it the truth of that great operation which did irreparable damage to the German right wing in its plan of campaign. The optimism with which this officer ended his tale makes one smile a little now, though in a pitiful way. The words in which he prophesied a quick finish to the war were spoken in September 1914, before the agony of the winter campaign, the awful monotony of that siege warfare, and the tides of blood that came in the spring of another year.

7

The retreat of the Germans to the Marne, when those columns of men turned their backs on Paris and trudged back along many roads down which they had come with songs of victory and across stony fields strewn already with the débris of fighting, on through villages where they burned and looted as they passed, left a trail of muck and blood and ruin. Five weeks before, when I had travelled through part of the countryside from the eastern frontier of France, the spirit of beauty dwelt in it. Those fields, without any black blotches on grass nibbled short by flocks of sheep, were fresh and green in the sunlight. Wild flowers spangled them with gold and silver. No horrors lurked in the woods, where birds sang shrill choruses to the humming undertone of nature's organists. Little French towns stood white on the hill-sides and in villages of whitewashed houses under thatch roofs, with deep, low barns filled with the firstfruits of the harvest, peasant girls laughed as they filled their jugs from the wells, and boys and girls played games in the market-places ; and old men and women, sitting in the cool gloom of their doorways, watched the old familiar things of peaceful life and listened to the chimes of the church clocks, without any terror in their hearts. War had been declared, but it seemed remote in its actual cruelty. There was only the faint thrill of unaccustomed drama in the scenes which passed through these village streets as guns rattled over the cobble-stones, or as a squadron of light blue cavalry streamed by, with bronzed men who grinned at the peasant girls, and horses still groomed and glossy. It is true that in some of these villages mothers of France had clasped their sons to their bosoms and wept a little over their nestling heads and wept still more in loneliness when the boys had gone away. The shadow of the war had crept into all these villages of France, but outwardly they were still at peace and untroubled by the far-off peril. Nature was indifferent to the stupid ways of men. Her beauty had the ripeness of the full-blown summer and the somnolence of golden days when the woods are very still in the shimmering heat and not a grass-blade moves except when a cricket stirs it with its chirruping.

Now, along the line of the retreat, nature itself was fouled and the old dwelling-places of peace were wrecked. Fighting their way back the enemy had burned many villages, or had defended them against a withering fire from the pursuing troops, so that their blackened stumps of timber, and charred, broken walls, with heaps of ashes which were once farmhouses and barns, remained as witnesses of the horror that had passed. Along the roadways were the bodies of dead horses. Swarms of flies were black upon them, browsing on their putrefying flesh, from which a stench came poisoning the air and rising above the scent of flowers and the sweet smell of hay in eddying waves of abominable odour. In villages where there had been street fighting, like those of Barcy, and Poincy, Neufmoutiers and Montlyon, Douy-la-Ramée and Chevre-ville, the whitewashed cottages and old farmsteads which were used as cover by the German soldiers before they were driven out by shell-fire or bayonet charges, were shattered into shapeless ruin. Here and there a house had escaped. It stood trim and neat amid the wreckage. A café restaurant still displayed its placards advertising Dubonnet and other *apéritifs*, peppered by shrapnel bullets, but otherwise intact. Here and there whole streets stood spared, without a trace of conflict, and in a street away the cottages had fallen down like card-houses toppled over by the hand of a petulant child. In other villages it was difficult to believe that war had passed that way. It was rather as though a plague had driven their inhabitants to flight. The houses were still shuttered as when the bourgeoisie and peasant had fled at the first news of the German advance. It was only by the intense solitude and silence that one realized the presence of some dreadful visitation, only that and a faint odour of corruption stealing from a dark mass of unknown beastliness huddled under a stone wall, and the deep ruts and holes in the roadway, made by gun-carriages and wagons.

Spent cartridges lay about, and fragments of shell, and here and there shells which had failed to burst until they buried their nozzles in the earth.

French peasants prowled about for these trophies, though legally they had no right to them, as they came under the penalties attached to loot. In many of the cottages which were used by the German officers there were signs of a hasty evacuation. Capes and leather pouches still lay about on chairs and bedsteads. Half finished letters, written to women in the Fatherland who will never read those words, had been trampled under heel by hurrying boots.

I saw similar scenes in Turkey when the victorious Bulgarians marched after the retreating Turks. I never dreamed then that such scenes would happen in France in the wake of a German retreat. It is a little thing, like one of those unfinished letters from a soldier to his wife, which overwhelms one with pity for all the tragedy of war.

"Meine liebe Frau." Somewhere in Germany a woman was waiting for the scrap of paper, wet with dew and half obliterated by mud, which I picked up in the Forest of

Compiègne   She would wait week after week for that letter
from the front, and day after day during those weeks she
would be sick at heart because no word came, no word which
would make her say, " Gott sei dank ! " as she knelt by the
bedside of a fair-haired boy so wonderfully like the man
who had gone away to that *unvermeidliche krieg* which had
come at last.   I found hundreds of letters like this, but so
soppy and trampled down that I could only read a word or
two in German script.   They fluttered about the fields and
lay in a litter of beef-tins left behind by British soldiers on
their own retreat over the same fields.

Yet I picked them up and stared at them and seemed to
come closer into touch with the tragedy which, for the most
part, up to now, I could only guess at by the flight of fugitives,
by the backwash of wounded, by the destruction of old houses,
and by the silence of abandoned villages.   Not yet had I seen
the real work of war, or watched the effects of shell-fire on
living men.   I was still groping towards the heart of the
business and wandering in its backyards.

I came closer to the soul of war on a certain Sunday in
September.   By that time the enemy's retreat had finished
and the German army under General von Kluck was at last
on the other side of the Aisne, in the strongholds of the hills
at which the French and British guns were vainly battering
at the beginning of a long and dreary siege against entrenched
positions.

All day long, on this Sunday in September, I trudged
over battlefields still littered with the horrors of recent
fighting, towards the lines, stretching northwards and eastwards from Vic-sur-Aisne to Noyon and Soissons, where for
six days without an hour's pause one of the greatest battles
in history had continued.

As I walked far beyond the rails from the town of Crépy-
en-Valois, which had suffered the ravages of the German
legions and on through the forest of Villers-Cotterets and
over fields of turnips and stubble. which only a few days ago
were trampled by French and British troops following the
enemy upon their line of retreat, to the north side of the Aisne,

the great guns of our heavy artillery shocked the air with thunderous reverberations.

Never for more than a minute or two did those thunderclaps cease. In those intervals the silence was intense, as though nature—the spirit of these woods and hills—listened with strained ears and a frightened hush for the next report. It came louder as I advanced nearer to the firing line, with startling crashes, as though the summits of the hills were falling into the deepest valleys. They were answered by vague, distant, murmurous echoes, which I knew to be the voice of the enemy's guns six miles further away, but not so far away that they could not find the range of our own artillery.

Presently, as I tramped on, splashing through waterpools and along rutty tracks ploughed up by the wheels of gun carriages, I heard the deeper, more sonorous booming of different guns, followed by a percussion of the air as though great winds were rushing into void spaces. These strange ominous sounds were caused by the heavy pieces which the enemy had brought up to the heights above the marshlands of the Aisne—the terrible 11-inch guns which outranged all pieces in the French or British lines. With that marvellous foresight which the Germans had shown in all their plans, these had been embedded in cement two weeks before in high emplacements, while their advanced columns were threatening down to Paris. The Germans even then were preparing a safe place of retreat for themselves in case their grand coup should fail, and our British troops had to suffer from this organization on the part of an enemy which was confident of victory but remembered the need of a safe way back.

I have been for many strange walks in my life with strange companions, up and down the world, but never have I gone for such a tramp with such a guide as on this Sunday within sound of the guns. My comrade of this day was a gravedigger.

His ordinary profession is that of a *garde champêtre,* or village policeman, but during the past three weeks he had been busy with the spade, which he carried across his shoulder by my side. With other peasants enrolled for the same tragic task he had followed the line of battle for twenty kilometres from his own village, Rouville, near Levignen, helping to bury the French ánd British dead, and helping to burn the German corpses.

His work was not nearly done when I met him, for during the fighting in the region round the forest of Villers-Cotterets, twice a battlefield, as the Germans advanced and then retreated, first pursuing and then pursued by the French and British, 3000 German dead had been left upon the way, and 1000 of our Allied troops. Dig as hard as he could my friendly gravedigger had been unable to cover up all those brothers-in-arms who lay out in the wind and the rain.

I walked among the fields where they lay, and among their roughly piled graves, and not far from the heaps of the enemy's dead who were awaiting their funeral pyres

My guide grasped my arm and pointed to a dip in the ground beyond the abandoned village of Levignen.

" See there," he said ; " they take some time to burn."

He spoke in a matter-of-fact way, like a gardener pointing to a bonfire of autumn leaves.

But there in line with his forefinger rose a heavy rolling smoke, sluggish in the rain under a leaden sky, and I knew that those leaves yonder had fallen from the great tree of human life, and this bonfire was made from an unnatural harvesting.

The French and British dead were laid in the same graves —" Are they not brothers ? " asked the man with the spade —and as soon as the peasants had courage to creep back to their villages and their woods they gathered leaves and strewed them upon those mounds of earth among which I wandered, as heroes' wreaths. But no such honour was paid to the enemy, and with a little petrol and straw they were put to the flames until only their charred ashes, wind-swept and wet with heavy rain, marked the place of their death.

It is the justice of men. It makes no difference. But as I stood and watched these smoky fires, between the beauty of great woods stretching away to the far hills, and close to a village which seemed a picture of human peace, with its old church-tower and red-brown roofs, I was filled with pity at all this misery and needless death which has flung its horror across the fair fields of France.

What was the sense of it ? Why, in God's name, or the devil's, were men killing each other like this on the fields of France, so that human life was of no more value than that of vermin slaughtered ruthlessly ? Each one of the German corpses whose flesh was roasting under those oily clouds of smoke had been a young man with bright hopes, and a gift of laughter, and some instincts of love in his heart. At least he had two eyes and a nose, and other features common to the brotherhood of man. Was there really the mark of the beast upon him so that he should be killed at sight, without pity ? I wondered if in that roasting mass of human flesh were any of the men who had been kind to me in Germany —the young poet whose wife had plucked roses for me in her garden, and touched them with her lips and said, " Take them to England with my love"; or the big Bavarian professor who had shared his food with me in the hills above Adrianople; or any of the Leipzig students who had clinked glasses with me in the beer-halls.

It was Germany's guilt—this war. Well, I could not read all the secrets of our Foreign Office for twenty years or more to know with what tact or tactlessness, with what honesty or charity, or with what arrogance or indifference our statesmen had dealt with Germany's claims or Germany's aspirations. But at least I knew, as I watched those smouldering death-fires, that no individual corpse among them could be brought in guilty of the crime which had caused this war, and that not a soul hovering above that mass of meat could be made responsible at the judgment seat of God. They had obeyed orders, they had marched to the hymn of the Fatherland, they believed, as we did, in the righteousness of their cause. But like the dead bodies of the Frenchmen and the Englishmen who lay quite close, they had been done to death by the villainy of statecraft and statesmen, playing one race against another as we play with pawns in a game of chess. The old witchcraft was better than this new witchcraft, and not so fraudulent in its power of duping the ignorant masses. . . .

My guide had no such sentiment. As he led me through a fringe of forest land he told me his own adventures, and heaped curses upon the enemy.

He had killed one of them with his own hand. As he was walking on the edge of a wood a solitary Uhlan came riding over the fields, below the crest of a little hill. He was one of the outposts of the strong force in Crépy-en-Valois, and had lost his way to that town. He demanded guidance, and to point his remarks pricked his lance at the chest of the *garde champêtre*.

But the peasant had been a soldier, and he held a revolver in the side pocket of his jacket. He answered civilly, but shot through his pocket and killed the man at the end of the lance. The Uhlan fell from his horse, and the peasant seized his lance and carbine as souvenirs of a happy moment.

But the moment was brief. A second later and the peasant was sick with fear for what he had done. If it should be discovered that he, a civilian, had killed a German soldier, every living thing in his village would be put to the sword—and among those living things were his wife and little ones.

` He dragged his trophies into the forest, and lay in hiding there for two days until the enemy had passed.

Afterwards I saw the lance—it reached from the floor to the ceiling of his cottage—and for years to come in the village of Rouville it will be the centre-piece of a thrilling tale.

Other peasants joined my friendly gravedigger, and one of them—the giant of his village—told me of his own escape from death. He was acting as the guide of four British officers through a part of the forest. Presently they stopped to study their maps ; and it was only the guide who saw at the other end of the glade a patrol of German cavalry. Before he could call out a warning they had unslung their carbines and fired. The British officers fell dead without a cry, and the peasant fell like a dead man also, rolling into a ditch, unwounded but paralysed with fear. They did not bother about him—that little German patrol. They rode off laughing, as though amused with this jest of death.

There have been many jests like that—though I see no mirth in them—and I could fill this chapter with the stories I have heard of this kind of death coming quite quickly in woods and fields where peasants raised their heads for a moment to find that the enemy was near. It is these isolated episodes among the homesteads of France, and in quiet villages girdled by silent woods, which seemed to reveal the spirit of war more even than the ceaseless fighting on the battle front with its long lists of casualties.

On that Sunday I saw the trail of this great spirit of evil down many roads.

I walked not only among the dead, but, what affected me with a more curious emotion, through villages where a few living people wrung their hands amidst the ruins of their homes.

Even in Crépy-en-Valois, which had suffered less than other towns through which the enemy had passed, I saw a wilful, wanton, stupid destruction of men—no worse I think than other men, but with their passions let loose and unrestrained. They had entered all the abandoned houses, and had found some evil pleasure in smashing chairs and tables and lampshades and babies' perambulators, and the cheap but precious ornaments of little homes. They had made a pigsty of many a neat little cottage, and it seemed as though an earthquake had heaped everything together into a shapeless, senseless litter. They entered a musical instrument shop, and diverted themselves, naturally enough, with gramophones and mouth-organs and trumpets and violins. But, unnaturally, with just a devilish mirth, they had then smashed all these things into twisted metal and broken strings. In one cottage an old man and woman, among the few inhabitants who remained, told me their story.

They are Alsatians, and speak German, and with the craftiness which accompanies the simplicity of the French peasant, made the most of this lucky chance.   Nine German soldiers were quartered upon them, and each man demanded and obtained nine eggs for the meal, which he washed down with the peasant's wine.   Afterwards, they stole everything they could find, and with their comrades swept the shops clean of shirts, boots, groceries, and everything they could lay their hands on.   They even took the hearses out of an undertaker's yard and filled them with loot.   Before they left Crépy-en-Valois, they fired deliberately, I was told, upon Red Cross ambulances containing French wounded.

Yet it was curious that the old Alsatian husband who told me some of these things had amusement rather than hatred in his voice when he described the German visit before their quick retreat from the advancing British.   He cackled with laughter at the remembrance of a moment of craftiness when he crept out of his back door and wrote a German sentence on his front door in white chalk.   It was to the effect that the inhabitants of his house were honest folk—*gute leute*—who were to be left in peace. . . .   He laughed in a high old man's treble at this wily trick.   He laughed again, until the tears came into his eyes, when he took me to a field where the French and British had blown up 3000 German shells abandoned by the enemy at the time of their retreat.   The field was strewn with great jagged pieces of metal, and to the old Alsatian it seemed a huge joke that the Germans had had to leave behind so much " food for the guns."   After all it was not a bad joke as far as we are concerned.

On that Sunday in September I saw many things which helped me to understand the meaning of war, and yet afterwards became vague memories of blurred impressions, half obliterated by later pictures.   I remember that I saw the movements of regiments moving up to support the lines of the Allies, and the carrying up of heavy guns for the great battle which had now reached its sixth day, and the passing, passing, of Red Cross trains bringing back the wounded from that terrible front between Vic and Noyon, where the trenches were being filled and refilled with dead and wounded, and regiments of tired men struggled forward with heroic endurance to take their place under the fire of those shells which had already put their souls to the test of courage beyond anything that might be demanded, in reason, from the strongest heart.

And through the mud and the water-pools, through the wet bracken and undergrowth, in a countryside swept by heavy rainstorms, I went tramping with the gravedigger, along the way of the German retreat, seeing almost in its nakedness the black ravage of war and its foul litter.

Here and there the highway was lined with snapped and twisted telegraph wires. At various places great water-tanks and reservoirs had been toppled over and smashed as though some diabolical power had made cockshies of them. I peered down upon the broken bridge of a railway line, and stumbled across uprooted rails torn from their sleepers and hurled about the track.

My gravedigger plucked my sleeve and showed me where he had buried a French cuirassier who had been shot as he kept a lonely guard at the edge of a wood.

He pointed with his spade again at newly-made graves of French and British. The graves were everywhere—mile after mile, on the slopes of the hills and in the fields and the valleys, though still on the battleground my friend had work to do.

I picked up bullets from shrapnels. They are scattered like peas for fifteen miles between Betz and Mortefontaine, and thicker still along the road to Vic. The jagged pieces of shell cut my boots. I carried one of the German helmets for which the peasants were searching among cabbages and turnips. And always in my ears was the deep rumble of the guns, those great booming thunder-blows, speaking from afar and with awful significance of the great battle, which seemed to be deciding the destiny of our civilization and the new life of nations which was to come perhaps out of all this death.

CHAPTER VI

INVASION

1

BEFORE this year has ended England will know something of what war means. In English country towns there will be many familiar faces missing, many widows and orphans, and many mourning hearts. Dimly and in a far-off way, the people who have stayed at home will understand the misery of war and its brutalities. But in spite of all our national effort to raise great armies, and our immense national sacrifice in sending the best of our young manhood to foreign battlefields, the imagination of the people as a whole will still fail to realize the full significance of war as it is understood in France and Belgium. They will not know the meaning of invasion.

It is a great luck to be born in an island. The girdle of sea is a safeguard which gives a sense of security to the whole psychology of a race, and for that reason there is a gulf of ignorance about the terrors of war which, happily, may never be bridged by the collective imagination of English and Scottish people. A continental nation, divided by a few hills, a river, or a line on the map, from another race with other instincts and ideals, is haunted throughout its history by a sense of peril. Even in times of profound peace, the thought is there, in the background, with a continual menace. It shapes the character of a people and enters into all their political and educational progress. To keep on friendly terms with a powerful next-door neighbour, or to build defensive works high enough to make hostility a safe game, is the lifework of its statesmen and its politicians. Great crises and agitations shake the nation convulsively when cowardice or treachery or laziness has allowed that boundary wall to crumble or has made a breach in it. The violence of the Dreyfus affair was not so much due to a Catholic detestation of the Jewish race, but in its root-instincts to a fear of the German people over the frontier making use of French corruption to sap the defensive works which had been raised against them.

The necessity of conscription is obvious beyond argument to a continental people still cherishing old traditions of nationality, and the military training which is compulsory for all young men of average health, not only shapes the bodies of their lads, but also shapes their minds, so that their outlook upon life is largely different from that of an island people protected by the sea. They know that they have been born of women for one primary object—to fight when the time comes in defence of the Fatherland, to make one more human brick in the great wall of blood and spirit dividing their country and race from some other country and race. At least that is the lesson taught them from first to last in the schools and in the national assemblies, and there are only a few minds which are able to see another way of life when the walls of division may be removed and when the fear of a next-door neighbour may be replaced by friendship and common interests.

The difference between the intellectual instincts of an island people and that of a continental race was the cause of the slow way in which England groped her way to an understanding of the present war, so that words of scorn and sarcasm, a thousand mean tricks of recruiting sergeants in high office, and a thousand taunts had to be used to whip up the young men of Great Britain, and induce them to join the Army. Their hearths and homes were not in immediate danger. They could not see any reasonable prospect of danger upon English soil. Their women were safe. Their property, bought on the hire system out of hard-earned wages, was not, they thought, in the least likely to be smashed into small bits or carried off as loot. They could not conceive the idea of jerry-built walls which enshrined all the treasures of their life suddenly falling with a crash like a house of cards, and burying their babies. The British Expeditionary Force which they were asked to join was after all only a sporting party going out to foreign fields for a great adventure.

2

In France there were no such illusions. As soon as war was imminent the people thought of their frontiers, and prayed God in divers ways that the steel hedges there were strong enough to keep back the hostile armies until the general call to the colours had been answered. Every able-bodied man in France was ready, whatever the cowardice in his heart, to fling himself upon the frontier to keep out, with his own body, the inrushing tide of German troops. The memory of 1870 had taught them the meaning of Invasion.

I saw the meaning of it during the first months of the war, when I wandered about France. In the north, nearest to the enemy, and along the eastern frontier, it was a great fear which spread like a plague, though more swiftly and terribly, in advance of the enemy's troops. It made the bravest men grow pale when they thought of their women and children. It made the most callous man pitiful when he saw those women with their little ones and old people, whose place was by the hearthside, trudging along the highroads, faint with hunger and weariness, or pleading for places in cattle-trucks already overpacked with fugitives, or wandering about un-lighted towns at night for any kind of lodging, and then, finding none, sleeping on the doorsteps of shuttered houses and under the poor shelter of overhanging gables.

For months, in every part of France there were thousands of husbands who had lost their wives and children, thousands of families who had been divided hopelessly in the wild confusion of retreats from a brutal soldiery. They had disappeared into the maelstrom of fugitives—wives, daughters, sisters, mothers, and old grandmother, most of them without money and all of them dependent for their lives upon the hazard of luck. Every day in the French newspapers there were long lists of inquiries.

" M. Henri Planchet would be deeply grateful to anyone who can inform him of the whereabouts of his wife, Suzanne, and of his two little girls, Berthe and Marthe, refugees from Armentières."

" Mme. Tardieu would be profoundly grateful for information about her daughter, Mme. des Rochers, who fled from the destroyed town of Albert on October 10, with her four children."

Every day I read some of these lists, finding a tragedy in every line, and wondering whether any of these missing people were among those whom I had met in the guard vans of troop trains, huddled among their bundles, or on wayside platforms, or in the long columns of retreating inhabitants from a little town deep in a wooded valley below the hills where German guns were vomiting their shrapnel.

Imagine such a case in England. A man leaves his office in London and takes the train to Guildford, where his wife and children are waiting supper for him. At Weybridge the train comes to a dead-halt. The guard runs up to the engine-driver, and comes back to say that the tunnel has been blown up by the enemy. It is reported that Guildford and all the villages around have been invaded. Families flying from Guildford describe the bombardment of the town. A part of it is in flames. The Guildhall is destroyed. Many inhabitants have been killed. Most of the others have fled.

The man who was going home to supper wants to set out to find his wife and children. His friends hold him back in spite of his struggles. " You are mad ! " they shout. " Mad ! " . . . He has no supper at home that night. His supper and his home have been burnt to cinders. For weeks he advertises in the papers for the whereabouts of his wife and babes. Nobody can tell him. He does not know whether they are dead or alive.

There were thousands of such cases in France. I have seen this tragedy—a man weeping for his wife and children swallowed up into the unknown after the destruction of Fives, near Lille. A new-born babe was expected. On the first day of life it would receive a baptism of fire. Who could tell this distracted man whether the mother or child were alive ?

3

There were many villages in France around Lille and Armentières, Amiens and Arras, and over a wide stretch of country in Artois and Picardy, where, in spite of all weariness, women who lay down beside their sleeping babes could find no sleep for themselves. For who could say what the night would bring forth ? Perhaps a patrol of Uhlans, who shot peasants like rabbits as they ran across the fields, and who demanded wine, and more wine, until in the madness of drink they began to burn and destroy for mere lust of ruin. So it was at Senlis, at Sermaize, and in many villages in the region through which I passed.

It was never possible to tell the enemy's next move. His cavalry came riding swiftly far from the main lines of the hostile troops, and owing to the reticence of official news, the inhabitants of a town or village found themselves engulfed in the tide of battle before they guessed their danger. They were trapped by the sudden tearing-up of railway lines and blowing-up of bridges, as I was nearly trapped one day when the Germans cut a line a few hundred yards away from my train.

Yet the terror was as great when no Germans were seen, and no shells heard. It was enough that they were coming. They had been reported—often falsely—across distant hills. So the exodus began and, with perambulators laden with bread and apples, in any kind of vehicle—even in a hearse— drawn by poor beasts too bad for army requisitions, ladies of quality left their châteaux and drove in the throng with peasant women from whitewashed cottages. Often in a little while both the château and the cottage were buried in the same heap of ruins.

In a week or two, the enemy was beaten back from some of these places, and then the most hardy of the townsfolk returned " home." I saw some of them going home—at

Senlis, at Sermaize, and other, places. They came back doubtful of what they would find, but soon they stood stupefied in front of some charred timbers which were once their house. They did not weep, but just stared in a dazed way. They picked over the ashes and found burnt bits of former treasures—the baby's cot, the old grandfather's chair, the parlour clock. Or they went into houses still standing neat and perfect, and found that some insanity of rage had smashed up all their household, as though baboons had been at play or fighting through the rooms. The chest of drawers had been looted or its contents tumbled out upon the floor. Broken glasses, bottles, jugs, were mixed up with a shattered violin, the medals of a grandfather who fought in '70, the children's broken toys, clothes, foodstuff, and picture frames. I saw many of such houses after the coming and going of the German soldiers.

Even for a correspondent in search of a vantage-ground from which he might see something of this war, with a reasonable chance of being able to tell the story afterwards, the situation in France during those early days was somewhat perilous.

It is all very well to advance towards the fighting lines when the enemy is opposed by allied forces in a known position, but it is a quite different thing to wander about a countryside with only the vaguest idea of the direction in which the enemy may appear, and with the disagreeable thought that he may turn up suddenly round the corner after cutting off one's line of retreat. That was my experience on more than one day of adventure when I went wandering with those two friends of mine, whom I have alluded to as the Strategist and the Philosopher. Not all the strategy of the one or the philosophy of the other could save us from unpleasant moments when we blundered close to the lines of an unexpected enemy.

That was our experience on an early day in October, when we decided to go to Béthune, which seemed an interesting place in the war-zone.

It may seem strange in England that railway trains

should still be running in the ordinary way, according to the time-tables of peace, in these directions, and that civilians should have been allowed to take their tickets without any hint as to the danger at the journey's end. But in spite of the horror of invasion, French railway officials showed an extraordinary *sang-froid* and maintained their service, even when they knew that their lines might be cut, and their stations captured, within an hour or two. Ignorance also helped their courage and, not knowing the whereabouts of the enemy even as well as I did, they ran their trains to places already threatened by advancing squadrons.

On this October day, for example, there was no sign of surprise on the part of the buxom lady behind the *guichet* of the booking-office when I asked for a ticket to Béthune, although there had been heavy fighting in that district only a few hours before, at the end of a great battle extending over several days.

In the train itself were several commercial gentlemen, on their way to Lille, by way of the junction at Arques, where they had to change; and with two or three French soldiers, and a lady entirely calm and self-possessed, they discussed the possibility of getting into a city round which the German cavalry were reported to be sweeping in a great tide. Another man who entered into conversation with me was going to Béthune. He had a wife and family there and hoped they were safe. It was only by a sudden thoughtfulness in his eyes that I could guess that behind that hope was a secret fear, which he did not express even to himself. We might have been a little party of people travelling, say, between Surbiton and Weybridge on an autumn afternoon, when the golf-ball flies across the links. Not one of them showed the least sign of anxiety, the least consciousness of peril close at hand.

Looking out of the carriage window I saw that trenches had been dug in all the adjacent fields, and that new trenches were being made hastily but efficiently by gangs of soldiers, who had taken off their blue coats for once, and were toiling

cheerily at their task. In all the villages we passed were
battalions of infantry guarding the railway bridges and
level crossings. Patrols of cavalry rode slowly down the
roads. Here and there some of them were dismounted,
with their horses tethered, and from behind the cover of
farmhouses or haystacks, looked across the country, with
their carbines slung across their shoulders, as though waiting
for any Uhlans that might appear that way.

All around us was the noise of guns, firing in great salvoes
across the hills, ten miles or more away. Suddenly, as we
approached the junction at Arques, there was an explosion
which sounded very close to us ; and the train came to a
dead stop on grinding brakes.

" What's that ? " asked a man in the carriage, sharply.

I thrust my head out of the carriage window and saw
that all along the train other faces were staring out. The
guard was running down the platform. The station-master
was shouting to the engine-driver. In a moment or two
we began to back, and kept travelling backwards until we
were out of the station. . . . The line had just been blown
up beyond Arques by a party of Uhlans, and we were able
to thank our stars that we had stopped in time. We could get
no nearer to Béthune, over which next day the tide of war
had rolled. I wondered what had happened to the wife and
children of the man who was in the carriage with me.

At Aire-sur-Lys there were groups of women and children
who, like so many others in those days, had abandoned
their houses and left all they had in the world save a few
bundles of clothes and baskets of food. I asked them what
they would do when the food was finished.

" There will always be a little charity, m'sieur," said one
woman, " and at least my children are safe."

After the first terror of the invasion those women were
calm and showed astounding courage and resignation.

It was more than pitiful to see the refugees on the roads
from Hazebrouck. There was a constant stream of them
in those two cross-currents, and they came driving slowly
along in bakers' carts and butchers' carts, with covered

hoods, in farm carts loaded up with several families or trudging along with perambulators and wheelbarrows. The women were weary. Many of them had babies in their arms. The elder children held on to their mother's skirts or tramped along together, hand in hand. But there was no trace of tears. I heard no wailing cry. Some of them seemed utterly indifferent to this retreat from home. They had gone beyond the need of tears.

From one of these women, a lady named Mme. Duterque, who had left Arras with a small boy and girl, I heard the story of her experiences in the bombarded town. There were hundreds of women who had similar stories, but this one is typical enough of all those individual experiences of women who quite suddenly, and almost without warning, found themselves victims of the Invasion.

She was in her dressing-room in one of the old houses of the Grande Place in Arras, when at half-past nine in the morning the first shell burst over the town very close to her own dwelling-place. For days there had been distant firing on the heights round Arras, but now this shell came with a different, closer, more terrible sound.

" It seemed to annihilate me for a moment," said Mme. Duterque. " It stunned all my senses with a frightful shock. A few moments later I recovered myself and thought anxiously of my little girl who had gone to school as usual a few streets away. I was overjoyed when she came trotting home, quite unafraid, although by this time the shells were falling in various parts of the town."

On the previous night Mme. Duterque had already made preparations in case the town should be bombarded. Her house, like most of the old houses in Arras, had a great cellar, with a vaulted roof, almost as strong as a castle dungeon. She had stocked it with a supply of sardines and bread and other provisions, and as soon as she had her little daughter safe indoors again she took her children and the nurse down to this subterranean hiding-place, where there was greater safety. The cave, as she called it, was dimly lighted with a paraffin lamp, and was very damp and chilly, but it was good to be there in this hiding-place, for at regular intervals she could hear the terrible buzzing noises of a shell, like some gigantic hornet, followed by its exploding boom ; and then, more awful still, the crash of a neighbouring house falling into ruins.

"Strange to say," said Mme. Duterque, " after my first shock I had no sense of fear, and listened only with an intense interest to the noise of these shells, estimating their distance by their sound.   I could tell quite easily when they were close overhead, and when they fell in another part of the town, and it seemed to me that I could almost tell which of my friends' houses had been hit.   My children, too, were strangely fearless.   They seemed to think it an exciting adventure to be here in the great cellar, making picnic meals by the light of a dim lamp.   My little boy amused himself by playing *carrés* (hop-scotch), and my daughter was very cheerful.   Still, after a little while we suffered. I had forgotten to bring down water or wine, and we also craved for something more comforting than cold sardines. In spite of the noise of houses falling into ruins—and at any moment mine might fall above my head—I went upstairs and began to cook some macaroni.   I had to retreat in a hurry, as a shell burst quite close to my house, and for a moment I thought that I should be buried under my own roof.   But I went up again in one of the intervals of silence, found the macaroni cooked to a turn and even ventured to peep out of doors.   There I saw a dreadful sight.   The whole of the Grande Place was littered with broken roofs and shattered walls, and several of the houses were burning furiously.   From other parts of the town there came up great volumes of smoke and the red glare of flames."

For three days Mme. Duterque kept to her cellar. Unknown to herself, her husband, who had come from Boulogne to rescue her, was watching the battle from one of the heights outside the town, which he was forbidden to enter by the soldiers.   On a Thursday morning she resolved to leave the shelter of her underground vault.   News had been brought to her by a daring neighbour that the Germans had worked round by the railway station and might enter the town.

" I had no fear of German shells," she said, " but I had a great fear of German officers and soldiers. Imagine my fate if I had been caught by them, with my little daughter. For the first time I was filled with a horrible fear, and I decided to fly from Arras at all costs.'"

With her children and the nurse, she made her way through the streets, above which the shells were still crashing, and glanced with horror at all the destruction about her. The Hôtel de Ville was practically destroyed, though at that time the famous belfry still stood erect above the ruined town, chiming out the hours of this tragedy.

Mme. Duterque told me her story with great simplicity and without any self-consciousness of her fine courage. She was only one of those thousands of women in France who, with a spiritual courage beyond one's understanding, endured the horrors of this war. It was good to talk with them, and I was left wondering at such a spirit.

It was with many of these fugitives that I made my way back. Away in the neighbourhood of Hazebrouck the guns were still booming, and across the fields the outposts of French cavalry were waiting for the enemy.

4

It was better for women and children to be in Arras under continual shell-fire than in some of those villages along the valleys of the Marne and the Meuse and in the Department of the Seine, through which the Germans passed on their first march across the French frontier. It was a nicer thing to be killed by a clean piece of shell than to suffer the foulness of men whose passions had been unleashed by drink and the devil and the madness of the first experience of war, and by fear which made them cruel as beasts.

I think fear was at the heart of a good deal of those atrocious acts by which the German troops stained the honour of their race in the first phases of the war. Advancing into a hostile country, among a people whom they knew to be reckless in courage and of a proud spirit, the generals and high officers were obsessed with the thought of peasant warfare, rifle-shots from windows, murders of soldiers billeted in farms, spies everywhere, and the peril of franc-tireurs, goading their troops on the march. Their text-books had told them that all this was to be expected from the French people and could only be stamped out by ruthlessness. The proclamations posted on the walls of invaded towns reveal fear as well as cruelty. The mayor and prominent citizens were to surrender themselves as hostages. If any German soldier were killed, terrible reprisals would be exacted. If there were any attempt on the part of the citizens to convey information to the French troops, or to disobey the regulations of the German commander, their houses would be burned and their property seized, and their lives would pay the forfeit. These bald-headed officers in pointed helmets, so scowling behind their spectacles, had fear in their hearts and concealed it by cruelty.

When such official proclamations were posted up on the walls of French villages, it is no wonder that the subordinate officers and their men were nervous of the dangers suggested in those documents, and found perhaps without any conscious dishonesty clear proof of civilian plots against them. A shot rang out down a village street. " The peasants are firing on us ! " shouted a German soldier of neurotic temperament. " Shoot them at sight ! " said an officer who had learnt his lesson of ruthlessness. " Burn these wasps out ! Lieber Gott, we will teach them a pretty lesson ! "

They had all the material for teaching the pretty lessons of war—inflammable tablets which would make a house blaze in less than five minutes after they had been strewn about the floors and touched by a lighted match (I have a few specimens of the stuff)—incendiary bombs which worked even more rapidly, torches for setting fire to old barns and thatched roofs. In the wonderful equipment of the German army in the field this material of destruction had not been forgotten and it was used in many little towns and villages where German soldiers heard real or imaginary shots, suspected betrayal from any toothless old peasant, and found themselves in the grip of fear because these Frenchwomen, these old men of the farm and the workshop, and even the children, stared at them as they passed with contemptuous eyes and kept an uncomfortable silence even when spoken to with cheerful Teuton greetings, and did not hide the loathing of their souls. All this silence of village people, all these black looks seemed to German soldiers like an evil spell about them. It got upon their nerves and made them angry. They had come to enjoy the fruits of victory in France, or at best the fruits of life before death came. So these women would not smile, eh ? Nor give their kisses nor their love with amiability ? Well, a German soldier would have his kisses.even though he had to hold a shrieking woman to his lips. He would take his love even though he had to kill the creature who refused it. These Frenchwomen were not so austere as a rule in times of peace. If they would not be fondled they should be forced. Herr Gott ! they should know their masters.

5

At the little town of Rebais in the department of Seine-et-Marne there was a pretty Frenchwoman who kept a grocer's shop and did not care for the way in which some German soldiers made free with her biscuits and sweetmeats. She was a proud and fearless young woman, and when the soldiers grinned at her and tried to put their arms about her she struck them and called them unpleasant names and drew an open knife. So she wanted her lesson ? Well, she had a soft white neck, and if they could not put their arms about it they would put a rope round it and hang her with her pride. But she was strong and quick as well as proud. She cut their rope with her knife and fought like a wild thing. So they slashed at her with their fists and bruised all her beauty by the time one of their officers came in and ordered them away. No one would court her after the lesson they had given her.

At Saint-Denis-en-Rebais, on September 7, an Uhlan who

was eager for a woman's love saw another pretty woman who tried to hide from him. There was a mother-in-law with her, and a little son, eight years of age. But in war-time one has to make haste to seize one's victim or one's loot. Death is waiting round the corner. Under the cover of his rifle—he had a restless finger on the trigger—the Uhlan bade the woman strip herself before him. She had not the pride or the courage of the other woman. She did not want to die, because of that small boy who stared with horror in his eyes. The mother-in-law clasped the child close and hid those wide staring eyes in her skirts, and turned her own face away from a scene of bestial violence, moaning to the sound of her daughter's cries.

6

At the town of Coulommiers on September 6 a German soldier came to the door of a small house where a woman and her husband were sitting with two little children, trying to hide their fear of this invasion of German troops. It was half-past nine in the evening and almost dark, except for a glow in the sky. The soldier was like a shadow on the threshold until he came in, and they saw a queer light in his eyes. He was very courteous, though rather gruff in his speech. He asked the husband to go outside in the street to find one of his comrades. The man, afraid to refuse, left the room on this errand, but before he had gone far heard piercing cries. It was his wife's voice, screaming in terror. He rushed back again and saw the German soldier struggling with his wife. Hearing her husband's shout of rage, the soldier turned, seized his rifle, and clubbed the man into an adjoining room, where he stayed with the two little children who had fled there, trying to soothe them in their fright and listening, with madness in his brain, to his wife's agony through the open door a yard away. The husband was a coward, it seems. But supposing he had flung himself upon the soldier and strangled him, or cut his throat ? We know what would have happened in the village of Coulommiers.

7

On September 7 ten German horsemen rode into the farm of Lamermont, in the commune of Lisle-en-Barrois. They were in good humour, and having drunk plenty of fresh milk, left the farmhouse in a friendly way. Shortly after their departure, when Farmer Elly and his friend, the sieur Javelot, breathed more easily and thanked God because the danger had passed, some rifle-shots rang out. Somewhere or other a dreadful thing was happening. A new danger came to the farm at Lamermont, with thirty men of a different patrol, who did not ask for milk but blood. They accused the farm people of having killed a German soldier, and in spite of the protests of the two men, who had been sitting quietly in the kitchen, they were shot in the yard.

8

At Triaucourt the Germans were irritated by the behaviour of a young girl named Mlle. Hélène Procès, who was bold enough to lodge a complaint to one of their officers about a soldier who had tried to make love to her in the German way. It was a fine thing if German soldiers were to be punished for a little sport like that in time of war ! " Burn them out ! " said one of the men. On a cold autumn night a bonfire would warm things up a little. . . . It was the house of M. Jules Gaude which started the bonfire. It blazed so quickly after the torch had touched his thatch that he had to leap through the flames to save himself, and as he ran the soldiers shot him dead. When the houses were burning the Germans had a great game shooting at the people who rushed about the streets. A boy of seventeen, named George Lecourtier, was killed as he thrust his way through the flames. A gentleman named Alfred Lallemand—his name ought to have saved him—was chased by some soldiers when he fled for refuge to the kitchen of his fellow-citizen Tautelier, and shot there on his hearthside. His friend had three bullet-wounds in the hand with which he had tried to protect the hunted man. Mlle. Procès, the young girl

who had made the complaint which led to this trouble, flea
into the garden with her mother and her grandmother and
an aunt named Mlle. Mennehard, who was eighty-one years
old. The girl was able to climb over the hedge into the
neighbour's garden, where she hid among the cabbages like
a frightened kitten. But the old people could not go so fast,
and as they tried to climb the hedge they were shot down
by flying bullets. The curé of the village crept out into
the darkness to find the bodies of those ladies, who had
been his friends. With both hands he scooped up the
scattered brains of Mlle. Mennehard, the poor old dame of
eighty-one, and afterwards brought her body back into her
house, where he wept at this death and destruction which
had made a hell of his little village in which peace had reigned
so long. And while he wept merry music played, and its
lively notes rattled out into the quiet night from an open
window quite close to where dead bodies lay. The German
soldiers enjoyed themselves that night in Triaucourt. Like
so many Neros on a smaller scale, they played and sang
while flames leapt up on either side of them. Thirty-five
houses in this village were burnt to cinders after their old
timbers had blazed fiercely with flying sparks which sparkled
above the helmets of drunken soldiery. An old man of
seventy named Jean Lecourtier, and a baby who had been
only two months in this strange world of ours were roasted
to death in the furnace of the village. A farmer named Igier,
hearing the stampede of his cattle, tried to save these poor
beasts, but he had to run the gauntlet of soldiers who shot
at him as he stumbled through the smoke, missing him only
by a hair's-breadth, so that he escaped as by a miracle, with
five holes in his clothes. The village priest, Père Viller,
leaving the body of his old friend, went with the courage of
despair to the Duke of Würtemberg, who had his lodging
near by, and complained to him passionately of all these
outrages. The Duke of Würtemberg shrugged his shoulders.
" Que voulez-vous ? " he said. " We have bad soldiers,
like you have ! "

9

At Montmirail a man named François Fontaine lived with his widowed daughter, Mme. Naudé, and his little grandchild Juliette. A German non-commissioned officer demanded lodging at the house, and on the night of September 5, when all was quiet, he came undressed into the young widow's room and, seizing her roughly, tried to drag her into his own chamber. She cried and struggled so that her father came running to her, trembling with fear and rage. The *Unteroffizier* seems to have given some signal, perhaps by the blowing of a whistle. It is certain that immediately after the old man had left his room fifteen or twenty German soldiers burst into the house and dragged him out into the street, where they shot him dead. At that moment the child Juliette opened her bedroom window, looking out into the darkness at this shadow scene. It was not Romeo but Death who called this little Juliette. A bullet hit her in the stomach, and twenty-four hours later she died in agony.

I need not add to these stories, nor plunge deeper into the vile obscenity of all those crimes which in the months of August and September set hell loose in the beautiful old villages of France along a front of five hundred miles. The facts are monotonous in the repetition of their horror, and one's imagination is not helped but stupefied by long records of outrages upon defenceless women, with indiscriminate shooting down village streets, with unarmed peasants killed as they trudged across their fields or burned in their own homesteads, with false accusations against innocent villagers, so that hostages were collected and shot in groups as a punishment for alleged attacks upon German soldiers, with old French châteaux looted of all their treasures by German officers in search of souvenirs and trophies of victory for their womenfolk, and with drunken orgies in which men of decent breeding became mere animals inflamed with lust.

K

10

The memory of those things has burnt deep into the brains of the French people, so deep that in some cases there is the fire of madness there.

In a small château in France an English friend of mine serving with a volunteer ambulance column with the French troops on the Meuse was sitting at ease one night with some of his comrades and fellow-countrymen. The conversation turned to England, because April was there, and after ten months of war the thoughts of these men yearned back to their homes. They spoke of their mothers and wives and children. One man had a pretty daughter, and read a piece of her latest letter, and laughed at her gay little jests and her descriptions of the old pony and the dogs and the antics of a black kitten. Other men gave themselves away and revealed the sentiment which as a rule Englishmen hide. In the room was a French officer, who sat very still, listening to these stories. The candles were burning dim on the table when he spoke at last in a strange, hard voice :

" It is good for you Englishmen when you go back home. Those who are not killed out here will be very happy to see their women again. You do not want to die, because of that. . . . If I were to go home now, gentlemen, I should not be happy. I should find my wife and my daughter both expecting babies whose fathers are German soldiers. . . . England has not suffered invasion."

11

The most complete destruction I saw in France was in Champagne, when I walked through places which had been the villages of Sermaize, Heiltz-le-Maurupt, Blesmes, and Huiron. Sermaize was utterly wiped out. As far as I could see, not one house was left standing. Not one wall was spared. It was laid flat upon the earth, with only a few charred chimney-stacks sticking out of the piles of bricks and cinders. Strange, piteous relics of pretty dwelling-places lay about in the litter, signifying that men and women with

some love for the arts of life had lived here in decent comfort.
A notice-board of a hotel which had given hospitality to
many travellers before it became a blazing furnace lay
sideways on a mass of broken bricks with a legend so frightfully ironical that I laughed among the ruins : " Chauffage
central "—the system of " central heating " invented by
Germans in this war had been too hot for the hotel, and had
burnt it to a wreck of ashes. Half a dozen peasants stood
in one of the " streets "—marked by a line of rubbish-heaps
which had once been their homes. Some of them had waited
until the first shells came over their chimney-pots before they
fled. Several of their friends, not so lucky in timing their
escape, had been crushed to death by the falling houses.
But it was not shell-fire which did the work. The Germans
strewed the cottages with their black inflammable tablets,
which had been made for such cases, and set their torches
to the window-curtains before marching away to make other
bonfires on their road of retreat. Sermaize became a street
of fire, and from each of its houses flames shot out like scarlet
snakes, biting through the heavy pall of smoke. Peasants
hiding in ditches a mile away stared at the furnace in which
all their household goods were being consumed. Something
of their own life seemed to be burning there, leaving the dust
and ashes of old hopes and happiness.

" That was mine," said one of the peasants, pointing to a
few square yards of wreckage. " I took my woman home
across the threshold that was there. She was a fine girl,
with hair like gold, Monsieur. Now her hair has gone quite
white, during these recent weeks. That's what war does
for women. There are many like that hereabouts, white-
haired before their time."

I saw some of those white-haired women in Blesmes and
Huiron and other scrap-heaps of German ruthlessness. They
wandered in a disconsolate way about the ruins, watching
rather hopelessly the building of wooden huts by a number
of English " Quakers " who had come here to put up shelters
for these homeless people of France. They were doing good
work—one of the most beautiful works of charity which

had been called out of this war, and giving a new meaning to their name of the Society of Friends. But though they were handy in the use of the wood given them by the French Government for this purpose, not all their industry nor all their friendliness could bring back the beauty of these old-world villages of Champagne, built centuries ago by men of art and craft, and chiselled by Time itself, so that the stones told tales of history to the villagers. It would be difficult to patch up the grey old tower of Huiron Church, through which shells had come crashing, or to rebuild its oak roof whose beams were splintered like the broken ribs of a rotting carcase. A white-haired priest passed up and down the roadway before the place in which he had celebrated Mass and praised God for the blessings of each day. His hands were clenched behind his bent back, and every now and then he thrust back his broad felt hat and looked up at the poor, battered thing which had been his church with immense sadness in his eyes.

There was an old château near Huiron in which a noble family of France had lived through centuries of war and revolution. It had many pointed gables and quaint turrets and mullioned windows, overlooking a garden in which there were arbours for love-in-idleness where ladies had dreamed awhile on many summer days in the great yesterday of history. When I passed it, after the Germans had gone that way, the gables and the turrets had fallen down, and instead of mullioned windows there were gaping holes in blackened walls. The gardens were a wild chaos of trampled shrubberies among the cinder-heaps, the twisted iron, and the wreckage of the old mansion. A flaming torch or two had destroyed all that time had spared, and the château of Huiron was a graveyard in which beauty had been killed, murderously, by outrageous hands.

In one of these villages of Champagne—I think it was at Blesmes—I saw one relic which had been spared by chance when the flames of the incendiaries had licked up all other things around, and somehow, God knows why, it seemed to me the most touching thing in this place of desolation.

It was a little stone fountain, out of which a jet of water rose playfully, falling with a splash of water-drops into the sculptured basin. While the furnace was raging in the village this fountain played and reflected the glare of crimson light in its bubbling jet. The children of many generations had dabbled their hands in its basin. Pretty girls had peeped into their own bright eyes mirrored there. On summer days the village folk had sauntered about this symbol of grace and beauty. Now it was as though I had discovered a white Venus in the dust-heap of a burying-place.

12

The great horror of Invasion did not reach only a few villages in France and blanch the hair of only a few poor women. During the long months of this stationary war there was a long black line on all the maps, printed day after day with depressing repetition in all the newspapers of the world. But I wonder how many people understood the meaning of that black line marking the length of the German front through France, and saw in their mind's eye the blackness of all those burnt and shattered villages, for ten miles in width, on that border-line of the war trail? I wonder how many people, searching for news of heroic bayonet charges or for thrilling stories of how Private John Smith kept an army corps at bay, single-handed, with a smile on his face, saw even faintly and from afar the flight of all the fugitives from that stricken zone, the terror of women and children trapped in its hell-fire, and the hideous obscenity of that long track across the fields of France, where dead bodies lay rotting in the rain and sun and the homesteads of a simple people lay in heaps from Artois to Lorraine?

Along the valley of the Aisne and of the Vesle the spirit of destruction established its kingdom. It was a valley of death. In the official reports only a few villages were mentioned by name, according to their strategical importance, but there were hundreds of hamlets, unrecorded in dispatches, which were struck by death and became the charnel-houses of bones and ruins.

In the single district of Vic-sur-Aisne, the little communities of Saconin, Pernant, Ambleny, and Ressons—beautiful spots in old days of peace, where Nature displayed all her graciousness along the winding river and where Time itself seemed to slumber—French soldiers stared upon broken roofs, shattered walls, and trampled gardens, upon the twisted iron of ploughs and the broken woodwork of farmers' carts, and all the litter of war's ruthless damage. Week after week, turn and turn about, German, French, and British shells crashed over these places, making dust and ashes of them. Peasants who clung to their cots, hid in their cellars and at last fled, described all this in a sentence or two when I questioned them. They had no grievance even against fate— their own misery was swallowed up in that of their neighbours; each family knew a worse case than its own, and so, with a shake of the head, they said there were many who suffered these things.

Shopkeepers and peasants of Celles, of Condé, of Attichy, along the way to Berry-au-Bac and from Billy to Sermoise, all those who have now fled from the Valley of the Vesle and the valley of the Aisne had just the same story to tell— monotonous, yet awful because of its tragedy. It was their fate to be along the line of death. One old fellow who came from Vailly had lived for two months in a continual cannonade. He had seen his little town taken and retaken ten times in turn by the French and the Germans.

When I heard of this eye-witness I thought: "Here is a man who has a marvellous story to tell. If all he has seen, all the horrors and heroism of great engagements were written down, just as he describes them in his peasant speech, it would make an historic document to be read by future generations."

But what did he answer to eager questions about his experience? He was hard of hearing and, with a hand making a cup for his right ear, stared at me a little dazed. He said at last, "It was difficult to get to sleep."

That was all he had to say about it, and many of these peasants were like him, repeating some trivial detail of their experience, the loss of a dog or the damage to an old teapot, as though that eclipsed all other suffering. But little by little, if one had the patience, one could get wider glimpses of the truth. Another old man from the village of Soupir told a more vivid tale. His dwelling-place sheltered some of the Germans when they traversed the district. The inhabitants of Soupir, he said, were divided into two groups. Able-bodied prisoners were sent off to Germany, and women and children who were carried off in the retreat were afterwards allowed to go back, but not until several poor little creatures had been killed, and pretty girls subjected to gross indignities by brutal soldiers. Upon entering Soupir the French troops found in cellars where they had concealed themselves thirty people who had gone raving mad and who cried and pleaded to remain so that they could still hear the shells and gibber at death. "War is so bracing to a nation," says the philosopher. "War purges peoples of their vanities." If there is a devil—and there must be many old-time sceptics who believe now not in one but in a hundred thousand devils—how the old rogue must chuckle at such words !

13

It was astounding to any student of psychology wandering in the war zone to see how many of the peasants of France clung to their houses, in spite of all their terror of German shells and German soldiers. When in the first month of 1915 the enemy suddenly swarmed over the ridges of Cuffies and Crouy, to the north of Soissons, and with overwhelming numbers smashed the French back across the Aisne at a time when the rising of the river had broken many pontoon bridges, so that the way of escape was almost cut off, they drove out crowds of peasant folk who had remained along this fifteen miles of front until actually shelled out in that last attack which put the ruins of their houses into the hands of the Germans. As long as three months before Crouy itself had been a target for the enemy's guns, so that hardly a cottage was standing with solid walls.

Nevertheless, with that homing instinct which is the strongest emotion in the heart of the French peasant, many of the inhabitants had been living an underground life in their cellars, obtaining food from French soldiers and cowering close together as shells came shrieking overhead, and as the shattered buildings collapsed into greater ruin.

So it was in Rheims and Arras and other towns which were not spared in spite of the glories of an architecture which can never be rebuilt in beauty. Only a few days before writing these lines, I stood on the edge of the greatest battlefield in France and from an observation post perched like an eyric in a tree above the valley, looked across to the cathedral of Rheims, that shrine of history, where the bones of kings lie, and where every stone speaks of saints and heroes and a thousand years of worship. The German shells were still falling about it, and its great walls stood grim and battered in a wrack of smoke. For nine months the city of Rheims has suffered the wounds of war. Shrapnel and air-bombs, incendiary shells and monstrous *marmites* had fallen within its boundaries week by week; sometimes only one or two on an idle day, sometimes in a raging storm of fire, but always killing a few more people, always shattering another house or two, always spoiling another bit of sculptured beauty. Nevertheless, there were thousands of citizens, women as well as men, who would not leave their city. They lived in cellars, into which they had dragged their beds and stores, and when the shell fire slackened they emerged, came out into the light of day, looked around at the new damage, and went about their daily business until cleared underground again by another storm of death. There were two old ladies with an elderly daughter who used to sit at table in the *salle-à-manger* of a hotel in Paris a week or two ago. I saw them arrive one day, and watched the placid faces of these stately old dames in black silk with little lace caps on their white hair. It was hardly possible to believe that for three months they had lived in a cellar at Rheims, listening through the day and night to the cannonading of the city, and to the rushing of the shells above their own house.

Yet I think that even in a cellar those old women of France preserved their dignity, and in spite of dirty hands (for water was very scarce) ate their meagre rations with a stately grace.

14

More miserable and less armed with courage were the people of France who lived in cities held by the enemy and secure from shell-fire—in Lille, and St. Quentin, and other towns of the North, where the Germans paraded in their pointed casques. For the most part in these great centres of population the enemy behaved well. Order was maintained among the soldiers with ruthless severity by German officers in high command. There were none of the wild and obscene acts which disgraced the German army in its first advance to and its retreat from the Marne. No torch bearers and tablet scatterers were let loose in the streets. On the contrary any German soldier misbehaving himself by looting, raping, or drunken beastliness found a quick death against a white wall. But to the French citizens it was a daily agony to see those crowds of hostile troops in their streets and houses, to listen to their German speech, to obey the orders of generals who had fought their way through Northern France across the bodies of French soldiers, smashing, burning, killing along the bloody track of war. These citizens of the captured soil of France knew bitterness of invasion more poignantly than those who hid in cellars under shell-fire. Their bodies were unwounded, but their spirits bled in agony. By official placards posted on the walls they read of German victories and French defeats. In the restaurants and cafés, and in their own houses, they had to serve men who were engaged in slaughtering their kinsfolk. It was difficult to be patient with those swaggering young officers who gave the glad eye to girls whose sweethearts lay dead somewhere between the French and German trenches.

From a lady who had been seven months in St. Quentin, I heard the story of how invasion came suddenly and took possession of the people. The arrival of the German troops was an utter surprise to the population, who had had no previous warning. Most of the French infantry had left the town, and there remained only a few detachments, and some English and Scottish soldiers who had lost their way in the great retreat, or who were lying wounded in the hospitals. The enemy came into the town at 4 P.M. on August 28, having completely surrounded it, so that they entered from every direction. The civil population, panic-stricken, remained for the most part in their houses, staring through their windows at the columns of dusty, sun-baked men who came down the streets. Some of the British soldiers, caught in this trap, decided to fight to the death, which they knew was inevitable. Several English and Scottish soldiers fired at the Germans as they advanced into the chief square and were instantly shot. One man, a tall young soldier, stationed himself at the corner of the Place du Huit Octobre, and with extraordinary coolness and rapidity fired shot after shot, so that several German soldiers were killed or wounded. The enemy brought up a machine gun and used it against this one man who tried to stop an army. He fell riddled with bullets, and was blown to pieces as he lay.

On the whole the Germans behaved well at St. Quentin. Their rule was stern but just, and although the civil population had been put on rations of black bread, they got enough and it was not, after all, so bad. As one of the most important bases of the German army in France, the town was continually filled with troops of every regiment, who stayed a little while and then passed on. Meanwhile the permanent troops in occupation of the town settled down and made themselves thoroughly at home. They established many of their own shops—bakeries, tailoring establishments, and groceries ; and in consequence of the lack of discipline and decency which prevailed in some of the cafés and restaurants, these places were conducted by German officers, who acted as censors of morals and professors of propriety.

Astounding as it seems, there were Frenchwomen in St. Quentin who sold themselves for German money and gave their kisses for a price to men who had ravaged France and killed the sons of France. Such outrageous scenes took place, that the German order to close some of the cafés was hailed as a boon by the decent citizens, who saw the women expelled by order of the German commandant with enormous thankfulness.

It is strange that the Huns, as they are called, should have been so strict in moral discipline. Many of them were not so austere in the villages when they let their passions loose and behaved like drunken demons or satyrs with flaming torches. There is a riddle in the psychology of all these contrasts between the iron discipline and perfect organization by which all outrage was repressed in the large towns occupied for any length of time by German troops, and the lawlessness and rapine of the same race in villages through which they passed hurriedly, giving themselves just time enough to wreak a cruel ferocity upon unoffending people. Riddle as it is, it holds perhaps the key to the mystery of the German character and to their ideal of war. Whenever there was time to establish discipline, the men were well behaved, and did not dare to disobey the orders of their chiefs. It was only when special orders for " frightfulness " had been issued, or when officers in subordinate command let their men get out of hand, or led the way to devilry by their own viciousness of action, that the rank and file of the enemy's army committed its brutalities. Even now, after all that I have seen in the ruined villages in France, I cannot bring myself to believe that the German race is distinguished from all other peoples in Europe by the mark of the beast, or that they are the exclusive possession of the devil. The prisoners I have spoken to, the blue-eyed Saxons and plump Bavarians with whom I travelled for awhile after the battle of Neuve Chapelle, seemed to me uncommonly like the yokels of our own Somersetshire and Devonshire. Their officers were polite and well-bred men in whom I saw no sign of fiendish lusts and cruelties. In normal moods they are a good-natured people, with a little touch of Teuton grossness perhaps, which makes them swill overmuch beer, and with an arrogance towards their women-folk which is not tolerable to Englishmen, unless they have revolted from the older courtesies of English life because the Suffragettes have challenged their authority.

It was in abnormal moods that they committed their atrocities, for in the hot sun of the first September of the war their blood was overheated, and in the first intoxication of their march through France, drunk with the thrill of butcher's work as well as with French wine, brought back suddenly to the primitive lusts of nature by the spirit of war, which strips men naked of all refinements and decent veils, they became for a time savages, with no other restraint than that of Red Indians on the warpath. They belonged to an Army of Invasion, marching through hostile territory, and the soul of war robbed the individual of his own separate soul and put a spell of madness on him, so that his eyes were bloodshot and his senses inflamed with lust. In the Peninsular War young Englishmen from decent villages in quiet countrysides, with pious mothers praying for them at home in grey old churches, and with pretty sisters engaged in hero-worship, were bewitched by the same spell of wizardry and did foul and frightful things which afterwards made them dream o' nights and wake in a cold sweat of shame and horror. There are many young Germans who will wake out of such dreams when they get back to Düsseldorf and Bingen-am-Rhein, searching back in their hearts to find a denial of the deeds which have become incredible after their awakening from the nightmare. For a little while they had been caught up in the soul of war and their heroism had been spoilt by obscenity, and their ideals debased by bestial acts. They will have only one excuse to their recaptured souls : " It was War." It is the excuse which man has made through all the ages of his history for the bloody thing which, in all those ages, has made him a liar to his faith and a traitor to the gentle gods.

CHAPTER VII

THE LAST STAND OF THE BELGIANS

1

DURING the first two and a half months of the war I was a wanderer in France, covering many hundreds of miles in zig-zag journeys between Nancy and the west coast, always on the move, backwards and forwards, between the lines of the French and British armies, and watching with a tireless though somewhat haggard interest the drama of a great people engaged in a life-and-death struggle against the most formidable army in the world. I had been in the midst of populations in flight, armies in retreat, and tremendous movements of troops hurled forward to new points of strategical importance. Now and again I had come in touch with the British army and had seen something of the men who had fought their way down from Mons to Meaux, but for the most part my experience had been with the French, and it was the spirit of France which I had done my best to interpret to the English people.

Now I was to see war, more closely and intimately than before, in another nation; and I stood with homage in my heart before the spirit of Belgium and that heroic people who, when I came upon them, had lost all but the last patch of territory, but still fought, almost alone, a tenacious, bloody and unending battle against the Power which had laid low their cities, mangled their ancient beauties, and changed their little land of peaceful industry into a muck-heap of slaughter and destruction.

Even in France I had this vision of the ruin of a nation, and saw its victims scattered. Since that day when I came upon the first trainload of Belgian soldiers near Calais, weary or lame dogs after their retreat, I had seen an interminable procession of fugitives from that stricken country and heard from them the tale of Alost, Louvain, Termonde and other towns where only horror dwelt above incinerated stones and scraps of human flesh.   The fall of Antwerp resounded into France, and its surrender after words of false hope that it would never fall shook the soul of the French people with a great dismay.   It was idle to disguise the importance of this German victory at the time when France, with every nerve strained and with England by her side, could hardly stem back the tide of those overflowing armies which had been thrust across the Marne but now pressed westward towards Calais with a smashing strength.   The capture of Antwerp would liberate large numbers of the enemy's best troops. Already, within a day of this disaster to the Allied armies, squadrons of German cavalry swept across the frontiers into France, forcing their way rapidly through Lille and Armentières towards Béthune and La Bassée, cutting lines which had already been cut and then repaired, and striking terror into French villages which had so far escaped from these hussars of death.   As a journalist, thwarted at every turn by the increasing severity of military orders for correspondent catching, the truth was not to be told at any cost.   I had suspected the doom of Antwerp some days before its fate was sealed, and I struck northward to get as near as possible to the Belgian frontier.   The nearest I could get was Dunkirk, and I came in time to see amazing scenes in that port of France.   They were scenes which, even now as I write months afterwards, stir me with pity and bring back to my imagination an immense tragedy of history.

2

The town of Dunkirk, from which I went out to many adventures in the heart of war, so that for me it will always hold a great memory, was on that day in October a place of wild chaos, filled with the murmur of enormous crowds, and with the steady tramp of innumerable feet which beat out a tragic march.   Those weary footsteps thumping the pavements and the cobble-stones, made a noise like the surging of waves on a pebble beach—a queer, muffled, shuffling sound, with a rhythm in it which stupefied one's senses if one listened to it long. I think something of this agony of a people in flight passed into my own body and brain that day. Some sickness of the soul took possession of me, so that I felt faint and overcome by black dejection. There was a physical evil among those vast crowds of Belgians who had come on foot, or in any kind of vehicle, down the big, straight roads which led to France, and now struggled down towards the docks, where thousands were encamped. From their weariness and inevitable dirtiness, from the sweat of their bodies, and the tears that had dried upon their cheeks, from the dust and squalor of bedraggled clothes, there came to one's nostrils a sickening odour. It was the stench of a nation's agony. Poor people of despair! There was something obscene and hideous in your miserable condition. Standing among your women and children, and your old grandfathers and grandmothers, I was ashamed of looking with watchful and observant eyes. There were delicate ladies with their hats awry and their hair dishevelled, and their beautiful clothes bespattered and torn, so that they were like the drabs of the slums and stews. There were young girls who had been sheltered in convent schools, now submerged in the great crowd of fugitives, so utterly without the comforts of life that the common decencies of civilization could not be regarded, but gave way to the unconcealed necessities of human nature. Peasant women, squatting on the dock-sides, fed their babes as they wept over them and wailed like stricken creatures. Children with scared eyes, as though they had been left alone in the horror of darkness, searched piteously for parents who had been separated from them in the struggle for a train or in the surgings of the crowds. Young fathers of families shouted hoarsely for women who could not be found. Old women, with shaking heads and trembling hands, raised shrill voices in the vain hope that they might hear an answering call from sons or daughters. Like people who had escaped from an earthquake to some seashore where by chance a boat might come for them all, these Belgian families struggled to the port of Dunkirk and waited desperately for rescue. They were in a worse plight than shipwrecked people, for no ship of good hope could take them home again. Behind them the country lay in dust and flames, with hostile armies encamped among the ruins of their towns.

For a little while I left these crowds and escaped to the quiet sanctuary of a restaurant in the centre of the town. I remember that some English officers came in and stared at me from their table with hard eyes, suspicious of me as a spy, or, worse still, as a journalist. (In those days, having to dodge arrest at every turn, I had a most unpatriotic hatred of those British officers whose stern eyes gimletted my soul. They seemed to me so like the Prussian at his worst. Afterwards, getting behind this mask of harness, by the magic of official papers, I abandoned my dislike and saw only the virtue of our men.) I remember also that I ate at table opposite a pretty girl, with a wanton's heart, who prattled to me, because I was an Englishman, as though no war had come to make a mockery of love-in-idleness. I stood up from the table, upsetting a glass so that it broke at the stem. Outside the restaurant was the tramp of another multitude. But the rhythm of those feet was different from the noise I had heard all day. It was sharper and more marked. I guessed at once that many soldiers were passing by, and that upon striding to the door I should see another tragedy. From the doorway I watched an army in retreat. It was the army of Antwerp marching into Dunkirk. I took off my hat and watched with bared head.

They were but broken regiments, marching disorderly for the most part, yet here and there were little bodies of men keeping step, with shouldered rifles, in fine, grim pride. The municipal guards came by, shoulder to shoulder, as on parade, but they were followed by long convoys of mounted men on stumbling horses, who came with heaps of disorderly salvage piled on to dusty wagons. Saddles and bridles and bits, the uniforms of many regiments flung out hurriedly from barrack cupboards; rifles, swords, and boots were heaped on to beds of straw, and upon the top of them lay men exhausted to the point of death, so that their heads flopped and lolled as the carts came jolting through the streets. Armoured cars with mitrailleuses, motor-cars slashed and plugged by German bullets, forage carts and ambulances, struggled by in a tide of traffic between bodies of foot-soldiers slouching along without any pride, but dazed with weariness. Their uniforms were powdered with the dust of the roads, their faces were blanched and haggard for lack of food and sleep. Some of them had a delirious look and they stared about them with rolling eyes in which there was a gleam of madness. Many of these men were wounded, and spattered with their blood. Their bandages were stained with scarlet splotches, and some of them were so weak that they left their ranks and sat in doorways, or on the kerb-stones, with their heads drooping sideways. Many another man, footsore and lame, trudged along on one boot and a bandaged sock, with the other boot slung to his rifle barrel.

Riding alone between two patrols of mounted men was a small boy on a high horse. He was a fair-haired lad of twelve or so, in a Belgian uniform, with a tasselled cap over one ear, and as he passed the Dunquerquoises clapped hands and called out: "Bravo! Bravo!" He took the ovation with a grin and held his head high.

The cafés in this part of France were crowded with Belgian officers of all grades. I had never seen so many generals together or such a medley of uniforms. They saluted each other solemnly, and there were emotional greetings between friends and brothers who had not seen each other after weeks of fighting in different parts of the lines, in this city across the border. Most of the officers were fine, sturdy, young fellows of stouter physique than the French among whom I had been roving. But others had the student look and stared mournfully from gold-rimmed spectacles. There were many middle-aged men among them who wore military uniforms, but without a soldier's ease or swagger. When Germany tore up that "scrap of paper" which guaranteed the integrity of Belgium, every patriotic man there volunteered for the defence of his country and shouldered a rifle, though he had never fired a blank cartridge, and put on some kind of uniform, though he had never drilled in a barrack square. Lawyers and merchants, schoolmasters and poets, actors and singers, farmers and peasants, rushed to take up arms, and when the vanguards of the German army struck across the frontier they found themselves confronted not only by the small regular army of Belgium, but by the whole nation. Even the women helped to dig the trenches at Liège, and poured boiling water over Uhlans who came riding into Belgian villages. It was the rising of a whole people which led to so much ruthlessness and savage cruelty. The German generals were afraid of a nation of franc-tireurs, where every man or boy who could hold a gun shot at the sight of a pointed helmet. Those high officers to whom war is a science without any human emotion or pity in its rules, were determined to stamp out this irregular fighting by blood and fire, and " frightfulness " became the order of the day. I have heard English officers uphold these methods and use the same excuse for all those massacres which has been put forward by the enemy themselves. " War is war. . . . One cannot make war with rosewater. . . . The franc-tireur has to be shot at sight. A civil population using arms against an invading army must be taught a bloody lesson. If ever we get into Germany we may have to face the same trouble, so it is no use shouting words of horror."

War is war, and hell is hell. Let us for the moment leave it at that, as I left it in the streets of Dunkirk, where the volunteer army of Belgium and their garrison troops had come in retreat after heroic resistance against overwhelming odds, in which their courage without science was no match for the greatest death machine in Europe, controlled by experts highly trained in the business of arms.

3

' That night I went for a journey in a train of tragedy I was glad to get into the train. Here, travelling through the clean air of a quiet night, I might forget for a little while the senseless cruelties of this war, and turn my eyes away from the suffering of individuals smashed by its monstrous injustice.

But the long train was packed tight with refugees. There was only room for me in the corridor if I kept my elbows close, tightly wedged against the door. Others tried to clamber in, implored piteously for a little space, when there was no space. The train jerked forward on uneasy brakes, leaving a crowd behind.

Turning my head and half my body round, I could see into two of the lighted carriages behind me, as I stood in the corridor. They were overfilled with various types of these Belgian people whom I had been watching all day—the fugitives of a ravaged country. For a little while in this French train they were out of the hurly-burly of their flight. For the first time since the shells burst over Antwerp they had a little quietude and rest.

I glanced at their faces, as they sat back with their eyes closed. · There was a young Belgian priest there, with a fair, clean-shaven face. He wore top boots splashed with mud, and only a silver cross at his breast showed his office. He had fallen asleep with a smile about his lips. But presently he awakened with a start, and suddenly there came into his eyes a look of indescribable horror. . . . He had remembered.

There was an old lady next to him. The light from the carriage lamp glinted upon her silver hair, and gave a Rembrandt touch to a fair old Flemish face. She was looking at the priest, and her lips moved as though in pity. Once or twice she glanced at her dirty hands, at her draggled dress, and then sighed, before bending her head, and dozing into forgetfulness.

A young Flemish mother cuddled close to a small boy with flaxen hair, whose blue eyes stared solemnly in front of him with an old man's gravity of vision. She touched the child's hair with her lips, pressed him closer, seemed eager to feel his living form, as though nothing mattered now that she had him safe.

On the opposite seat were two Belgian officers—an elderly man with a white moustache and grizzled eyebrows under his high *képi* and a young man in a tasselled forage cap, like a boy-student. They both sat in a limp, dejected way. There was defeat and despair in their attitude It was only when the younger man shifted his right leg with a sudden grimace of pain that I saw he was wounded.

Here in these two carriages through which I could glimpse were a few souls holding in their memory all the sorrow and suffering of poor, stricken Belgium. Upon this long train were a thousand other men and women in the same plight and with the same grief.

Next to me in the corridor was a young man with a pale beard and moustache and fine delicate features. He had an air of distinction, and his clothes suggested a man of some wealth and standing. I spoke to him, a few common-place sentences, and found, as I had guessed, that he was a Belgian refugee.

" Where are you going ? " I asked.

He smiled at me and shrugged his shoulders slightly.

" Anywhere. What does it matter ? I have lost everything. One place is as good as another for a ruined man."

He did not speak emotionally. There was no thrill of despair in his voice. It was as though he were telling me that he had lost his watch.

" That is my mother over there," he said presently, glancing towards the old lady with the silver hair. " Our house has been burnt by the Germans and all our property was destroyed. We have nothing left. May I have a light for this cigarette ? "

One young soldier explained the reasons for the Belgian debacle. They seemed convincing

" I fought all the way from Liège to Antwerp. But it was always the same. When we killed one German, five appeared in his place. When we killed a hundred, a thousand followed. It was all no use. We had to retreat and retreat. That is demoralizing."

"England is very kind to the refugees," said another man. "We shall never forget these things."

The train stopped at wayside stations. Sometimes we got down to stamp our feet. Always there were crowds of Belgian refugees on the platforms—shadow figures in the darkness or silhouetted in the light of the station lamps. They were encamped there with their bundles and their babies.

On the railway lines were many trains, shunted into sidings. They belonged to the Belgian State Railways, and had been brought over the frontier away from German hands—hundreds of them. In their carriages little families of refugees had made their homes. They are still living in them, hanging their washing from the windows, cooking their meals in these narrow rooms. They have settled down as though the rest of their lives is to be spent in a siding. We heard their voices, speaking Flemish, as our train passed on. One woman was singing her child to sleep with a sweet old lullaby. In my train there was singing also. A party of four young Frenchmen came in, forcing their way hilariously into a corridor which seemed packed to the last inch of space. I learnt the words of the refrain which they sang at every station :

> *A bas Guillaume !*
> *C'est un filou*
> *Il faut le pendre*
> *Il faut le pendre*
> *La corde à son cou !*

The young Fleming with a pale beard and moustache smiled as he glanced at the Frenchmen.

"They have had better luck," he said. "We bore the first brunt."

I left the train and the friends I had made. We parted with an "Au revoir" and a "Good luck !" When I went down to the station the next morning I learnt that a train of refugees had been in collision at La Marquise, near Boulogne. Forty people had been killed and sixty injured.

After their escape from the horrors of Antwerp the people on this train of tragedy had been struck again by a blow from the clenched fist of fate.

4

I went back to Dunkirk again and stayed there for some days in the hope of getting a pass which would allow me to cross the Belgian frontier and enter the zone of battle. Even to get out of the railway station into this fortified town required diplomacy bordering upon dishonesty, for since the retreat of the Belgian army of volunteers, Dunkirk had an expectation of a siege and bombardment and no civilian strangers were allowed to enter. Fortunately I was enabled to mention a great name, with the implied and utterly untruthful suggestion that its influence extended to my humble person, so that a French gentleman with a yard-long bayonet withdrew himself from the station doorway and allowed me to pass with my two friends.

It struck me then, as it has a thousand times since the war began, how all precautions must fail to keep out a spy who has a little tact and some audacity. My two friends and I were provided with worthless passes which failed to comply with official regulations. We had no authorized business in Dunkirk, and if our real profession had been known we should have been arrested by the nearest French or British officer, sent down to British headquarters under armed guard and, after very unpleasant experiences as criminals of a dangerous and objectionable type, expelled from France with nasty words on our passports. Yet in spite of spy-mània and a hundred methods of spy-catching, we who were classed with spies—passed all barriers and saw all the secrets of the town's defence. If instead of being a mild and inoffensive Englishman I had been a fierce and patriotic German, I might have brought away a mass of military information of the utmost value to General von Kluck ; or, if out for blood, I might have killed some very distinguished officers before dying as a faithful son of the Fatherland. No sentries at the door of the Hôtel des Arcades, in the Place Jean-Bart, challenged three strangers of shabby and hungry look when they passed through in search of food. Waiters scurrying about with dishes and plates did not look askance at them when they strolled into a dining-room crowded with French and British staff officers. At the far end of the room was a great general—drinking *croûte-au-pot* with the simple appetite of a French *poilu*—who would have been a splendid mark for anyone careless of his own life and upholding the law of frightfulness as a divine sanction for assassination. It was "Soixante-dix Pau," and I was glad to see that brave old man who had fought through the terrible year of 1870, and had been *en retraite* in Paris when, after forty-four years, France was again menaced by German armies. Left "on the shelf" for a little while, and eating his heart out in this inactivity while his country was bleeding from the first wounds of war, he had been called back to repair the fatal blunders in Alsace. He had shown a cool judgment and a masterly touch. From Alsace, after a reorganization of the French plan of attack, he came to the left centre and took part in the councils of war, where General Joffre was glad of this shrewd old comrade and gallant heart. He was given an advisory position, unhampered by the details of a divisional command, and now it seemed to me that his presence in Dunkirk hinted at grave possibilities in this fortified town. He had not come merely to enjoy a good luncheon at the Hôtel des Arcades.

The civilian inhabitants of Dunkirk were beginning to feel alarmed. They knew that only the last remnant of the active Belgian army stood between their great port and the enemy's lines. Now that Antwerp had fallen they were beginning to lose faith in their girdle of forts and in their garrison artillery. The German guns had assumed a mythical and monstrous significance in the popular imagination. It seemed that they could smash the strongest defences with their far-reaching thunderbolts. There was no outward panic in the town and the citizens hid their fears under a mask of contempt for the "sacrés Boches." But on some faces—of people who had no fear of death except for those they loved

—it was a thin mask, which crumbled and let through terroi when across the dykes and ramparts the rumours came that the German army was smashing forward, and closer.

The old landlady of the small hotel in which I stayed had laughed very heartily with her hands upon her bulging stays when a young Belgian officer flirted in a comical way with her two pretty daughters—a blonde and a brunette, whose real beauty and freshness and simplicity redeemed the squalor of their kitchen.

But presently she grabbed me by the arm, closing the door with the other hand.

"Monsieur, I am an old fool of a woman, because I have those two beauties there. It is not of myself that I am afraid. If I could strangle a German and wring his neck, I would let the rest cut me into bits. But those girls of mine—those two roses! I can't let *them* take risks! You understand—those Germans are a dirty race. Tell me, is it time for us to go?"

I could not tell her if it were time to go. With two such girls I think I should have fled, panic-stricken. And yet I did not believe the Germans would find Dunkirk an easy place to take. I had been round its fortifications, and had seen the details of elaborate works which even against German guns might prove impregnable. Outside the outer forts the ground was bare and flat, so that not a rabbit could scuttle across without being seen and shot. Sandbag entrenchments and earthworks, not made recently, because grass had clothed them, afforded splendid cover for the French batteries. Bomb-proof shelters were dotted about the fields, and for miles away, as far as the Belgian frontier, were lines of trenches and barbed-wire entanglements. To the eye of a man not skilled in military science all these signs of a strong defence were comforting. And yet I think they were known to be valueless if the enemy broke through along the road to Dunkirk.

A cheerful priest whom I met across an iron bridge told me the secret of Dunkirk's real defences.

"We have just to turn on a tap or two," he said, laughing

at the simplicity of the operation, "and all those fields for miles will be flooded within an hour or two. Look, that low-lying land is under water already. The enemy's guns would sink in it."

He pointed away to the south-west, and I saw that many of the fields were all moist and marshy, as though after torrential rain. Nearer to us, on the dry land, a body of soldiers marched up and down, drilling industriously.

The priest pointed to them.

"They fought untrained, those Belgian boys. Next time they will fight with greater discipline. But not with greater courage, Monsieur! I lift my hat to the heroic spirit of brave little Belgium, which as long as history tells a splendid tale, will be remembered. May God bless Belgium and heal its wounds!"

He took off his broad black hat and stood bareheaded, with a great wind blowing his *soutane*, gazing at those Belgian soldiers who, after the exhaustion of retreat, gathered themselves into rank again and drilled so that they might fight once more for the little kingdom they had lost.

A few days later I saw how Belgians were still fighting on their own soil, miserable but magnificent, sick at heart but dauntless in spirit.

5

It was in Calais, to which I had gone back for a day or two, that I found my chance to get into the firing lines in Belgium. I was sitting at an open window with my two friends when I saw a lady's face in the street. The last time I had seen it was in an old English mansion, filled with many gallant and gentle ghosts of history, and with laughing girls who went scampering out to a game of tennis on the lawn below the terrace from which a scent of roses and climbing plants was wafted up on the drowsy air of an English summer. It was strange to see one of those girls in Calais, where such a different game was being played. She had a gravity in her eyes which I had not seen before in England, and yet, after-wards, I heard her laughter ring out within a little distance of bursting shells. She had a motor-car and a pass to the Belgian front, and a good nature which gave me a free seat, provided I was "jolly quick." I was so quick that, with a few things scrambled into a handbag, I was ready in two shakes of a jiffy, whatever that may be, and had only time to give a hasty grip to the hands of the two friends who had gone along many roads with me in this adventure of war, watching its amazing dramas. The Philosopher and the Strategist are but shadows in this book, but though I left them on the kerbstone, I took with me the memory of a comradeship which had been good to have.

6

The town of Furnes, in Belgium, into which I came when dusk crept into its streets and squares, was the headquarters of King Albert and his staff, and its people could hear all day long the roll of guns a few kilometres away, where the remnant of their army held the line of the Yser canal and the trenches which barred the roads to Dixmude, Pervyse and other little towns and villages on the last free patch of Belgian soil.

I drove into the Grande Place and saw the beauty of this old Flemish square, typical of a hundred others, not less quaint and with not less dignity, which had been smashed to pieces by German guns. Three great buildings dominated its architecture—the Town Hall, with a fine stately façade, and two ancient churches, with massive brick towers, overshadowing the narrow old houses and timber-front shops with stepped gables and wrought-iron signs. For three centuries or more time had slept here, and no change of modern life had altered the character of this place, where merchant princes had dwelt around the market. If there had been peace here in that velvety twilight which filled the square when I first passed through it, I should have expected to see grave burghers in furred hoods pacing across the cobble stones to the Hôtel de Ville, and the florid-faced knights whom Franz Hals loved to paint, quaffing wine inside the Hotel de la Couronne, and perhaps a young king in exile known as the Merry Monarch smiling with a roguish eye at some fair-haired Flemish wench as he leaned on the arm of my lord of Rochester on his way to his lodging on the other side of the way. But here was no peace. It was a backyard of war, and there was the rumble of guns over the stones, and a litter of war's munitions under the church wall. Armoured cars were parked in the centre of the square, a corps of military cyclists had propped their machines against gun wagons and forage carts, out of the black shadows under high walls poked the snouts of guns, wafts of scented hay came from carts with their shafts down in the gutters, sentries with bayonets which caught the light of old lanterns paced up and down below the Town Hall steps, Belgian soldiers caked in the mud of the trenches slouched wearily in the side streets, and staff officers in motor-cars with glaring headlights and shrieking horns threaded their way between the wagons and the guns. From beyond the town dull shocks of noise grumbled, like distant thunder-claps, and through the tremulous dusk of the sky there came an irregular repetition of faint flashes.

As the twilight deepened and the shadows merged into a general darkness I could see candles being lit through the bull's-eye windows of small shops, and the rank smell of paraffin lamps came from vaulted cellars, into which one descended by steps from the roadway, where soldiers were drinking cups of coffee or cheap wine in a flickering light which etched Rembrandt pictures upon one's vision.

A number of staff officers came down the steps of the Town Hall and stood at the foot of the steps as though waiting for some one. They had not long to wait, for presently a very tall soldier came out to join them. For a moment he stood under the portico lighting a cigarette, and the flare of his match put a glamour upon his face. It was the King of the Belgians, distinguished only by his height from the simple soldiers who stood around him, and as he came down the steps he had the dignity of his own manhood but no outward sign of royalty. I could hardly see his face then, but afterwards in the daylight I saw him pass down the lines of some of his heroic regiments and saw his gravity and the sadness of his eyes, and his extreme simplicity. . . . The first time I had seen him was in a hall in Brussels, when he opened the Great Exhibition in royal state, in the presence of many princes and ministers and all his Court. Even then it seemed to me he had a look of sadness—it may have been no more than shyness—as though the shadow of some approaching tragedy touched his spirit. I spoke of it at the time to a friend of mine and he smiled at the foolishness of the remark.

Here in Furnes his personality was touched with a kind of sanctity because his kingship of the last piece of Belgian soil symbolized all the ruin and desolation of his poor country and all the heroism of its resistance against an overpowering enemy and all the sorrows of those scattered people who still gave him loyalty. Men of Republican instincts paid a homage in their hearts to this young king, sanctified by sorrow and crowned with martyrdom. Living plainly as a simple soldier, sharing the rations, the hardships and the dangers of his men, visiting them in their trenches and in their field-hospitals, steeling his nerves to the sight of bloody things and his heart to the grim task of fighting to the last ditch of Belgian ground, he seemed to be the type of early kingship, as it was idealized by poets and minstrels, when those who were anointed by the Church dedicated their souls to the service of the people and their swords to justice. He stood in this modern world and in this modern war as the supreme type of the Hero, and mythical stories are already making a legend of his chivalrous acts and virtue, showing that in spite of all our incredulities and disillusions hero-worship is still a natural instinct in the minds of men.

7

I had a job to do on my first night in Furnes, and earned a dinner, for a change, by honest work. The staff of an English hospital with a mobile column attached to the Belgian cavalry for picking up the wounded on the field, had come into the town before dusk with a convoy of ambulances and motor-cars. They established themselves in an old convent with large courtyards and many rooms, and they worked hurriedly as long as light would allow, and afterwards in darkness, to get things ready for their tasks next day, when many wounded were expected. This party of doctors and nurses, stretcher-bearers and chauffeurs, had done splendid work in Belgium. Many of them were in the siege of Antwerp, where they stayed until the wounded had to be taken away in a hurry ; and others, even more daring, had retreated from town to town, a few kilometres in advance of the hostile troops. I had met some of the party in Malo-les-Bains, where they had reassembled before coming to Furnes, and I had been puzzled by them. In the "flying column," as they called their convoy of ambulances, were several ladies very practically dressed in khaki coats and breeches, and very girlish in appearance and manners. They did not seem to me at first sight the type of woman to be useful on a battlefield or in a field-hospital. I should have expected them to faint at the sight of blood, and to swoon at the bursting of a shell. Some of them at least were too pretty, I thought, to play about in fields of war among men and horses smashed to pulp. It was only later that I saw their usefulness and marvelled at the spiritual courage of these young women, who seemed not only careless of shell-fire but almost unconscious of its menace, and who, with more nervous strength than that of many men, gave first-aid to the wounded without shuddering at sights of agony which might turn a strong man sick.

It is not an easy task to settle down into a new hospital, especially in time of war not far from the enemy's lines, and as a volunteer in the work I was able to make myself useful by lending a hand with mattresses and beds and heavy cases of medical material. It was a strange experience, as far as I was concerned, and sometimes seemed a little unreal as, with a bed on my head, I staggered across dark courtyards, or with my arms full of lint and dressings, I groped my way down the long, unlighted corridors of a Flemish convent. Nurses chivvied about with little squeals of laughter as they bumped into each other out of the shadow world, but not losing their

heads or their hands, with so much work to do. Framed
in one or other of the innumerable doorways stood a Belgian
nun, with a white face, staring out upon those flitting shadows.
The young doctors had flung their coats off and were handling
the heaviest stuff like dock labourers at trade union rates,
though with more agility. I made friends with them on
the other side of cases too heavy for one man to handle—with
a golden-haired, blue-eyed boy from Bart.'s (I think), who
made the most preposterous jokes in the darkness, so that
I laughed and nearly dropped my end of the box (I saw
him in the days to come doing heroic and untiring work in the
operating theatre), and with another young surgeon whose
keen, grave face lighted up marvellously when an ironical
smile caught fire in his brooding eyes, and with other men
in this hospital and ambulance column who will be remembered in Belgium as fine and fearless men. With the super-
intendent of the commissariat department—an Italian lady
with a pretty sense of humour and a devil-may-care courage
which she inherited from Stuart ancestors—I went on a
shopping expedition into the black gulfs of Furnes, stumbling
into holes and jerking up against invisible gun-wagons, but
bringing back triumphantly some fat bacon and, more precious
still, some boxes of tallow candles, of great worth in a town
which had lost its gas.

I lighted dozens of these candles, like an acolyte in a
Catholic church, setting them in their own grease on windowsills and ledges of the long corridors, so that the work of
moving might go on more steadily. But there was a wind
blowing, and at the bang of distant doors out went one
candle after another, and nurses carrying other candles and
shielding the little flames with careful hands cried in laughing
dismay as they were puffed out by malicious draughts.

There was chaos in the kitcheh, but out of it came order
and a good meal, served in the convent refectory, where the
flickering light of candles in beer-bottles sheltered from the
wind, gleamed upon holy pictures of the Sacred Heart and
the Madonna and Child and glinted upon a silver crucifix
where the Man of Sorrows looked down upon a supper party

of men and women who, whatever their creed or faith or unbelief, had dedicated themselves to relieve a suffering humanity with a Christian chivalry—which did not prevent the blue-eyed boy from making most pagan puns, or the company in general from laughing as though war were all a jest.

Having helped to wash up—the young surgeons fell into queue before the washtubs—I went out into the courtyard again. Horses were stabled there, guarded by a man who read a book by the rays of an old lantern, which was a little oasis of light in this desert of darkness. The horses were listening. Every now and then they jerked their heads up in a frightened way. From a few miles away came the boom of great guns, and the black sky quivered with tremulous bars of light as shell after shell burst somewhere over the heads of men waiting for death. With one of the doctors, two of the nurses, and a man who led the way, I climbed up to a high room in the convent roof. Through a dormer window we looked out across the flat country beyond Furnes and saw, a few miles away, the lines of battle. Some village was burning there, a steady torch under a heavy cloud of smoke made rosy and beautiful as a great flower over the scarlet flames. Shells were bursting with bouquets of light and then scattered stars into the sky. Short, sharp stabs revealed a Belgian battery, and very clearly we could hear the roll of field guns, followed by enormous concussions of heavy artillery.

" There will be work to do to-morrow ! " said one of the nurses. Work came before it was expected in the morning Quite early some Belgian ambulances came up to the great gate of the convent loaded with wounded. A few beds were made ready for them and they were brought in by the stretcher-bearers and dressers. Some of them could stagger in alone, with the help of a strong arm, but others were at the point of death as they lay rigid on their stretchers, wet with blood. For the first time I felt the weight of a man who lies unconscious, and strained my stomach as I helped to carry these poor Belgian soldiers. And for the first

time I had round my neck the arm of a man who finds each
footstep a torturing effort, and who after a pace or two
halts and groans, and loses the strength of his legs, so that
all his weight hangs upon that clinging arm.   Several times
I nearly let these soldiers fall, so great was the burden
weighing down my shoulders.   It was only by a kind of
prayer that I could hold them up and guide them to the great
room where stretchers were laid out for lack of beds.

In a little while the great hall where I had helped to
sort out packages was a hospital ward where doctors and
nurses worked very quietly and from which there came
faint groans of anguish, horrible in their significance.   Already
it was filled with that stench of blood and dirt and iodoform
which afterwards used to sicken me as I helped to carry in
the wounded or carry out the dead.

8

In the courtyard the flying column was getting ready to
set out in search of other wounded men, not yet rescued
from the firing line.   The officer in command was a young
Belgian gentleman, Lieutenant de Broqueville, the son of the
Belgian Prime Minister, and a man of knightly valour.   He
was arranging the order of the day with Dr. Munro, who had
organized the ambulance convoy, leading it through a series
of amazing adventures and misadventures—not yet to be
written in history—to this halting-place at Furnes.   Three
ladies in field kit stood by their cars waiting for the day's
commands, and there were four stretcher-bearers, of whom
I was the newest recruit.   Among them was an American
journalist named Gleeson, who had put aside his pen for
a while to do manual work in fields of agony, proving himself
to be a man of calm and quiet courage, always ready to take
great risks in order to bring in a stricken soldier.   I came
to know him as a good comrade, and in this page greet him
again

The story of the adventure which we went out to meet
that day was written in the night that followed it, as I lay
on straw with a candle by my side, and because it was

written with the emotion of a great experience still thrilling in my brain and with its impressions undimmed by any later pictures of the war I will give it here again as it first appeared in the columns of the *Daily Chronicle*, suppressing only a name or two because those whom I wished to honour hated my publicity.

9

We set out before noon, winding our way through the streets of Furnes, which were still crowded with soldiers and wagons. In the Town Hall square we passed through a mass of people who surrounded a body of 150 German prisoners who had just been brought in from the front. It was a cheering sight for Belgians who had been so long in retreat before an overpowering enemy. It was a sign that the tide of fortune was changing. Presently we were out in open country, by the side of the Yser Canal. It seemed very peaceful and quiet. Even the guns were silent now, and the flat landscape, with its long, straight lines of poplars between the low-lying fields, had a spirit of tranquillity in the morning sunlight. It seemed impossible to believe that only a few kilometres away great armies were ranged against each other in a death-struggle. But only for a little while. The spirit of war was forced upon our imagination by scenes upon the roadside. A squadron of Belgian cavalry rode by on tired horses. The men were dirty in the service of war, and haggard after long privations in the field. Yet they looked hard and resolute, and saluted us with smiles as we passed. Some of them shouted out a question: " Anglais ? " They seemed surprised and glad to see British ambulances on their way to the front. Belgian infantrymen trudged with slung rifles along the roads of the villages through which we passed. At one of our halts, while we waited for instructions from the Belgian headquarters, a group of these soldiers sat in the parlour of an inn singing a love-song in chorus. One young officer swayed up and down in a rhythmic dance, waving his cigarette. He had been wounded in the arm, and knew the horror of the

M

trenches; but for a little while he forgot, and was very gay because he was alive.

Our trouble was to know where to go. The fighting on the previous night had covered a wide area, but a good many of the wounded had been brought back. Where the wounded still lay the enemy's shell-fire was so heavy that the Belgian ambulances could get nowhere near. Lieutenant de Broqueville was earnestly requested not to lead his little column into unnecessary risks, especially as it was difficult to know the exact position of the enemy until reports came in from the field officers.

It was astonishing—as it is always in war—to find how soldiers quite near to the front are in utter ignorance of the course of a great battle. Many of the officers and men with whom we talked could not tell us where the allied forces were, nor where the enemy was in position, nor whether the heavy fighting during the last day and night had been to the advantage of the Allies or the Germans. They believed, but were not sure, that the enemy had been driven back many kilometres between Nieuport and Dixmude.

At last, after many discussions and many halts, we received our orders. We were asked to get into the town of Dixmude, where there were many wounded.

It was about sixteen kilometres away from Furnes, and about half that distance from where we had halted for lunch. Not very far away, it will be seen, yet, as we went along the road, nearer to the sound of great guns which for the last hour or two had been firing incessantly again, we passed many women and children. It had only just occurred to them that death was round the corner, and that there was no more security in those little stone or plaster houses of theirs, which in time of peace had been safe homes against all the evils of life. It had come to their knowledge, very slowly, that they were of no more protection than tissue paper under a rain of lead. So they were now leaving for a place at longer range. Poor old grandmothers in black bonnets and skirts trudged under the lines of poplars, with younger women who clasped their babes tight in one hand while with the other they carried heavy bundles of household goods. They did not walk very fast. They did not seem very much afraid. They had a kind of patient misery in their look. Along the road came some more German prisoners, marching rapidly between mounted guards. Many of them were wounded, and all of them had a wild, famished, terror-stricken look. I caught the savage glare of their eyes as they stared into my car. There was something beast-like and terrible in their gaze like that of hunted animals caught in a trap.

At a turn in the road the battle lay before us, and we were in the zone of fire. Away across the fields was a line of villages, with the town of Dixmude a little to the right of us, perhaps two kilometres away. From each little town smoke was rising in separate columns, which met at the top in a great pall of smoke, as a heavy black cloud cresting above the light on the horizon line. At every moment this blackness was brightened by puffs of electric blue, extraordinarily vivid, as shells burst in the air. Then the colour gradually faded out, and the smoke darkened and became part of the pall. From the mass of houses in each town came jabs of flame, following the explosions which sounded with terrific, thudding shocks.

Upon a line of fifteen kilometres there was an incessant cannonade and in every town there was a hell. The furthest villages were already alight. I watched how the flames rose, and became great glowing furnaces, terribly beautiful. Quite close to us—only a kilometre away across the fields to the left—there were Belgian batteries at work, and rifle-fire from many trenches. We were between two fires, and the Belgian and German shells came screeching across our heads. The enemy's shells were dropping close to us, ploughing up the fields with great pits. We could hear them burst and scatter, and could see them burrow. In front of us on the road lay a dreadful barrier, which brought us to a halt. An enemy's shell had fallen right on top of an ammunition convoy. Four horses had been blown to pieces, and lay strewn across the road. The ammunition wagon had been broken into fragments, and smashed and burnt to cinders by the explosion of its own shells. A Belgian soldier lay dead, cut in half by a great fragment of steel. Further along the road were two other dead horses in pools of blood. It was a horrible and sickening sight from which one turned away shuddering with a cold sweat. But we had to pass after some of this dead flesh had been dragged away. Further down the road we had left two of the cars in charge of the three ladies. They were to wait there until we brought back some of the wounded, whom they would take from us so that we could fetch some more out of Dixmude. The two ambulances came on with our light car, commanded by Lieutenant de Broqueville and Dr. Munro. Mr. Gleeson asked me to help him on the other end of his own stretcher.

I think I may say that none of us quite guessed what was in store for us. At least I did not guess that we had been asked to go into the open mouth of Death. I had only a vague idea that Dixmude would be just a little worse than the place at which we now halted for final instructions as to the geography of the town.

It was a place which made me feel suddenly cold, in spite of a little sweat which made my hands moist.

It was a halt between a group of cottages, where Belgian soldiers were huddled close to the walls under the timber beams of the barns. Several of the cottages were already smashed by shell-fire. There was a great gaping hole through one of the roofs. The roadway was strewn with bricks and plaster, and every now and then a group of men scattered as shrapnel bullets came pattering down. We were in an inferno of noise. It seemed as though we stood in the midst of the guns within sight of each other's muzzles. I was deafened and a little dazed, but very clear in the head, so that my thoughts seemed extraordinarily vivid. I was thinking, among other things, of how soon I should be struck by one of those flying bullets, like the men who lay moaning inside the doorway of one of the cottages. On a calculation of chances it could not be long.

The Belgian official in charge of this company was very courteous and smiling. It was only by a sudden catch of the breath between his words that one guessed at the excitement of his brain. He explained to us, at what seemed to me needless length, the ease with which we could get into Dixmude, where there were many wounded. He drew a map of the streets, so that we could find the way to the Hôtel de Ville, where some of them lay. We thanked him, and told the chauffeurs to move on. I was in one of the ambulances and Gleeson sat behind me in the narrow space between the stretchers. Over my shoulder he talked in a quiet voice of the job that lay before us. I was glad of that quiet voice, so placid in its courage.

We went forward at what seemed to me a crawl, though I think it was a fair pace. The shells were bursting round us now on all sides. Shrapnel bullets sprayed the earth about us. It appeared to me an odd thing that we were still alive.

Then we came into Dixmude. It was a fair-sized town, with many beautiful buildings, and fine old houses in the Flemish style—so I was told. When I saw it for the first time it was a place of death and horror. The streets through which we passed were utterly deserted and wrecked from end to end as though by an earthquake. Incessant explosions of shell-fire crashed down upon the walls which still stood. Great gashes opened in the walls, which then toppled and fell. A roof came tumbling down with an appalling clatter. Like a house of cards blown down by a puff of wind a little shop suddenly collapsed into a mass of ruins. Here and there, further into the town, we saw living figures. They ran swiftly for a moment and then disappeared into dark caverns under toppling porticoes. They were Belgian soldiers.

We were now in a side street leading into the Town Hall square. It seemed impossible to pass owing to the wreckage strewn across the road.

" Try to take it," said Dr. Munro, who was sitting beside the chauffeur.

We took it, bumping over the high débris, and then swept round into the square. It was a spacious place, with the Town Hall at one side of it, or what was left of the Town Hall. There was only the splendid shell of it left, sufficient for us to see the skeleton of a noble building which had once been the pride of Flemish craftsmen. Even as we turned towards it parts of it were falling upon the ruins already on the ground. I saw a great pillar lean forward and then topple down. A mass of masonry crashed down from the portico. Some stiff, dark forms lay among the fallen stones. They were dead soldiers. I hardly glanced at them, for we were in search of living men. The cars were brought to a halt outside the building and we all climbed down. I lighted a cigarette, and I noticed two of the other men fumble for matches for the same purpose. We wanted something to steady us. There was never a moment when shell-fire was not bursting in that square about us. The shrapnel bullets whipped the stones. The enemy was making a target of the Hôtel de Ville, and dropping their shells with dreadful exactitude on either side of it. I glanced towards a flaring furnace to the right of the building. There was a wonderful glow at the heart of it. Yet it did not give me any warmth at that moment.

Dr. Munro and Lieutenant de Broqueville mounted the steps of the Town Hall, followed by another *brancardier* and myself. Gleeson was already taking down a stretcher. He had a little smile about his lips.

A French officer and two men stood under the broken archway of the entrance between the fallen pillars and masonry. A yard away from them lay a dead soldier—a handsome young man with clear-cut features turned upwards to the gaping roof. A stream of blood was coagulating round his head, but did not touch the beauty of his face. Another dead man lay huddled up quite close, and his face was hidden.

"Are there any wounded here, sir?" asked our young lieutenant.

The other officer spoke excitedly. He was a brave man, but could not hide the terror of his soul because he had been standing so long waiting for death which stood beside him but did not touch him. It appeared from his words that there were several wounded men among the dead, down in the cellar. He would be obliged to us if we could rescue them.

We stood on some steps looking down into that cellar. It was a dark hole—illumined dimly by a lantern, I think. I caught sight of a little heap of huddled bodies. Two soldiers still unwounded, dragged three of them out, handed them up, delivered them to us. The work of getting those three men into the first ambulance seemed to us interminable. It was really no more than fifteen to twenty minutes, while they were being arranged. During that time Dr. Munro was moving about the square in a dreamy sort of way, like a poet meditating on love or flowers in May. Lieutenant de Broqueville was making inquiries about other wounded in other houses. I lent a hand to one of the stretcher-bearers. What others were doing I don't know, except that Gleeson's calm face made a clear-cut image on my brain. I had lost consciousness of myself. Something outside myself, as it seemed, was talking now that there was no way of escape, that it was monstrous to suppose that all these bursting shells would not smash the ambulances to bits and finish the agony of the wounded, and that death is very hideous. I remember thinking also how ridiculous it is for men to kill each other like this, and to make such hells.

Then Lieutenant de Broqueville spoke a word of command. "The first ambulance must now get back."

I was with the first ambulance, in Gleeson's company. We had a full load of wounded men—and we were loitering. I put my head outside the cover and gave the word to the chauffeur. As I did so a shrapnel bullet came past my head, and, striking a piece of ironwork, flattened out and fell at my feet. I picked it up and put it in my pocket—though God alone knows why, for I was not in search of souvenirs. So we started with the first ambulance, through those frightful streets again, and out into the road to the country.

"Very hot," said one of the men. I think it was the chauffeur. Somebody else asked if we should get through with luck.

Nobody answered the question. The wounded men with us were very quiet. I thought they were dead. There was only the incessant cannonade and the crashing of buildings. Mitrailleuses were at work now spitting out bullets. It was a worse sound than the shells. It seemed more deadly in its rattle. I stared back behind the car and saw the other ambulance in our wake. I did not see the motor-car. Along the country road the fields were still being ploughed by shell, which burst over our heads. We came to a halt again at the place where the soldiers were crouched under the cottage walls. There were few walls now, and inside some of the remaining cottages many wounded men. Their own comrades were giving them first aid, and wiping the blood out of their eyes. We managed to take some of these on board. They were less quiet than the others we had, and groaned in a heartrending way.

And then, a little later, we made a painful discovery. Lieutenant de Broqueville, our gallant young leader, was missing. By some horrible mischance he had not taken his place in either of the ambulances or the motor-car. None of us had the least idea what had happened to him. We had all imagined that he had scrambled up like the rest of us, after giving the order to get away. We looked at each other in dismay. There was only one thing to do, to get back in search of him. Even in the half-hour since we had left the town Dixmude had burst into flames and was a great blazing torch. If young de Broqueville were left in that furnace he would not have a chance of life.

It was Gleeson and another stretcher-bearer who with great gallantry volunteered to go back and search for our leader. They took the light car and sped back towards the burning town.

The ambulances went on with their cargo of wounded, and I was left in a car with one of the ladies while Dr. Munro was ministering to a man on the point of death. It was the girl whom I had seen on the lawn of an old English house in the days before the war. She was very worried about the fate of de Broqueville, and anxious beyond words as to what would befall the three friends who were now missing. We drove back along the road towards Dixmude, and rescued another wounded man left in a wayside cottage. By this time there were five towns blazing in the darkness, and in spite of the awful suspense which we were now suffering, we could not help staring at the fiendish splendour of that sight. Dr. Munro joined us again, and after a consultation we decided to get as near Dixmude as we could, in case our friends had to come out without their car or wounded.

The enemy's bombardment was now terrific. All its guns were concentrated upon Dixmude and the surrounding trenches. In the darkness close under a stable wall I stood listening to the great crashes for an hour, when I had not expected such a grace of life. Inside the stable, soldiers were sleeping in the straw, careless that any moment a shell might burst through upon them and give them unwaking sleep. The hour seemed a night. Then we saw the gleam of head-lights, and an English voice called out.

Our two friends had come back. They had gone to the entry of Dixmude, but could get no further owing to the flames and shells. They, too, had waited for an hour, but had not found de Broqueville. It seemed certain that he was dead, and very sorrowfully, as there was nothing to be done, we drove back to Furnes.

At the gate of the convent were some Belgian ambulances which had come from another part of the front with their wounded. I helped to carry one of them in, and strained my shoulders with the weight of the stretcher. Another wounded man put his arm round my neck, and then, with a dreadful cry, collapsed, so that I had to hold him in a strong grip. A third man, horribly smashed about the head, walked almost unaided into the operating-room. Gleeson and I led him, with just a touch on his arm. Next morning he lay dead on a little pile of straw in a quiet corner of the courtyard.

I sat down to a supper which I had not expected to eat. There was a strange excitement in my body, which trembled a little after the day's adventures. It seemed very strange to be sitting down to table with cheerful faces about me. But some of the faces were not cheerful. Those of us who knew of the disappearance of de Broqueville sat silently over our soup.

Then suddenly there was a sharp exclamation of surprise —of sheer amazement—and Lieutenant de Broqueville came walking briskly forward, alive and well. . . . It seemed a miracle.

It was hardly less than that. For several hours after our departure from Dixmude he had remained in that inferno. He had missed us when he went down into the cellars to haul out another wounded man, forgetting that he had given us the order to start. There he had remained with the buildings crashing all around him until the enemy's fire had died down a little. He succeeded in rescuing his wounded, for whom he found room in a Belgian ambulance outside the town, and walked back along the road to Furnes. So we gripped his hands and were thankful for his escape.

10

Early next morning I went into Dixmude again with some of the men belonging to the " flying column." It was more than probable that there were still a number of wounded men there, if any of them were left alive after that night of horror when they lay in cellars or under the poor shelter of broken walls. Perhaps also there were men but lately wounded, for before the dawn had come some of the Belgian infantry had been sent into the outlying streets with mitrailleuses, and on the opposite side German infantry were in possession of other streets or of other ruins, so that bullets were ripping across the mangled town. The artillery was fairly quiet. Only a few shells were bursting over the Belgian lines—enough to keep the air rumbling with irregular thunderclaps. But as we approached the corner where we had waited for news of de Broqueville one of these shells burst very close to us and ploughed up a big hole in a field across the roadside ditch. We drove more swiftly with empty cars and came into the streets of Dixmude. They were sheets of fire, burning without flame but with a steady glow of embers. They were but cracked shells of houses, unroofed and swept clean of their floors and furniture, so that all but the bare walls and a few charred beams had been consumed by the devouring appetite of fire. Now and again one of the beams broke and fell with a crash into the glowing heart of the furnace, which had once been a Flemish house, raising a fountain of sparks. Further into the town, however, there stood, by the odd freakishness of an artillery bombardment, complete houses hardly touched by shells and, very neat and prim, between masses of shapeless ruins. One street into which I drove was so undamaged that I could hardly believe my eyes, having looked back the night before to one great torch which men called " Dixmude." Nevertheless some of its window-frames had bulged with heat, and panes of glass fell with a splintering noise on to the stone pavement. As I passed a hail of shrapnel was suddenly flung upon the wall on one side of the street and the bullets played at marbles in the roadway. In this street some soldiers were grouped about two wounded men, one of them only lightly touched, the other—a French marine—at the point of death, lying very still in a huddled way with a clay-coloured face smeared with blood. We picked them up and put them into one of the ambulances, the dying man groaning a little as we strapped him on the stretcher.

The Belgian soldiers who had come into the town at dawn stood about our ambulances as though our company gave them a little comfort. They did not speak much, but had grave wistful eyes like men tired of all this misery about them but unable to escape from it. They were young men with a stubble of fair hair on their faces and many days' dirt.

" Vous êtes très aimable," said one of them when I handed him a cigarette, which he took with a trembling hand. Then he stared up the street as another shower of shrapnel swept it, and said in a hasty way, " C'est l'enfer. . . . Pour trois mois je reste sous feu. C'est trop, n'est-ce pas ? "

But there was no time for conversation about war and

the effects of war upon the souls of men. The German guns were beginning to speak again, and unless we made haste we might not rescue the wounded men.

"Are there many *blessés* here ? " asked our leader.

One of the soldiers pointed to a house which had a tavern sign above it.

"They've been taken inside," he said. "I helped to carry them." We dodged the litter in the roadway, where, to my amazement, two old ladies were searching in the rubbish-heaps for the relics of their houses. They had stayed in Dixmude during this terrible bombardment, hidden in some cellar, and now had emerged, in their respectable black gowns, to see what damage had been done. They seemed to be looking for something in particular—some little object not easy to find among these heaps of calcined stones and twisted bars of iron. One old woman shook her head sadly as though to say, "Dear me, I can't see it anywhere." I wondered if they were looking for some family photograph— or for some child's cinders. It might have been one or the other, for many of these Belgian peasants had reached a point of tragedy when death is of no more importance than any trivial loss. The earth and sky had opened, swallowing up all their little world in a devilish destruction. They had lost the proportions of everyday life in the madness of things.

In the tavern there was a Belgian doctor with a few soldiers to help him, and a dozen wounded in the straw which had been put down on the tiled floor. Another wounded man was sitting on a chair, and the doctor was bandaging up a leg which looked like a piece of raw meat at which dogs had been gnawing. Something in the straw moved and gave a frightful groan. A boy soldier with his back propped against the wall had his knees up to his chin and his face in his grimy hands through which tears trickled. There was a soppy bandage about his head. Two men close to where I stood lay stiff and stark, as though quite dead, but when I bent down to them I heard their hard breathing and the snuffle of their nostrils. The others more lightly wounded watched us like animals, without curiosity but with a horrible sort of patience in their eyes, which seemed to say, "Nothing matters. . . . Neither hunger nor thirst nor pain. We are living but our spirit is dead."

The doctor did not want us to take away his wounded at once. The German shells were coming heavily again, on the outskirts of the town through which we had to pass on our way out. An officer had just come in to say they were firing at the level crossing to prevent the Belgian ambulances from coming through. It would be better to wait a while before going back again. It was foolish to take unnecessary risks.

I admit frankly that I was anxious to go as quickly as possible with these wounded A shell burst over the houses on the opposite side of the street. When I stood outside watching two soldiers who had been sent further down to bring in two other wounded men who lay in a house there, I saw them dodge into a doorway for cover as another hail of shrapnel whipped the stones about them. Afterwards they made an erratic course down the street like drunken men, and presently I saw them staggering back again with their wounded comrades, who had their arms about the necks of their rescuers. . . . I went out to aid them, but did not like the psychology of this street, where death was teasing the footsteps of men, yapping at their heels.

I helped to pack up one of the ambulances and went back to Furnes sitting next to the driver, but twisted round so that I could hold one of the stretcher poles which wanted to jolt out of its strap so that the man lying with a dead weight on the canvas would come down with a smash upon the body of the man beneath.

"Ça y est," said my driver friend, very cheerfully. He was a gentleman volunteer with his own ambulance and looked like a seafaring man in his round yachting cap and blue jersey. He did not speak much French, I fancy, but I loved to hear him say that " Ça y est," when he raised a stretcher in his hefty arms and packed a piece of bleeding flesh into the top of his car with infinite care lest he should give a jolt to broken bones.

One of the men behind us had his leg smashed in two places. As we went over roads with great stones and the rubbish of ruined houses he cried out again and again in a voice of anguish :

" Pas si vite ! Pour l'amour de Dieu. . . . Pas si vite ! "

Not so quickly. But when we came out of the burnt streets towards the level crossing of the railway it seemed best to go quickly. Shells were falling in the fields quite close to us. One of them dug a deep hole in the road twenty yards ahead of us. Another burst close behind. Instinctively I yearned for speed. I wanted to rush along that road and get beyond the range of fire. But the driver in the blue jersey, hearing that awful cry behind him, slowed down and crawled along.

" Poor devil," he said. " I can imagine what it feels like when two bits of broken bone get rubbing together. Every jolt and jar must give him hell."

He went slower still, at a funeral pace, and looking back into the ambulance said " Ça y est, mon vieux. . . . Bon courage ! "

Afterwards, this very gallant gentleman was wounded himself, and lay in one of the ambulances which he had often led towards adventure, with a jagged piece of steel in his leg, and two bones rasping together at every jolt. But when he was lifted up, he stifled a groan and gave his old cheerful cry of " Ça y est ! "

11

During the two days that followed the convent at Furnes was overcrowded with the wounded. All day long and late into the night they were brought back by the Belgian ambulances from the zone of fire, and hardly an hour passed without a bang at the great wooden gates in the courtyard which were flung open to let in another tide of human wreckage.

The Belgians were still holding their last remaining ground—it did not amount to more than a few fields and villages between the French frontier and Dixmude—with a gallant resistance which belongs without question to the heroic things of history. During these late days in October, still fighting almost alone, for there were no British soldiers to help them and only a few French batteries with two regiments of French marines, they regained some of their soil and beat back the enemy from positions to which it had advanced. In spite of the most formidable attacks made by the German troops along the coastline between Westende and Ostende, and in a crescent sweeping round Dixmude for about thirty kilometres, those Belgian soldiers, tired out by months of fighting with decimated regiments and with but the poor remnant of a disorganized army, not only stood firm, but inflicted heavy losses upon the enemy and captured four hundred prisoners. For a few hours the Germans succeeded in crossing the Yser, threatening a general advance upon the Belgian line. Before Nieuport their trenches were only fifty metres away from those of the Belgians, and on the night of October 22 they charged eight times with the bayonet in order to force their way through.

Each assault failed against the Belgian infantry, who stayed in their trenches in spite of the blood that eddied about their feet and the corpses that lay around them. Living and dead made a rampart which the Germans could not break. With an incessant rattle of mitrailleuses and rifle-fire, the Belgians mowed down the German troops as they advanced in solid ranks, so that on each of those eight times the enemy's attack was broken and destroyed. They fell like the leaves which were then being scattered by the autumn wind and their bodies were strewn between the trenches. Some of them were the bodies of very young men—poor boys of sixteen and seventeen from German high schools and universities who were the sons of noble and well-to-do families, had been accepted as volunteers by Prussian war-lords ruthless of human life in their desperate gamble with fate. Some of these lads were brought to the hospitals in Furnes, badly wounded. One of them carried into the convent courtyard smiled as he lay on his stretcher and spoke imperfect French very politely to Englishwomen who bent over him, piteous as girls who see a wounded bird. He seemed glad to be let off slightly with only a wound in his foot which would make him limp for life ; very glad to be out of all the horror of those trenches on the German side of the Yser. One could hardly call this boy an " enemy." He was just a poor innocent caught up by a devilish power, and dropped when of no more use as an instrument of death. The pity that stirs one in the presence of one of these broken creatures does not come to one on the field of battle, where there is no single individuality, but only a grim conflict of unseen powers, as inhuman as thunderbolts, or as the destructive terror of the old nature gods. The enemy, then, fills one with a hatred based on fear. One rejoices to see a shell burst over his batteries and is glad at the thought of the death that came to him of that puff of smoke. But I found that no such animosity stirs one in the presence of the individual enemy or among crowds of their prisoners. One only wonders at the frightfulness of the crime which makes men kill each other without a purpose of their own, but at the dictate of powers far removed from their own knowledge and interests in life.

12

That courtyard in the convent at Furnes will always haunt my mind as the scene of a grim drama. Sometimes, standing there alone, in the darkness, by the side of an ambulance, I used to look up at the stars and wonder what God might think of all this work if there were any truth in old faiths. A pretty mess we mortals made of life ! I might almost have laughed at the irony of it all, except that my laughter would have choked in my throat and turned me sick. They were beasts, and worse than beasts, to maim and mutilate each other like this, having no real hatred in their hearts for each other, but only a stupid perplexity that they should be hurled in masses against each other's ranks, to slash and shoot and burn in obedience to orders by people who were their greatest enemies—Ministers of State, with cold and calculating brains, high inhuman officers who studied battlefields as greater chessboards. So I—a little black ant in a shadow on the earth under the eternal sky—used to think like this, and to stop thinking these silly irritating thoughts turned to the job in hand, which generally was to take up one end of a stretcher laden with a bloody man, or to give my shoulder to a tall soldier who leaned upon it and stumbled forward to an open door which led to the operating-table and an empty bed, where he might die if his luck were out.

The courtyard was always full of stir and bustle in the hours when the ambulance convoys came in with their cargoes of men rescued from the firing zone. The headlights of the cars thrust shafts of blinding light into the darkness as they steered round in the steep and narrow road which led to the convent gates between two high thick walls, and then, with a grinding and panting, came inside to halt beside cars already at a standstill. The cockney voices of the chauffeurs called to each other.

" Blast yer, Bill . . . Carn't yer give a bit of elber room ? Gord almighty, 'ow d'yer think I can get in there ? "

Women came out into the yard, their white caps touched by the light of their lanterns, and women's voices spoke quietly.

" Have you got many this time ? " . . . " We can hardly find an inch of room." . . . " It's awful having to use stretchers for beds. . . " " There were six deaths this afternoon."

Then would follow a silence or a whispering of stretcher-bearers, telling their adventures to a girl in khaki breeches, standing with one hand in her jacket pocket, and with the little flare of a cigarette glowing upon her cheek and hair.

" All safe ? . . . That was luck ! "

" O mon Dieu ! O, cré nom ! O ! O ! "

It was a man's voice crying in agony, rising to a shuddering, blood-curdling scream :

" O Jésus ! O ! O ! "

One could not deafen one's ears against that note of

N

human agony. It pierced into one's soul. One could only stand gripping one's hands in this torture chamber, with darkness between high walls, and with shadows making awful noises out of the gulfs of blackness.

The cries of the wounded men died down and whimpered out into a dull faint moaning.

A laugh came chuckling behind an ambulance.

" Hot ? . . . I should think it was ! But we picked the men up and crossed the bridge all right. . . . The shells were falling on every side of us. . . . I was pretty scared, you bet. . . . It's a bit too thick, you know ! "

Silence again. Then a voice speaking quietly across the yard :

" Anyone to lend a hand ? There's a body to be carried out."

I helped to carry out the body, as every one helped to do any small work if he had his hands free at the moment. It was the saving of one's sanity and self-respect. Yet to me, more sensitive perhaps than it is good to be, it was a moral test almost greater than my strength of will to enter that large room where the wounded lay, and to approach a dead man through a lane of dying. (So many of them died after a night in our guest-house. Not all the skill of surgeons could patch up some of those bodies, torn open with ghastly wounds from German shells.) The smell of wet and muddy clothes, coagulated blood and gangrened limbs, of iodine and chloroform, sickness and sweat of agony, made a stench which struck one's senses with a foul blow. I used to try and close my nostrils to it, holding my breath lest I should vomit. I used to try to keep my eyes upon the ground, to avoid the sight of those smashed faces, and blinded eyes, and tattered bodies, lying each side of me in the hospital cots, or in the stretchers set upon the floor between them. I tried to shut my eyes to the sounds in this room, the hideous snuffle of men drawing their last breaths, the long-drawn moans of men in devilish pain, the ravings of fever-stricken men crying like little children—" Maman ! O Maman ! "—or repeating over and over again some angry protest against a distant comrade.

But sights and sounds and smells forced themselves upon one's senses. I had to look and to listen and to breathe in the odour of death and corruption. For hours afterwards I would be haunted with the death face of some young man, lying half-naked on his bed while nurses dressed his horrible wounds. What waste of men ! What disfigurement of the beauty that belongs to youth ! Bearded soldier faces lay here in a tranquillity that told of coming death. They had been such strong and sturdy men, tilling their Flemish fields, and living with a quiet faith in their hearts. Now they were dying before their time, conscious, some of them, that death was near, so that weak tears dropped upon their beards, and in their eyes was a great fear and anguish.

"Je ne veux pas mourir ! " said one of them. "O ma pauvre femme ! . . . Je ne veux pas mourir ! "

He did not wish to die . . . but in the morning he was dead.

The corpse that I had to carry out lay pinned up in a sheet. The work had been very neatly done by the nurse. She whispered to me as I stood on one side of the bed, with a friend on the other side.

"Be careful. . . . He might fall in half."

I thought over these words as I put my hands under the warm body and helped to lift its weight on to the stretcher. Yes, some of the shell wounds were rather big. One could hardly sew a man together again with bits of cotton. . . . It was only afterwards, when I had helped to put the stretcher in a separate room on the other side of the courtyard, that a curious trembling took possession of me for a moment. . . . The horror of it all ! . . . Were the virtues which were supposed to come from war, "the binding strength of nations," "the cleansing of corruption," all the falsities of men who make excuses for this monstrous crime, worth the price that was being paid in pain and tears and death ? It is only the people who sit at home who write these things. When one is in the midst of war false heroics are blown out of one's soul by all its din and tumult of human agony. One learns that courage itself exists, in most cases, as the pride in the heart of men very much afraid—a pride which makes them hide their fear. They do not become more virtuous in war, but only reveal the virtue that is in them. The most heroic courage which came into the courtyard at Furnes was not that of the stretcher-bearers who went out under fire, but that of the doctors and nurses who tended the wounded, toiling ceaselessly in the muck of blood, amidst all those sights and sounds. My spirit bowed before them as I watched them at work. I was proud if I could carry soup to any of them when they came into the refectory for a hurried meal, or if I could wash a plate clean so that they might fill it with a piece of meat from the kitchen stew. I would have cleaned their boots for them if it had been worth while cleaning boots to tramp the filthy yard.

" It's not surgery ! " said one of the young surgeons, coming out of the operating-theatre and washing his hands at the kitchen sink ; " it's butchery ! "

He told me that he had never seen such wounds or imagined them, and as for the conditions in which he worked —he raised his hands and laughed at the awfulness of them, because it is best to laugh when there is no remedy. There was a scarcity of dressings, of instruments, of sterilizers. The place was so crowded that there was hardly room to turn, and wounded men poured in so fast that it was nothing but hacking and sewing.

" I'm used to blood," said the young surgeon. " It's some years now since I was put through my first ordeal, of dissecting dead bodies and then handling living tissue. You know how it's done—by gradual stages until a student no longer wants to faint at the sight of raw flesh, but regards it as so much material for scientific work. But this ! "—he looked towards the room into which the wounded came— " It's getting on my nerves a little. It's the sense of wanton destruction that makes one loathe it, the utter senselessness of it all, the waste of such good stuff. War is a hellish game . . and I'm so sorry for all the poor Belgians who are getting it in the neck. *They* didn't ask for it ! "

The wooden gates opened to let in another ambulance full

of Belgian wounded, and the young surgeon nodded to me with a smile.

"Another little lot ! I must get back into the slaughter-house. So long ! "

I helped out one of the " sitting-up " cases—a young man with a wound in his chest, who put his arm about my neck and said, "Merci ! Merci ! " with a fine courtesy, until suddenly he went limp, so that I had to hold him with all my strength, while he vomited blood down my coat. I had to get help to carry him indoors.

And yet there was laughter in the convent where so many men lay wounded. It was only by gaiety and the quick capture of any jest that those doctors and nurses and ambulance girls could keep their nerves steady. So in the refectory, when they sat down for a meal, there was an endless fire of raillery, and the blue-eyed boy with the blond hair used to crow like Peter Pan and speak a wonderful mixture of French and English, and play the jester gallantly. There would be processions of plate-bearers to the kitchen next door, where a splendid Englishwoman—one of those fine square-faced, brown-eyed, cheerful souls—had been toiling all day in the heat of oven and stoves to cook enough food for fifty-five hungry people who could not wait for their meals. There was a scramble between two doctors for the last potatoes, and a duel between one of them and myself in the slicing up of roast beef or boiled mutton, and amorous advances to the lady cook for a tit-bit in the baking-pan. There never was such a kitchen, and a County Council inspector would have reported on it in lurid terms. The sink was used as a wash-place by surgeons, chauffeurs, and stretcher-bearers. Nurses would come through with bloody rags from the ward, which was only an open door away. Lightly wounded men, covered with Yser mud, would sit at a side table, eating the remnants of other people's meals. Above the sizzling of sausages and the clatter of plates one could hear the moaning of the wounded and the incessant monologue of the fever-stricken. And yet it is curious I look back upon that convent kitchen as a place of gaiety, holding many memories of comradeship, and as a little sanctuary from the misery of war. I was a scullion in it, at odd hours of the day and night when I was not following the ambulance wagons to the field, or helping to clean the courtyard or doing queer little jobs which some one had to do.

" I want you to dig a hole and help me to bury an arm," said one of the nurses. " Do you mind ? "

I spent another hour helping a lady to hang up blankets, not very well washed, because they were still stained with blood, and not very sanitary, because the line was above a pile of straw upon which men had died. There were many rubbish heaps in the courtyard near which it was not wise to linger, and always propped against the walls were stretchers soppy with blood, or with great dark stains upon them where blood had dried. It was like the courtyard of a shambles, this old convent enclosure, and indeed it was exactly that, except that the animals were not killed outright, but lingered in their pain.

13

Early each morning the ambulances started on their way to the zone of fire, where always one might go gleaning in the harvest fields of war. The direction was given us, with the password of the day, by young de Broqueville, who received the latest reports from the Belgian headquarters staff. As a rule there was not much choice. It lay somewhere between the roads to Nieuport on the coast, and inland, to Pervyse, Dixmude, St. Georges, or Ramscapelle where the Belgian and German lines formed a crescent down to Ypres.

The centre of that half-circle girdled by the guns was an astounding and terrible panorama, traced in its outline by the black fumes of shell-fire above the stabbing flashes of the batteries. Over Nieuport there was a canopy of smoke, intensely black, but broken every moment by blue glares of light as a shell burst and rent the blackness. Villages were burning on many points of the crescent, some of them smouldering drowsily, others blazing fiercely like beacon fires.

Dixmude was still alight at either end, but the fires seemed to have burnt down at its centre. Beyond, on the other horn of the crescent, were five flaming torches, which marked what were once the neat little villages of a happy Belgium. It was in the centre of this battleground, and the roads about me had been churned up by shells and strewn with shrapnel bullets. Close to me in a field, under the cover of a little wood, were some Belgian batteries. They were firing with a machine-like regularity, and every minute came the heavy bark of the gun, followed by the swish of the shell, as it flew in a high arc and then smashed over the German lines. It was curious to calculate the length of time between the flash and the explosion. Further away some naval guns belonging to the French marines were getting the range of the enemy's positions, and they gave a new note of music to this infernal orchestra. It was a deep, sullen crash, with a tremendous menace in its tone. The enemy's shells were bursting incessantly, and at very close range, so that at times they seemed only a few yards away. The Germans had many great howitzers, and the burst of the shell was followed by enormous clouds which hung heavily in the air for ten minutes or more. It was these shells which dug great holes in the ground deep enough for a cart to be buried. Their moral effect was awful, and one's soul was a shuddering coward before them.

The roads were encumbered with long convoys of provisions for the troops, ambulances, Red Cross motor-cars, gun-wagons, and farm carts. Two regiments of Belgian cavalry—the chasseurs à cheval—were dismounted and bivouacked with their horses drawn up in single line along the roadway for half a mile or more. The men were splendid fellows, hardened by the long campaign, and amazingly careless of shells. They wore a variety of uniforms, for they were but the gathered remnants of the Belgian cavalry division which had fought from the beginning of the war. I was surprised to see their horses in such good condition, in spite of a long ordeal which had so steadied their nerves that they paid not the slightest heed to the turmoil of the guns.

Near the line of battle, through outlying villages and past broken farms, companies of Belgian infantry were huddled under cover out of the way of shrapnel bullets if they could get the shelter of a doorway or the safer side of a brick wall. I stared into their faces and saw how dead they looked. It seemed as if their vital spark had already been put out by the storm of battle. Their eyes were sunken and quite expressionless. For week after week, night after night, they had been exposed to shell-fire, and something had died within them—perhaps the desire to live. Every now and then some of them would duck their heads as a shell burst within fifty or a hundred yards of them, and I saw then that fear could still live in the hearts of men who had become accustomed to the constant chance of death. For fear exists with the highest valour, and its psychological effect is not unknown to heroes who have the courage to confess the truth.

14

" If any man says he is not afraid of shell-fire," said one of the bravest men I have ever met—and at that moment we were watching how the enemy's shrapnel was ploughing up the earth on either side of the road on which we stood— " he is a liar ! " There are very few men in this war who make any such pretence. On the contrary, most of the French, Belgian, and English soldiers with whom I have had wayside conversations since the war began, find a kind of painful pleasure in the candid confession of their fears.

" It is now three days since I have been frightened," said a young English officer, who, I fancy, was never scared in his life before he came out to see these battlefields of terror.

" I was paralysed with a cold and horrible fear when I was ordered to advance with my men over open ground under the enemy's shrapnel," said a French officer with the steady brown eyes of a man who in ordinary tests of courage would smile at the risk of death.

But this shell-fire is not an ordinary test of courage. Courage is annihilated in the face of it. Something else takes its place—a philosophy of fatalism, sometimes an utter boredom with the way in which death plays the fool with men, threatening but failing to kill; in most cases a strange extinction of all emotions and sensations, so that men who have been long under shell-fire have a peculiar rigidity of the nervous system, as if something has been killed inside them, though outwardly they are still alive and untouched.

The old style of courage, when man had pride and confidence in his own strength and valour against other men, when he was on an equality with his enemy in arms and intelligence, has almost gone. It has quite gone when he is called upon to advance or hold the ground in face of the enemy's artillery. For all human qualities are of no avail against those death-machines. What are quickness of wit, the strength of a man's right arm, the heroic fibre of his heart, his cunning in warfare, when he is opposed by an enemy's batteries which belch out bursting shells with frightful precision and regularity? What is the most courageous man to do in such an hour? Can he stand erect and fearless under a sky which is raining down jagged pieces of steel? Can he adopt the pose of an Adelphi hero, with a scornful smile on his lips, when a yard away from him a hole large enough to bury a taxicab is torn out of the earth, and when the building against which he has been standing is suddenly knocked into a ridiculous ruin?

It is impossible to exaggerate the monstrous horror of the shell-fire, as I knew when I stood in the midst of it, watching its effect upon the men around me, and analysing my own psychological sensations with a morbid interest. I was very much afraid—day after day I faced that music and hated it—but there were all sorts of other sensations besides fear which worked a change in me. I was conscious of great physical discomfort which reacted upon my brain. The noises were even more distressing to me than the risk of death. It was terrifying in its tumult. The German batteries were hard at work round Nieuport, Dixmude, Pervyse, and other towns and villages, forming a crescent, with its left curve sweeping away from the coast. One could see the stabbing flashes from some of the enemy's guns and a loud and unceasing roar came from them with regular rolls of thunderous noise interrupted by sudden and terrific shocks, which shattered into one's brain and shook one's body with a kind of disintegrating tumult. High above this deep-toned concussion came the cry of the shells—that long carrying buzz—like a monstrous, angry bee rushing away from a burning hive—which rises into a shrill singing note before ending and bursting into the final boom which scatters death. But more awful was the noise of our own guns. At Nieuport I stood only a few hundred yards away from the warships lying off the coast. Each shell which they sent across the dunes was like one of Jove's thunderbolts, and made one's body and soul quake with the agony of its noise. The vibration was so great that it made my skull ache as though it had been hammered. Long afterwards I found myself trembling with those waves of vibrating sounds. Worse still, because sharper and more piercingly staccato, was my experience close to a battery of French *cent-vingt*. Each shell was fired with a hard metallic crack, which seemed to knock a hole into my ear-drums. I suffered intolerably from the noise, yet—so easy it is to laugh in the midst of pain—I laughed aloud when a friend of mine, passing the battery in his motor-car, raised his hand to one of the gunners, and said, " Un moment, s'il vous plaît ! " It was like asking Jove to stop his thunderbolts.

Some people get accustomed to the noise, but others never. Every time a battery fired simultaneously one of the men who were with me, a hard, tough type of mechanic, shrank and ducked his head with an expression of agonized horror. He confessed to me that it " knocked his nerves to pieces." Three such men out of six or seven had to be invalided home in one week. One of them had a *crise de nerfs,* which nearly killed him. Yet it was not fear which was the matter with them. Intellectually they were brave men and coerced themselves into joining many perilous adventures. It was the intolerable strain upon the nervous system that made wrecks of them. Some men are attacked with a kind of madness in the presence of shells. It is what a French friend of mine called *la folie des obus*. It is a kind of spiritual exultation which makes them lose self-consciousness and be caught up, as it were, in the delirium of those crashing, screaming things. In the hottest quarter of an hour in Dixmude one of my friends paced about aimlessly with a dreamy look in his eyes. I am sure he had not the slightest idea where he was or what he was doing. I believe he was "outside himself," to use a good old-fashioned phrase. And at Antwerp, when a convoy of British ambulances escaped with their wounded through a storm of shells, one man who had shown a strange hankering for the heart of the inferno, stepped off his car, and said: "I must go back, I must go back! Those shells call to me." He went back and has never been heard of again.

Greater than one's fear, more overmastering in one's interest is this shell-fire. It is frightfully interesting to watch the shrapnel bursting near bodies of troops, to see the shells kicking up the earth, now in this direction and now in that; to study a great building gradually losing its shape and falling into ruins; to see how death takes its toll in an indiscriminate way—smashing a human being into pulp a few yards away and leaving oneself alive, or scattering a roadway with bits of raw flesh which a moment ago was a team of horses, or whipping the stones about a farmhouse with shrapnel bullets which spit about the crouching figures of soldiers who stare at these pellets out of sunken eyes. One's interest holds one in the firing zone with a grip from which one's intelligence cannot escape whatever may be one's cowardice. It is the most satisfying thrill of horror in the world. How foolish this death is! How it picks and chooses, taking a man here and leaving a man there by just a hair's-breadth of difference. It is like looking into hell and watching the fury of supernatural forces at play with human bodies, tearing them to pieces with great splinters of steel and burning them in the furnace-fires of shell-stricken towns, and in a devilish way obliterating the image of humanity in a welter of blood.

There is a beauty in it too, for the æstheticism of a Nero.
Beautiful and terrible were the fires of those Belgian towns
which I watched under a star-strewn sky. There was a
pure golden glow, as of liquid metal, beneath the smoke
columns and the leaping 'tongues of flame. And many
colours were used to paint this picture of war, for the enemy
used shells with different coloured fumes, by which I was
told they studied the effect of their fire. Most vivid is the
ordinary shrapnel, which tears a rent through the black
volumes of smoke rolling over a smouldering town with a
luminous sphere of electric blue. Then from the heavier
guns come dense puff-balls of tawny orange, violet, and
heliotrope, followed by fleecy little cumuli of purest white.
One's mind is absorbed in this pageant of shell-fire, and
with a curious intentness, with that rigidity of nervous
and muscular force which I have described, one watches
the zone of fire sweeping nearer to oneself, bursting quite
close, killing people not very far away.

Men who have been in the trenches under heavy shell-fire,
sometimes for as long as three days, come out of their torment
like men who have been buried alive. They have the
brownish, ashen colour of death. They tremble as through
anguish. They are dazed and stupid for a time. But they
go back. That is the marvel of it. They go back day after
day, as the Belgians went day after day. There is no fun
in it, no sport, none of that heroic adventure which used
perhaps—gods know—to belong to warfare when men were
matched against men, and not against unapproachable
artillery. This is their courage, stronger than all their fear.
There is something in us, even divine pride of manhood,
a dogged disregard of death, though it comes from an unseen
enemy out of a smoke-wracked sky, like the thunderbolts
of the gods, which makes us go back, though we know the
terror of it. For honour's sake men face again the music
of that infernal orchestra, and listen with a deadly sickness
in their hearts to the song of the shell screaming the French
word for kill, which is *tue! tue!*

It was at night that I used to see the full splendour of

the war's infernal beauty. After a long day in the fields
travelling back in the repeated journeys to the station of
Fortem, where the lightly wounded men used to be put on
a steam tramway for transport to the Belgian hospitals, the
ambulances would gather their last load and go homeward
to Furnes. It was quite dark then, and towards nine
o'clock the enemy's artillery would slacken fire, only the
heavy guns sending out long-range shots. But five towns
or more were blazing fiercely in the girdle of fire, and the
sky throbbed with the crimson glare of their furnaces, and
tall trees to which the autumn foliage clung would be touched
with light, so that their straight trunks along a distant
highway stood like ghostly sentinels. Now and again,
above one of the burning towns a shell would burst as
though the enemy were not content with their fires and
would smash them into smaller fuel.

As I watched the flames, I knew that each one of those
poor burning towns was the ruin of something more than
bricks and mortar. It was the ruin of a people's ideals,
fulfilled throughout centuries of quiet progress in arts and
crafts. It was the shattering of all those things for which
they praised God in their churches—the good gifts of home-
life, the security of the family, the impregnable stronghold,
as it seemed, of prosperity built by labour and thrift now
utterly destroyed.

15

I motored over to Nieuport-les-Bains, the seaside resort
of the town of Nieuport itself, which is a little way from the
coast. It was one of those Belgian watering-places much
beloved by the Germans before their guns knocked it to bits
—a row of red-brick villas with a few pretentious hotels
utterly uncharacteristic of the Flemish style of architecture,
lining a promenade and built upon the edge of dreary and
monotonous sand-dunes. On this day the place and its
neighbourhood were utterly and terribly desolate. The
only human beings I passed on my car were two seamen
of the British Navy, who were fixing up a wireless apparatus

on the edge of the sand. They stared at our ambulances curiously, and one of them gave me a prolonged and strenuous wink, as though to say, "A fine old game, mate, this bloody war!" Beyond, the sea was very calm, like liquid lead, and a slight haze hung over it, putting a gauzy veil about a line of British and French monitors which lay close to the coast. Not a soul could be seen along the promenade of Nieuport-les-Bains, but the body of a man—a French marine—whose soul had gone in flight upon the great adventure of eternity, lay at the end of it with his sightless eyes staring up to the grey sky. Presently I was surprised to see an elderly civilian and a small boy come out of one of the houses. The man told me he was the proprietor of the Grand Hotel, "but," he added, with a gloomy smile, "I have no guests at this moment. In a little while, perhaps my hotel will have gone also." He pointed to a deep hole ploughed up an hour ago by a German "Jack Johnson." It was deep enough to bury a taxicab.

For some time, as I paced up and down the promenade, there was no answer to the mighty voices of the naval guns firing from some British warships lying along the coast. Nor did any answer come for some time to a French battery snugly placed in a hollow of the dunes, screened by a few trees. I listened to the overwhelming concussion of each shot from the ships, wondering at the mighty flight of the shell, which travelled through the air with the noise of an express train rushing through a tunnel. It was curious that no answer came! Surely the German batteries beyond the river would reply to that deadly cannonade.

I had not long to wait for the inevitable response. It came with a shriek, and a puff of bluish smoke, as the German shrapnel burst a hundred yards from where I stood. It was followed by several shells which dropped into the dunes, not far from the French battery of *cent-vingt*. Another knocked off the gable of a villa.

I had been pacing up and down under the shelter of a red-brick wall leading into the courtyard of a temporary hospital, and presently, acting upon orders from Lieutenant de Broqueville, I ran my car up the road with a Belgian medical officer to a place where some wounded men were lying. When I came back again the red-brick wall had fallen into a heap. The Belgian officer described the climate as " quite unhealthy," as I went away with two men dripping blood on the floor of the car. They had been brought across the ferry, further on, where the Belgian trenches were being strewn with shrapnel. Another little crowd of wounded men was there. Many of them had been huddled up all night, wet to the skin, with their wounds undressed, and without any kind of creature comfort. Their condition had reached the ultimate bounds of misery, and with two of these poor fellows I went away to fetch hot coffee for the others, so that at last they might get a little warmth if they had strength enough to drink. . . . That evening, after a long day in the fields of death, and when I came back from the village where men lay waiting for rescue or the last escape, I looked across to Nieuport-les-Bains. There were quivering flames above it and shells were bursting over it with pretty little puffs of smoke which rested in the opalescent sky. I thought of the proprietor of the Grand Hotel, and wondered if he had insured his house against " Jack Johnsons." . . .

<h2 style="text-align:center">16</h2>

Early next morning I paid a visit to the outskirts of Nieuport town, inland. It was impossible to get further than the outskirts at that time, because in the centre houses were falling and flames were licking each other across the roadways. It was even difficult for our ambulances to get so far, because we had to pass over a bridge to which the enemy's guns were paying great attention. Several of their thunderbolts fell with a hiss into the water of the canal where some Belgian soldiers were building a bridge of boats. It was just an odd chance that our ambulance could get across without being touched, but we took the chance and dodged between two shell-bursts. On the other side, on the outlying streets, there was a litter of bricks and broken glass, and a number of stricken men lay huddled in the parlour of a small house to which they had been carried.   One man was holding his head to keep his brains from spilling, and the others lay tangled amidst upturned chairs and cottage furniture. There was the photograph of a family group on the mantel-piece, between cheap vases which had been the pride, perhaps, of this cottage home.   On one of the walls was a picture of Christ with a bleeding heart.

I remember that at Nieuport there was a young Belgian doctor who had established himself at a dangerous post within range of the enemy's guns, and close to a stream of wounded who came pouring into the little house which he had made into his field hospital.   He had collected also about twenty old men and women who had been unable to get away when the first shells fell.   Without any kind of help he gave first aid to men horribly torn by the pieces of flying shell, and for three days and nights worked very calmly and fearlessly, careless of the death which menaced his own life.

Here he was found by the British column of field ambu-lances, who took away the old people and relieved him of the last batch of *blessés*.   They told the story of that doctor over the supper-table that night, and hoped he would be remem-bered by his own people. . . .

17

There were picnic parties on the Belgian roadsides. Looking back now upon those luncheon hours, with khaki ambulances as shelters from the shrewd wind that came across the marshes, I marvel at the contrast between their gaiety and the brooding horror in the surrounding scene. Bottles of wine were produced and no man thought of blood when he drank its redness, though the smell of blood reeked from the stretchers in the cars.   There were hunks of good Flemish cheese with fresh bread and butter, and it was extraordinary what appetites we had, though guns were booming a couple of kilometres away and the enemy was smashing the last strongholds of the Belgians.   The women in their field kit, so feminine though it included breeches, gave a grace to those wayside halts, and gave to dirty men the chance of little courtesies which brought back civilization to their thoughts, even though life had gone back to primitive things with just life and death, hunger and thirst, love and courage, as the laws of existence. The man who had a cork-screw could command respect. A lady with gold-spun hair could gnaw a chicken bone without any loss of beauty. The chauffeurs munched solidly, making cockney jokes out of full mouths and abolishing all distinctions of caste by their comradeship in great adventures when their courage, their cool nerve, their fine endurance at the wheel, and their skill in taking heavy ambulances down muddy roads with skidding wheels, saved many men's lives and won a heartfelt praise. Little groups of Belgian soldiers came up wistfully and lingered round us as though liking the sight of us, and the sound of our English speech, and the gallantry of those girls who went into the firing-lines to rescue their wounded.

" They are wonderful, your English ladies," said a bearded man. He hesitated a moment and then asked timidly : " Do you think I might shake hands with one of them ? "

I arranged the little matter, and he trudged off with a flush on his cheeks as though he had been in the presence of a queen, and graciously received.

The Belgian officers were eager to be presented to these ladies and paid them handsome compliments. I think the presence of these young women with their hypodermic syringes and first-aid bandages, and their skill in driving heavy motor-cars, and their spiritual disregard of danger, gave a sense of comfort and tenderness to those men who had been long absent from their women-folk and long-suffering in the bleak and ugly cruelty of war. There was no false sentiment, no disguised gallantry, in the homage of the Belgians to those ladies. It was the simple, chivalrous respect of soldiers to dauntless women who had come to help them when they were struck down and needed pity.

Women, with whom for a little while I could call myself comrade, I think of you now and marvel at you ! The call of the wild had brought some of you out to those fields of death. The need of more excitement than modern life gives in time of peace, even the chance to forget, had been the motives with which two or three of you, I think, came upon these scenes of history, taking all risks recklessly, playing a man's part with a feminine pluck, glad of this liberty, far from the conventions of the civilized code, yet giving no hint of scandal to sharp-eared gossip. But most of you had no other thought than that of pity and helpfulness, and with a little flame of faith in your hearts you bore the weight of bleeding men, and eased their pain when it was too intolerable. No soldiers in the armies of the Allies have better right to wear the decorations which a king of sorrow gave you for your gallantry in action.

18

The Germans were still trying to smash their way through the lines held by the Belgians, with French support. They were making tremendous attacks at different places, searching for the breaking-point by which they could force their way to Furnes and on to Dunkirk. It was difficult to know whether they were succeeding or failing. It is difficult to know anything on a modern battlefield where men holding one village are ignorant of what is happening in the next, and where all the sections of an army seem involved in a bewildering chaos, out of touch with each other, waiting for orders which do not seem to come, moving forward for no apparent reason, retiring for other reasons hard to find, or resting, without firing a shot, in places searched by the enemy's fire.

The enemy had built eight pontoon bridges over the Yser canal, but all of them had been destroyed. This was a good piece of news. But against it was the heavy loss of a Belgian company holding another bridge further down the river. At Dixmude the Belgians held the outer streets. Outside there had been heavy trench fighting. The enemy had charged several times with the bayonet, but had been raked back by the mitrailleuses.

Things were going on rather well at most parts of the line.

The French batteries were getting the range every time, and their gunners were guessing at heaps of German dead. The Belgian infantry was holding firm. Their cavalry was out of action for the time, trying to keep warm on the roadsides.

That was all the truth that I could get out of a tangle of confused details. All through another day I watched the business of battle—a strange, mysterious thing in which one fails to find any controlling brain. Regiments came out of the trenches and wandered back, caked with clay, haggard for lack of sleep, with a glint of hunger in their eyes. Guns passed along the roads with ammunition wagons, whose axles shrieked over the stones. For an hour a Belgian battery kept plugging shots towards the enemy's lines. The artillerymen were leisurely at their work, handling their shells with interludes of conversation. At luncheon time they lay about behind the guns smoking cigarettes, and I was glad, for each of their shots seemed to wreck my own brain. At a neighbouring village things were more lively. The enemy was turning his fire this way. A captive balloon had signalled the position, and shrapnels were bursting close. One shell tore up a great hole near the railway line.

Shell after shell fell upon one dung-heap—mistaken perhaps for a company of men. Shrapnel bullets pattered into the roadway, a piece of jagged shell fell with a clatter.

My own chauffeur—a young man of very cool nerve and the best driver I have known—picked it up with a grin, and then dropped it, with a sharp cry. It was almost red-hot. The flames of the enemy's batteries could be seen stabbing through a fringe of trees, perhaps two kilometres away, by Pervyse. Their shells were making puff-balls of smoke over neighbouring farms, and for miles round I could see the clouds stretching out into long, thin wisps. The air throbbed with horrible concussions, the dull full boom of big guns, the sharp staccato of the smaller shell, and the high singing note of it as it came soaring overhead. Gradually one began to realize the boredom of battle, to acquire some of that fantastic indifference to the chance of death which enables the soldiers to stir their soup without an upward glance at a skyful of jagged steel. Only now and then the old question came to one, " This—or the next ? "

It was only the adventure of searching out the wounded that broke the monotony for the Belgian ambulance men. At first they were not hard to find—they were crowded upon the straw in cottage parlours, cleared of all but the cheap vases on the mantelshelf and family photographs tacked upon walls that had not been built for the bloody mess of tragedy which they now enclosed. On their bodies they bore the signs of the tremendous accuracy of the enemy's artillery, and by their number, increasing during the day, one could guess at the tragic endurance of the Belgian infantry in the ring of iron which was closing upon them ; drawing just a little nearer by half a village or half a road as the hours passed. The ambulances carried them away to the station of Fortem, where those who could still sit up were packed into a steam tram, and where the stretcher-cases were taken to the civil hospital at Furnes by motor transport. But in outlying farmsteads in the zone of fire, and in isolated cottages which had been struck by a chance shot, were other wounded men difficult to get. It was work for scouting cars, and too dangerous for ambulances.

Some volunteers made several journeys down the open roads to places not exactly suitable for dalliance. Lieutenant de Broqueville called upon me for this purpose several times because I had a fast little car. I was glad of the honour, though when he pointed to a distant roof where a wounded man was reported to be lying, it looked to me a long, long way in the zone of fire. Two houses blown to pieces by the side of a ditch showed that the enemy's shells were dropping close, and it was a test of nerves to drive deliberately through the flat fields with sharp, stabbing flashes on their frontiers, and right into the middle of an infernal tumult of guns.

It was in the darkness that I went back to Furnes again, with the last of the wounded—a French corporal, who groaned in anguish at every jolt in the road, and then was silent with his head flopping sideways in a way that frightened me. Several times I called back to him, " Courage, mon vieux ! . . . Comment allez vous ? " But he made no answer and there were times when I thought I had a dead man behind me. A biting wind was blowing, and I leaned over his seat to put a blanket over him. But it always blew off that dead-grey face and blood-stained body. Once he groaned, and I was glad to hear the sound and to know that he was still alive. Another man trudging along the highway, using his rifle as a crutch, called out. He spoke the word *blessé,* and I stopped to take him up and sped on again, glancing to right and left at the villages on fire, at the quick flashes of Belgian and German artillery signalling death to each other in the night. The straight trees rushed by like tall, hurrying ghosts. For most of the way we drove without our head-lights through tunnels of darkness. "Queer, isn't it ? " said my driver, and it was his only comment on this adventure in the strangest drama of his life

19

That night the wind came howling across the flat fields into Furnes and a rain-storm broke in fierce gusts upon the convent walls. In this old building with many corridors and innumerable windows, panes of glass rattled and window-sashes creaked and doors banged like thunderclaps. It was impossible to keep a candle alight down any of the passages unless it were protected in a lantern, and a cold mist crept into the house, stealthily striking one with a clammy chill. I stayed up most of the night in the kitchen, having volunteered to stoke the fires and fill hot-water bottles for the wounded. Most of the nurses had gone to bed utterly exhausted. Only two or three of them remained in the wards with one of the doctors. Every now and then the outer bell would jangle, and I would hear the wheels of an ambulance crunching into the courtyard.

"Blessés ! " said a woman who was watching the fires with me.

But we could not take in another *blessé* as there were no more beds or bed-spaces, and after despairing conversations Belgian ambulance officers at the front door of the convent went elsewhere. The house became very quiet except for the noise of the wind and the rain. In the scullery where I sat by the stoves which were in my charge, I could only hear one voice speaking. It was speaking two rooms away, in a long, incessant monologue of madness. Now and again a white-faced nurse came out for newly-filled water-bottles, and while I scalded my fingers with screws which would not fit and with boiling water poured into narrow necks, she told me about a French officer who was dying.

"He wants his wife so badly. He would die quite happily if he could only see her for a minute. But she is in Paris, and he will be dead before the morning comes. . . . I have written a letter for him, and he kissed it before I wrote his wife's address. He keeps calling out her name."

The scullery was warm and cosy, in spite of all the draughts. Sitting back in a wooden chair, I nearly fell asleep, because I had had a long day in the fields and fatigue threatened to overwhelm me. But I wakened with a start when a door opened, letting in a sudden blast of cold air and the noise of the beating rain, and then banged with violence. I seemed to hear footsteps coming across the kitchen floor, and, with an eerie feeling of some new presence in the convent, I strode out of the scullery. A queer little figure startled me. It was a girl in man's clothes, except for a white cap on her head, tight-fitting above her eyes. She was dripping wet and caked in slimy mud, and she faltered forward a little and spoke in French.

"I am very wet. And so tired and hungry! If I could sleep here, on the floor, and dry myself a little——"

"Who are you?" I asked. There seemed something uncanny in this little figure coming out of the wild night.

It appeared that she was one of two Belgian girls who since the beginning of the war had acted as *infirmières* with the Belgian troops, giving the first aid in the trenches, carrying hot soup to them, and living with them under fire. She seemed hardly more than a child, and spoke childishly in a pitiful way, while she twisted the corner of her jacket so that water came out and made a pool about her on the boards. She dried herself in front of the fire and ate—ravenously—some food which had been left on a side-table, and then lay down in a corner of the refectory, falling into the deepest sleep as soon as her head had touched the mattress. She did not wake next morning, though fifty-five people made a clatter at the breakfast-table, and at four in the afternoon she was still sleeping, like a sick child, with her head drooping over the mattress.

20

That day, owing to the heavy rain in the night, the roads were slimy with mud, so that the cars skidded almost over the brim of the dykes. There was more movement among the troops, less sitting about for orders. Officers were riding up and down the roads, and wheeling into little groups for quick discussion. Something was happening—something more than the ding-dong slam of the guns. A regiment of Belgian infantry came plodding through the mud, covered with whitish clay even to their top-hats. They were earthmen, with the blanched look of creatures who live below ground. The news was· whispered about that the enemy was breaking through along one of the roads between Nieuport and Furnes. Then the report came through that they had smashed their way to Wulpen.

"We hope to hold them," said an officer, "but Furnes is in danger. It will be necessary to clear out."

In consequence of this report, it was necessary to be quick in the search for the wounded who had been struck down in the night. The medical men were resolute not to go until they had taken in all that could be removed in time. A little crowd of them were in a small villa along the road. They were wet to the skin and quite famished, without food or drink. A car went back for hot coffee and bread. There was another group of wounded in the church of Oudecapelle.

They were bad cases, and lay still upon the straw. I shall never forget the picture of that church with its painted statues huddled together and toppled down. St. Antony of Padua and St. Sebastian were there in the straw, and crude pictures of saints on the walls stared down upon those bodies lying so quiet on the floor. It was the house of God, but it was filled with the cruelty of life, and those statues seemed to mock at men's faith.

In Furnes the news of the danger seemed to have been scented by the people. They had packed a few things into bundles and made ready to leave their homes. In the convent where I had helped to wash up and to fill the part of odd-job man when I was not out with the " flying column," the doctors and nurses were already loading the ambulances with all their cases. The last of the wounded was sent away to a place of safety. He was a man with a sabre-cut on his head, who for four days had lain quite still, with a grave Oriental face, which seemed in the tranquillity of death.

A group of nuns pleaded to be taken with the doctors and nurses. They could help in the wards or in the kitchen —if only they might go and escape the peril of the German soldiery.

I went across the square to my own room in the Hôtel de la Couronne, and put a few things together. A friend of mine who helped me told the story of a life—the mistakes that had nearly ruined it, the adventures of a heart. A queer conversation at a time when the enemy was coming down the road. The guns were very loud over Wulpen way. They seemed to be coming closer. Yet there was no panic. There was even laughter in the courtyard of the hospital, where the doctors tossed blankets, mattresses, food stores and stoves into the motor ambulances. They were in no hurry to go. It was not the first or the second time they had to evacuate a house menaced by the enemy. They had made a habit of it, and were not to be flurried. I helped the blue-eyed boy to lift the great stoves. They were " some " weight, as an American would say, and both the blue-eyed boy and myself were plastered with soot, so that we looked like sweeps calling round for orders. I lifted packing-cases which would have paralysed me in times of peace and scouted round for some of the thousand and one things which could not be left behind without a tragedy. But at last the order was given to start, and the procession of motor-cars started out for Poperinghe, twenty-five kilometres to the south. Little by little the sound of the guns died away, and the cars passed through quiet fields where French troops bivouacked round their camp fires. I remember that we passed a regiment of Moroccans half-way to Poperinghe, and I looked back from the car to watch them pacing up and down between their fires, which glowed upon their red cloaks and white robes and their grave, bearded Arab faces. They looked miserably cold as the wind flapped their loose garments, but about these men in the muddy field there was a sombre dignity which took one's imagination back to the day when the Saracens held European soil.

21

It was dark when we reached Poperinghe and halted our cars in the square outside the Town Hall, among a crowd of other motor-cars, naval lorries, mitrailleuses, and wagons. Groups of British soldiers stood about smoking cigarettes and staring at us curiously through the gloom as though not quite sure what to make of us. And indeed we must have looked an odd party, for some of us were in khaki and some of us in civilian clothes with Belgian caps, and among the crowd of nurses was a carriage-load of nuns, huddled up in their black cloaks. Warning of our arrival in Poperinghe should have been notified to the municipal authorities, so that they might find lodgings for us ; and the Queen of the Belgians had indeed sent through a message to that effect. But there seemed to be some trouble about finding a roof under which to lay our heads, and an hour went by in the square while the lady in charge of the domesticity department interviewed the mayor, cajoled the corporation, and inspected convents down side streets. She came back at last with a little hopelessness in her eyes.

" Goodness knows where we can go ! There doesn't seem room for a mouse in Poperinghe, and meanwhile the poor nurses are dying of hunger.   We must get into some kind of shelter."

I was commissioned to find at least a temporary abode and to search around for food ; not at all an easy task in a dark town where I had never been before and crowded with the troops of three nations.   I was also made the shepherd of all these sheep, who were commanded to keep their eyes upon me and not to go astray but to follow where I led.   It was a most ridiculous position for a London journalist of a shy and retiring nature, especially as some of the nurses were getting out of hand and indulging in private adventures.   One of them, a most buxom and jolly soul, who, as she confided to me, " didn't care a damn," had established friendly relations with a naval lieutenant, and I had great trouble in dragging her away from his engaging conversation.   Others had discovered a shop where hot coffee was being served to British soldiers who were willing to share it with attractive ladies.   A pretty shepherd I looked when half my flock had gone astray !   Then one of the chauffeurs had something like an apoplectic stroke in the street—the effect of a nervous crisis after a day under shell-fire—and with two friendly " Tommies " I helped to drag him into the Town Hall.   He was a very stout young man, with well-developed muscles, and having lain for some time in a state of coma, he suddenly became delirious and tried to fight me.   I disposed of him in a backyard, where he gradually recovered, and then I set out again in search of my sheep.   After scouting about Poperinghe in the darkness, I discovered a beer tavern with a fair-sized room in which the party might be packed with care, and then, like a pocket patriarch with the children of Israel, I led my ladies on foot to the place of sanctuary and disposed the nuns round the bar, with the reverend mother in the centre of them, having a little aureole round her head from the glamour of the pewter pots.   The others crowded in anyhow and said in a dreadful chorus, like Katherine in " The Taming of the Shrew," " We want our supper ! "

A brilliant inspiration came to me.   As there were British troops in Poperinghe, there must also be British rations, and I had glorious visions of Maconochie and army biscuits. Out into the dark streets again I went with my little car, and after wayside conversations with British soldiers who knew nothing but their own job, found at last the officer in charge of the commissariat. He was a tall fellow and rather haughty in the style of a British officer confronted abruptly with an unusual request. He wanted to know who the devil I was, not liking my civilian clothes and suspecting a German spy. But he became sympathetic when I told him, quite dishonestly, that I was in charge of a British field ambulance under the Belgian Government, which had been forced to evacuate Furnes as the enemy had broken through the Belgian lines. I expressed my gratitude for his kindness, which I was sure he would show, in providing fifty-five army rations for fifty-five doctors and nurses devilishly hungry and utterly destitute. After some hesitation he consented to give me a " chit," and turning to a sergeant who had been my guide down a dark street, said : " Take this officer to the depot and see that he gets everything he wants." It was a little triumph not to be appreciated by readers who do not know the humiliations experienced by corre-spondents in time of war.

A few minutes later the officer came padding down the street after me, and I expected instant arrest and solitary confinement to the end of the war. But he was out for information.

" I beg your pardon, sir," he said, very politely, " but would you mind giving me a sketch of the military situation round your part ? "

I gave him an outline of the affair which had caused the Belgian headquarters staff to shift from Furnes, and though it was, I fancy, slightly over-coloured, he was very much obliged. . . . So, gloriously, I drove back to the beer-tavern with the fifty-five army rations which were enough to feed fifty-five starving people for a week, and was received with cheers. That night, conscious of good deeds, I laid down in the straw of a school-house which had been turned into a barracks, and by the light of several candle-ends, scribbled a long dispatch, which became a very short one when the British censor had worked his will with it.

22

After all, the ambulance column did not have to stay in Poperinghe, but went back to their old quarters, with doctors, nurses and nuns, and all their properties. The enemy had not followed up its advantages, and the Belgian troops, aided by French marines and other French troops who now arrived in greater numbers, thrust them back and barred the way to Dunkirk. The waters of the Yser had helped to turn the tide of war. The sluice-gates were opened and flooded the surrounding fields, so that the enemy's artillery was bogged and could not move. For a little while the air in all that region between Furnes and Nieuport, Dixmude and Pervyse, was cleansed of the odour and fume of battle. But there were other causes of the German withdrawal after one day, at least, when it seemed that nothing short of miraculous aid could hold them from a swift advance along the coast. The chief cause was to be found at Ypres, where the British army sustained repeated and most desperate onslaughts. Ypres was now the storm centre in a ten-days' battle of guns, which was beyond all doubt the most ferocious and bloody episode in the first year of war on the Western side of operations. Repeatedly, after being checked in their attacks by a slaughter which almost annihilated entire regiments, the Germans endeavoured to repair their shattered strength by bringing up every available man and gun for another bout of blood. We know now that it was one of the most awful conflicts in which humanity has ever agonized. Heroism shone through it on both sides. The resistance and nerve strength of the British troops were almost superhuman ; and in spite of losses which might have demoralized any army, however splendid in valour, they fought on with that dogged spirit which filled the trenches at Badajoz and held the lines of Torres Vedras, a hundred years before, when the British race seemed to be stronger than its modern generation.

There were hours when all seemed lost, when it was impossible to bring up reserves to fill the gaps in our bleeding battalions, when so many dead and wounded lay about and so few remained to serve the guns and hold the trenches that another attack pushed home would have swept through our lines and broken us to bits. The cooks and the commissariat men took their places in the trenches, and every man who could hold a rifle fired that day for England's sake, though England did not know her peril.

But the German losses were enormous also, and during those ten days they sacrificed themselves with a kind of Oriental valour, such as heaped the fields of Omdurman with Soudanese. The Kaiser was the new Mahdi for whom men died in masses, going with fatalistic resignation to inevitable death. After a lull for burning and burial, for the refilling of great gaps in regiments and divisions, the enemy moved against us with new masses, but again death awaited them, in spite of all their guns, and the British held their ground.

They held their ground with superb and dauntless valour, and out of the general horror of it all there emerges the fine, bright chivalry of young officers and men who did amazing deeds, which read like fairy tales, even when they are told soberly in official dispatches. In this slaughter field the individual still found a chance now and then of personal prowess, and not all his human qualities had been annihilated or stupefied by the overwhelming power of artillery.

23

The town of Ypres was added to the list of other Belgian towns like those in which I saw the ruin of a nation.

It existed no longer as a place of ancient beauty in which men and women made their homes, trustful of fate. Many of its houses had fallen into the roadways and heaped them high with broken bricks and shattered glass. Others burned with a fine, fierce glow inside the outer walls. The roofs had crashed down into the cellars. All between, furniture and panelling and household treasures, had been burnt out into black ash or mouldered in glowing embers.

The great Cloth Hall, which had been one of the most magnificent treasures of ancient architecture in Europe, was smashed and battered by incessant shells, so that it became one vast ruin of broken walls and fallen pillars framed about a scrapheap of twisted iron and calcined statues, when one day later in the war I wandered for an hour or more, groping for some little relic which would tell the tale of this tragedy.

On my desk now at home there are a few long, rusty nails, an old lock of fifteenth-century workmanship, and a little broken window with leaded panes, which serve as mementoes of this destruction.

The inhabitants of Ypres had gone, unless some of them were hiding, or buried in their cellars. A few dogs roamed about, barking or whining at the soldiers who passed through the outskirts staring at all this destruction with curious eyes, and storing up images for which they will never find the right words.

Two young naval officers who went into Ypres one day tried to coax one of the dogs to come with them. "Might have brought us luck," they said, hiding their pity for a poor beast. But it slunk back into the ruin of its master's house, distrustful of men who did things not belonging to the code of beasts.

24

Human qualities were not annihilated, I have said. Yet in a general way that was the effect of modern weapons, and at Ypres masses of men did not fight so much as stand until they died.

"We just wait for death," said a Belgian officer one night, "and wonder if it doesn't reach us out of all this storm of shells. It is a war without soul or adventure. In the early days, when I scoured the country with a party of motor scouts there was some sport in it. Any audacity we had, or any cunning, could get some kind of payment. The individual counted.

"But now, in the business round Ypres, what can men do —infantry, cavalry, scouts ? It is the gun that does all the business heaving out shells, delivering death in a merciless way. It is guns, with men as targets, helpless as the leaves that are torn from these autumn trees around us by a storm of hail. Our men are falling like the leaves, and the ground is heaped with them, and there is no decisive victory on either side. One week of death is followed by another week of death. The position changes a little, that is all, and the business goes on again. It is appalling."

The same words were used to me on the same night by a surgeon who had just come from the station of Dunkirk, where the latest batch of wounded—a thousand of them— were lying on the straw. " It is appalling," he said. " The destruction of this shell-fire is making a shambles of human bodies. How can we cope with it ? What can we do with such a butchery ? "

Round about Furnes there was a fog in the war zone. In the early dawn until the morning had passed, and then again as the dusk fell and the mists crept along the canals and floated over the flat fields, men groped about it like ghosts, with ghostly guns.

Shells came hurtling out of the veil of the mist and burst in places which seemed hidden behind cotton-wool. An unseen enemy was killing unseen men, and other guns replied into this grim, grey mystery, not knowing what destruction was being done.

It was like the war itself, which was utterly shrouded in these parts by a fog of mystery. Watching it close at hand (when things are more difficult to sort into any order of logic) my view was clouded and perplexed by the general confusion. A few days previously, it seemed that the enemy had abandoned his attack upon the coast-line and the country between Dixmude and Nieuport. There was a strange silence behind the mists, but our aeroplanes, reconnoitring the enemy's lines, were able to see movements of troops drifting south- wards towards the region round Ypres.

Now there was an awakening of guns in places from which they seemed to be withdrawn. Dixmude, quiet in its ruins, trembled again, and crumbled a little more, under the vibration of the enemy's shells, firing at long range towards the Franco-Belgian troops.

Here and there, near Pervyse and Ramscapelle, guns, not yet located, fired " pot shots " on the chance of killing something—soldiers or civilians, or the wounded on their stretchers.

Several of them came into Furnes, bursting quite close to the convent, and one smashed into the Hôtel de la Noble Rose, going straight down a long corridor and then making a great hole in a bedroom wall. Some of the officers of the Belgian staff were in the room downstairs, but not a soul was hurt.

French and Belgian patrols thrusting forward cautiously found themselves under rifle-fire from the enemy's trenches which had previously appeared abandoned. Something like an offensive developed again, and it was an unpleasant surprise when Dixmude was retaken by the Germans.

As a town its possession was not of priceless value to the enemy. They had retaken a pitiful ruin, many streets of skeleton houses filled with burnt-out ashes, a Town Hall with gaping holes in its roof, an archway which thrust up from a wreck of pillars like a gaunt rib, and a litter of broken glass, bricks and decomposed bodies.

If they had any pride in the capture it was the completeness of their destruction of this fine old Flemish town.

But it was a disagreeable thing that the enemy, who had been thrust back from this place and the surrounding neighbourhood, and who had abandoned their attack for a time in this region, should have made such a sudden hark-back in sufficient strength to regain ground which was won by the Belgian and French at the cost of many thousands of dead and wounded

The renewed attack was to call off some of the allied troops from the lines round Ypres, and was a part of the general shock of the offensive all along the German line in order to test once more the weakest point of the Allies' strength through which to force a way.

The character of the fighting in this part of Flanders entered into the monotone of the winter campaign and, though the censorship was blamed for scarcity of news, there was really nothing to conceal in the way of heroic charges by cavalry, dashing bayonet attacks, or rapid counter-movements by infantry in mass. Such things for which public imagination craved were not happening.

What did happen was a howling gale shrieking across the dunes, and swirling up the sands into blinding· clouds, and tearing across the flat marshlands as though all the invisible gods of the old ghost world were racing in their chariots.

In the trenches along the Yser men crouched down close to the moist mud to shelter themselves from a wind which was harder to dodge than shrapnel shells. It lashed them with a fierce cruelty. In spite of all the woollen comforters and knitted vests made by women's hands at home, the wind found its way through to the bones and marrow of the soldiers so that they were numbed. At night it was an agony of cold, preventing sleep, even if men could sleep while shells were searching for them with a cry of death.

The gunners dug pits for themselves, and when they ceased fire for a time crawled to shelter, smoking through little outlets in the damp blankets in which they had wrapped their heads and shoulders. They tied bundles of straw round their legs to keep out the cold and packed old newspapers inside their chests as breast-plates, and tried to keep themselves warm, at least in imagination.

There was no battlefield in the old idea of the world. How often must one say this to people at home who think that a modern army is encamped in the fields with bivouac fires and bell tents? The battle was spread over a wide area of villages and broken towns and shattered farmhouses, and neat little homesteads yet untouched by fire or shell. The open roads were merely highways between these points of shelter, in which great bodies of troops were huddled—

the internal lines of communication connecting various parts of the fighting machine.

It was rather hot, as well as cold, at Oudecapelle and Nieucapelle, and along the line to Styvekenskerke and Lombardtzyde. The enemy's batteries were hard at work again belching out an inexhaustible supply of shells. Over there, the darkness was stabbed by red flashes, and the sky was zigzagged by waves of vivid splendour, which shone for a moment upon the blanched faces of men who waited for death.

Through the darkness, along the roads, infantry tramped towards the lines of trenches, to relieve other regiments who had endured a spell in them. They bent their heads low, thrusting forward into the heart of the gale, which tore at the blue coats of these Frenchmen and plucked at their red trousers, and slashed in their faces with cruel whips. Their side-arms jingled against the teeth of the wind, which tried to snatch at their bayonets and to drag the rifles out of their grip. They never raised their heads to glance at the Red Cross carts coming back.

Some of the French officers, tramping by the side of their men, shouted through the swish of the gale :

" Courage, mes petits ! "

" Il fait mauvais temps pour les sales Boches ! "

In cottage parlours near the fighting lines—that is to say in the zone of fire, which covered many villages and farmsteads, French doctors, buttoned up to the chin in leather coats, bent over the newest batches of wounded.

" Shut that door ! Sacred name of a dog ; keep the door shut ! Do you want the gale to blow us up the chimney ? "

But it was necessary to open the door to bring in another stretcher where a man lay still.

" Pardon, mon capitaine," said one of the stretcher-bearers, as the door banged to, with a frightful clap.

Yesterday the enemy reoccupied Dixmude.

So said the official bulletin, with its incomparable brevity of eloquence.

26

For a time, during this last month in the first year of the war, I made my headquarters at Dunkirk, where without stirring from the town there was always a little excitement to be had. Almost every day, for instance, a German aeroplane—one of the famous Taube flock—would come and drop bombs by the Town Hall or the harbour, killing a woman or two and a child, or breaking many panes of glass, but never destroying anything of military importance (for women and children are of no importance in time of war), although down by the docks there were rich stores of ammunition, petrol, and material of every kind. These birds of death came so regularly in the afternoon that the Dunquerquoises, who love a jest, even though it is a bloody one, instead of saying " Trois heures et demie," used to say, " Taube et demie " and know the time.

There was a window in Dunkirk which looked upon the chief square. In the centre of the square is the statue of Jean-Bart, the famous captain and pirate of the seventeenth century, standing in his sea-boots (as he once strode into the presence of the Sun-King) and with his sword raised above his great plumed hat. I stood in the balcony of the window looking down at the colour and movement of the life below, and thinking at odd moments—the thought always thrust beneath the surface of one's musings—of the unceasing slaughter of the war not very far away across the Belgian frontier. All these people here in the square were in some way busy with the business of death. They were crossing these flagged stones on the way to the shambles, or coming back from the shell-stricken towns, *là bas*, as the place of blood is called, or taking out new loads of food for guns and men, or bringing in reports to admirals and the staff, or going to churches to pray for men who have done these jobs before, and now, perhaps, lie still, out of it.

This square in Dunkirk contained many of the elements which go to make up the actions and reactions of this war. It seemed to me that a clever stage manager desiring to present

to his audience the typical characters of this military drama
—leaving out the beastliness, of course—would probably
select the very people and groups upon whom I was now
looking down from the window. Motor-cars came whirling
up with French staff officers in dandy uniforms (the stains of
blood and mud would only be omitted by Mr. Willie Clarkson).
In the centre, just below the statue of Jean-Bart, was an
armoured-car which a Belgian soldier, with a white rag round
his head, was explaining to a French cuirassier whose long
horse-hair queue fell almost to his waist from his linen-
covered helm. Small boys mounted the step and peered into
the wonder-box, into the mysteries of this neat death-
machine, and poked grubby fingers into bullet-holes which
had scored the armour-plates. Other soldiers—Chasseurs
Alpins in sky-blue coats, French artillery men in their dark-
blue jackets, Belgian soldiers wearing shiny top-hats with
eye-shades, or dinky caps with gold or scarlet tassels, and
English Tommies in mud-coloured khaki—strolled about the
car, and nodded their heads towards it as though to say, " That
has killed off a few Germans, by the look of it. Better sport
than trench digging."

The noise of men's voices and laughter—they laugh a
good deal in war time, outside the range of shells—came up
to the open window; overpowered now and then by the
gurgles and squawks of motor-horns, like beasts giving
their death-cries. With a long disintegrating screech there
came up a slate-grey box on wheels. It made a semicircular
sweep, scattering a group of people, and two young gentlemen
of the Royal Naval Air Service sprang down and shouted
" What-ho ! " very cheerily to two other young gentlemen
in naval uniforms who shouted back " Cheer-o ! " from the
table under my balcony.

I knew all of them, especially one of the naval airmen
who flies what he calls a motor-bus and drops bombs with
sea curses upon the heads of any German troops he can find
on a morning's reconnaissance. He rubs his hand at the
thought that he has " done in " quite a number of the
" German blighters." With a little luck he hopes to nobble

a few more this afternoon. A good day's work like this bucks him up wonderfully, he says, except when he comes down an awful whop in the darned old motor-bus, which is all right while she keeps going but no bloomin' use at all when she spreads her skirts in a ploughed field and smashes her new set of stays. Oh, a bad old vixen, that seaplane of his ! Wants a lot of coaxin'.

A battery of French artillery rattled over the cobblestones. The wheels were caked with clay, and the guns were covered with a grey dust. They were going up Dixmude way, or along to Ramscapelle. The men sat their horses as though they were glued to the saddles. One of them had a loose sleeve pinned across his chest, but a strong grip on his bridle with his left hand. The last wheels rattled round the corner, and a little pageant, more richly coloured, came across the stage. A number of Algerian Arabs strode through the square, with a long swinging gait. They were wearing blue turbans above the flowing white " haik " which fell back upon their shoulders, and the white burnous which reached to their ankles. They were dark, bearded men ; one of them at least with the noble air of Othello, the Moor, and with his fine dignity.

They stared up at the statue of Jean-Bart, and asked a few questions of a French officer who walked with a shorter step beside them. It seemed to impress their imagination, and they turned to look back at that figure with the raised sword and the plumed hat. Three small boys ran by their side and held out grubby little hands, which the Arabs shook, with smiles that softened the hard outlines of their faces.

Behind them a cavalcade rode in. They were Arab chiefs, on little Algerian horses, with beautifully neat and clean limbs, moving with the grace of fallow deer across the flagged stones of Dunkirk. The bridles glistened and tinkled with silver plates. The saddles were covered with embroidered cloths. The East came riding to the West. These Mohammedans make a religion of fighting. It has its ritual and its ceremony—even though shrapnel makes such a nasty mess of men.

So I stood looking down on these living pictures of a city in the war zone. But now and again I glanced back into the room behind the window, and listened to the scraps of talk which came from the lounge and the scattered chairs. There was a queer collection of people in this room. They, too, had some kind of business in the job of war, either to kill or to cure. Among them was a young Belgian lieutenant who used to make a " bag " of the Germans he. killed each day with his mitrailleuse until the numbers bored him and he lost count. Near him were three or four nurses discussing wounds and dying wishes and the tiresome hours of a night when a thousand wounded streamed in suddenly, just as they were hoping for a quiet cup of coffee. A young surgeon spoke some words which I heard as I turned my head from the window.

" It's the frightful senselessness of all this waste of life which makes one sick with horror . . ."

Another doctor came in with a tale from Ypres, where he had taken his ambulances under shell-fire.

" It's monstrous," he said, " all the red tape ! Because I belong to a volunteer ambulance the officers wanted to know by what infernal impudence I dared to touch the wounded. I had to drive forty miles to get official permission, and could not get it then. . . . And the wounded were lying about everywhere, and it was utterly impossible to cope with the numbers of them. . . . They stand on etiquette when men are crying out in agony ! The Prussian caste isn't worse than that."

I turned and looked out of the window again. But I saw nothing of the crowd below. I saw only a great tide of blood rising higher and higher, and I heard, not the squawking of motor-horns, but the moans of men in innumerable sheds, where they lie on straw waiting for the surgeon's knife and crying out for morphia. I saw and heard, because I had seen and heard these things before in France and Belgium.

In the room there was the touch of quiet fingers on a piano not too bad. It was the music of deep, soft chords. A woman's voice spoke quickly, excitedly.

" Oh ! some one can play. Ask him to play ! It seems a thousand years since I heard some music. I'm thirsty for it ! "

A friend of mine who had struck the chords while standing before the piano, sat down, and smiled a little over the notes.

" What shall it be ? " he asked, and then, without waiting for the answer, played. It was a reverie by Chopin, I think, and somehow it seemed to cleanse our souls a little of things seen and smelt. It was so pitiful that something broke inside my heart a moment. I thought of the last time I had heard some music. It was in a Flemish cottage, where a young lieutenant, a little drunk, sang a love-song among his comrades, while a little way off men were being maimed and killed by bursting shells.

The music stopped with a slur of notes. Somebody asked, " What was that ? "

There was the echo of a dull explosion and the noise of breaking glass. I looked out into the square again from the open window, and saw people running in all directions.

Presently a man came into the room and spoke to one of the doctors, without excitement.

" Another Taube. Three bombs, as usual, and several people wounded. You'd better come. It's only round the corner."

It was always round the corner, this sudden death. Just a step or two from any window of war.

27

Halfway through my stay at Dunkirk I made a trip to England and back, getting a free passage in the Government ship *Invicta*, which left by night to dodge the enemy's submarines, risking their floating mines. It gave me one picture of war which is unforgettable. We were a death-ship that night, for we carried the body of a naval officer who had been killed on one of the monitors which I had seen in action several times off Nieuport. With the corpse came also several seamen, wounded by the same shell. I

did not see any of them until the *Invicta* lay alongside the
Prince of Wales pier.   Then a party of marines brought up
the officer's body on a stretcher.   They bungled the job
horribly, jamming the stretcher poles in the rails of the
gangway, and, fancying myself an expert in stretcher work,
for 1 had had a little practice, I gave them a hand and
helped to carry the corpse to the landing-stage.   It was
sewn up tightly in canvas, exactly like a piece of meat
destined for Smithfield market, and was treated with no
more ceremony than such a parcel by the porters who
received it.

"Where are you going to put that, Dick ?"

"Oh, stow it over there, Bill ! "

That was how a British hero made his home-coming.

But I had a more horrible shock, although I had been
accustomed to ugly sights.   It was when the wounded
seamen came up from below.   The lamps on the landing-
stage, flickering in the high wind, cast their white light
upon half a dozen men walking down the gangway in Indian
file.   At least I had to take them on trust as men, but they
looked more like spectres who had risen from the tomb,
or obscene creatures from some dreadful underworld.   When
the German shell had burst on their boat, its fragments
had scattered upwards, and each man had been wounded
in the face, some of them being blinded and others scarred
beyond human recognition.   Shrouded in ship's blankets,
with their heads swathed in bandages, their faces were
quite hidden behind masks of cotton-wool coming out to
a point like beaks and bloody at the tip.   I shuddered at
the sight of them, and walked away, cursing the war and
all its horrors.

After my return to Dunkirk, I did not stay very long
there.   There was a hunt for correspondents, and my name
was on the black list as a man who had seen too much.
I found it wise to trek southwards, turning my back on
Belgium, where I had had such strange adventures in the
war-zone.   The war had settled down into its winter campaign, utterly dreary and almost without episodes in the

country round Furnes. But I had seen the heroism of the Belgian soldiers in their last stand against the enemy who had ravaged their little kingdom, and as long as life lasts the memory of these things will remain to me like a tragic song. I had been sprinkled with the blood of Belgian soldiers, and had helped to carry them, wounded and dead. I am proud of that, and my soul salutes the spirit of those gallant men—the remnants of an army—who, without much help from French or English, stood doggedly in their last ditches, refusing to surrender, and with unconquerable courage until few were left, holding back the enemy from their last patch of soil. It was worth the risk of death to see those things.

CHAPTER VIII

THE SOUL OF PARIS

1

In the beginning of the war it seemed as though the soul had gone out of Paris and that it had lost all its life.

I have already described those days of mobilization when an enormous number of young men were suddenly called to the colours out of all their ways of civil life, and answered that summons without enthusiasm for war, hating the dreadful prospect of it and cursing the nation which had forced this fate upon them. That first mobilization lasted for twenty-one days, and every day one seemed to notice the difference in the streets, the gradual thinning of the crowds, the absence of young manhood, the larger proportion of women and old fogeys among those who remained. The life of Paris was being drained of its best blood by this vampire, war. In the Latin Quarter most of the students went without any preliminary demonstrations in the café d'Harcourt, or speeches from the table-tops in the cheaper restaurants along the Boul' Miche, where in times of peace any political crisis or intellectual drama produces a flood of fantastic oratory from young gentlemen with black hair, burning eyes, and dirty finger-nails. They had gone away silently, with hasty kisses to little mistresses, who sobbed their hearts out for a night before searching for any lovers who might be left.

In all the streets of Paris there was a shutting up of shops. Every day put a new row of iron curtains between the window panes, until at the end of the twelfth day the city seemed as dismal as London on a Sunday, or as though

234

all the shops were closed for a public funeral. Scraps of paper were pasted on the barred-up fronts.

" *Le magasin est fermé à cause de la mobilisation.*"
" *M. Jean Cochin et quatre fils sont au front des armées.*"
" *Tout le personel de cet établissement est mobilisé.*"

A personal incident brought the significance of the general mobilization sharply to my mind. I had not realized till then how completely the business of Paris would be brought to a standstill, and how utterly things would be changed. Before leaving Paris for Nancy and the eastern frontier, I left a portmanteau and a rug in a hotel where I had become friendly with the manager and the assistant manager, with the hall porter, the liftman, and the valet de chambre. I had discussed the war with each of these men and from each of them had heard the same expressions of horror and dismay. The hall porter was a good-humoured soul, who confided to me that he had a pretty wife and a new-born babe, who reconciled him to the disagreeable side of a life as the servant of any stranger who might come to the hotel with a bad temper and a light purse. . . .

On coming back from Nancy I went to reclaim my bag and rug. But when I entered the hotel something seemed different. At first I could not quite understand this difference. It seemed to me for a moment that I had come to the wrong place. I did not see the hotel porter nor the manager and assistant manager. There was only a sharp-featured lady sitting at the desk in loneliness, and she looked at me, as I stared round the hall, with obvious suspicion. Very politely I asked for my bag and rug, but the lady's air became more frigid when I explained that I had lost the cloak-room ticket and could not remember the number of the room I had occupied a few days before.

" Perhaps there is some means by which you could prove that you stayed here ? " said the lady.

" Certainly. I remember the hall porter. His name is Pierre, and he comes from the Midi."

She shook her head.

"There is no hall porter, Monsieur. He has gone."

"And then the valet de chambre. His name is François. He has curly hair and a short brown moustache."

The lady shook her head in a most decided negative.

"The present valet de chambre is a bald-headed man, and clean-shaven, monsieur. It must have been another hotel where you stayed."

I began to think that this must undoubtedly be the case, and yet I remembered the geography of the hall, and the pattern of the carpet, and the picture of Mirabeau in the National Assembly.

Then it dawned on both of us.

"Ah! Monsieur was here before August 1. Since then everyone is mobilized. I am the manager's wife, Monsieur, and my husband is at the front, and we have hardly any staff here now. You will describe the shape of your bag...."

2

The French Government was afraid of the soul of Paris. Memories of the Commune haunted the minds of men who did not understand that the character of the Parisian has altered somewhat since 1870. Ministers of France who had read a little history, were terribly afraid that out of the soul of Paris would come turbulence and mob-passion, *crises de nerfs*, rioting, political strife, and panics. Paris must be handled firmly, sobered down by every possible means, kept from the knowledge of painful facts, spoon-fed with cheerful communiqués whatever the truth might be, guarded by strong but hidden force, ready at a moment's notice to smash up a procession, to arrest agitators, to quell a rebellion, and to maintain the strictest order.

Quietly, but effectively, General Galièni, the military governor of "the entrenched camp of Paris," as it was called, proceeded to place the city under martial law in order to strangle any rebellious spirit which might be lurking in its hiding places. Orders and regulations were issued in a rapid volley fire which left Paris without any of its old life or liberty. The *terrasses* were withdrawn from the cafés. No longer could the philosophic Parisian sip his *petit verre* and watch the drama of the boulevards from the shady side of a marble-topped table. He must sit indoors like an Englishman, in the darkness of his public-house, as though ashamed of drinking in the open. Absinthe was banned by a thunderstroke from the Invalides, where the Military Governor had established his headquarters, and Parisians who had acquired the absinthe habit trembled in every limb at this judgment which would reduce them to physical and moral wrecks, as creatures of the drug habit suddenly robbed of their nerve-controlling tabloids. It was an edict welcomed by all men of self-control who knew that France had been poisoned by this filthy liquid, but they too became a little pale when all the cafés of Paris were closed at eight o'clock.

"Sapristi ! Qu'est qu'on peut faire les soirs ? On ne peut pas dormir tout le temps ! Et la guerre durera peut-être trois mois ! "

To close the cafés at eight o'clock seemed a tragic infliction to the true Parisian, for whom life only begins after that hour, when the stupidity of the day's toil is finished and the mind is awakened to the intellectual interests of the world, in friendly conversation, in philosophical discussions, in heated arguments, in wit and satire. How then could they follow the war and understand its progress if the cafés were closed at eight o'clock ? But the edict was given and Paris obeyed, loyally and with resignation.

Other edicts followed, or arrived simultaneously like a broadside fired into the life of the city. Public processions " with whatever patriotic motive " were sternly prohibited. " Purveyors of false news, or of news likely to depress the public spirit " would be dealt with by courts-martial and punished with the utmost severity. No musical instruments were to be played after ten o'clock at night, and orchestras were prohibited in all restaurants. Oh, Paris, was even your laughter to be abolished, if you had any heart for laughter while your sons were dying on the fields of battle ?

The newspaper censors had put a strangle grip upon the press, not only upon news of war but also upon expressions of opinion.   Gustave Hervé signed his name three days a week to blank columns of extraordinary eloquence.   Georges Clemenceau had a series of striking head-lines which had been robbed of all their text.   The intellectuals of Paris might not express an opinion save by permission of the military censors, most of whom, strangely enough, had German names.

The civil police under direction of the Military Governor were very busy in Paris during the early days of the war. Throughout the twenty-four hours, and especially in the darkness of night, the streets were patrolled by blue-capped men on bicycles, who rode, four by four, as silently as shadows, through every quarter of the city.   They had a startling habit of surrounding any lonely man who might be walking in the late hours and interrogating him as to his nationality, age and business.

Several times I was arrested in this way and never escaped the little *frousse* which came to me when these dark figures closed upon me, as they leapt from their bicycles and said with grim suspicion :

" Vos papiers, s'il vous plait ! "

My pockets were bulging with papers, which I thrust hurriedly into the lantern-light for a close-eyed scrutiny.

They were very quick to follow the trail of a stranger, and there was no sanctuary in Paris in which he might evade them.   Five minutes after calling upon a friend in the fifth floor flat of an old mansion at the end of a courtyard in the Rue de Rivoli, there was a sharp tap at his door, and two men in civil clothes came into the room, with that sleuth-hound look which belongs to stage, and French, detectives. They forgot to remove their bowler hats, which seemed to me to be a lamentable violation of French courtesy.

" Vos papiers, s'il vous plait ! "

Again I produced bundles of papers—*permis de séjour* in Paris, Amiens, Rouen, Orleans, Le Mans ; *laisser-passer* to Boulogne, Dieppe, Havre, Dunkirk, Aire-sur-Lys, Béthune and Hazebrouck ; British passports and *papiers visés* by French consuls, French police, French generals, French mayors, and

French stationmasters. But they were hardly satisfied. One man with an ugly bulge in his side-pocket—you have seen at Drury Lane how quickly the revolver comes out ?— suggested that the whole collection was not worth an old railway ticket because I had failed to comply with the latest regulation regarding a photograph on the *permis de séjour*. . . . We parted, however, with mutual confidence and an expression of satisfaction in the Entente Cordiale.

8

One scene is clear cut in my memory, as it was revealed in a narrow street of Paris where a corner lantern flung its rays down upon the white faces of two men and two women. It was midnight, and I was waiting outside the door of a newspaper office, where my assistant was inquiring for the latest bulletins of war. For some minutes I watched this little group with an intuition that tragedy was likely to leap out upon them. They belonged to the apache class, as it was easy to see by the cut of the men's trousers tucked into their boots, with a sash round the waist, and by the velvet bonnets pulled down sideways over their thin-featured faces and sharp jaws. The women had shawls over their heads and high-heeled shoes under their skirts. At the Alhambra in London the audience would have known what dance to expect when such a group had slouched into the glamour of the footlights. They were doing a kind of slow dance now, though without any music except that of women's sobs and a man's sibilant curses. The younger of the two men was horribly drunk, and it was clear that the others were trying to drag him home before trouble came. They swayed with him up and down, picked him up when he fell, swiped him in the face when he tried to embrace one of the women, and lurched with him deeper into the throat of the alley. Then suddenly the trouble came. Four of those shadows on bicycles rode out of the darkness and closed in.

As sharp and distinct as pistol shots two words came to my ears out of the sudden silence and stillness which had arrested the four people :

" Vos papiers ! "

There was no " s'il vous plait " this time.

It was clear that one at least of the men—I guessed it was the drunkard—had no papers explaining his presence in Paris, and that he was one of the *embusqués* for whom the Military Governor was searching in the poorer quarters of the city (in the richer quarters there was not such a sharp search for certain young gentlemen of good family who had failed to answer the call to the colours), and for whom there was a very rapid method of punishment on the sunny side of a white wall.   Out of the silence of that night came shriek after shriek.   The two women abandoned themselves to a wild and terror-stricken grief.   One of them flung herself on to her knees, clutching at an *agent de police*, clasping him with piteous and pleading hands, until he jerked her away from him.   Then she picked herself up and leant against a wall, moaning and wailing like a wounded animal.   The drunkard was sobered enough to stand upright in the grasp of two policemen while the third searched him.   By the light of the street lamp I saw his blanched face and sunken eyes.   Two minutes later the police led both men away, leaving the women behind, very quiet now, sobbing in their shawls.

It was the general belief in Paris that many apaches were shot *pour encourager les autres*.   I cannot say that is true—the police of Paris keep their own secrets—but I believe a front place was found for some of them in the fighting lines.   Paris lost many of its rebels, who will never reappear in the Place Pigalle and the Avenue de Clichy on moonless nights.   Poor devils of misery !   They did but make war on the well-to-do, and with less deadly methods, as a rule, than those encouraged in greater wars when, for trade interests also, men kill each other with explosive bombs and wrap each other's bowels round their bayonets and blow up whole companies of men in trenches which have been sapped so skilfully that at the word " Fire ! " no pair of arms or legs remains to a single body and God Himself would not know His handiwork.

4

For several months there was a spy mania in Paris, and the police, acting under military orders, showed considerable activity in " Boche " hunting. It was a form of chase which turned me a little sick when I saw the captured prey, just as I used to turn sick as a boy when I saw a rat caught in a trap and handed over to the dogs, or any other animal run to earth. All my instincts made me hope for the escape of the poor beast, vermin though it might be.

One day as I was sitting in the Café Napolitain on one of my brief excursions to Paris from the turmoil in the wake of war, I heard shouts and saw a crowd of people rushing towards a motor-car coming down the Boulevard des Italiens. One word was repeated with a long-drawn sibilance :

" *Espion ! Espion !* "

The spy was between two *agents de police*. He was bound with cords and his collar had been torn off, so that his neck was bare, like a man ready for the guillotine. Somehow, the look of the man reminded me in a flash of those old scenes in the French Revolution, when a French aristocrat was taken in a tumbril through the streets of Paris. He was a young man with a handsome, clear-cut face, and though he was very white except where a trickle of blood ran down his cheek from a gash on his forehead, he smiled disdainfully with a proud curl of the lip. He knew he was going to his death, but he had taken the risk of that when he stayed in Paris for the sake of his country. A German spy ! Yes, but a brave man who went rather well to his death through the sunlit streets of Paris, with the angry murmurs of a crowd rising in waves about him.

On the same night I saw another episode of this spy-hunting period, and it was more curious. It happened in a famous restaurant not far from the Comédie Française, where a number of French soldiers in a variety of uniforms dined with their ladies before going to the front after a day's leave from the fighting lines. Suddenly, into the buzz of voices and above the tinkle of glasses and coffee-cups one voice spoke in a formal way, with clear, deliberate words. I saw that it was the manager of the restaurant addressing his clients.

" Messieurs et Mesdames,—My fellow-manager has just been arrested on a charge of espionage. I have been forbidden to speak more than these few words, to express my personal regret that I am unable to give my personal attention to your needs and pleasure."

With a bow this typical French " patron "—surely not a German spy !—turned away and retreated from the room. A look of surprise passed over the faces of the French soldiers. The ladies raised their pencilled eyebrows, and then—so quickly does this drama of war stale after its first experience —continued their conversation through whiffs of cigarette smoke.

5

But it was not of German spies that the French Government was most afraid. Truth to tell, Paris was thronged with Germans, naturalized a week or two before the war and by some means or other on the best of terms with the police authorities, in spite of spy-hunts and spy-mania, which sometimes endangered the liberty of innocent Englishmen, and Americans more or less innocent. It was only an accident which led to the arrest of a well-known milliner whose afternoon-tea parties among her mannequins were attended by many Germans with business in Paris of a private character. When this lady covered up the Teutonic name of her firm with a Red Cross flag and converted her show-rooms into a hospital ward, excellently supplied except with wounded men, the police did not inquire into the case until a political scandal brought it into the limelight of publicity.

The French Government was more afraid of the true Parisians. To sober them down in case their spirit might lead to trouble, the streets of Paris were kept in darkness and all places of amusement were closed as soon as war was declared. In case riots should break forth from secret lairs of revolutionary propaganda, squadrons of Gardes Republicains patrolled the city by day and night, and the *agents de police* were reinforced by *fusiliers marins* with loaded rifles, who—simple fellows as they are—could hardly direct a stranger to the Place de la Concorde or find their own way to the Place de la Bastille.

At all costs Paris was not to learn the truth about the war if there were any unpleasant truths to tell. For Paris there must always be victories and no defeats. They must not even know that in war time there were wounded men ; otherwise they might get so depressed or so enraged that (thought the French Government) there might be the old cry of " Nous sommes trahis ! " with a lopping off of Ministers' heads and dreadful orgies in which the streets of Paris would run red with blood. This reason alone—so utterly unreasonable, as we now know—may explain the farcical situation of the hospitals in Paris during the first two months of the war. Great hotels like the Astoria, Claridge's, and the Majestic had been turned into hospitals magnificently equipped and over-staffed. Nothing that money could buy was left unbought, so that these great palaces might be fully provided with all things necessary for continual streams of wounded men. High society in France gave away its wealth with generous enthusiasm. Whatever faults they might have they tried to wash them clean by charity, full-hearted and overflowing, for the wounded sons of France. Great ladies who had been the beauties of the salons, whose gowns had been the envy of their circles, took off their silks and chiffons and put on the simple dress of the *infirmière* and volunteered to do the humblest work, the dirty work of kitchen-wenches and scullery-girls and bedroom-maids, so that their hands might help, by any service, the men who had fought for France. French doctors, keen and brilliant men who hold a surgeon's knife with a fine and delicate skill, stood in readiness for the maimed victims of the war. The best brains of French medical science were mobilized in these hospitals of Paris. But the wounded did not come to Paris until the war had dragged on for weeks. After the battle of the Marne, when the wounded were pouring into Orleans and other towns at the rate of seven thousand a day, when it was utterly impossible for the doctors there to deal with all that tide of agony, and when the condition of the French wounded was a scandal to the name of a civilized country, the hospitals of Paris remained empty, or with a few lightly wounded men in a desert of beds. Because they could not speak French, perhaps, these rare arrivals were mostly Turcos and Senegalese, so that when they awakened in these wards and their eyes rolled round upon the white counterpanes, the exquisite flowers and the painted ceilings, and there beheld the beauty of women bending over their bedsides—women whose beauty was famous through Europe—they murmured " Allahu akbar " in devout ecstasy and believed themselves in a Mohammedan paradise.

It was a comedy in which there was a frightful tragedy. The doctors and surgeons standing by these empty beds, wandering through operating-theatres magnificently appointed, asked God why their hands were idle when so many soldiers of France were dying for lack of help, and why Paris, the nerve-centre of all railway lines, so close to the front, where the fields were heaped with the wreckage of the war, should be a world away from any work of rescue. It was the same old strain of falsity which always runs through French official life. " Politics ! " said the doctors of Paris ; " those cursed politics ! "

But it was fear this time. The Government was afraid of Paris, lest it should lose its nerve, and so all trains of wounded were diverted from the capital, wandering on long and devious journeys, side-tracked for hours, and if any ambulances came it was at night, when they glided through back streets under cover of darkness, afraid of being seen.

They need not have feared, those Ministers of France. Paris had more courage than some of them, with a greater dignity and finer faith. When the French Ministry fled to Bordeaux without having warned the people that the enemy was at their gates, Paris remained very quiet and gave no sign of wild terror or of panic-stricken rage. There was no political cry or revolutionary outburst. No mob orator sprang upon a café chair to say "Nous sommes trahis !" . . . There was not even a word of rebuke for those who had doctored the official communiqués and put a false glamour of hope upon hideous facts. Hurriedly and dejectedly over a million people of Paris fled from the city, now that the Government had led the way of flight. They were afraid, and there was panic in their exodus, but even that was not hysterical, and men and women kept their heads, though they had lost their hopes. It was rare to see a weeping woman. There was no wailing of a people distraught. Sadly those fugitives left the city which had been all the world to them, and the roads to the south were black with their multitudes, having left in fear but full of courage on the road, dejected, but even then finding a comedy in the misery of it, laughing—as most French women will laugh in the hour of peril—even when their suffering was greatest and when there was a heartache in their humour.

6

After all the soul of Paris did not die, even in those dark days when so many of its inhabitants had gone, and when, for a little while, it seemed a deserted city. Many thousands of citizens remained, enough to make a great population, and although for a day or two they kept for the most part indoors, under the shadow of a fear that at any moment they might hear the first shells come shrieking overhead, or even the clatter of German cavalry, they quickly resumed the daily routine of their lives, as far as it was possible at such a time. The fruit- and vegetable-stalls along the Rue St. Honoré were thronged as usual by frugal housewives who do their shopping early, and down by Les Halles, to which I wended my way through the older streets of Paris, to note any change in the price of food, there were the usual scenes of bustling activity among the baskets and the litter of the markets. Only a man who knew Paris well could detect a difference in the early morning crowds—the absence of many young porters who used to carry great loads on their heads before quenching their thirst at the Chien Qui Fume, and the presence of many young girls of the midinette class, who in normal times lie later in bed before taking the *métro* to their shops.

The shops were closed now. Great establishments like the Galeries Lafayette had disbanded their armies of girls and even many of the factories in the outer suburbs, like Charenton and La Villette, had suspended work, because their mechanics and electricians and male factory hands had been mobilized at the outset of the war. The women of Paris were plunged into dire poverty, and thousands of them into idleness, which makes poverty more awful. Even now I can hardly guess how many of these women lived during the first months of the war. There were many wives who had been utterly dependent for the upkeep of their little homes upon men who were now earning a sou a day as soldiers of France, with glory as a *pourboire*. So many old mothers had been supported by the devotion of sons who had denied themselves marriage, children, and the little luxuries of life in order that out of their poor wages in Government offices they might keep the woman to whom they owed their being. Always the greater part of the people of Paris lives precariously on the thin edge of a limited income, stinting and scraping, a sou here, a sou there, to balance the week's accounts and eke out a little of that *joie de vivre,* which to every Parisian is an essential need. Now by the edict of war all life's economies had been annihilated. There were no more wages out of which to reckon the cost of an extra meal, or out of which to squeeze the price of a seat at a Pathé cinema. Mothers and wives and mistresses had been abandoned to the chill comfort of national charity, and oh, the coldness of it !

The French Government had promised to give an allowance of 1 franc 25 centimes a day to the women who were dependent on soldier husbands. Perhaps it is possible to live on a shilling a day in Paris, though, by Heaven, I should hate to do it. Nicely administered it might save a woman from rapid starvation and keep her thin for quite a time. But even this measure of relief was difficult to get. French officials are extraordinarily punctilious over the details of their work, and it takes them a long time to organize a system which is a masterpiece of safeguards and regulations and subordinate clauses. So it was with them in the first weeks of the war, and it was a pitiable thing to watch the long queues of women waiting patiently outside the *mairies*, hour after hour and sometimes day after day, to get that one franc twenty-five which would buy their children's bread. Yet the patience of these women never failed, and with a resignation which had something divine in it, they excused the delays, the official deliberations, the infinite vexations which they were made to suffer, by that phrase which has excused everything in France : " C'est la guerre ! " Because it was war, they did not raise their voices in shrill protest, or wave their skinny arms at imperturbable men who said, "Attendez, s'il vous plaît ! " with damnable iteration, or break the windows of Government offices in which bewildering regulations were drawn up in miles of red tape.

" C'est la guerre ! " and the women of Paris, thinking of their men at the front, dedicated themselves to suffering and were glad of their very hunger pains, so that they might share the hardships of the soldiers.

By good chance, a number of large-hearted men and women, more representative of the State than the Ministry in power, because they had long records of public service and united all phases of intellectual and religious activity in France, organized a system of private charity to supplement the Government doles, and under the title of the Sécours Nationale, relieved the needs of the destitute with a prompt and generous charity in which there was human love beyond the skinflint justice of the State. It was the Sécours Nationale which saved Paris in those early days from some of the worst miseries of the war and softened some of the inevitable cruelties which it inflicted upon the women and children. Their organization of *ouvroirs*, or workshops for unemployed girls, where a franc a day (not much for a long day's labour, yet better than nothing at all) saved many midinettes from sheer starvation.

There were hard times for the girls who had not been trained to needlework or to the ordinary drudgeries of life, though they toil hard enough in their own professions. To the dancing girls of Montmartre, the singing girls of the cabarets, and the love girls of the streets, Paris with the Germans at its gates was a city of desolation, so cold as they wandered with questing eyes through its loneliness, so cruel to those women of whom it has been very tolerant in days of pleasure. They were unnecessary now to the scheme of things. Their merchandise—tripping feet and rhythmic limbs, shrill laughter and roguish eyes, carmined lips and pencilled lashes, singing voices and cajoleries—had no more value, because war had taken away the men who buy these things, and the market was closed. These commodities of life were no more saleable than paste diamonds, spangles, artificial roses, the vanities of fashion showrooms, the trinkets of the jeweller in the Rue de la Paix, and the sham antiques in the Rue Mazarin. Young men, shells, hay, linen for bandages, stretchers, splints, hypodermic syringes were wanted in enormous quantities, but not light o' loves, with cheap perfume on their hair, or the fairies of the footlights with all the latest tango steps. The dance music of life had changed into a funeral march, and the alluring rhythm of the tango had been followed by the steady tramp of feet, in common time, to the battlefields of France. Virtue might have hailed it as a victory. Raising her chaste eyes, she might have cried out a prayer of thankfulness that Paris had been cleansed of all its vice, and that war had purged a people of its carnal weakness, and that the young manhood of the nation had been spiritualized and made austere. Yes, it was true. War had captured the souls and bodies of men, and under her discipline of blood and agony men's wayward fancies, the seductions of the flesh, the truancies of the heart were tamed and leashed.

Yet a Christian soul may pity those poor butterflies of life who had been broken on the wheels of war. I pitied them, unashamed of this emotion, when I saw some of them flitting through the streets of Paris on that September eve

when the city was very quiet, expecting capture, and afterwards through the long, weary weeks of war. They had a
scared look, like pretty beasts caught in a trap. They had
hungry eyes, filled with an enormous wistfulness. Their
faces were blanched, because rouge was dear when food had
to be bought without an income, and their lips had lost
their carmine flush. Outside the Taverne Royale one day
two of them spoke to me—I sat scribbling an article for
the censor to cut out. They had no cajoleries, none of
the little tricks of their trade. They spoke quite quietly and
gravely.

"Are you an Englishman ? "

"Yes."

"But not a soldier ? "

"No. You see my clothes ! "

"Have you come to Paris for pleasure ? That is strange,
for now there is nothing doing in that way."

"Non, c'est vrai. Il n'y a rien à faire dans ce
genre."

I asked them how they lived in war time.

One of the girls—she had a pretty delicate face and a
serious way of speech—smiled, with a sigh that seemed to
come from her little high-heeled boots.

"It is difficult to live. I was a singing girl at Montmartre. My lover is at the war. There is no one left. It is
the same with all of us. In a little while we shall starve to
death. *Mais, pourquoi pas ?* A singing girl's death does
not matter to France, and will not spoil the joy of her
victory ! "

She lifted a glass of *amer picon*—for the privilege of
hearing the truth she could tell me I was pleased to pay
for it—and said in a kind of whisper, " Vive la France ! "
and then, touching her glass with her lips : " Vive l'Angleterre ! "

The other girl leaned forward and spoke with polite and
earnest inquiry.

"Monsieur would like a little love ? "

I shook my head.

" Ça ne marche pas. Je suis un homme serieux."

" It is very cheap to-day," said the girl.   " Ça ne coute pas cher, en temps de guerre."

7

After the battle of the Marne the old vitality of Paris was gradually restored.   The people who had fled by hundreds of thousands dribbled back steadily from England and provincial towns where they had hated their exile and had been ashamed of their flight.   They came back to their small flats or attic room rejoicing to find all safe under a layer of dust—shedding tears, some of them, when they saw the children's toys, which had been left in a litter on the floor, and the open piano with a song on the music-rack, which a girl had left as she rose in the middle of a bar, wavering off into a cry of fear, and all the domestic treasures which had been gathered through a life of toil and abandoned—for ever it seemed—when the enemy was reported within twenty miles of Paris in irresistible strength.   The city had been saved.   The Germans were in full retreat.   The great shadow of fear had been lifted and the joy of a great hope thrilled through the soul of Paris, in spite of all that death *là-bas*, where so many young men were making sacrifices of their lives for France.

As the weeks passed the streets became more thronged, and the shops began to re-open, their business conducted for the most part by women and old people.   A great hostile army was entrenched less than sixty miles away.   A ceaseless battle, always threatening the roads to Paris, from Amiens and Soissons, Rheims and Vic-sur-Aisne, was raging night and day, month after month.   But for the moment when the enemy retreated to the Aisne, the fear which had been like a black pall over the spirit of Paris, lifted as though a great wind had blown it away, and the people revealed a sane, strong spirit of courage and confidence and patience, amazing to those who still believed in the frivolity and nervousness and unsteady emotionalism of the Parisian population.

Yet though normal life was outwardly resumed (inwardly all things had changed), it was impossible to forget the war or to thrust it away from one's imagination for more than half an hour or so of forgetfulness. Those crowds in the streets contained multitudes of soldiers of all regiments of France, coming and going between the base depots and the long lines of the front. The streets were splashed with the colours of all those uniforms—crimson of Zouaves, azure of chasseurs d'Afrique, the dark blue of gunners, marines. Figures of romance walked down the boulevards and took the sun in the gardens of the Tuileries. An Arab chief in his white burnous and flowing robes padded in soft shoes between the little crowds of cocottes who smiled into his grave face with its dark liquid eyes and pointed beard, like Othello the Moor. Senegalese and Turcos with rolling eyes and wreathed smiles sat at the tables in the Café de la Paix, paying extravagantly for their fire-water, and exalted by this luxury of life after the muddy hell of the trenches and the humid climate which made them cough consumptively between their gusts of laughter. Here and there a strange uniform of unusual gorgeousness made all men turn their heads with a " Qui est ça ? " such as the full dress uniform of a dandy flight officer of cardinal red from head to foot, with a golden wing on his sleeve. The airman of ordinary grade had no such magnificence, yet in his black leather jacket and blue breeches above long boots was the hero of the streets and might claim any woman's eyes, because he belonged to a service which holds the great romance of the war, risking his life day after day on that miracle of flight which has not yet staled in the imagination of the crowd, and winging his way god-like above the enemy's lines, in the roar of their pursuing shells.

Khaki came to Paris, too, and although it was worn by many who did not hold the King's commission but swaggered it as something in the Red Cross—God knows what !—the drab of its colour gave a thrill to all those people of Paris who, at least in the first months of the war, were stirred with an immense sentiment of gratitude because England had come to the rescue in her hour of need, and had given her blood generously to France, and had cemented the Entente Cordiale with deathless ties of comradeship.

"Comme ils sont chics, ces braves anglais ! "

They did not soon tire of expressing their admiration for the " chic " style of our young officers, so neat and clean-cut and workmanlike, with their brown belts and brown boots, and khaki riding breeches.

"Ulloh. . . . Engleesh boy ? Ahlright, eh ? "

The butterfly girls hovered about them, spread their wings before those young officers from the front and those knights of the Red Cross, tempted them with all their wiles, and led them, too many of them, to their mistress Circe, who put her spell upon them.

At every turn in the street, or under the trees of Paris, some queer little episode, some startling figure from the great drama of the war arrested the interest of a wondering spectator. A glimpse of tragedy made one's soul shudder between two smiles at the comedy of life. Tears and laughter chased each other through Paris in this time of war.

"Coupé gorge, comme ça. Sale boche, mort. Sa tête, voyez. Tombé à terre. Sang ! Mains, en bain de sang. Comme ça ! "

So the Turco spoke under the statue of Aphrodite in the gardens of the Tuileries to a crowd of smiling men and girls. He had a German officer's helmet. He described with vivid and disgusting gestures how he had cut off the man's head— he clicked his tongue to give the sound of it—and how he had bathed his hands in the blood of his enemy, before carrying this trophy to his trench. He held out his hands, staring at them, laughing at them as though they were still crimson with German blood. . . . A Frenchwoman shivered a little and turned pale. But another woman laughed—an old creature with toothless gums—with a shrill, harsh note.

"*Sale race !* " she said ; "a dirty race ! I should be glad to cut a German throat ! "

Outside the Invalides, motor-cars were always arriving at the headquarters of General Galièni. French staff officers came at full speed, with long shrieks on their motor-horns, and little crowds gathered round the cars to question the drivers.

"Ça marche, la guerre ? Il y a du progrès ? "

British officers came also, with dispatches from head-quarters, and two soldiers with loaded rifles in the back seats of cars that had been riddled with bullets and pock-marked with shrapnel.

Two of these men told their tale to me. They had left the trenches the previous night to come on a special mission to Paris, and they seemed to me like men who had been in some torture chamber and suffered unforgettable and name-less horrors. Splashed with mud, their faces powdered with a greyish clay and chilled to the bone by the sharp shrewd wind of their night near Soissons and the motor journey to Paris, they could hardly stand, and trembled and spoke with chattering teeth.

" I wouldn't have missed it," said one of them, " but I don't want to go through it again. It's absolutely infernal in those trenches, and the enemy's shell-fire breaks one's nerves."

They were not ashamed to confess the terror that still shook them, and wondered, like children, at the luck—the miracle of luck—which had summoned them from their place in the firing-line to be the escort of an officer to Paris, with safe seats in his motor-car.

8

For several weeks of the autumn while the British were at Soissons, many of our officers and men came into Paris like this, on special missions or on special leave, and along the boulevards one heard all accents of the English tongue from John o' Groats to Land's End and from Peckham Rye to Hackney Downs. The Kilties were the wonder of Paris, and their knees were under the fire of a multitude of eyes as they went swinging to the Gare du Nord The shopgirls of Paris screamed with laughter at these brawny lads in " jupes," and surrounded them with shameless mirth, while

Jock grinned from ear to ear and Sandy, more bashful, coloured to the roots of his fiery hair. Cigarettes were showered into the hands of these soldier lads. They could get drunk for nothing at the expense of English residents of Paris—the jockeys from Chantilly, the bank clerks of the Imperial Club, the bar loungers of the St. Petersbourg. The temptation was not resisted with the courage of Christian martyrs. The Provost-Marshal had to threaten some of his own military police with the terrors of court-martial.

The wounded were allowed at last to come to Paris, and the surgeons who had stood with idle hands found more than enough work to do, and the ladies of France who had put on nurses' dresses walked very softly and swiftly through long wards, no longer thrilled with the beautiful sentiment of smoothing the brows of handsome young soldiers, but thrilled by the desperate need of service, hard and ugly and terrible, among those poor bloody men, agonizing through the night, helpless in their pain, moaning before the rescue of death. The faint-hearted among these women fled panic-stricken, with blanched faces, to Nice and Monte Carlo and provincial châteaux, where they played with less unpleasant work. But there were not many like that. Most of them stayed, nerving themselves to the endurance of those tragedies, finding in the weakness of their womanhood a strange new courage, strong as steel, infinitely patient, full of pity cleansed of all false sentiment. Many of these fine ladies of France, in whose veins ran the blood of women who had gone very bravely to the guillotine, were animated by the spirit of their grandmothers and by the ghosts of French womanhood throughout the history of their country, from Geneviève to Sister Julie, and putting aside the frivolity of life which had been their only purpose, faced the filth and horrors of the hospitals without a shudder and with the virtue of nursing nuns.

Into the streets of Paris, therefore, came the convalescents and the lightly wounded, and one-armed or one-legged officers or simple *poilus* with bandaged heads and hands could be seen in any restaurant among comrades who had not yet received their baptism of fire, had not cried " Touché ! " after the bursting of a German shell.

It was worth while to spend an evening, and a louis, at Maxim's, or at Henry's, to see the company that came to dine there when the German army was still entrenched within sixty miles of Paris. They were not crowded, those places of old delight, and the gaiety had gone from them, like the laughter of fair women who have passed beyond the river. But through the swing doors came two by two, or in little groups, enough people to rob these lighted rooms of loneliness. Often it was the woman who led the man, lending him the strength of her arm. Yet when he sat at table—this young officer of the Chasseurs in sky-blue jacket, or this wounded Dragoon with a golden casque and long horse-hair tail—hiding an empty sleeve against the woman's side, or concealing the loss of a leg beneath the table cloth, it was wonderful to see the smile that lit up his face and the absence of all pain in it.

" Ah ! comme il fait bon ! "

I heard the sigh and the words come from one of these soldiers—not an officer but a fine gentleman in his private's uniform—as he looked round the room and let his brown eyes linger on the candle-lights and the twinkling glasses and snow-white table-cloths.   Out of the mud and blood of the trenches, with only the loss of an arm or a leg, he had come back to this sanctuary of civilization from which ugliness is banished and all grim realities.

So, for this reason, other soldiers came on brief trips to Paris from the front. They desired to taste the fine flavour of civilization in its ultra-refinement, to dine delicately, to have the fragrance of flowers about them, to sit in the glamour of shaded lights, to watch a woman's beauty through the haze of cigarette-smoke, and to listen to the music of her voice.   There was always a woman by the soldier's side, propping her chin in her hands and smiling into the depths of his eyes.   For the soul of a Frenchman demands the help of women, and the love of women, however strong his courage or his self-reliance. The beauty of life is to him a feminine thing, holding the spirit of motherhood, romantic love and comradeship more intimate and tender than between man and man. Only duty is masculine and hard. . . .

9

The theatres and music-halls of Paris opened one by one in the autumn of the first year of war. Some of the dancing girls and the singing girls found their old places behind the footlights, unless they had coughed their lungs away, or grown too pinched and plain. But for a long time it was impossible to recapture the old spirit of these haunts, especially in the music-halls, where ghosts passed in the darkness of deserted *promenoirs*, and where a chill gave one goose-flesh in the empty stalls.

Paris was half ashamed to go to the Folies Bergères or the Renaissance, while away *là-bas* men were lying on the battlefields or crouching in the trenches. Only when the monotony of life without amusement became intolerable to people who have to laugh so that they may not weep, did they wend their way to these places for an hour or two. Even the actors and actresses and playwrights of Paris felt the grim presence of death not far away. The old Rabelaisianism was toned down to something like decency and at least the grosser vulgarities of the music-hall stage were banned by common consent.

The little indecencies, the sly allusions, the candour of French comedy remained, and often it was only stupidity which made one laugh. Nothing on earth could have been more ridiculous than the little lady who strutted up and down the stage, in the uniform of a British Tommy, to the song of "Tipperary," which she rendered as a sentimental ballad, with dramatic action. When she lay down on her front buttons and died a dreadful death from German bullets, still singing in a feeble voice : "Good-bye, Piccadilly ; farewell, Leicester Square," there were British officers in the boxes who laughed until they wept, to the great astonishment of a French audience, who saw no humour in the exhibition.

The kilted ladies of the Olympia would have brought a blush to the cheeks of the most brazen-faced Jock from the slums of Glasgow, though they were received with great applause by respectable French bourgeois with elderly wives. And yet the soul of Paris, the big thing in its soul, the spirit which leaps out to the truth and beauty of life, was there even in Olympia, among the women with the roving eyes, and amidst all those fooleries.

Between two comic " turns " a patriotic song would come. They were not songs of false sentiment, like those patriotic ballads which thrill the gods in London, but they had a strange and terrible sincerity, not afraid of death nor of the women's broken hearts, nor of the grim realities of war, but rising to the heights of spiritual beauty in their cry to the courage of women and the pity of God. They sang of the splendours of sacrifice for France and of the glory of that young manhood which had offered its blood to the Flag. The old Roman spirit breathed through the verses of these music-hall songs, written perhaps by hungry poets *au sixième étage*, but alight with a little flame of genius. The women who sang them were artists. Every gesture was a studied thing. Every modulation of the voice was the result of training and technique. But they too were stirred with a real emotion, and as they sang something would change the audience, some thrill would stir them, some power, of old ideals, of traditions strong as natural instinct, of enthusiasm for their country of France, for whom men will gladly die and women give their heart's blood, shook them and set them on fire.

10

The people of Paris, to whom music is a necessity of life, were not altogether starved, though orchestras had been abolished in the restaurants. One day a well-known voice, terrific in its muscular energy and emotional fervour, rose like a trumpet-call in a quiet courtyard off the Rue St. Honoré. It was the voice of " Bruyant Alexandre "—" Noisy Alexander "—who had new songs to sing about the little

soldiers of France and the German vulture and the glory of the
Tricolour.   Giving part of his proceeds to the funds for the
wounded, he went from courtyard to courtyard—one could
trace his progress by vibration of tremendous sound—and
other musicians followed him, so that often when I came
up the Rue Royale or along quiet streets between the boulevards, I was tempted into the courts by the tinkle of guitars
and women's voices singing some ballad of the war with
a wonderful spirit and rhythm which set the pulses beating at
a quicker pace.   In the luncheon hour crowds of midinettes
surrounded the singers, joining sometimes in the choruses,
squealing with laughter at jests in verse not to be translated
in sober English prose and finding a little moisture in their
eyes after a song of sentiment which reminded them of the
price which must be paid for glory by young men for whose
homecoming they had waited through the winter and the
spring.

11

No German soldier came through the gates of Paris, and
no German guns smashed a way through the outer fortifications.   But now and then an enemy came over the gates and
high above the ramparts, a winged messenger of death, coming
very swiftly through the sky, killing a few mortals down below
and then retreating into the hiding-places behind the clouds.
There were not many people who saw the " Taube "—the
German dove—make its swoop and hurl its fire-balls.   There
was just a speck in the sky, a glint of metal, and the far-
humming of an aerial engine.   Perhaps it was a French
aviator coming back from a reconnaissance over the enemy's
lines on the Aisne, or taking a joy ride over Paris to stretch
his wings.   The little shop-girls looked up and thought how
fine it would be to go riding with him, as high as the stars—
with one of those keen profiled men who have such roguish
eyes when they come to earth.   Frenchmen strolling down the
boulevards glanced skywards and smiled.   They were brave
lads who defended the air of Paris.   No Boche would dare to
poke the beak of his engine above the housetops. . . . But

one or two men were uneasy and stood with strained eyes. There was something peculiar about the cut of those wings *en haut*. They seemed to bend back at the tips, unlike a Blériot, with its straight spread of canvas.

"Sapristi! une Taube! . . . Attention, mon vieux!"

In some side streets of Paris a hard thing hit the earth and opened it with a crash. A woman crossing the road with a little girl—she had just slipped out of her courtyard to buy some milk—felt the ground rise up and hit her in the face. It was very curious. Such a thing had never happened to her before. "Suzette?" She moaned and cried, "Suzette?" . . . But Suzette did not answer. The child was lying sideways, with her face against the kerbstone. Her white frock was crimsoning with a deep and spreading stain. Something had happened to one of her legs. It was broken and crumpled up, like a bird's claw.

"Suzette! Ma petite! . . . O, mon Dieu!"

A policeman was bending over little Suzette. Then he stood straight and raised a clenched fist to the sky.

"Sale Boche! . . . Assassin! . . . Sale cochon!"

People came running up the street and out of the courtyards. An ambulance glided swiftly through the crowd. A little girl whose name was Suzette was picked up from the edge of the kerbstone out of a pool of blood. Her face lay sideways on the policeman's shoulder, as white as a sculptured angel on a tombstone. It seemed that she would never walk again, this little Suzette, whose footsteps had gone dancing through the streets of Paris. It was always like that when a Taube came. That bird of death chose women and children as its prey, and Paris cursed the cowards who made war on their innocents.

But Paris was not afraid. The women did not stay indoors because between one street and another they might be struck out of life, without a second's warning. They glanced up to the sky and smiled disdainfully. They were glad even that a Taube should come now and then, so that they, the women of Paris, might run some risks in this war and share its perils with their men, who every day in the trenches *là-bas*, faced death for the sake of France. " Our chance of death is a million to one," said some of them. " We should be poor things to take fright at that ! "

12

But there were other death-ships that might come sailing through the sky on a fair night without wind or moon. The enemy tried to affright the soul of Paris by warnings of the destruction coming to them with a fleet of Zeppelins. But Paris scoffed. " Je m'en fiche de vos Zeppelins ! " said the spirit of Paris. As the weeks passed by and the months, and still no Zeppelins came, the menace became a jest. The very word of Zeppelin was heard with hilarity. There were comic articles in the newspapers, taunting the German Count who had made those gas-bags. There were also serious articles proving the impossibility of a raid by airships. They would be chased by French aviators as soon as they were sighted. They would be like the Spanish Armada, surrounded by the little English warships, pouring shot and shell into their unwieldy hulks. Not one would escape down the wind.

The police of Paris, more nervous than the public, devised a system of signals if Zeppelins were sighted. There were to be bugle-calls throughout the city, and the message they gave would mean "lights out ! " in every part of Paris. For several nights there were rehearsals of darkness, without the bugle-calls, and the city was plunged into abysmal gloom, through which people who had been dining in restaurants lost themselves in familiar streets and groped their way with little shouts of laughter as they bumped into substantial shadows.

Paris enjoyed the adventure, the thrill of romance in the mystery of darkness, the weird beauty of it. The Tuileries gardens, without a single light except the faint gleams of star-dust, was an enchanted place, with the white statues of the goddesses very vague and tremulous in the shadow world above banks of invisible flowers which drenched the still air with sweet perfumes. The narrow streets were black tunnels into which Parisians plunged with an exquisite *frisson* of romantic fear. High walls of darkness closed about them, and they gazed up to the floor of heaven from enormous gulfs. A man on a balcony *au cinquième* was smoking a cigarette, and as he drew the light made a little beacon-flame, illumining his face before dying out and leaving a blank wall of darkness. Men and women took hands like little children playing a game of bogey-man. Lovers kissed each other in this great hiding-place of Paris, where no prying eyes could see. Women's laughter, whispers, swift scampers of feet, squeals of dismay made the city murmurous. La Ville Lumière was extinguished and became an unlighted sepulchre thronged with ghosts. But the Zeppelins had not come, and in the morning Paris laughed at last night's jest and said, " C'est idiot ! "

But one night—a night in March—people who had stayed up late by their firesides, talking of their sons at the front or dozing over the *Temps*, heard a queer music in the streets below, like the horns of elf-land blowing. It came closer and louder, with a strange sing-song note in which there was something ominous.

" What is that ? " said a man sitting up in an easy-chair and looking towards a window near the Boulevard St. Germain.

The woman opposite stretched herself a little wearily.

" Some drunken soldier with a bugle. . . . Good gracious, it is one o'clock and we are not in bed ! "

The man had risen from his chair and flung the window open.

" Listen ! . . . They were to blow the bugles when the Zeppelins came. . . . Perhaps. . . ."

There were other noises rising from the streets of Paris. Whistles were blowing, very faintly, in far places. Firemen's bells were ringing, persistently.

" L'alerte ! " said the man. " The Zeppelins are coming ! "

The lamp at the street corner was suddenly extinguished, leaving absolute darkness.

" Fermez vos rideaux ! " shouted a hoarse voice.

Footsteps went hurriedly down the pavement and then were silent.

" It is nothing ! " said the woman ; " a false alarm ! "

" Listen ! "

Paris was very quiet now.   The bugle-notes were as faint as far-off bells against the wind.   But there was no wind, and the air was still.   It was still except for a peculiar vibration, a low humming note, like a great bee booming over clover fields.   It became louder and the vibration quickened, and the note was like the deep stop of an organ.   Tremendously sustained was the voice of a great engine up in the sky, invisible.   Lights were searching for it now.   Great rays, like immense white arms, stretched across the sky, trying to catch that flying thing.   They crossed each other, flying backwards and forwards, travelled softly and cautiously across the dark vault as though groping through every inch of it for that invisible danger.   The sound of guns shocked into the silence, with dull reports.   From somewhere in Paris a flame shot up, revealing in a quick flash groups of shadow figures at open windows and on flat roofs.

" Look ! " said the man who had a view across the Boulevard St. Germain.

The woman drew a deep breath.

" Yes, there is one of them ! . . . And another ! . . . How fast they travel ! "

There was a black smudge in the sky, blacker than the darkness.   It moved at a great rate, and the loud vibrations followed it.   For a moment or two, touched by one of the long rays of light it was revealed—a death-ship, white from stem to stern and crossing the sky like a streak of lightning. It went into the darkness again and its passage could only be seen now by some little flames which seemed to fall from it. They went out like French matches, sputtering before they died.

In all parts of Paris there were thousands of people watching the apparition in the sky.   On the heights of the Sacré Cœur inhabitants of Montmartre gathered and thrilled to the flashing of the searchlights and the bursting of shrapnel.

The bugle-calls bidding everybody stay indoors had brought Paris out of bed and out of doors. The most bad-tempered people in the city were those who had slept through the *alerte*, and in the morning received the news with an incredulous " Quoi ?   Non, ce n'est pas possible !   Les Zeppelins sont venus ?   Je n'ai pas entendu le moindre bruit ! "

Some houses were smashed in the outer suburbs.   A few people had been wounded in their beds.   Unexploded bombs were found in gardens and rubbish heaps.   After all, the Zeppelin raid had been a grotesque failure in the fine art of murder, and the casualty list was so light that Paris jeered at the death-ships which had come in the night.   Count Zeppelin was still the same old *blagueur*.   His precious airships were ridiculous.

A note of criticism crept into the newspapers and escaped the censor.   Where were the French aviators who had sworn to guard Paris from such a raid ?   There were unpleasant rumours that these adventurous young gentlemen had taken the night off with the ladies of their hearts.   It was stated that the telephone operator who ought to have sent the warning to them was also making *la bombe*, or sleeping away from his post.   It was beyond a doubt that certain well-known aviators had been seen in Paris restaurants until closing time. . . . Criticism was killed by an official denial from General Galièni, who defended those young gentlemen under his orders, and affirmed that each man was at the post of duty.   It was a denial which caused the scandalmongers to smile as inscrutably as Mona Lisa.

13

The shadow of war crept through every keyhole in Paris, and no man or woman shut up in a high attic with some idea or passion could keep out the evil genii which dominated the intellect and the imagination, and put its cold touch upon the senses, through that winter of agony when the best blood in France slopped into the waterlogged trenches from Flanders to the Argonne.   Yet there were coteries in Paris which thrust the Thing away from them as much as possible, and tried to pretend that art was still alive, and that philosophy was untouched by these brutalities.

In the Restaurant des Beaux-Arts and other *boîtes* where men of ideas pander to the baser appetites for 1 franc 50 (*vin compris*), old artists, old actors, sculptors whose beards seemed powdered with the dust of their *ateliers,* and *littérateurs* who will write you a sonnet or an epitaph, a wedding speech, or a political manifesto in the finest style of French poesy and prose (a little archaic in expression) assembled nightly just as in the days of peace. Some of the youngest faces who used to be grouped about the tables had gone, and now and then there was silence for a second as one of the habitués would raise his glass to the memory of a soldier of France (called to the colours on that fatal day in August) who had fallen on the Field of Honour. The ghost of war stalked even into the Restaurant des Beaux-Arts, but his presence was ignored as much as might be by these long-haired Bohemians with grease-stained clothes and unwashed hands who discussed the spirit of Greek beauty, the essential viciousness of women, the vulgarity of the bourgeoisie, the prose of Anatole France, the humour of Rabelais and his successors, and other eternal controversies with a pretext of their old fire. If the theme of war slipped in it was discussed with an intellectual contempt, and loose-lipped old men found a frightful mirth in the cut-throat exploits of Moroccans and Senegalese, in the bestial orgies of drunken Boches, and in the most revolting horrors of bayonet charges and the *corps-à-corps*. It was as though they wanted to reveal the savagery of war to the last indescribable madness of its lust.

" Pah ! " said an old *cabotin,* after one of these word-pictures. " This war is the last spasm of the world's barbarity. Human nature will finish with it this time. . . . Let us talk of the women we have loved. I knew a splendid creature once—she had golden hair, I remember——"

One of these shabby old gentlemen touched me on the arm.

" Would Monsieur care to have a little music ? It is

quite close here, and very beautiful. It helps one to forget the war, and all its misery."

I accepted the invitation. I was more thirsty for music than for vin ordinaire or cordiale Médoc. Yet I did not expect very much round the corner of a restaurant frequented by shabby intellectuals. . . . That was my English stupidity.

A little group of us went through a dark courtyard lit by a high dim lantern, touching a sculptured figure in a far recess.

" Pas de bruit," whispered a voice through the gloom.

Up four flights of wooden stairs we came to the door of a flat which was opened by a bearded man holding a lamp.

" Soyez les bienvenus ! " he said, with a strongly foreign accent.

It was queer, the contrast between the beauty of his salon into which we went and the crudeness of the restaurant from which we had come. It was a long room, with black wall-paper, and at the far end of it was a shaded lamp on a grand piano. There was no other light, and the faces of the people in the room, the head of a Greek god on a pedestal, some little sculptured figures on an oak table, and some portrait studies on the walls, were dim and vague until my eyes became accustomed to this yellowish twilight. No word was spoken as we entered, and took a chair if we could find one. None of the company here seemed surprised at this entry of strangers—for two of us were that—or even conscious of it. A tall, clean-shaven young man with a fine, grave face—certainly not French—was playing the violin, superbly ; I could not see the man at the piano who touched the keys with such tenderness. Opposite me was another young man, with the curly hair and long, thin face of a Greek faun nursing a violoncello, and listening with a dream in his eyes. A woman with the beauty of some northern race sat in an oak chair with carved arms, which she clasped tightly. I saw the sparkle of a ring on her right hand. The stone had caught a ray from the lamp and was alive with light. Other people with strange, interesting faces were grouped about this salon, absorbed in that music of the violin, which played something of spring, so lightly, so delicately, that our spirit danced to it, and joy came into one's senses as on a sunlit day, when the wind is playing above fields of flowers. Afterwards the 'cellist drew long, deep chords from his great instrument, and his thin fingers quivered against the thick strings, and made them sing grandly and nobly. Then the man at the piano played alone, after five minutes of silence, in which a few words were spoken, about some theme which would work out with strange effects.

"I will try it," said the pianist. "It amuses me to improvise. If it would not worry you——"

It was not wearisome. He played with a master-touch, and the room was filled with rushing notes and crashing harmonies. For a little time I could not guess the meaning of their theme. Then suddenly I was aware of it. It was the tramp of arms, the roar of battle, the song of victory and of death. Wailing voices came across fields of darkness, and then, with the dawn, birds sang, while the dead lay still.

The musician gave a queer laugh.

"Any good ? "

"C'est la guerre ! " said a girl by my side. She shivered a little.

They were Danes, Norwegians, and Swedes in that room, with a few Parisians among them. Students to whom all life is expressed in music, they went on with their work in spite of the war. But war had touched their spirit too, with its great tragedy, and found expression in their art. It was but one glimpse behind the scenes of Paris, in time of war, and in thousands of other rooms, whose window-curtains were drawn to veil their light from hostile aircraft, the people who come to Paris as the great university of intellect and emotion, continued their studies and their way of life, with vibrations of fiddle-strings and scraping of palettes and adventures among books.

Even the artists' clubs had not all closed their doors,

though so many young painters were mixing blood with mud and watching impressionistic pictures of ruined villages through the smoke of shells. Through cigarette smoke I gazed at the oddest crowd in one of these clubs off the Boulevard Saint-Germain. Slavs with matted hair, American girls in Futurist frocks, Italians like figures out of pre-Raphaelite frescoes, men with monkey faces and monkey manners, men with the faces of mediæval saints a little debauched by devilish temptations, filled the long bare room, spoke in strange tongues to each other, and made love passionately in the universal language and in dark corners provided with ragged divans. A dwarf creature perched on a piano stool teased the keys of an untuned piano and drew forth adorable melody, skipping the broken notes with great agility. . . . It was the same old Paris, even in time of war.

14

The artists of neutral countries who still kept to their lodgings in the Quartier Latin and fanned the little flame of inspiration which kept them warm though fuel is dear, could not get any publicity for their works. There was no autumn or spring salon in the Palais des Beaux-Arts, where every year till war came one might watch the progress of French art according to the latest impulse of the time stirring the emotions of men and women who claim the fullest liberties even for their foolishness. War had killed the Cubists, and many of the Futurists had gone to the front to see the odd effects of scarlet blood on green grass. The Grand Palais was closed to the public. Yet there were war pictures here, behind closed doors, and sculpture stranger than anything conceived by Marinetti. I went to see the show, and when I came out again into the sunlight of the gardens, I felt very cold, and there was a queer trembling in my limbs.

The living pictures and the moving statuary in the Grand Palais exhibited the fine arts of war as they are practised by civilized men using explosive shells, with bombs, shrapnel, hand-grenades, mitrailleuses, trench-mines, and other ingenious instruments by which the ordinary designs of God may be re-drawn and re-shaped to suit the modern tastes of men. I saw here the Spring Exhibition of the Great War, as it is catalogued by surgeons, doctors, and scientific experts in wounds and nerve diseases.

It was not a pretty sight, and the only thing that redeemed its ugliness was the way in which all those medical men were devoting themselves to the almost hopeless task of untwisting the contorted limbs of those victims of the war spirit, and restoring the shape of man botched by the artists of the death machines.

In the Great Hall through which in the days of peace pretty women used to wander with raised eyebrows and little cries of " Ciel ! " (even French women revolted against the most advanced among the Futurists), there was a number of extraordinary contrivances of a mechanical kind which shocked one's imagination, and they were being used by French soldiers in various uniforms and of various grades, with twisted limbs, and paralytic gestures. One young man, who might have been a cavalry officer, was riding a queer bicycle which never moved off its pedestal, though its wheels revolved to the efforts of its rider. He pedalled earnestly and industriously, though obviously his legs had stiffened muscles, so that every movement gave him pain. Another man, " bearded like the pard," sat with his back to the wall clutching at two rings suspended from a machine and connected with two weights. Monotonously and with utterly expressionless eyes, he raised and lowered his arms a few inches or so, in order to bring back their vitality, which had been destroyed by a nervous shock. Many wheels were turning in that great room and men were strapped to them, as though in some torture chamber, devilishly contrived. In this place, however, the work was to defeat the cruelties of War the Torturer, after it had done its worst with human flesh.

The worst was in other rooms, where poor wrecks of men lay face downwards in hot-air boxes, where they stayed

immovable and silent as though in their coffins, or with half
their bodies submerged in electrolysed baths. Nurses were
massaging limbs which had been maimed and smashed by
shell-fire, and working with fine and delicate patience at the
rigid fingers of soldiers, some of whom had lost their other
arms, so that unless they could use their last remaining
fingers, three or four to a hand, they would be useless for any
work in the world. But most pitiable of all were the long
rows of the paralysed and the blind, who lay in the hospital
ward, motionless and sightless, with smashed faces. In
the Palace of Fine Arts this statuary might have made the
stones weep.

15

At last the spring song sounded through the streets of
Paris with a pagan joy.

There was a blue sky over the city—so clear and cloudless
that if any Zeppelin came before the night, it would have
been seen a mile high, as a silver ship, translucent from stem
to stern, sailing in an azure sea. One would not be scared
by one of these death-ships on such a day as this, nor believe,
until the crash came, that it would drop down destruction
upon this dream city, all aglitter in gold and white, with all
its towers and spires clean-cut against the sky.

It was hard to think of death and war ; because spring
had come with its promise of life. There was a thrill of new
vitality throughout the city. I seemed to hear the sap rising
in the trees along the boulevards. Or was it only the wind
plucking at invisible harp-strings, or visible telephone wires,
and playing the spring song in Parisian ears ?

In the Tuileries gardens, glancing aslant the trees, I
saw the first green of the year, as the buds were burgeoning and
breaking into tiny leaves. The white statues of goddesses
—a little crumbled and weather-stained after the winter—
were bathed in a pale sunshine. Psyche stretched out her
arms, still half-asleep, but waking at the call of spring.
Pomona offered her fruit to a young student, who gazed at
her with his black hat pushed to the back of his pale forehead.

Womanhood, with all her beauty carved in stone, in laughing and tragic moods, in the first grace of girlhood, and in full maturity, stood poised here in the gardens of the Tuileries, and seemed alive and vibrant with this new thrill of life which was pulsing in the moist earth and whispering through the trees, because spring had come to Paris.

There was no doubt about it. The flower girls who had been early to les Halles came up the rue Royale one morning with baskets full of violets, so that all the street was perfumed as though great ladies were passing and wafting scent in their wake.   Even the old *cocher* who drove me down the rue Cambon had put on a new white hat.   He had heard the glad tidings, this old wrinkled man, and he clacked his whip to let others know, and gave the glad-eye—a watery, wicked old eye—to half a dozen midinettes who came dancing along the rue St. Honoré.   They knew without his white hat, and the clack of his whip.   The *ichor* of the air had got into their blood.   They laughed without the reason for a jest, and ran, in a skipping way, because there was the spring-song in their feet.

Along the Champs Élysées there was the pathway of the sun.   Through the Arc de Triomphe there was a glamorous curtain of cloth of gold, and arrows of light struck and broke upon the golden figures of Alexander's Bridge.   Looking back I saw the dome of the Invalides suspended in space, like a cloud in the sky.   It was painted over to baffle the way of hostile aircraft, but the paint was wearing off, and the gold showed through again, glinting and flashing in the air-waves.

The Seine was like molten liquid and the bridges which span it a dozen times or more between Notre Dame and the Pont de l'Alma were as white as snow, and unsubstantial as though they bridged the gulfs of dreams.   Even the great blocks of stone and the balks of timber which lie on the mud banks below the Quai d'Orsay—it is where the bodies of suicides float up and bring new tenants to the Morgue— were touched with the beauty of this lady day, and invited an artist's brush.

The Eiffel Tower hung a cobweb in the sky. Its wires had been thrilling to the secrets of war, and this signal station was barricaded so that no citizens might go near, or pass the sentries pacing there with loaded rifles. But now it was receiving other messages, not of war. The wireless operator with the receiver at his ears must have heard those whispers coming from the earth: "I am spring. . . . The earth is waking. . . . I am coming with the beauty of life. . . . I am gladness and youth. . . ."

Perhaps even the sentry pacing up and down the wooden barricade heard the approach of some unseen presence when he stood still that morning and peered through the morning sunlight. "Halt! who goes there?" . . . "A friend." . . . "Pass, friend, and give the countersign."

The countersign was "Spring," and where the spirit of it stepped, golden crocuses had thrust up through the warming earth, not far from where, a night or two before, fire-balls dropped from a hostile air-craft.

Oh, strange and tragic spring, of this year 1915! Was it possible that, while Nature was preparing her beauty for the earth, and was busy in the ways of life, men should be heaping her fields with death, and drenching this fair earth with blood?

· One could not forget. Even in Paris away from the sound of the guns which had roared in my ears a week before, and away from the moan of the wounded which had made my ears ache worse than the noise of battle, I could not forget the tragedy of all this death which was being piled up under the blue sky, and on fields all astir with the life of the year.

In the Tuileries gardens the buds were green. But there were black figures below them. The women who sat there all the afternoon, sewing, and knitting, or with idle hands in their laps, were clothed in widows' black. I glanced into the face of one of these figures as I passed. She was quite a girl to whom the spring-song should have called with a loud, clear note of joy. But her head drooped and her eyes were steadfast as they stared at the pathway, and the sunshine brought no colour into her white cheeks. . . . She shivered a little, and pulled her crêpe veil closer about her face.

Down the broad pathway between the white statues came a procession of cripples. They wore the uniforms of the French army, and were mostly young men in the prime of life, to whom also the spring should have brought a sense of vital joy, of intense and energetic life. But they dragged between their crutches while their lopped limbs hung free. A little further off in a patch of sunshine beyond the wall of the Jeu de Paumes, sat half a dozen soldiers of France with loose sleeves pinned to their coats, or with only one leg to rest upon the ground. One of them was blind and sat there with his face to the sun, staring towards the fountain of the nymphs with sightless eyes. Those six comrades of war were quite silent, and did not "fight their battles o'er again." Perhaps they were sad because they heard the spring-song, and knew that they could never step out again to the dance-tune of youth.

And yet, strangely, there was more gladness than sadness in Paris now that spring had come, in spite of the women in black, and the cripples in the gardens. Once again it brought the promise of life. "Now that the spring is here," said the old cab-driver in the white hat, "France will soon be free and the war will soon be over."

This hopefulness that the fine weather would end the war quickly was a splendid superstition which buoyed up many hearts in France. Through the long, wet months of winter the women and the old people had agonized over the misery of their soldiers in the trenches. Now that the earth was drying again, and the rain clouds were vanishing behind a blue sky, there was new hope, and a wonderful optimism in the spirit of the people. "The spring will bring victory to France" was an article of faith which comforted the soul of the little midinette who sang on her way to the Rue Lafayette, and the French soldier who found a wild flower growing in his trench.

16

I have written many words about the spirit of Paris in war. Yet all these little glimpses I have given reveal only the trivial characteristics of the city. Through all these episodes and outward facts, rising above them to a great height of spirituality, the soul of Paris was a white fire burning with a steady flame. I cannot describe the effect of it upon one's senses and imagination. I was only conscious of it, so that again and again, in the midst of the crowded boulevards, or in the dim aisles of Notre Dame, or wandering along the left bank of the Seine, I used to say to myself, silently or aloud : " These people are wonderful ! . . . They hold the spirit of an unconquerable race. . . . Nothing can smash this city of intellect, so gay, and yet so patient in suffering, so emotional and yet so stoical in pride and courage ! " There was weakness, and vanity, in Paris. The war had not cleansed it of all its vice or of all its corruption, but this burning wind of love for *La Patrie* touched the heart of every man and woman, and inflamed them so that self-interest was almost consumed, and sacrifice for the sake of France became a natural instinct. The ugliest old hag in the markets shared this love with the most beautiful woman of the salons ; the demi-mondaine with her rouged lips, knelt in spirit, like Mary Magdalene before the cross, and was glad to suffer for the sake of a pure and uncarnal love, symbolized to her by the folds of the Tricolour or by the magic of that word, " La France ! " which thrilled her soul, smirched by the traffic of the streets. The most money-loving bourgeois, who had counted every sou and cheated every other one, was lifted out of his meanness and materialism and did astounding things, without a murmur, abandoning his business to go back to the colours as a soldier of France, and regarding the ruin of a life's ambitions without a heartache so that France might be free. There were *embusqués* in Paris—perhaps hundreds, or even thousands of young men who searched for soft jobs which would never take them to the firing-line, or who pleaded ill-health with the successful influence of a family or political " pull." Let that be put down honestly, because nothing matters save the truth. But the manhood of Paris as a whole, after the first shudder of dismay, the first agonies of this wrench from the safe, familiar ways of life, rose superbly to the call of *la Patrie en danger !* The middle-aged fathers of families and the younger sons marched away singing and hiding their sadness under a mask of careless mirth. The boys of eighteen followed them in the month of April, after nine months of war, and not a voice in Paris was raised to protest against this last and dreadful sacrifice. Paris cursed the stupidity of the war, cried " How long, O Lord, how long ? " as it dragged on in its misery, with accumulating sums of death, was faint at the thought of another winter campaign, and groaned in spirit when its streets were filled with wounded men and black-garbed women. But though Paris suffered with the finer agonies of the sensitive intelligence, it did not lose faith or courage, and found the heart to laugh sometimes, in spite of all its tears.

City of beauty, built out of the dreams of great artists and great poets, I have watched you through this time of war, walking through your silent streets in the ordeal of most dreadful days, mingling with your crowds when a multitude of cripples dragged their lopped limbs through the sunlight, studying your moods of depression, and hopefulness, and passionate fervour, wandering in your churches, your theatres and your hospitals, and lingering on mild nights under the star-strewn sky which made a vague glamour above your darkness ; and always my heart has paid a homage to the spirit which after a thousand years of history and a thousand million crimes, still holds the fresh virtue of ardent youth, the courage of a gallant race, and a deathless faith in the fine, sweet, gentle things of art and life. The Germans, however great their army, could never have captured the soul of Paris.

CHAPTER IX

THE SOLDIERS OF FRANCE

1

WHEN in the first days of the war I saw the soldiers of France on their way to the front, I had even then a conviction that the fighting qualities of the nation had not degenerated in forty-four years of peace, after the downfall in which the courage of the men had been betrayed by the corruption of a Government. Afterwards, during many months as a wanderer in this war, I came to know the French soldier with the intimacy of long conversations to the sound of guns, in the first line of trenches facing the enemy, in hospitals, where he spoke quietly while comrades snored themselves to death, in villages smashed to pieces by shell-fire, in troop trains overcrowded with wounded, in woods and fields pock-marked by the holes of *marmites*, and in the restaurants of Paris and provincial towns where, with an empty sleeve or one trouser-leg dangling beneath the tablecloth, he told me his experiences of war with a candour in which there was no concealment of truth ; and out of all these friendships and revelations of soul the character of the soldiers of France stands before my mind in heroic colours.

Individually, of course, the qualities of these men differ as one man from another in any nation or class. I have seen the neurasthenic, quivering with agony in his distress of imaginary terrors, and the man with steady nerves, who can turn a deaf ear to the close roar of guns and eat a hunk of bread-and-cheese with an unspoilt appetite within a yard or two of death ; I have seen the temperament of the aristocrat and the snob in the same carriage with the sons of the soil and the factory whose coarse speech and easy-going manners jarred upon his daintiness. War does not entirely anni-hilate all distinctions of caste even in France, where Equality is a good word, and it does not blend all intellectual and moral qualities into one type of character, in spite of the discipline of compulsory service and the chemical processes which mix flesh and blood together in the crucible of a battle-field. So it is impossible to write of the French soldier as a single figure, or to make large generalizations about the armies of France. The coward skulks by the side of the war. The priestly spirit in the ranks is outraged by the obscenities of the debauchee.

Yet out of those great masses of men who have fought for France there does emerge a certain definite character overwhelming the details of their individual differences, and I have seen certain qualities of temperament which belong to the majority of them, as essential elements of the national spirit of France. The quality of their patriotism, for example, shines very clear above all these millions of men who have abandoned all their small self-interests for the supreme purpose of defending France. England has her patriotism—we give a great proof of it in blood—but it is not like that of France, not so religious in its sentiment, not so passionate in its convictions, not so feminine a thing. To most of these French soldiers, indeed to all that I have talked with, the love of France is like the faith of a devout Catholic in his church. It is not to be argued about. It holds the very truth of life. It enshrines all the beauty of French ideals, all the rich colour of imagination, all the poetry and music that has thrilled through France-since the beginning of our civilization, all her agonies and tears. To the commonest soldier of France, "La Patrie" is his great mother, with the tenderness of motherhood, the authority of motherhood, the sanctity of motherhood, as to a Catholic the Blessed Virgin is the mother of his soul. Perhaps as one of her children he has been hardly dealt with, has starved and struggled and received many whippings, but he does not lose his mother-love. The thought of outrageous hands plucking at her garments, of hostile feet trampling upon her, of foul attempts upon her liberty and honour, stirs him to just that madness he would feel if his individual mother, out of whose womb he came, were threatened in the same way. He does not like death—he dreads the thought of it—but without questioning his soul he springs forward to save this mother-country of his and dies upon her bosom with a cry of " Vive la France ! "

2

The French soldier, whatever his coarseness or his delicacy, needs feminine consolation, and all his ideals and his yearnings and his self-pity are intimately associated with the love of women, and especially of one woman—his mother. When Napoleon, in the island of St. Helena, used to talk about the glories of his victorious years, and then brooded over the tragedy of his overthrow so that all his soul was clouded with despair, he used to rouse himself after the silence which followed those hours of self-analysis and say, " Let us talk about women—and love." Always it is the feminine spirit in which a Frenchman bathes his wounds. One small incident I saw a year or two ago gave me the clue to this quality in the French character. It was when Védrines, the famous airman, was beaten by only a few minutes in the flight round England. Capitaine Conneau—" Beaumont," as he called himself—had outraced his rival and waited, with French gallantry, to shake the hand of the adversary he had defeated on untiring wings. A great crowd of smart men and women waited also at Brooklands to cheer the second in the race, who in England is always more popular than the prize-winner. But when Védrines came to earth out of a blue sky he was savage and bitter. The loss of the prize-money was a great tragedy to this mechanic who had staked all his ambition on the flight. He shouted out harsh words to those who came to cheer him, and shook them off violently when they tried to clap him on the back. He was savagely angry. Then suddenly something seemed to break in his spirit, and his face quivered.

" Is there any woman to embrace me ? " he asked. Out

of the crowd came a pretty Frenchwoman and, understanding the man, though she had not met him before, she held out her arms to him and raised her face.

" Allons-donc, mon vieux ! " she said.

The man put his arms about her and kissed her, while tears streamed down his face, covered in sweat and dust. He was comforted, like a boy who had hurt himself, in his mother's arms. It was a queer little episode—utterly impossible in the imagination of an Englishman—but a natural thing in France.

So when a Frenchman lies dying, almost unconscious before the last breath, it is always a woman's name that he cries out, or whispers, though not always the name of his wife or mistress.   One word is heard again and again in the hospital wards, where the *poilus* lie, those bearded fellows, so strong when they went out to the war, but now so weak and helpless before death.

" Maman !   Maman ! "

It is to the bosom of motherhood that the spirit of the Frenchman goes in that last hour

" Oh, my dear little mamma," writes a young lieutenant of artillery, " it would be nice to be in my own room again, where your picture hangs over my bed looking down on the white pillows upon which you used to make the sign of the Cross before I went to sleep.   I often try to dream myself into that bedroom again, but the cold is too intense for dreams, and another shell comes shrieking overhead.   War is nothing but misery, after all."

8

Yet if any English reader imagines that because this thread of sentiment runs through the character of France there is a softness in the qualities of French soldiers, he does not know the truth.   Those men whom I saw at the front and behind the fighting lines were as hard in moral and spiritual strength as in physical endurance.   It was this very hardness which impressed me even in the beginning of the war, when I did not know the soldiers of France as well as I do now.

After a few weeks in the field these men, who had been labourers and mechanics, clerks and journalists, artists and poets, shop assistants and railway porters, hotel waiters, and young aristocrats of Paris who had played the fool with pretty girls, were fined down to the quality of tempered steel. With not a spare ounce of flesh on them—the rations of the French army are not as rich as ours—and tested by long marches down dusty roads, by incessant fighting in retreat against overwhelming odds, by the moral torture of those rearguard actions, and by their first experience of indescribable horrors, among dead and dying comrades, they had a beauty of manhood which I found sublime. They were bronzed and dirty and hairy, but they had the look of knighthood, with a calm light shining in their eyes and with resolute lips. They had no gaiety in those days, when France was in gravest peril, and they did not find any kind of fun in this war. Out of their baptism of fire they had come with scorched souls, knowing the murderous quality of the business to which they were apprenticed; but though they did not hide their loathing of it, nor the fears which had assailed them, nor their passionate anger against the people who had thrust this thing upon them, they showed no sign of weakness. They were willing to die for France, though they hated death, and in spite of the first great rush of the German legions, they had a fine intellectual contempt of that army, which seemed to me then unjustified, though they were right, as history now shows. Man against man, in courage and cunning they were better than the Germans, gun against gun they were better, in cavalry charge and in bayonet charge they were better, and in equal number irresistible.

There was in England a hidden conviction, expressed privately in clubs and by women over their knitting, that the French soldiers were poor fellows as fighting men, filled with sentimentality, full of brag, with fine words on their lips, but with no strength of courage or endurance. British soldiers coming back wounded from the first battles and a three weeks' rearguard action, spread abroad the tale that

" those French fellows were utterly useless and had run like rabbits before the German advance." They knew nothing but what they' had seen in their own ditches on the fighting ground, they were sick with horror at the monstrous character of the war, and they had a rankling grudge against the French because they had not been supported strongly enough during those weeks in August between Charleroi and Compiègne. Later the English Press, anxious, naturally enough, to throw into high relief the exploits of our own troops in France, and getting only scraps of news from the French lines, gave a distorted view of the general situation, and threw the whole picture of the war out of perspective, like the image of a man in a convex mirror. The relative importance of the British Expedition was vastly exaggerated, not because its particular importance was over-estimated, but because the French operations received very scant notice. There are still people in England who believe with a pious and passionate faith that our soldiers sustained the entire and continual attack of the German army, while the French looked on and thanked God for our work of rescue. The fact that we only held a front of thirty miles, at most, during the first nine months of war, and that the French were successfully holding a line of five hundred miles through which the Germans were trying to smash their way by repeated attacks of ferocious character, never took hold of the imagination of many honest souls at home, who thrilled with patriotic pride at the heroism of the British troops, according to the old tradition of " How England saved Europe."

4

Well, nothing will ever minimise our services to France. The graves of our men will stand as records of the help we gave, paying our debt of honour with priceless blood. But England must know what France did in self-defence and understand the fine enduring heroism of those armies of France which, after the first mistakes, built a wall of steel against which the greatest fighting machine in Europe shattered itself in vain.

Not a mile along all that five hundred miles of front was without its battle, and not a mile there but is the grave of young Frenchmen who fought with a martyr's faith and recklessness of life. As far back as the last days of September 1914 I met men of the eastern frontier who had a right already to call themselves veterans because they had been fighting continuously for two months in innumerable engagements—for the most part unrecorded in the public Press.

At the outset they were smart fellows, clean-shaven and even spruce in their new blue coats and scarlet trousers. Now the war had put its dirt upon them and seemed to have aged them by fifteen years, leaving its ineffaceable imprint upon their faces. They had stubble beards upon their chins, and their cheeks were sunken and hollow, after short rations in the trenches and sleepless nights on the battlefields, with death as their bedfellow. Their blue coats had changed to a dusty grey. Their scarlet trousers had deep patches of crimson, where the blood of comrades had splashed them. They were tattered and torn and foul with the muck and slime of their frontier work. But they were also hard and tough for the most part—though here and there a man coughed wheezily with bronchitis or had the pallor of excessive fatigue—and Napoleon would not have wished for better fighting-men.

In the wooded country of the two " Lost Provinces " there was but little time or chance to bury the dead encumbering the hills and fields. Even six weeks after the beginning of the war horror made a camping ground of the regions which lay to the east of the Meurthe, between the villages of Blamont and Badonviller, Cirey les Forges and Arracourt, Chateau Salins and Baudrécourt. The slopes of Hartmansweilerkopf were already washed by waves of blood which surged round it for nine months and more, until its final capture by the French. St. Mihiel and Les Eparges and the triangle which the Germans had wedged between the French lines were a shambles before the leaves had fallen from the autumn trees in the first year of war. In the country of the Argonne men fought like wolves and began a guerilla warfare with smaller bodies of men, fighting from wood to wood, from village to village, the forces on each side being scattered over a wide area in advance of their main lines.   Then they dug themselves into trenches from which they came out at night, creeping up to each other's lines, flinging themselves upon each other with bayonets and butt-ends, killing each other as beasts kill, without pity and in the mad rage of terror which is the fiercest kind of courage.   In Lorraine the tide of war ebbed and flowed over the same tracts of ground, and neither side picked up its dead or its wounded.   Men lay there alive for days and nights, bleeding slowly to death.   The hot sun glared down upon them and made them mad with thirst, so that they drank their own urine and jabbered in wild delirium.   Some of them lay there for as long as three weeks, still alive, with gangrened limbs in which lice crawled, so that they stank abominably.

"I cannot tell you all the things I saw," said one of the young soldiers who talked to me on his way back from Lorraine.   He had a queer look in his eyes when he spoke those words which he tried to hide from me by turning his head away.   But he told me how the fields were littered with dead, decomposing and swarmed with flies, lying here in huddled postures, yet some of them so placed that their fixed eyes seemed to be staring at the corpses near them. And he told me how on the night he had his own wound French and German soldiers not yet dead talked together by light of the moon, which shed its pale light upon all those prostrate men, making their faces look very white.   He heard the murmurs of voices about him, and the groans of the dying, rising to hideous anguish as men were tortured by ghastly wounds and broken limbs.   In that night enmity was forgotten by those who had fought like beasts and now lay together.   A French soldier gave his water-bottle to a German officer who was crying out with thirst.   The German sipped a little and then kissed the hand of the man who had been his enemy.   "There will be no war on the other side," he said.

Another Frenchman—who came from Montmartre—found lying within a yard of him a Luxembourgeois whom he had known as his *chasseur* in a big hotel in Paris. The young German wept to see his old acquaintance. " It is stupid," he said, " this war. You and I were happy when we were good friends in Paris. Why should we have been made to fight with each other ? " He died with his arms round the neck of the soldier who told me the story, unashamed of his own tears.

Round this man's neck also were clasped the arms of a German officer when a week previously the French *pioupiou* went across the field of a battle—one of the innumerable skirmishes—which had been fought and won four days before another French retirement. The young German had had both legs broken by a shell, and was wounded in other places. He had strength enough to groan piteously, but when my friend lifted him up death was near to him.

" He was all rotten," said the soldier, " and there came such a terrible stench from him that I nearly dropped him, and vomited as I carried him along."

I learnt something of the psychology of the French soldier from this young infantryman with whom I travelled in a train full of wounded soon after that night in Lorraine, when the moon had looked down on the field of the dead and dying in which he lay with a broken leg. He had passed through a great ordeal, so that his nerves were still torn and quivering, and I think he was afraid of going mad at the memory of the things he had seen and suffered, because he tried to compel himself to talk of trivial things, such as the beauty of the flowers growing on the railway banks and the different badges on English uniforms. But suddenly he would go back to the tale of his fighting in Lorraine and resume a long and rapid monologue in which little pictures of horror flashed after each other as though his brain were a cinematograph recording some melodrama. Queer bits of philosophy jerked out between this narrative. " This war is only endurable because it is for a final peace in Europe." " Men will refuse to suffer these things again. It is the end of militarism." " If I thought that a child of mine would have to go through all that I have suffered during these last weeks, I would strangle him in his cradle to save him from it."

Sometimes he spoke of France with a kind of religion in his eyes.

" Of course, I am ready to die for France. She can demand my life as a right. I belong to her and she can do with me what she likes. It's my duty to fight in her defence, and although I tell you all the worst of war, monsieur, I do not mean that I am not glad to have done my part. In a few weeks this wound of mine will be healed and I shall go back, for the sake of France, to that Hell again. It is Hell, *quand même* ! "

He analysed his fears with simple candour and confessed' that many times he had suffered most from imaginary terrors. After the German retreat from Lunéville, he was put on a chain of outposts linked up with the main French lines. It was at night, and as he stood leaning on his rifle he saw black figures moving towards him. He raised his rifle, and his finger trembled on the trigger. At the first shot he would arouse the battalion nearest to him. They were sleeping, but as men sleep who may be suddenly attacked. They would fire without further question, and probably he would be the first to die from their bullets. Was it the enemy ? They were coming at right angles to the French lines. The foremost were even within twenty yards of him now. His nerves were all trembling. He broke out into a hot sweat. His eyes straining through the darkness were shot through with pain. He had almost an irresistible desire to fire and shout out, so as to end the strain of suspense which racked his soul. At last he gave the challenge, restraining himself from firing that first shot. It was well he did so. For the advancing French troops belonged to a French regiment changing their position under cover of darkness. If my little friend had lost his nerve and fired too soon they would have been shot down by their own comrades.

" It's one's imagination that gives one most trouble," he said, and I thought of the words of an English officer, who

told me one day that " No one with an imagination ought to
come out to this war." It is for that reason—the possession
of a highly developed imagination—that so many French
soldiers have suffered more acutely than their English allies.
They see the risks of war more vividly, though they take them
with great valour. They are more sensitive to the sights and
sounds of the fighting lines than the average English
" Tommy," who has a tougher temperament and does not
allow his mind to brood over blood and agony. They have
the gift, also, of self-analysis and self-expression, so that
they are able to translate their emotions into vivid words,
whereas our own men are taciturn for the most part about
their side of the business and talk objectively, looking outwards, and not inwards.

5

Some of the letters from French soldiers, scrawled in the
squalor of the trenches by men caked in filth and mud, are
human documents in which they reveal themselves with
extraordinary intimacy, and in which they put the whole
truth, not disguising their terror or their blood-lust in the
savage madness of a bayonet charge, or the heartache which
comes to them when they think of the woman they love, or
the queer little emotions and sentiments which come to them
in the grim business of war. They watch the dawn, and in a
line or two put some of its beauty into their letters home.
They describe with a literary skill that comes from strong
emotions the gloom and horror of long nights near the
enemy's trenches from which at any moment a new attack
may come. And yet, though they do not hide their moments
of spiritual misery or despair, there is in all these letters the
splendid courage of men who are ready for the last sacrifice
and eager for their chance of honour.

" I send this letter," writes a young Zouave, " as I sit
huddled under an earth-heap at twenty yards from a German
trench, less to be envied than a rabbit in its burrow, because
when the hunter is far away it can come out and feed at
pleasure. You who live through the same agonies, old friend,

must learn and rejoice that I have been promoted adjutant on the night of November 13 on the banks of the Yser. There were seventy men out of 250—the rest of the company sleep for ever round that ferryman's house which the papers have made famous. . . . What moral sufferings I have endured! We have now been brought to the south of Ypres and continue this depressing life in advanced trenches. Not a quarter of an hour's respite : shells, shrapnels, bombs and bullets fall around us continuously. How courage has changed with this modern war! The hero of olden times was of a special type, who put on a fine pose and played up to the gallery because he fought before admiring spectators. Now, apart from our night attacks, always murderous, in which courage is not to be seen, because one can hardly discern one's neighbour in the darkness, our valour consists in a perfect stoicism. Just now I had a fellow killed before a loophole His comrades dragged him away, and with perfect quietude replaced the man who is eternally out of action. Isn't that courage? Isn't it courage to get the brains of one's comrade full in the face, and then to stand on guard in the same place while suffering the extremes of cold and dampness? . . . On the night of the 13th I commanded a section of corpses which a mitrailleuse had raked. I had the luck to escape, and I shouted to these poor devils to make a last assault. Then I saw what had happened and found myself with a broken rifle and a uniform in rags and tatters. My commandant spoke to me that night, and said : ' You had better change those clothes. You can put on an adjutant's stripes.' "

One passage in this young Zouave's letter reveals the full misery of the war to a Frenchman's spirit : " Our courage consists in a perfect stoicism." It is not the kind of courage which suits his temperament, and to sit in a trench for months, inactive, waiting for death under the rain of shells, is the worst ordeal to which the soul of the French soldier is asked to submit. Yet he has submitted, and held firm, along lines of trenches, 500 miles from end to end, with a patience in endurance which no critics of France would have believed possible until the proof was given. Above the parapet lie the corpses of comrades and of men who were his enemies until they became poor clay.

" The greater number of the bodies," writes a soldier, " still lie between the trenches, and we have been unable to withdraw them. We can see them always, in frightful quantity, some of them intact, others torn to bits by the shells which continue to fall upon them. The stench of this corruption floats down upon us with foul odours. Bits of their rotting carcases are flung into our faces and over our heads as new shells burst and scatter them. It is like living in a charnel house where devils are at play flinging dead men's flesh at living men, with fiendish mockery. The smell of this corruption taints our food, and taints our very souls, so that we are spiritually and physically sick. That is war ! "

" This horrible game of war," writes another man, "goes on passionately in our corner. In seventy-four days we have ' progressed ' about 1200 yards. That tells you everything. Ground is gained, so to speak, by the inch, and we all know now how much it costs to get back a bit of free France."

6

Along the French lines Death did not rest from his harvesting whatever the weather, and although for months there was no general advance on either side, not a day passed without new work for the surgeons, the stretcher-bearers, and the gravediggers. One incident is typical of a hospital scene near the front. It was told in a letter from a hospital nurse to a friend in Paris.

" About midday we received a wounded general, whom we made as comfortable as possible in a little room. Although he suffered terribly, he would submit to no special care, and only thought of the comfort of two of his officers. By an extraordinary chance a soldier of his own regiment was brought in a few moments later. Joy of the general, who wanted to learn at once what had happened to his children. He asked to see the soldier immediately :

" ' Tell me—the commandant ? '

" ' Dead, mon général.'

" ' And the captain ? '

" ' Dead, mon général.'

" Four times questions were asked, and four times the soldier, whose voice became lower, made his answer of death. Then the general lowered his head and asked no more. We saw the tears running down his scarred old face, and we crept out of the room on tip-toe."

7

In spite of all this tragedy, the French soldier into whose soul it sank, and who will never forget, wrote home with a gaiety which gleamed through the sadness of his memories. There was a new series of " Lettres de mon moulin " from a young officer of artillery keeping guard in an old mill-house in an important position at the front. They were addressed to his " dearest mamma," and, thoughtful of all the pretty hands which had been knitting garments for him, he described his endeavours to keep warm in them :

" To-night I have piled on to my respectable body a flannel waistcoat, a flannel shirt, and a flannel belt going round three times, a jacket with sleeves sent by mamma herself, a leather waistcoat from Aunt Charlotte, a woollen vest which came to me from the unknown mother of a young dragoon, a warm undercoat recently received from my tailor, and a woollen jacket and wrap knitted by Madame P. J. So I prepare to sleep in peace, if the ' Boches ' will kindly allow me."

The enemy did not often allow the young gentleman to sleep, and about the windmill the shells were bursting.

They reached one Sunday morning almost as far as the little twelfth-century church to which the young officer had stepped down from his windmill to hear Mass in the middle of a crowd of soldiers chanting the office, recited by a soldier, accompanied by a harmonium played by another soldier. The windows were shattered, and a beautiful old house next to the church lay in ruins.

The officer spent lonely hours in the windmill in charge of the telephone exchange, from which the batteries were worked. The men in the trenches and the gun-pits pitied his loneliness, and invented a scheme to cheer him up. So after dark, when the cannonade slackened, he put the receiver to his ears and listened to a Tyrolese ballad sung by an orderly, and to the admirable imitation of a barking dog performed by a sapper, and to a Parisian *chanson* delightfully rendered by the aviator.

"Bonne nuit, maman," wrote the officer of artillery at the end of each letter from his windmill.

8

The front did not change its outline on the map, except by hairbreadths, for months at a stretch, yet at many points of the line there were desperate battles, a bayonet charge now and then, and hours of frightful slaughter, when men saw red and killed with joy.

There was a little farm near Steinbach round which a battle raged for many days. Leading to it was a sunken road, defended by the enemy, until one day they put up a number of non-combatants from captured villages to prevent a French attack.

"Among them we could distinguish a woman, with her hair falling to her shoulders and her hands tied behind her back. This new infamy inflamed the courage of our soldiers. A company rushed forward with fixed bayonets. The road to the farm was swept by the enemy's fire, but nothing stopped our men. In spite of our losses we carried the position and are masters of the farm. There was no mercy in those moments of triumph. The ghastly business of war was done to the uttermost."

There were ghastly things in some of the enemy's trenches. One of the worst of them was seen in the forest of Apremont, in the district of Woevre, where the enemy was strongly entrenched in some quarries quite close to the French trenches, which sapped their way forward to those pits. When the guns ceased firing the French soldiers often heard the sound of singing. But above the voices of the Germans there came sometimes a series of piercing cries like the screeching

T

of an owl in a terrible plaint, followed by strange and blood-curdling laughter. It was the voice of a mad woman who was one of those captured from neighbouring villages and brought into the trenches by the Germans. One day the German soldiers carried her the length of their own trenches. Only her head was visible above the ground. She wore a German helmet above the wild hair which blew in wisps about her death-white face, and it seemed like a vision of hell as she passed shrieking with the laughter of insanity.

One turns from such horrors to the heroism of the French soldier, his devotion to his officers, his letters to that *chère maman* before whom his heart is always that of a little child, to the faith which saves men from at least the grosser brutalities of war.

9

One of the tragic ironies of the war was that men whose lives had been dedicated to the service of Christ, and whose hands should be clean of blood, found themselves compelled by the law of France (and in many cases urged by their own instincts of nationality) to serve as soldiers in the fighting ranks. Instead of denouncing from every pulpit the shamefulness of this butchery, which has made a mockery of our so-called civilization and involved all humanity in its crime, those priests and monks put themselves under discipline which sent them into the shambles in which they must kill or be killed. When the mobilization orders were issued, the call to the colours was sent to young curés and abbés throughout the country, and to monks belonging to religious orders banished by its politicians. Jesuits and Dominicans, Franciscans and Carmelites, who had been exiled from France for conscience' sake, hurried back at the first summons, dispensed from that Canon Law which forbids them to shed blood, and as Frenchmen, loving their country though it expelled them, rallied to the flag in the hour of peril. They were Christian priests, but they were also patriots, and Christianity is not so instinctive in its emotion as the spirit of nationality which, by some natural law, makes men on one side of a frontier eager to fight till death when they are challenged by men across the boundary line, forgetting their principles of peace and the command, "Thou shalt not kill," in their loyalty to their own soil, crown, or national ideas. There were twenty thousand priests in the French army, and although many of them were acting according to their religious vocations as chaplains, or stretcher-bearers, the great majority were serving as simple soldiers in the ranks or as officers who had gained promotion by merit.

Although nothing may explain away the paradox that those whose duty it seems to preach the gospel of peace and charity should be helping to heap up the fields of Christendom with the corruption of dead bodies, there is at least this to be said : the priest-soldier in France has been a spiritual influence among his comrades, so that some of them fought with nobler motives than that of blood-lust, and went to death or victory, influenced not with hatred of fellow men, but with a conviction that out of all that death there would come a new life to nations, and that in killing their enemy they were killing a brutal tyranny with its grip upon the world, and a barbarism which would make human life a slavery.

A young priest who said his prayers before lying down on his straw mattress or in the mud of his trench, put a check upon blasphemy, and his fellows—anti-clericals perhaps in the old days or frank materialists—watched him curiously and were thoughtful after their watchfulness. It was easy to see that he was eager to give up his life as a sacrifice to the God of his faith. His courage had something supernatural in it, and he was careless of death. Then, again, he was the best comrade in the company. Never a grumble came from his lips, though he was as cold and wet and hungry as the others. He did a thousand little acts of service to his fellow soldiers, and especially to those who were most sullen, most brutal or most miserable. He spoke sometimes of the next life with a cheerful certainty which made death seem less than an end of things, and he was upborne with a strange fervour which gave a kind of glory to the most wretched toil.

Not a week passed without some priest being cited in the Order of the Day.

"Corporal Delabre Alphonse (priest of the diocese of Puy) and Private Miolane Antoine (priest of the diocese of Clermont) belonging to the 292nd Regiment of Infantry, distinguished themselves throughout the battle by an untiring gallantry and devotion, going to collect the wounded in the line and afterwards spending their nights in assisting the wounded and dying."

That is one notice out of hundreds which I had in official documents.

"M. l'Abbé Martin," says another, "having been wounded in the hand by a bursting shell, remained at his post in the line of fire, prodigal in his help to the wounded and in his consolations to the dying."

The Abbé Bertrand, vicar of St. Germain de Coulamer, was mobilized on the outbreak of war, and for his gallantry in the field promoted successively to the ranks of sergeant, sergeant-major, sub-lieutenant, and lieutenant. He fell on November 4 at the battle of Audrechy, leading his men to the assault. A few days before his death he wrote: "I always look upon this war as an expiation, and I am proud to be a victim." And again: "Oh, how cold the rain is, and how severe the weather! For our faith in France I have offered God to let me be wet and soaked to the very bones."

The story of the Abbé Armand, in the 14th battalion of the Chasseurs Alpins, is that of a hero. A simple man, he used to open his heart to his rough comrades, and often in the trenches, under shell-fire, he would recite the Psalms in a clear voice so that they could hear him. On November 17, to the south of Ypres, his company was selected to hold a dangerous position, swept by the heavy guns of the Germans and near the enemy's trenches. All day until the evening the priest and his comrades stayed there, raked by a hideous shell-fire. At last nearly all the men were killed, and on his side of the emplacement the Abbé Armand was left with two men alive. He signalled the fact to those below by raising three fingers, but shortly afterwards a bullet struck him so that he fell and another hit him in the stomach. It was impossible to send help to him at the time, and he died half an hour later on the tumulus surrounded by the dead bodies of his comrades. They buried him up there, and that night his loss was mourned, not without tears, by many rough soldiers who had loved the man for his cheeriness, and honoured him for the simple faith, which seemed to put a glamour about the mud-stained uniform of a soldier of France.

There were scores of stories like that, and the army lists contained the names of hundreds of these priest-soldiers decorated with the Legion of Honour or mentioned in dispatches for gallant acts.

The character of these men was filled with the spirit of Christian faith, though the war in which they sacrificed their lives was an outrage against Christianity itself. The riddle of it all bewilders one's soul, and one can only go groping in the dark of despair, glad of the little light which comes to the trench of the battlefield, because men like these still promise something better than hatred and blood, and look beyond the gates of death, to peace.

10

Not all French soldiers are like these priests who were valiant with the spirit of Christian faith. Side by side with the priest was the apache, or the slum-dweller, or the peasant from the fields, who in conversation was habitually and unconsciously foul. Not even the mild protest of one of these priests could check the flow of richly imagined blasphemies which are learnt in the barracks during the three years' service, and in the *bistros* of the back streets of France from Cherbourg to Marseilles. But, as a rule, the priest did not protest, except by the example of keeping his own tongue clean. "What is the use ?" said one of them. "That kind of thing is second nature to the men and, after all, it is part of my sacrifice."

Along the roads of France, swinging along to dig a new line of trenches, or on a march from a divisional headquarters to the front, the soldiers would begin one of their Rabelaisian songs which have no ending, but in verse after verse roam further into the purlieus of indecent mirth, so that, as one French officer told me, "these ballads used to make the heather blush." After the song would come the great game of French soldiers on the march. The humorist of the company would remark upon the fatigued appearance of a *sous-officier* near enough to hear.

"He is not in good form to-day, our little corporal. Perhaps it has something to do with his week-end in Paris ! "

Another humorist would take up the cue.

"He has a great thirst, our corporal. His first bottle of wine just whets his whistle. At the sixth bottle he begins to think of drinking seriously ! "

"He is a great amourist, too, they tell me, and very passionate in his love-making ! "

So the ball is started and goes rolling from one man to another in the ranks, growing in audacity and wallowing along filthy ways of thought, until the *sous-officier*, who had been grinning under his *képi*, suddenly turns red with anger and growls out a protest.

"Taisez-vous, cochons. Foutez-moi la paix ! "

All this obscenity of song and speech spoils tne heroic picture a little, and yet does not mean very much in spite of its outrageous heights and depths. It belongs to the character of men who have faced all the facts of life with frank eyes, and find laughter in the grossest humours without losing altogether the finer sentiments of the heart and little delicacies of mind which seem untarnished by the rank weeds which grow in human nature. Laughter is one of the great needs of the French soldier. In war he must laugh or lose all courage. So if there is a clown in the company he may be as coarse as one of Shakespeare's jesters as long as he be funny, and it is with the boldness of one of Shakespeare's heroes—like Benedick—that a young Frenchman, however noble in his blood, seizes the ball of wit and tosses it higher. Like D'Artagnan, he is not squeamish, though a very gallant gentleman.

11

The spirit of D'Artagnan is not dead. Along many roads of France I have met gay fellows whose courage has the laughing quality of that Musketeer, and his Gascon audacity which makes a jest of death itself. In spite of all the horrors of modern warfare, with its annihilating shell-fire and the monstrous ruthlessness of great guns, the French soldier at his best retains that quality of youth which soars even above the muck and misery of the trenches.

The character of a young lieutenant of artillery, who came to fill the place of a poor fellow killed at the side of his *caisson*, is typical of innumerable soldiers of France. He presented himself with a jaunty good humour, made a little speech to his battery which set all the men laughing, and then shook hands with them one by one. Next day he knew each man by name, used the familiar " thee " and " thou " to them, and won their hearts by his devil-may-care manners and the smile which came from a heart amused by life. Everything was a joke to him. He baptized his four guns by absurd nicknames, and had a particular affection for old " Bumps," which had been scarred by several shells. The captain called this young gentleman Lieutenant Mascot, because he had a lucky way with him. He directed the aim of his guns with astounding skill. A German battery had to shift very quickly five minutes after his first shell had got away, and when the enemy's fire was silenced, he would call out, " Don't chuck any more," to the telephone operator. That was his way of ordering the cease-fire.

But Lieutenant " Mascot," one day jumped on the top of a hayrick to direct the marksmanship of his battery, and a moment later a German shell burst above him and scattered part of the rick in all directions. It was a moment of anguish for the onlookers. The captain became as pale as death, and the gunners went on plugging out shells in an automatic way with grief-stricken faces. The telephone man put his head out of his dugout. He stared at the broken rick. Beyond doubt Monsieur Mascot was as dead as mutton. Suddenly, with the receiver at his ear and trans-figured, he began to shout : " Don't chuck any more ! " It was the lieutenant who had sent him the usual order. Ten minutes later the lieutenant came back laughing gaily and, after shaking some straw out of his muddy uniform, gave a caressing touch to old " Bumps," who had got the enemy's range to perfection. . . Then the captain embraced him.

12

The spirit of youth and the spirit of faith cannot rob war of its horrors, nor redeem the crime in which all humanity is involved, nor check the slaughter that goes on incessantly. But they burn with a bright light out of the darkness, and make the killing of men less beastlike. The soul of France has not been destroyed by this war, and no German guns shattering the beauty of old towns and strewing the northern fields with the bodies of beautiful young manhood could be victorious over this nation, which, with all her faults, her incredulities and passions, has at the core a spiritual fervour which lifts it above the clay of life.

The soldiers of France have learnt the full range of human suffering, so that one cannot grudge them their hours of laughter, however coarse their mirth. There were many armies of men from Ypres to St. Mihiel who were put to greater tasks of courage than were demanded of the human soul in mediæval torture chambers, and they passed through the ordeal with a heroism which belongs to the splendid things of history. As yet the history has been written only in brief bulletins stating facts baldly, as when on a Saturday in March of 1915 it was stated that " In Malancourt Wood, between the Argonne and the Meuse, the enemy sprayed one of our trenches with burning liquid so that it had to be abandoned. The occupants were badly burnt." That official account does not convey in any way the horror which over-whelmed the witnesses of the new German method of attacking trenches by drenching them with inflammatory liquid. A more detailed narrative of this first attack by liquid fire was given by one of the soldiers :

"It was yesterday evening, just as night fell, that it happened. The day had been fairly calm, with the usual quantity of bursting shells overhead, and nothing forewarned us of a German attack. Suddenly one of my comrades shouted, ' Hallo ! what is this coming down on us ? Anyone would think it was petroleum.' At that time we could not believe the truth, but the liquid which began to spray on us was certainly some kind of petroleum. The Germans were pumping it from hoses. Our sub-lieutenant made us put out our pipes. But it was a useless precaution. A few seconds later incendiary bombs began to rain down on us and the whole trench burst into flame. It was like being in hell. Some of the men began to scream terribly, tearing off their clothes, trying to beat out the flames. Others were cursing and choking in the hot vapour which stifled us. ' Oh, my Christ ! ' cried a comrade of mine. ' They've blinded me ! ' In order to complete their work those German bandits took advantage of our disturbance by advancing on the trench and throwing burning torches into it. None of us escaped that torrent of fire. We had our eyebrows and eyelashes burnt off, and clothes were burnt in great patches and our flesh was sizzling like roasting meat. But some of us shot through the greasy vapour which made a cloud about us and some of those devils had to pay for their game."

Although some of them had become harmless torches and others lay charred to death, the trench was not abandoned until the second line were ready to make a counter-attack, which they did with fixed bayonets, frenzied by the shrieks which still came from the burning pit where those comrades lay, and flinging themselves with the ferocity of wild beasts upon the enemy, who fled after leaving three hundred dead and wounded on the ground.

13

Along five hundred miles of front such scenes took place week after week, month after month, from Artois to the Argonne, not always with inflammatory liquid, but with hand grenades, bombs, stink-shells, fire balls, smoke balls, and a storm of shrapnel. The deadly monotony of the life in wet trenches, where men crouched in mud, cold, often hungry, in the abyss of misery, unable to put their heads above ground for a single second without risk of instant death, was broken only by the attacks and counter-attacks when the order was given to leave the trench and make one of those wild rushes for a hundred yards or so in which the risks of death were at heavy odds against the chances of life.   Let a French soldier describe the scene :

"Two sections of infantry have crouched since morning on the edge of a wood, waiting for the order which hurls them to the assault of that stupid and formidable position which is made up of barbed wire in front of the advanced trenches. Since midday the guns thunder without cessation, sweeping the ground.   The Germans answer with great smashing blows, and it is the artillery duel which precedes heroic work. Every one knows that when the guns are silent the brief order which will ring out above the huddled men will hold their promise of death.   Yet those men talk quietly, and there are some of them who in this time of danger find some poignant satisfaction, softening their anguish, in calling up the memory of those dear beings whom perhaps they will never see again. With my own ears I have heard a great fair-headed lad expatiate to all his neighbours on the pretty ways of his little daughter who is eight years old. A kind of dry twittering interrupts his discourse. The field telegraph, fixed up in a tree, has called the lieutenant.   At the same moment the artillery fired a few single shots and then was silent.   The officer drew his watch, let ten minutes pass, and then said, ' Get up,' in the same tranquil and commonplace tones with which a corporal says ' attention ' on parade ground.   It was the order to go forward.   Every one understood and rose up, except five men whom a nervous agony chained to their ground.   They had been demoralized by their long wait and weakened by their yearnings for the abandoned homes, and were in the grip of fear.   The lieutenant—a reservist who had a little white in his beard—looked at the five defaulters without anger. Then he drew, not his sword from its scabbard, but a cigarette from its case, lighted it, and said simply:

"'Eh bien?'

"Who can render the intonation of that 'Eh bien'? What actor could imitate it? In that 'Eh bien?' there was neither astonishment nor severity, nor brusque recall to duty, but rather the compassionate emotion of an elder brother before a youngster's weakness which he knows is only a passing mood. That 'Eh bien?'—how he put into it, this elder of ours, so much pitiful authority, such sweetness of command, such brotherly confidence, and also such strength of will. The five men sprang up. . . . And you know that we took the village after having fought from house to house. At the angle of two alleys the lieutenant was killed, and that is why the two notes of his 'Eh bien?' will always echo in my heart as the fine call of an unrecorded heroism. It appears that this war must be impersonal—it is the political formula of the time—and it is forbidden to mention names. Eh bien? Have I named any one?"

14

Out of the monotonous narratives of trench-warfare, stories more horrible than the nightmare phantasies of Edgar Allen Poe, stories of men buried alive by sapping and mining, and of men torn to bits by a subterranean explosion which leaves one man alive amidst the litter of his comrades' limbs so that he goes mad and laughs at the frightful humour of death, come now and then to reveal the meaning of this modern warfare which is hidden by censors behind decent veils. It is a French lieutenant who tells this story, which is heroic as well as horrid:

"We were about to tidy up a captured trench. At the barrier of sand-bags which closed up one end of it, two sentinels kept a sharp look-out so that we could work in peace of mind. Suddenly from a tunnel, hidden by a fold in the ground, an avalanche of bombs was hurled over our heads, and before we could collect our wits ten of our men had fallen dead and wounded, all hugger-mugger. I opened my

mouth to shout a word of command when a pebble, knocked
by a piece of shell, struck me on the head and I fell, quite
dazed. But my unconsciousness only lasted a second or two.
A bursting shell tore off my left hand and I was awakened by
the pain of it. When I opened my eyes and groaned, I saw
the Germans jump across the sand-bags and invade the trench.
There were twenty of them. They had no rifles, but each man
carried a sort of wicker basket filled with bombs. I looked
round to the left. All our men had fled except those who were
lying in their blood. And the Germans were coming on.
Another slip or two and they would have been on the top of
me. At that moment one of my men, wounded in the forehead, wounded in the chin, and with his face all in a pulp
of blood, sat up, snatched at a bag of hand grenades, and
shouted out :

　" Arise, ye dead ! "

He got on his knees, and began to fling his bombs into
the crowd of Germans. At his call, the other wounded men
struggled up. Two with broken legs grasped their rifle and
opened fire. The hero with his left arm hanging limp,
grabbed a bayonet. When I stood up, with all my senses
about me now, some of the Germans were wounded and
others were scrambling out of the trench in a panic. But
with his back to the sand-bags stayed a German *Unteroffizier*, enormous, sweating, apoplectic with rage, who fired
two revolver shots in our direction. The man who had first
organized the defence of the trench—the hero of that " Arise,
ye dead ! "—received a shot full in the throat and fell. But
the man who held the bayonet and who had dragged himself
from corpse to corpse, staggered up at four feet from the
sand-bags, missed death from two shots, and plunged his
weapon into the German's throat. The position was saved,
and it was as though the dead had really risen.

15

The French soldier, as I have said, is strangely candid
in the analysis of his emotions, and is not ashamed of con-
fessing his fears. I remember a young lieutenant of Dragoons

who told me of the terror which took possession of him when the enemy's shrapnel first burst above his head.

" As every shell came whizzing past, and then burst, I ducked my head and wondered whether it was this shell which was going to kill me, or the next. The shrapnel bullets came singing along with a ' Tue ! Tue ! ' Ah, that is a bad song ! But most of all I feared the rifle-shots of an infantry attack. I could not help glancing sideways at the sound of that ' Zip ! zip ! zip ! ' There was something menacing and deadly in it, and one cannot dodge the death which comes with one of these little bullets. It is horrible ! "

And yet this man, who had an abscess in his leg after riding for weeks in his saddle and who had fought every day and nearly every night for a fortnight, was distressed because he had to retire from his squadron for awhile until his leg healed. In five days at the most he would go back again to hell— hating the horror of it all, fearing those screeching shells and hissing bullets, yet preferring to die for France rather than remain alive and inactive when his comrades were fighting.

Imagine the life of one of these cavalrymen, as I heard it described by many of them in the beginning of the war.

They were sent forward on a reconnaissance—a patrol of six or eight. The enemy was known to be in the neighbourhood. It was necessary to get into touch with him, to discover his strength, to kill some of his outposts, and then to fall back to the division of cavalry and report the facts. Not an easy task ! It quite often happened that only one man out of six came back to tell the tale, surprised at his own luck. The German scouts had clever tricks.

One day near Béthune they played one of them—a favourite one. A friend of mine led six of his dragoons towards a village where Uhlans had been seen. They became visible at a turn of the road, and after firing a few shots with . their carbines turned tail and fled. The French dragoons gave chase, across some fields and round the edge of a quiet wood. Suddenly at this point the Uhlans reined in their horses and out of the wood came the sudden shattering fire of a German quickfirer. Fortunately it was badly aimed, and my friend with his six dragoons was able to gallop away from that infernal machine which had so cleverly ambushed them.

There was no rest for the cavalry in those first days of the war. The infantry had its bivouac every day, there was rest sometimes in the trenches, but the cavalry had to push on always upon new adventures to check the enemy in his advance.

A young Russian officer in the French dragoons told me that he had been fighting since the beginning of the war with never more than three hours sleep a night and often no sleep at all. On many nights those brief hours of rest were in beetroot fields in which the German shrapnel had been searching for victims, and he awakened now and then to listen to the well-known sound of that singing death before dozing off again.

It was " Boot and saddle " at four o'clock in the morning, before the dawn. It was cold then—a cold which made men tremble as with an ague. A cup of black coffee was served, and a piece of bread.

The Russian officer of French dragoons, who has lived in British Colonies, saw a vision then—a false mirage—of a British breakfast. It was the thought of grilled bloaters, followed by ham and eggs, which unmanned him for a moment. Ten minutes later the cavalry was moving away. A detachment was sent forward on a mission of peril, to guard a bridge. There was a bridge near Béthune one night guarded by a little patrol. It was only when the last man had been killed that the Germans made their way across.

Through the darkness these mounted men leaned forward over their saddles, peering for the enemy, listening for any jangle of stirrup or clink of bit. On that night there came a whisper from the cavalry leader.

" They are coming ! . . . Quiet there ! "

A file of dark shadows moved forward. The dragoons swung their carbines forward. There was a volley of shots before a cry rang out.

" Cessez feu ! Cessez feu ! "

The cry had been heard before from German officers

speaking excellent French, but this time there was no treachery in it. The shadows who moved forward through the night were Frenchmen changing from one trench to another.

16

The infantryman had a hard time, too. It was true that theoretically he might sometimes snatch a few hours of sleep in a trench or out in an open field, but actually the coldness of the night was often an acute agony, which kept him awake. The food question was a difficult one. When there was heavy fighting to be done, and rapid marching, the provisions became as theoretical as the hours of sleep.

I heard the graphic recital of a sergeant of infantry, which was typical of many others in those early days.

His section awakened one morning near Armentières with a famishing hunger, to find an old peasant woman coming up with a great barrow-load of potatoes.

" These are for your breakfast, my little ones," she said. " See, I have some faggots here. If you care to make a fire there will be roast potatoes for you in twenty minutes."

" Madame, you are too kind," said my sergeant. He helped to make the fire, to pack it with potatoes. He added his eloquence to that of his comrades when the fragrant smell made his nostrils quiver. And just as the potatoes were nearly done up came a motor cyclist with orders that the section was to move on immediately to a place fifteen kilometres away. It was a tragedy ! There were tearful farewells to those potatoes. Fifteen kilometres away there was a château, and a friendly lady, and a good cook who prepared a dinner of excellent roast beef and most admirable fried potatoes. And just as the lady came to say " Mes amis, le diner est servi," up panted a Belgian cyclist with the news that German cavalry was advancing in strong force accompanied by 500 motor-cars with mitrailleuses and many motor-cycles, and a battery of horse artillery. It was another tragedy ! And the third took place sixteen hours later, when this section of infantry which had been marching most of that time lay down on an open field to sleep without a supper.

Yet—" Nothing matters except the rain," said a friend of mine in the French artillery. He shrugged his shoulders as he spoke, and an expression of disgust came upon his bearded face. He was thinking, perhaps, of his beloved guns which lose their mobility in the quagmires of the fields. But the rain is bad also for men and beasts. It takes eight days for a French overcoat to get thoroughly dry after a bad wetting. Even the cavalryman's cloak is a poor shield against the driving rain, and at night wet straw or a water pool in a trench is not a pleasant kind of bed.

" War," said one of the French officers with whom I have chatted, " is not only fighting, as some people seem to think. The physical discomforts are more dangerous to one's health than shrapnel. And it is—*par exemple*—the impossibility of changing one's linen for weeks and weeks which saps one's moral fibre more than the·risk of losing one's head."

The risk of death is taken lightly by all these men. It is curious, indeed, that almost every French soldier has a conviction that he will die in battle sooner or later. In moments of imagination he sees his own corpse lying out in the field, and is full of pity for his wife and children. But it does not destroy his courage or his gift of gaiety or his desire to fight for France or his sublime endurance of pain.

The wounded men who pour down from the battlefields are incredibly patient. I have seen them stand on a wounded leg to give their places in a railway-carriage to peasant women with their babies. They have used their bandaged hands to lift up the baskets of refugees. They forget their wounds in remembering their adventures, and the simple soldier describes his combats with a vivid eloquence not to be attained by the British Tommy, who has no gift of words.

The French soldier has something in his blood and strain which uplifts him as a fighting man, and gives him the quality of chivalry. Peasant or bourgeois or of patrician stock he has always the fine manners of a gentleman, and to know him in the field is to love the humour and temper of the man.

17

Yet there were some men in the French army, as in our own, who showed how thin is the veneer which hides the civilized being from the primitive savage, to whom there is a joy in killing, like the wild animal who hunts his prey in the jungles and desert places. One such man comes to my mind now. He was in the advanced lines near Albert, but was always restless in the trench. As soon as darkness came he would creep out and crawl on his belly across the swampy ground to a deep hole dug by the explosion of a *marmite* quite close to the German lines. Here he found a hiding-place from which he could take " pot shots " at any German soldiers who under cover of darkness left their burrows to drag in the bodies of their comrades or to gather bits of wood with which to make a floor to their trenches. They were quite unconscious of that man in the hole staring down the length of his rifle, and listening intently for any sound which would betray an enemy. Every night he shot two or three men, perfectly patient in his long cold vigil if he could have that " luck." Then at dawn he would crawl back again, bringing a helmet or two with him, a cartridge belt or some other trophy as a sign of his success. One night he shot a man who had stumbled quite close to his pit, and some great instinct of pity for his victim stirred in him, so that he risked a double journey over the open ground to fetch a spade with which he buried the man. But soon afterwards he added to his " bag " of human life. In his own trench he spoke very little and always seemed to be waiting for the hour when he could crawl out again like a Red Indian in search of scalps. He was the primitive man, living like one of his ancestors of the Stone Age, except for the fire-stick with which he was armed and the knowledge of the arts and beauties of modern life in his hunter's head. For he was not a French Canadian from the backwoods, or an Alpine chasseur from lonely mountains, but a well-known lawyer from a French

U

provincial town, with the blood and education of a gentleman.   As a queer character this man is worth remembering by
those who study the psychology of war, but he is not typical
of the soldiers of France, who in the mass have no blood-lust,
and hate butchering their fellow beings, except in their
moments of mad excitement, made up of fear as well as of
rage, when to the shout of " En avant ! " they leap out of the
trenches and charge a body of Germans, stabbing and slashing
with their bayonets, clubbing men to death with the butt-
ends of their rifles, and for a few minutes of devilish intoxication, with the smell of blood in their nostrils, and with blood-
shot eyes, rejoicing in slaughter.

" We did not listen to the cries of surrender or to the
beseeching plaints of the wounded," said a French soldier,
describing one of these scenes.   " We had no use for
prisoners and on both sides there was no quarter given in this
Argonne wood.   Better than fixed bayonets was an unfixed
bayonet grasped as a dagger.   Better than any bayonet was a
bit of iron or a broken gun-stock, or a sharp knife.   In that
hand-to-hand fighting there was no shooting but only the
struggling of interlaced bodies, with fists and claws grabbing
for each other's throats.   I saw men use teeth and bite
their enemy to death with their jaws, gnawing at their wind-
pipes.   This is modern war in the twentieth century—or one
scene in it—and it is only afterwards, if one escapes with life,
that one is stricken with the thought of all that horror which
has debased us as low as the beasts—lower than beasts,
because we have an intelligence and a soul to teach us better
things."

The soldiers of France have an intelligence which makes
them, or most of them, revolt from the hideous work they
have to do and cry out against this infamy which has been
thrust upon them by a nation which compelled the war.
Again and again, for nine months and more, I have heard
French soldiers ask the question, " Why are such things
allowed by God ?   What is the use of civilization if it leads to
this ? "   And, upon my soul, I could not answer them.

18

The mobilization of all the manhood of France, from boys of eighteen and nineteen to men of forty-five, was a demonstration of national unity and of a great people rising as one man in self-defence, which to the Englishman was an astounding and overwhelming phenomenon. Though I knew the meaning of it and it had no real surprises for me, I could never avoid the sense of wonderment when I met young aristocrats marching in the ranks as common soldiers, professors, poets, priests and painters, as hairy and dirty as the *poilus* who had come from the farms and the meat markets, millionaires and the sons of millionaires driving automobiles as military chauffeurs or as orderlies to officers upon whom they waited respectfully, forbidden to sit at table with them in public places, and having to " keep their place " at all times. Even now I am astonished at a system which makes young merchants abandon their businesses at a moment's notice to serve in the ranks, and great employers of labour go marching with their own labourers, giving only a backward glance at the ruin of their property and their trade. There is something magnificent in this, but all one's admiration of a universal military service which abolishes all distinctions of class and wealth—after all there were not many *embusqués*, or privileged *exemptés*—need not blind one to abuses and unnecessary hardships inflicted upon large numbers of men. Abuses there have been in France, as was inevitable in a system like this, and this general call to the colours inflicted an enormous amount of suffering upon men who would have suffered more willingly if it had been to serve France usefully. But in thousands and hundreds of thousands of cases there was no useful purpose served. General Joffre had as many men as he could manage along the fighting lines. More would have choked up his lines of communication and the whole machinery of the war. But behind the front there were millions of men in reserve, and behind them vast bodies of men idling in depots, crowded into barracks, and eating their hearts out for lack of work. They had been forced to abandon their homes and their professions, and yet during the whole length of the war they found no higher duty to do for France than sweep out a barrack-yard or clean out a military latrine. It was especially hard upon the *réformés*—men of delicate health who had been exempted from their military service in their youth but who now were re-examined by the Conseil de Revision and found "good for auxiliary service in time of war."

To the old soldiers who have done their three years a return to the barracks is not so distressing. They know what the life is like and the rude discipline of it does not shock them. But to the *réformé*, sent to barracks for the first time at thirty-five or forty years of age, it is a moral sacrifice which is almost unendurable. After the grief of parting from his wife and children and the refinements of his home, he arrives at the barracks inspired by the best sentiments, happy in the idea of being useful to his country, of serving like other Frenchmen. But when he has gone through the great gate, guarded by soldiers with loaded rifles, when he has changed his civil clothes for an old and soiled uniform, when he has found that his bed is a filthy old mattress in a barn where hundreds of men are quartered, when he has received for the first time certain brief and harsh orders from a *sous-officier*, and finally, when he goes out again into the immense courtyard, surrounded by high grey walls, a strange impression of solitude takes hold of him, and he finds himself abandoned, broken and imprisoned.

Many of these *réformés* are men of delicate health, suffering from heart or chest complaints, but in these barracks there is no comfort for the invalid. I know one of them in which nearly seven hundred men slept together in a great garret, with only one window and a dozen narrow skylights, so that the atmosphere was suffocating above their rows of straw trusses, rarely changed and of indescribable filth. But what hurts the spirits of men who have attained good positions in civil life, who have said to this man " Go ! " and he goeth, and to that man "Come !" and he cometh, is to find their positions reversed and to be under the orders of a corporal or sergeant with a touch of the bully about him, happy to dominate men more educated and more intelligent than himself. I can quote an example of an aristocrat who, in spite of his splendid château in the country, was mobilized as a *simple soldat*. At the barracks this gentleman found that his corporal was a labourer in the village where the old château stands. In order to amuse himself the corporal made M. le Chatelain do all the dirtiest jobs, such as sweeping the rooms, cleaning the staircases and the lavatories. At the same barracks were a number of priests, including an *archiprêtre*, who was about to become a bishop. Even the most ferocious anti-clericals in the *caserne* had to acknowledge that these men were excellent soldiers and good comrades. They submitted to all inconveniences, did any task as though it were a religious duty, and submitted to the rough life among men of foul speech with a wonderful resignation. But that did not save them from the tyranny of a *sous-officier*, who called them the hardest names his tongue could find when they made any *faux pas* in their barrack drill, and swore as terribly as those in Flanders when they did not obey his commands with the lightning rapidity of soldiers who have nothing more to learn. These cases could be multiplied by hundreds of thousands, and for men of refinement there was a long torture in their barracks when there was no mental satisfaction in useful work for France. Yet their sacrifice has not been in vain perhaps. " They serve who only stand and wait," and they proved by their submission to the system a loyalty and a patriotism equal to those who went into the trenches. They, too, who know what war means—for war is not only at the front—will come back with a deep-rooted hatred of militarism which will make it more difficult in future for politicians who breathe out fire and slaughter and urge a people to take up arms for any other cause than that of self-defence.

19

It is curious how long the song of La Marseillaise has held its power. It has been like a leit-motif through all the drama of this war in France, through the spirit of the French people waiting patiently for victory, hiding their tears for the dead, consoling their wounded and their cripples, and giving their youngest and their manhood to the God of War. What is the magic in this tune so that if one hear it even on a cheap piano in an auxiliary hospital, or scraped thinly on a violin in a courtyard of Paris, it thrills one horribly ? On the night of August 2, when I travelled from Paris to Nancy, it seemed to me that France sang La Marseillaise—the strains of it rose from every wayside station—and that out of its graveyards across those dark hills and fields, with a thin luminous line on the far horizon the ghosts of slain soldiers rose to sing it to those men who were going to fight again for liberty.

Since then it has always been in my ears. I heard it that night in Amiens when the French army was in retreat, and when all the young men of the city, not yet called to the colours because of their youth, escaped hurriedly on truck trains before a bridge was blown up, so that if they stayed they would be prisoners in German hands. It was these boys who sang it, with fresh, clear voices, joining in a fine chorus, though not far away the soldiers of France were limping through the night from abandoned positions :

Entendez-vous, dans les campagnes,
Mugir ces féroces soldats ?
Ils viennent jusque dans nos bras
Egorger nos fils, nos compagnes !
Aux armes, citoyens !
Formez vos bataillons !
Marchons ! . . .

I listened to those boys' voices, and something of the history of the song put its spell upon me then. There was the passion of old heroism in it, of old and bloody deeds, with the wild wars of revolution and lust for liberty. Rouget de Lisle wrote it one night at Strasburg, when he was drunk, says the legend. But it was not the drunkenness of wine which inspired his soul. It was the drunkenness of that year

1792, when the desire of liberty made Frenchmen mad. . . The men of Marseilles came singing it into Paris. The Parisians heard and caught up the strains. It marched to the victories of the Republican armies. " We fought one against ten," wrote a French general, " but La Marseillaise was on our side." " Send us," wrote another general, " ten thousand men and one copy of La Marseillaise, and I will answer for victory."

A hundred years and more have passed since then, but the tune has not gone stale. Again and again in the Orders of the Day one read that " the company went into action singing La Marseillaise, Lieutenant X was still singing when, after carrying the enemy's position, he was shot in the throat " ; or " the Chasseurs Alpins climbed the ridge to the song of La Marseillaise."

The spirit of it runs through the narrative of a French infantryman who described an action in the Argonne, where his regiment held a village heavily attacked by the enemy. There was street-fighting of the fiercest kind, and hand-to-hand combats in the houses and even in the cellars. " Blood," he wrote, " ran in the gutters like water on a rainy day." The French soldiers were being hard pressed and reserves came with their new regiments in the nick of time.

" Suddenly the Marseillaise rang out while the bugles of the three regiments sounded the charge. From where we stood by the fire of burning houses we could see the action very clearly, and never again shall I see anything more fantastic than those thousands of red legs charging in close ranks. The grey legs began to tremble (they do not love the bayonet), and the Marseillaise continued with the bugles, while our guns vomited without a pause. Our infantry had closed with the enemy. Not a shot now, but cold steel. . . . Suddenly the charge ceased its bugle-notes. They sounded instead the call to the flag. *Au drapeau!* Our flag was captured ! Instinctively we ceased fire, thunderstruck. Then very loud and strong the Marseillaise rang out above the music of the bugles, calling *Au drapeau* again and again. We saw the awful melée, the struggle to the death with that song above all the shouting and the shrieks. . . . You who imagine you know La Marseillaise because you have heard it played at prize distributions must acknowledge your error. In order to know it you must have heard it as I have tried to tell you, when blood is flowing and the flag of France is in danger."

To this soldier it is an intolerable thought that he should hear the hymn of victory sung at a " prize distribution," or in a music-hall scented with the perfume of women. But even in a music-hall in Paris, or in a third-rate *cabaret* in a provincial town, the song may be heard with all its magic. I heard it one night in such a place, where the song was greater than the singer. French *poilus* were in the hall, crippled or convalescent, after their day of battle, and with their women around them they stood at attention while the national hymn was sung. They knew the meaning of it, and the women knew. Some of them became quite pale, with others faces flushed. Their eyes were grave, but with a queer fire in them as the verses rang out. . . . It seemed to me as I stood there in this hall, filled with stale smoke and woman's scent, that I smelt blood, and gunpowder, and heard through the music of the Marseillaise the shouts of hoarse voices, charging with the bayonet, the screams of wounded, and then the murmur of a battlefield when dawn comes, lighting the tattered flags of France.

20

The soldiers of France in that strange land called *là-bas* had one consolation which should have helped them a little —did help them, I think, more than a little—to endure the almost intolerable misery of their winter quarters at the front in one of the wettest half years within living memory. They stood in the waterlogged trenches, shivering and coughing, they tramped through cotton-wool mists with heavy overcoats which had absorbed many quarts of rain, they slept at nights in barns through which the water dripped on to puddled straw, or in holes beneath the carts with dampness oozing through the clay walls, or in boggy beet-root fields under a hail of shrapnel, and their physical discomfort of coldness and humidity was harder to bear than their fear of death or mutilation. But throughout those months of mud and blood a spirit came to visit them in their trenches, and though it could not cure frozen feet or put a healing touch for men spitting blood and coughing their lungs away, it warmed the hearts of men who other-wise would have been chilled to a moral death. The love of women and of all those people who had not been called upon to fight went out to those *poilus* at the front, in waves of emotion which reached as far as the advanced trenches. By millions of letters, which in spite of an almost hopeless muddle of the postal service did at last reach the soldier, they knew that France, the very heart of France, was full of pity and hero-worship and yearning for them. By the gifts which came to them—after months of delay, some-times—not only from their own kinsfolk but from unknown benefactors, school children, convents, societies, and all classes of men and women, they knew that their sufferings were understood and that throughout the country there was a great prayer going up—from freethinkers as well as from Catholic souls—that the soldiers of France might be blessed with victory and that they might have the strength to endure the cruelties of war. It may be thought that this sentiment would not comfort a man lying on his stomach as sentinel on outpost duty, staring through the mist and rain, and listening for the slightest sound of an approaching enemy, or a man crouching beneath a ledge of earth, waiting for the quiet words of *En avant!* which would make him scramble up and go into a storm of shells with a fair chance of being cut to bits by flying scythes. But in truth the sentiment that came welling up to those men at the front was of infinite comfort and kept alight a flame in them which no winter wind could douse. That sentinel on his stomach, gripping a cold rifle with numbed hands, and cursing silently the fate which had brought him to this agony, checked the fear that was creeping up to his heart—

was that a line of Boches stealing through the mist ?—
when he thought that the women he knew, the folk in the
Normandy village, the old *curé*, and all the spirit of France
had made a hero of him and expected him to bear himself
bravely, and in imagination stood beside him to share his
vigil. In order not to spoil the image they had made of
him, to live up to their ideals of him he must hold on and
kill these little devils of fear, and die, if need be, as a gallant
soldier of France. It would be fine to come back with a
stripe on his arm, perhaps with the military medal on his
breast. . . . But oh, the pain in those frozen feet of his !
and the coldness of this bed of mud !

Poor devils ! hundreds of them have told me their
stories and at the end of a tale of misery have said : " I do
not complain, you know. It's war, and I am glad to do my
duty for the sake of France." And yet sometimes, when
they thought back, to the homes they had left, and their
old ways of civil life, they had moments of weakness in
which all the strength of their souls seemed to ebb away.

" It's fatal to think of one's life before the war," said a
young Frenchman who sat with me at the table of a little
café not far from the front. He was a rich young man, with
a great business in Paris which had been suspended on the
first day of mobilization, and with a pretty young wife who
had just had her first baby. Now he was a simple soldier,
and for nine months he had not seen Paris or his home or his
pretty wife. The baby's eyes were grey-blue, it seemed, but
he had not been able to test the truth of that description.

" As a rule," he said, " one doesn't think back to one's
old life. A great gulf lies between us and the past and it is
as though one had been born again just to be a soldier in this
war. The roots of our former existence have been torn up.
All one's old interests have been buried. My wife ? I
hardly ever think of her. My home ? Is there such a place ?
. . . It is only at night, or suddenly, sometimes, as one goes
marching with one's company that one's thoughts begin to
roam back over old grounds for a moment or two. The other
fellows know what one's silence means, and one's deafness,

so that one doesn't hear a neighbour's joke or answer his question. It gives one a horrible heartache and one is over-whelmed with depression. . . Great God, how long is this war going to last ? "

21

It is only those who have been to the front in France who can realize the life of the men there as it went on month after month—the misery of it, the dreariness of it, the lack of any thrill except that of fear. At the end of April in this year 1915 I went to the most desolate part of the French front, along the battlefields of Champagne, where after nine months of desperate fighting the guns were still at work ceaselessly and great armies of France and Germany were still divided from each other by a few barren meadows, a burnt wood or two, a river bank, a few yards of trenches and a zone of Death.

It was in Champagne-Pouilleuse—mangy Champagne it is called, because it has none of the richness of the vineyard country, but is a great stretch of barren land through which the chalk breaks out in bald patches. The spirit of war brooded over all this countryside, and I passed through many ruined villages, burnt and broken by incendiarism and shell-fire. Gradually as we approached nearer to the front, the signs of ordinary life were left behind, and we came into a region where all the activities of men were devoted to one extraordinary purpose, and where they lived in strange con-ditions.

No civilian came this way unless as a correspondent under the charge of a staff officer. The labourers on the roadside—carting stones to this country of chalk—were all in uniform. No women invaded this territory except, where, here and there, by rare chance, a wrinkled dame drove a plough across a lonely field. No children played about the brooks or plucked the wild flowers on the hillsides. The inhabitants of this country were all soldiers, tanned by months of hard weather, in war-worn clothes, dusty after marching down the long, white roads, hard and tough in spite of a winter's misery, with calm, resolute eyes in spite of the daily peril of death in which they live.

They lived in a world which is as different from this known world of ours as though they belonged to another race of men inhabiting another planet, or to an old race far back behind the memory of the first civilization.   For in this district of Champagne, the soldiers of France were earth-men or troglodytes, not only in the trenches, but for miles behind the trenches.   When the rains came last autumn they were without shelter, and there were few villages on this lonely stretch of country in which to billet them.   But here were soft, chalky ridges and slopes in which it was not difficult to dig holes and caverns.   The troops took to picks and shovels, and very soon they built habitations for themselves in which they have been living ever since when not in the trenches.

I was invited into some of these subterranean parlours, and ducked my head as I went down clay steps into dim caves where three or four men lived in close comradeship in each of them.   They had tacked the photographs of their wives or sweethearts on the walls, to make these places " homelike," and there was space in some of them for wood fires, which burned with glowing embers and a smoke that made my eyes smart, so that by the light of them these soldiers would see the portraits of those who wait for them to come back, who have waited so patiently and so long through the dreary months.

But now that spring had come the earth-men had emerged from their holes to bask in the sun again, and with that love of beauty which is instinctive in a Frenchman's heart, they were planting gardens and shrubberies outside their chalk dwellings with allegorical designs in cockle-shells or white stones.

" Très chic ! " said the commandant to a group of soldiers proud to their handicraft.

And chic also, though touching in its sentiment, was a little graveyard behind a fringe of branches which mask a French battery.   The gunners were still at work plugging out shells over the enemy's lines, from which came answering shells with the challenge of death, but they had found time to decorate the graves of the comrades who had been "unfortunate." They had twined wild flowers about the wooden crosses and made borders of blossom about those mounds of earth. It was the most beautiful cemetery in which I have ever stood with bared head. Death was busy not far away. Great guns were speaking in deep, reverberating tones, which gave a solemn import to the day ; but Nature was singing to a different tune.

"It is strange, is it not," said our commandant, "this contrast between war and peace ? Those cherry trees comfort one's spirit."

He was a soldier in every fibre of his being, but behind those keen, piercing eyes of his there was the sentiment of France stirred now by the beauty through which we passed, in spite of war. We drove for a mile or more down a long, straight road which was an avenue of cherry trees. They made an archway of white blossom above our heads, and the warm sun of the day drew out their perfume. Away on either side of us the fields were streaked with long rays of brilliant yellow where saffron grew as though the sun had split bars of molten metal there, and below the hillside the pear-blossom and cherry-blossom which bloomed in deserted orchards lay white and gleaming like snow on the Swiss peaks in summer.

"Even war is less horrible now that the sun shines," said a French officer.

The sky was cloudlessly blue, but as I gazed up into a patch of it, where a winged machine flew high with a humming song, five tiny white clouds appeared quite suddenly.

"They are shelling him," said the commandant. "Pretty close too."

Invisible in the winged machine was a French aviator, reconnoitring the German lines away over Beauséjour. Afterwards he became visible, and I talked with him when he had landed in the aviation field, where a number of aeroplanes stood ready for flight.

"They touched her three times," he said, pointing to his machine. "You can see the holes where the shrapnel bullets pierced the metal sheath."

He showed me how he worked his mitrailleuse, and then strolled away to light a cigarette against the wind. He had done his morning job, and had escaped death in the air by half an inch or so. But in the afternoon he would go up again —2000 feet up above the German guns—and thought no more of it than of just a simple duty with a little sport to keep his spirits up.

"We are quite at home here," said one of the French officers, leading the way through a *boyau*, or tunnel, to a row of underground dwellings which had been burrowed out of the earth below a high ridge overlooking the German positions opposite Perthes, Mesnil-lez-Hurlus, and Beauséjour, where there had been some of the most ferocious fighting in the war, so that the names of those places have been written in blood upon the history of France.

"You see we have made ourselves as comfortable as possible," said the general, who received us at the doorway of the little hole which, with delightful irony, he called his "palace." He is an elderly man, this general who has held in check some of the most violent assaults of the German army, but there was a boyish smile in his eyes and none of the harshness of old age in the sweetness of his voice. He lived in a hole in the earth with just a peep-hole out of which he could see the German lines on the opposite hills and his won trenches down below. As he spread out his maps and explained the positions of his batteries and lines, I glanced round his room—at the truckle-bed which filled the length of it, and the deal table over which he was bending, and the wooden chair in which he sat to think out the problems of his task. There was only one touch of colour in this hole in the hillside, and it belonged to a bunch of carnations placed in a German shell and giving out a rich odour so that some of the beauty of spring had come into this hiding-place where an old man directed the operations of death.

"Look," said the general, pointing to the opposite lines,

"here is Crest 196, about which you gentlemen have written so much in newspapers." It was just a rise in the ground above the ravine which divided us from the German ridges, but I gazed at it with a thrill, remembering what waves of blood have washed around this hillock, and how many heroes of France have given their lives to gain that crest. Faintly I could see the lines of German trenches with their earthworks thrown up along the hillsides and along the barren fields on each side of the ravine, where French and German soldiers are very close to each other's tunnels. From where we stood subterranean passages led to the advanced trenches down there, and to a famous "trapeze" on the right of the German position, forming an angle behind the enemy's lines, so that now and again their soldiers might be seen.

"It is not often in this war that we can see our enemy unless we visit them in their trenches, or they come to us," said the general, "but a few days ago, when I was in the trapeze, I saw one of them stooping down as though gathering something in his hands or tying up his boot-laces." Those words were spoken by a man who had commanded French troops for nine months of incessant fighting which reveal the character of this amazing war. He was delighted because he had seen a German soldier in the open and found it a strange unusual thing. Not a sign of any human being could I see as I gazed over the great battlefields of France. There was no glint of helmets, no flash of guns, no movements of regiments, no stirring of the earth. There was a long tract of country in which no living thing moved : utterly desolate in its abandonment. Yet beneath the earth here, close to us as well as far away, men crouched in holes waiting to kill or to be killed, and all along the ridges, concealed in dug-outs or behind the low-lying crests, great guns were firing so that their thunder rolled across the ravines, and their smoke-clouds rested for a little while above the batteries.

The general was pointing out a spot on Hill 196 where the Germans still held a ridge. I could not see it very clearly, or at least the general thought my eyes were wandering too much to the right.

"I will drop a shell there," he said, and then turned to a telephone operator who was crouched in a hole in the wall, and gave an order to him.

The man touched his instrument and spoke in the mouth-piece.

"C'est la batterie?"

There was a little crackling in the telephone, like twigs under a pot, and it seemed as though a tiny voice were speaking from a great distance.

"Now!" said the general, pointing towards the crest.

I stared intently, and a second later, after a solitary thunderstroke from a heavy gun, I saw a shell burst and leave a soft white cloud at the very spot indicated by the old man at my side. I wondered if a few Germans had been killed to prove the point for my satisfaction. What did it matter—a few more deaths to indicate a mark on the map? It was just like sweeping a few crumbs off the table in an argument on strategy.

In another hole to which the general took me was the officers' mess—about as large as a suburban bathroom. At the end of the dining-table the captain was shaving himself, and laughed with embarrassment at our entry. But he gave me two fingers of a soapy hand and said " Enchanté " with fine courtesy.

Outside, at the top of the tunnel, was another group of officers, who seemed to me cheery men in spite of all the hardships of their winter in a subterranean world. The spring had warmed their spirits, and they laughed under the blue sky. But one of them, who stood chatting with me, had a sudden thrill in his voice as he said, "How is Paris?" He spoke the word again and said, "Paris!" as though it held all his soul.

22

There was the real spirit of old-world chivalry in a château of France which I visited two days ago. This old building, with its high gables and pointed roofs, holds the memory of many great chapters in French history. Attila the Hun came this way with his hordes, checked and broken at last, as centuries later, not far away, 100,000 Germans were checked and broken by Dumouriez and the French army of 1792 on the plain of Valmy.

A French officer pointed to a tablet on the wall of the château commemorating that victory, and said : " Perhaps history will be repeated here by the general whom you will see later on." He stooped down and rubbed some dust off a stone, revealing a tracing of the footprint of Henri IV, who once crossed this threshold, and on the way upstairs pointed to other memorial tablets of kings and princes, statesmen and soldiers, who had received the hospitality of this old house.

There are many châteaux of this kind in Champagne, and in one of them we entered a long, bare room, where a French general stood with some of his officers, and I knew that the old spirit of France and its traditions of chivalry have not died. This general, with a silver star on his breast, seemed to me like one of those nobles who fought in the wars of the sixteenth century under the Duc de Guise.

He is a man of less than fifty years of age, with a black beard and steel-blue eyes, extraordinarily keen and piercing, and a fine poise of the head, which gives him an air of dignity and pride, in spite of the simplicity and charm of his manners.

I sat opposite to him at table, and in this old room, with stone walls, he seemed to me like the central figure of some mediæval painting. Yet there was nothing mediæval except the touch of chivalry and the faith of France in the character of this general and his officers. Men of modern science and trained in a modern school of thought, their conversation ranged over many subjects both grave and gay, and, listening to them, I saw the secret of Germany's failure to strike France to her knees.

With such men as these in command, with that steel-eyed general on the watch—energy and intellectual force personified in his keen, vivacious face—the old faults of 1870 could not happen so easily again, and Germany counted without this renaissance of France. These men do not

x

minimize the strength of the German defensive, but there is no fear in their hearts about the final issue of the war, and they are sure of their own position along this front in Champagne.

It was to the first lines of defence along that front that I went in the afternoon with other officers. Our way was through a wood famous in this war because it has been the scene of heavy fighting, ending in its brilliant capture by the French. It has another interest, because it is one of the few places along the front—as far as I know the only place—where troops have not entrenched themselves.

This was an impossibility, because the ground is so moist that water is reached a few feet down. It was necessary to build shell-proof shelters above-ground, and this was done by turning the troops into an army of wood-cutters.

This sylvan life of the French troops here is not without its charm, apart from the *marmites* which come crashing through the trees, and shrapnel bullets which whip through the branches. The ground has dried up during recent days, so that the long boarded paths leading to the first lines are no longer the only way of escape from bogs and swamps.

It might have been the scene of " A Midsummer Night's Dream " as I made my way through thickets all aglint with the first green of the spring's foliage, treading on a carpet of white and yellow flowers and accompanied on my way by butterflies and flying beetles.

But a tremendous noise beyond the stage would have spoilt the play. French batteries were hard at work and their shells came rushing like fierce birds above the trees. The sharp " tang " of the French " Soixante-quinze " cracked out between the duller thuds of the " Cent-vingt " and other heavy guns, and there were only brief moments of silence between those violent explosions and the long-drawn sighs of wind as the shells passed overhead and then burst with that final crash which scatters death.

In one of the silences, when the wood was very still and murmurous with humming insects, I heard a voice call. It was not a challenge of " Qui va là ?" or " Garde à vous," but the voice of spring. It called "Cuckoo! Cuckoo!" and mocked at war.

A young officer with me was more interested in the voices of the guns. He knew them all, even when they spoke from the enemy's batteries, and as we walked he said alternately, "Départ . . . Arrivé . . . Départ . . . Arrivé . . ." as one of the French shells left and one of the German shells arrived.

The enemy's shells came shattering across the French lines very frequently, and sometimes as I made my way through the trees towards the outer bastions I heard the splintering of wood not far away.

But the soldiers near me seemed quite unconscious of any peril overhead. Some of them were gardening and making little bowers about their huts. Only a few sentinels were at their posts, along the bastions built of logs and clay, behind a fringe of brushwood which screened them from the first line of German trenches outside this boundary of the wood. .

"Don't show your head round that corner," said an officer, touching me on the sleeve, as I caught a glimpse of bare fields and, a thousand yards away, a red-roofed house. There was nothing much to see—although the enemies of France were there with watchful eyes for any movement behind our screen.

"A second is long enough for a shot in the forehead," said the officer, "and if I were you I would take that other path. The screen has worn a bit thin just there."

It was curious. I found it absolutely impossible to realize, without an intellectual effort, that out of the silence of those flat fields death would come instantly if I showed my head. But I did not try the experiment to settle all doubts.

23

In the heart of the wood was a small house, spared by some freak of chance by the German shells which came dropping on every side of it. Here I took tea with the officers, who used it as their headquarters, and never did tea taste better than on that warm spring day, though it was served with a ladle out of a tin bowl to the music of many guns. The officers were a cheery set who had become quite accustomed to the menace of death which at any moment might shatter this place and make a wreckage of its peasant furniture. The colonel sat back in a wooden arm-chair, asking for news about the outer world as though he were a shipwrecked mariner on a desert isle ; but every now and then he would listen to the sound of the shells and say, " Départ ! . . . Arrivé ! " just like the officer who had walked with me through the wood. Two of the younger officers sat on the edge of a truckle-bed beneath the portrait of a buxom peasant woman, who was obviously the wife of the late proprietor. Two other officers lounged against the door-posts, entertaining the guests of the day with droll stories of death. Another came in with the latest communiqué received by the wireless station outside, and there was a " Bravo ! bravo ! " from all of us because it had been a good day for France. They were simple fellows, these men, and they had the manners of fine gentlemen in spite of their mud-stained uniforms and the poverty of the cottage in which they lived. Hardly a day passed without one of their comrades being killed or wounded, but some officer came to take his place and his risk, and they made him welcome to the wooden chair and his turn of the truckle-bed. I think in that peasant's hut I saw the whole spirit of the French army in its surrender of self-interest and its good-humoured gallantry.

The guns were still thundering as I drove back from the wood. The driver of the car turned to me for a moment with a smile and pointed a few yards away.

" Did you see that shell burst then ? It was pretty close."

Death was always pretty close when one reached the fighting-lines of France.

Soldiers of France, for nearly a year of war I have been walking among you with watchful eyes, seeing you in all your moods, of gaiety and depression, of youthful spirits and middle-aged fatigues, and listening to your tales of war along the roads of France, where you have gone marching to the zone of death valiantly. I know some of your weaknesses and the strength of the spirit that is in you, and the sentiment that lies deep and pure in your hearts in spite of the common clay of your peasant life or the cynical wit you learnt in Paris. Sons of a great race, you have not forgotten the traditions of a thousand years, which makes your history glorious with the spirit of a keen and flashing people, which century after century has renewed its youth out of the weariness of old vices and reached forward to new beauties of science and art with quick intelligence.

This monstrous war has been your greatest test, straining your moral fibre beyond even the ordeal of those days when your Republican armies fought in rags and tatters on the frontiers and swept across Europe to victories which drained your manhood. The debacle of 1870 was not your fault, for not all your courage could save you from corruption and treachery, and in this new war you have risen above your frailties with a strength and faith that have wiped out all those memories of failure. It is good to have made friends among you, to have clasped some of your brown hands, to have walked a little along the roads with you. Always now the name of France will be like a song in my heart, stirring a thousand memories of valour and fine endurance, and of patience in this senseless business of slaughter, which made you unwilling butchers and victims of a bloody sacrifice. *Bonne chance, soldats de France!*

CHAPTER X

THE MEN IN KHAKI

1

WHEN our little professional army landed on the coast of France there was not one in a thousand soldiers who had more than the vaguest idea as to why he was coming to fight the Germans or as to the character of the fighting in which he was to be engaged. If one asked him "Why are we at war with Germany" this regular soldier would scratch his head, struggle to find a reasonable answer, and mutter something about "them bloody Germans," and "giving a hand to the Froggies." Of international politics, world-problems, Teutonic ambitions, Slav perils, White Papers or Yellow Papers, he knew nothing and cared nothing. As a professional soldier it was his duty to fight anybody he was told to fight, of whatever colour he might be, or of whatever country. For some months it had been in his mind that he might have to do a bit of shooting in Ireland, and on the whole he was glad that this enemy was to speak a foreign language. It made the game seem more as it should be. What was it Blatchford had said about the Germans ? He couldn't quite remember the drift of it, except that they had been preparing for years to have a smack at England. Wanted to capture all our Colonies, and were building ships like blazes. Of course our Government had been asleep as usual, and didn't care a damn. No British Government ever did, as far as he could remember. Anyhow, the Germans were his enemy, and the French were our friends—which was queer—and the British army was going to save Europe again according to its glorious traditions as mentioned more than once by the Colonel. It had been a fine time before saying good-bye to the wife and kids. Every man had been a hero to his fellow citizens, who had clapped him on the back and stood free drinks in great style. "Bring us back some German helmets, Jock!" the girls had shouted out, "And mind your P's and Q's with them French hussies."

It would be a bit of a change to see the Continental way of doing things. They spoke a queer lingo, the French, but were all right. Quite all right, judging from the newspapers, and a fellow who had gone out as a chauffeur and had come back with fancy manners. "After you, Monsieur. Pardonney-more." There would be some great adventures to tell the lads when the business was over. Of course there would be hot work, and some of the boys would never come back at all —accidents did happen even in the best regulated wars—but with a bit of luck there would be a great home-coming with all the bells ringing, and crowds in the streets, and the band playing "See the conquering hero comes," or " when Tommy comes marching home." We had learnt a thing or two since South Africa, and the army was up to scratch. These Germans would have to look out for themselves.

2

I think that represents fairly enough the mental attitude of the average British soldier who came out to France into an unknown land in which he was to do "his bit." The younger men knew nothing of the psychological effect of shell-fire, and their imagination was not haunted by any fear. The older men, brought back to the Colours after a spell of civil life, judged of war according to the standards of the South African campaign or Omdurman, and did not guess that this war was to be a more monstrous thing, which would make that little affair in the Transvaal seem a picnic for boys playing at the game. Not yet had they heard the roar of Germany's massed artillery or seen the heavens open and rain down death.

The British officer was more thoughtful, and did not reveal his thoughts to the men. Only in quiet conversation in his own mess did he reveal the forebodings which made his soul gloomy.

" There is no doubt the German army is the greatest fighting machine in Europe. We might dislike some of their methods, their cast-iron system and all that—oh, I know what the *Times* man said about their last manœuvres—but they have been preparing for this war for years, and their organization is all cut and dried. How about the French ? Yes, they have plenty of pluck, and I've seen something of their gunners—quite marvellous !—but have they got any staying power ? Are they ready ? How about their politicians ? I don't like the look of things, altogether. We have joined in this infernal war—had to, of course—but if things go wrong in France we haven't anything like an army to tackle a job like this. . . . Not that I'm a pessimist, mind you."

No, they were not pessimists, these British officers, when they first came out to France ; and the younger men, all those lieutenants who had come quite recently from Sandhurst and Stonyhurst, and public schools in England, with the fine imperturbable manner of their class and caste, hiding their boyishness under a mask of gravity, and not giving themselves away by the slightest exuberance of speech or gesture, but maintaining stiff upper lips under a square quarter of an inch of fair bristles, went into this war with unemotional and unconscious heroism. Unlike the French officer, who had just that touch of emotionalism and self-consciousness which delights in the hero-worship in the streets, the cheers of great crowds, the fluttering of women's handkerchiefs, and the showering of flowers from high balconies, these English boys had packed up their traps and gone away from homes just as they had got back to school after the holidays, a little glum, and serious, at the thought of work.

" Good-bye, mother."

The embrace had lasted a few seconds longer than usual. This mother had held her son tight, and had turned a little pale. But her voice had been steady and she had spoken familiar words of affection and advice, just as if her boy were off to the hunting-fields, or a polo match.

" Good-bye, darling. Do be careful, won't you ? Don't take unnecessary risks."

"Right-o ! . . . Back soon, I hope."

That was all, in most cases. No sobs or heartbreaks. No fine words about patriotism, and the sweetness of death for the Mother Country, and the duty of upholding the old traditions of the Flag. All that was taken for granted, as it had been taken for granted when this tall fellow in brand new khaki with nice-smelling belts of brown leather, was a bald-headed baby on a lace pillow in a cradle, or an obstreperous boy in a big nursery. The word patriotism is never spoken in an English household of this boy's class. There are no solemn discourses about duty to the Mother Country. Those things have always been taken for granted, like the bread and butter at the breakfast table, and the common decencies of life, and the good manners of well-bred people. When his mother had brought a man-child into the world she knew that this first-born would be a soldier, at some time of his life. In thousands of families it is still the tradition. She knew also that if it were necessary, according to the code of England, to send a punitive expedition against some native race, or to capture a new piece of the earth for the British Empire, this child of hers would play his part, and take the risks, just as his father had done, and his grandfather. The boy knew also, though he was never told. The usual thing had happened at the usual age.

"I suppose you will soon be ready for Sandhurst, Dick ?"

"Yes, I suppose so, father."

So when the war came these young men who had been gazetted six months or so before went out to France as most men go to do their job, without enthusiasm, but without faltering, in the same matter-of-fact way as a bank clerk catches the 9.15 train to the city. But death might be at the end of the journey ? Yes. Quite likely. They would die in the same quiet way. It was a natural incident of the job. A horrid nuisance, of course, quite rotten, and all that, but no more to be shirked than the risk of taking a toss over an ugly fence. It was what this young man had been born for. It was the price he paid for his caste.

3

There were some undercurrents of emotion in the British army not to be seen on the surface. There had been private dramas in private drawing-rooms. Some of the older men had been " churned up," as they would say, because this sudden war had meant a leave-taking from women, who would be in a deuce of a fix if anything happened to certain captains and certain majors. Love affairs which had been somewhat complicated were simplified too abruptly by a rapid farewell, and a " God bless you, old girl. . . . I hate to leave you with such ragged ends to the whole business. But perhaps after all it's a way out—for both of us. Eh ? " The war offered a way out for all sorts of men with complicated lives, with debts that had been rather a worry, and with bills of folly that could not be paid at sight, and with skeletons in the cupboard rattling their bones too loudly behind the panels. Well, it was a case of cut and run. Between the new life and the old there would be no bridge, across which a woman or a ghost could walk. War is always a way of escape even though it be through the dark valley of death.

Nothing of this private melodrama was visible among those men who came to France. When they landed at Boulogne there was no visible expression on faces which have been trained to be expressionless. At Rouen, at Le Mans, at St. Omer, and many other towns in France I watched our British officers and tried to read their character after getting a different point of view among the French troops. Certainly in their way they were magnificent— the first gentlemen in the world, the most perfect type of aristocratic manhood. Their quietude and their coldness struck me as remarkable, because of the great contrast in the character of the people around them. For the first time I saw the qualities of my own race, with something like a foreigner's eyes, and realized the strength of our racial character. It was good to see the physique of these men, with their clear-cut English faces, and their fine easy swagger, utterly unconscious and unaffected, due to having played all manner of games since early boyhood, so that their athletic build was not spoilt by deliberate development. And I gave homage to them because of the perfect cut and equipment of their uniforms, so neat and simple, and workmanlike for the job of war. Only Englishmen could look so well in these clothes. And even in these French towns I saw the influence of English school life and of all our social traditions standing clear-cut against the temperament of another nation with different habits and ideals. They were confident without any demonstrative sign that they were superior beings destined by God, or the force of fate, to hold the fullest meaning of civilization. They were splendidly secure in this faith, not making a brag of it, not alluding to it, but taking it for granted, just as they had taken for granted their duty to come out to France and die if that were destined. And studying them, at café tables, at the base, or in their depots, I acknowledged that, broadly, they were right. In spite of an extraordinary ignorance of art and letters (speaking of the great majority), in spite of ideas stereotyped by the machinery of their schools and universities, so that one might know precisely their attitude to such questions as social reform, internationalism, Home Rule for Ireland, or the Suffragettes— any big problem demanding freedom of thought and unconventionality of discussion—it was impossible to resist the conviction that these officers of the British army have qualities, supreme of their kind, which give a mastery to men. Their courage was not a passion, demanding rage or religious fervour, or patriotic enthusiasm, for its inspiration. It was the very law of their life, the essential spirit in them. They were unconscious of it as a man is unconscious of breathing, unless diseased. Their honour was not a thing to talk about. To prate about the honour of the army or the honour of England was like talking about the honour of their mother. It is not done. And yet, as Mark Antony said, "They were all honourable men," and there seemed an austerity of virtue in them which no temptation would betray—the virtue of men who have a code admitting of certain easy vices, but not of treachery, or cowardice, or corruption. They had such good form, these young men who had come out to a dirty devilish war. It was enormously good to hear them talking to each other in just the same civil, disinterested, casual way which belongs to the conversational range of St. James's Street clubs. Not once—like French soldiers—did they plunge into heated discussions on the ethics of war, or the philosophy of life, or the progress of civilization, or the rights of democracies. Never did they reveal to casual strangers like myself—and hundreds of French soldiers did—the secret affections of their hearts, flowing back to the women they had left, or their fears of death and disablement, or their sense of the mystery of God. Not even war, with its unloosing of old restraints, its smashing of conventionalities, could break down the code of these young English gentlemen whose first and last lessons had been those of self-concealment and self-control. In England these characteristics are accepted, and one hardly thinks of them. It is the foreigner's point of view of us. But in France, in war time, in a country all vibrant with emotionalism, this restraint of manner and speech and utter disregard of all " problems " and mysteries of life, and quiet, cheerful acceptation of the job in hand, startled the imagination of Englishmen who had been long enough away from home to stand aloof and to study those officers with a fresh vision. There was something superb in those simple, self-confident, normal men, who made no fuss, but obeyed orders, or gave them, with a spirit of discipline which belonged to their own souls and was not imposed by a self-conscious philosophy. And yet I could understand why certain Frenchmen, in spite of their admiration, were sometimes irritated by these British officers. There were times when the similarity between them, the uniformity of that ridiculous little moustache on the upper lip, the intonation of voices with the peculiar timbre of the public school drawl, sound to them rather tiresome. They had the manners of a caste, the touch of arrogance which belongs to a caste, in power. Every idea they had was a caste idea, contemptuous in a civil way of poor devils who had other ideas and who were therefore guilty—not by their own fault of course—of shocking bad form. To be a Socialist in such company would be worse than being drunk. To express a belief in democratic liberty would cause a silence to fall upon a group of them as though some obscenity beyond the limits allowed in an officers' mess-room had been uttered by a man without manners.

Their attitude to French officers was, in the beginning of the war, calculated to put a little strain upon the Entente Cordiale. It was an attitude of polite but haughty condescension. A number of young Frenchmen of the best families had been appointed as interpreters to the British Expedition. There were aristocrats among them whose names run like golden threads through the pages of French history. It was therefore disconcerting when the young Viscomte de Chose and a certain Marquis de Machin found that their knowledge of English was used for the purpose of buying a packet of cigarettes for a lieutenant who knew no French, and of running errands for British officers who accepted such services as a matter of course. The rank-and-file of the British army which first came into France was also a little careless of French susceptibilities. After the first rapture of that welcome which was extended to anyone in khaki, French citizens began to look a little askance at the regiments from the Highlands and Lowlands, some of whose men demanded free gifts in the shops, and, when a little drunk, were rather crude in their amorous advances to girls of decent up-bringing. These things were inevitable. In our regular army there were the sweepings of many slums, as well as the best blood of our peasantry and our good old families. Tough and hardened fellows called to the Colours again from Glasgow and Liverpool, Cardiff and Limehouse, had none of the refinements of the younger generation of soldiers who prefer lemonade to whisky, and sweetmeats to shag. It was these who in the first Expeditionary Force gave most trouble to the military police and found themselves under the iron heel of a discipline which is very hard and very necessary in time of war.

4

These men were heroic soldiers, yet our hero-worship need not blind us to the truth of things. There is nothing more utterly false than to imagine that war purges human nature of all its frailties and vices, and that under the shadow of death a great body of men gathered like this from many classes and cities, become suddenly white knights, *sans peur et sans reproche*, inspired by the highest ideals of faith and chivalry. If only some new Shakespeare would come out of the ranks after this war to give us immortal portraits of a twentieth-century Falstaff, with a modern Nym, Pistol, and Bardolph—what a human comedy would be there in the midst of all this tragedy in France and Flanders, setting off the fine exalted heroism of all those noble and excellent men who, like the knights and men-at-arms of Henry at Agincourt, thought that "the fewer men the greater share of honour," and fought for England with a devotion that was careless of death. After the British retreat from Mons, when our regular troops realized very rapidly the real meaning of modern warfare, knowing now that it was to be no "picnic," but a deadly struggle against great odds, and a fight of men powerless against infernal engines, there came out to France by every ship the oddest types of men who had been called out to fill up the gaps and take a share in the deadly business. These "dug-outs" were strange fellows, some of them. Territorial officers who had held commissions in the Yeomanry, old soldiers who had served in India, Egypt, and South Africa, before playing interminable games of chess in St. James's Street, or taking tea in country rectories and croquet mallets on country lawns; provincial schoolmasters who had commanded an O.T.C. with high-toned voices which could recite a passage from Ovid with cultured diction; purple-faced old fellows who for years had tempted Providence and apoplexy by violence to their valets; and young bloods who had once "gone through the

Guards," before spending their week-ends at Brighton with little ladies from the Gaiety chorus, came to Boulogne or Havre by every boatload and astonished the natives of those ports by their martial manners. The Red Cross was responsible for many astounding representatives of the British race in France, and there were other crosses—purple, green, blue, and black—who contributed to this melodrama of mixed classes and types. Benevolent old gentlemen, garbed like second-hand Field Marshals, tottered down the quaysides and took the salutes of startled French soldiers with bland but dignified benevolence. The Jewish people were not only generous to the Red Cross work with unstinted wealth which they poured into its coffers, but with rich young men who offered their lives and their motor-cars in this good service—though the greater part of them never went nearer to the front (through no fault of their own) than Rouen or Paris, where they spent enormous sums of money at the best hotels, and took lady friends for joy rides in ambulances of magnificent design. Boulogne became overcrowded with men and women wearing military uniforms of no known design with badges of mysterious import. Even the Scotland Yard detectives were bewildered by some of these people whose passports were thoroughly sound, but whose costumes aroused deep suspicion. What could they do, for instance, with a young Hindu, dressed as a boy-scout, wearing tortoise-shell spectacles, and a field kit of dangling bags, water-bottles, maps, cooking utensils, and other material suitable for life on a desert isle ? Or what could they say to a lady in breeches and top-boots, with a revolver stuck through her belt, and a sou'wester on her head, who was going to nurse the wounded in a voluntary hospital at Nice ? Contingents of remarkable women invaded the chief tea-shops in Boulogne and caused a panic among the waitresses. They wore Buffalo Bill hats and blue uniforms with heavy blue coats, which were literally spangled with brass buttons. Upon their stalwart bosoms were four rows of buttons, and there was a row of brass on each side of their top-coats, on their shoulders, and at the back of their waist-belts. In the light of the tea-shop, where they consumed innumerable buns, one's eyes became dizzy with all these bits of shining metal. To a wounded man the sight of one of these ladies must have been frightening, as though a shell had burst near his bedside, with the glint of broken steel. Young officers just drafted out with commissions on which the ink was hardly dry, plucked at their budding moustaches and said " War is hell."

Some of the older officers, who had been called out after many years of civilian ease, found the spirit of youth again as soon as they set foot on the soil of France, and indulged in the follies of youth as when they had been sub-lieutenants in the Indian hills. I remember one of these old gentlemen who refused to go to bed in the Hôtel Tortoni at Havre, though the call was for six o'clock next morning with quite a chance of death before the week was out. Some younger officers with him coaxed him to his room just before midnight, but he came down again, condemning their impudence, and went out into the great silent square, shouting for a taxi. It seemed to me pitiful that a man with so many ribbons on his breast, showing distinguished service, should be wandering about a place where many queer characters roam in the darkness of night. I asked him if I could show him the way back to the Hôtel Tortoni. " Sir," he said, " I desire to go to Piccadilly Circus, and if I have any of your impertinence I will break your head." Two apaches lurched up to him, a few minutes later, and he went off with them into a dark ally, speaking French with great deliberation and a Mayfair accent. He was a twentieth century Falstaff, and the playwright might find his low comedy in a character like this thrust into the grim horror of the war.

5

One's imagination must try to disintegrate that great collective thing called an army and see it as much as possible as a number of separate individualities, with their differences of temperament and ideals and habits of mind. There has been too much of the impersonal way of writing of our

British Expeditionary Force as though it were a great human machine impelled with one idea and moving with one purpose. In its ranks was the coster with his cockney speech and cockney wit, his fear of great silences and his sense of loneliness and desolation away from the flare of gas-lights and the raucous shouts of the crowds in Petticoat Lane—so that when I met him in a field of Flanders with the mist and the long, flat marshlands about him he confessed to the almighty Hump. And there was the Irish peasant who heard the voice of the Banshee calling through that mist, and heard other queer voices of supernatural beings whispering to the melancholy which had been bred in his brain in the wilds of Connemara. Here was the English mechanic, matter-of-fact, keen on his job, with an alert brain and steady nerves ; and with him was the Lowland `Scot, hard as nails, with uncouth speech and a savage fighting instinct. Soldiers who had been through several battles and knew the tricks of old campaigners were the stiffening in regiments of younger men whose first experience of shell-fire was soul-shattering, so that some of them whimpered and were blanched with fear. In the ranks were men who had been mob-orators, and who had once been those worst of pests, "barrack-room lawyers." They talked Socialism and revolution in the trenches to comrades who saw no use to alter the good old ways of England and "could find no manner of use" for political balderdash. Can you not see all these men, made up of every type in the life of the British Isles, suddenly transported to the Continent and thence into the zone of fire of massed artillery which put each man to the supreme test of courage, demanding the last strength of his soul ? Some of them had been slackers, rebels against discipline, "hard cases." Some of them were sensitive fellows with imaginations over-developed by cinematograph shows and the unhealthiness of life in cities. Some of them were no braver than you or I, my readers. And yet out of all this mass of manhood, with all their faults, vices, coward instincts, pride of courage, unexpressed ideals, unconscious patriotism, old traditions of pluck, untutored faith in things more precious than self-interest—the mixture

Y

that one finds in any great body of men—there was made an army, that "contemptible little army" of ours which has added a deathless story of human valour to the chronicles of our race. These men who came out with the first Expeditionary Force had to endure a mode of warfare more terrible than anything the world has known before, and for week after week, month after month, they were called upon to stand firm under storms of shells which seemed to come from no human agency, but to be devilish in intensity and frightfulness of destruction. Whole companies of them were annihilated, whole battalions decimated, yet the survivors were led to the shambles again. Great gaps were torn out of famous regiments and filled up with new men, so often that the old regiment was but a name and the last remaining officers and men were almost lost among the new-comers. Yet by a miracle in the blood of the British race, in humanity itself, if it is not decadent beyond the point of renaissance, these cockneys and peasants, Scotsmen and Irishmen, and men from the Midlands, the North, and the Home Counties of this little England faced that ordeal, held on, and did not utter aloud (though sometimes secretly) one wailing cry to God for mercy in all this hell. With a pride of manhood beyond one's imagination, with a stern and bitter contempt for all this devilish torture, loathing it but "sticking" it, very much afraid yet refusing to surrender to the coward in their souls (the coward in our souls which tempts all of us), sick of the blood and the beastliness, yet keeping sane (for the most part) with the health of normal minds and bodies in spite of all this wear and tear upon the nerves, the rank-and-file of that British Expedition in France and Flanders, under the leadership of young men who gave their lives, with the largess of great prodigals, to the monstrous appetite of Death, fought with something like superhuman qualities.

6

Although I spent most of my time on the Belgian and French side of the war, I had many glimpses of the British troops who were enduring these things, and many conversations with officers and men who had come, but a few hours ago, from the line of fire. I went through British hospitals and British ambulance trains where thousands of them lay with new wounds, and I dined with them when after a few weeks of convalescence they returned to the front to undergo the same ordeal. Always I felt myself touched with a kind of wonderment at these men. After many months of war the unwounded men were still unchanged, to all outward appearance, though something had altered in their souls. They were still quiet, self-controlled, unemotional. Only by a slight nervousness of their hands, a slightly fidgety way so that they could not sit still for very long, and by sudden lapses into silence, did some of them show the signs of the strain upon them. Even the lightly wounded men were astoundingly cheerful, resolute, and unbroken. There were times when I used to think that my imagination exaggerated the things I had seen and heard, and that after all war was not so terrible, but a rather hard game with heavy risks. It was only when I walked among the wounded who had been more than " touched," and who were the shattered wrecks of men, that I realized again the immensity of the horror through which these other men had passed and to which some of them were going back. When the shrieks of poor tortured boys rang in my ears, when one day I passed an officer sitting up in his cot and laughing with insane mirth at his own image in a mirror, and when I saw men with both legs amputated up to the thighs, or with one leg torn to ribbons, and another already sawn away, lying among blinded and paralysed men, and men smashed out of human recognition but still alive, that I knew the courage of those others, who having seen and known, went back to risk the same frightfulness.

7

There was always a drama worth watching at the British base, for it was the gate of those who came in and of those who went out, " the halfway house" as a friend of mine called another place in France, between the front and home.

Everything came here first—the food for guns and men, new boots for soldiers who had marched the leather off their feet ; the comforters and body-belts knitted by nimble-fingered girls, who in suburban houses and country factories had put a little bit of love into every stitch ; chloroform and morphia for army doctors who have moments of despair when their bottles get empty ; ambulances, instruments, uniforms, motor lorries ; all the letters which came to France full of prayers and hopes ; and all the men who came to fill up the places of those for whom there are still prayers, but no more hope on this side of the river.   It was the base of the British Expeditionary Force, and the Army in the field would be starved in less than a week if it were cut off from this port of supplies.

There was a hangar here, down by the docks, half a mile long.   I suppose it was the largest shed in the world, and it was certainly the biggest store-cupboard ever kept under lock and key by a Mother Hubbard with a lot of hungry boys to feed.   Their appetites were prodigious, so that every day thousands of cases were shifted out of this cupboard and sent by train and motor-car to the front.   But always new cases were arriving in boats that are piloted into harbour across a sea where strange fish came up from the deeps at times.   So the hangar was never empty, and on the signature of a British officer the British soldiers might be sure of their bully beef, and fairly sure of a clean shirt or two when the old ones had been burnt by the order of a medical officer with a delicate nose and high ideals in a trench.

New men as well as new stores came in the boats to this harbour, which was already crowded with craft not venture-some in a sea where one day huge submarine creatures lurked about.   I watched some Tommies arrive.   They had had a nasty " dusting " on the voyage, and as they marched through the streets of the port some of them looked rather washed out.   They carried their rifles upside down as though that might ease the burden of them, and they had that bluish look of men who have suffered a bad bout of sea-sickness.   But they pulled themselves up when they came into the chief square where the French girls at the flower stalls, and ladies at the hotel windows, and a group of French and Belgian soldiers under the shelter of an arcade, watched them pass through the rain.

" Give 'em their old tune, lads," said one of the men, and from this battalion of new-comers who had just set foot in France to fill up gaps in the ranks, out there, at the front, there came a shrill whistling chorus of La Marseillaise. Yorkshire had learnt the hymn of France, her song of victory, and I heard it on the lips of Highlanders and Welshmen, who came tramping through the British base to the camps outside the town where they waited to be sent forward to the fighting line.

" Vive les Anglais ! " cried a French girl, in answer to the whistling courtesy. Then she laughed, with her arm round the waist of a girl friend, and said, " They are all the same, these English soldiers. In their khaki one cannot tell one from the other, and now that I have seen so many thousands of them—Heaven ! hundreds of thousands !—I have exhausted my first enthusiasm. It is sad : the new arrivals do not get the same welcome from us."

That was true. So many of our soldiers had been through the British base that they were no longer a novelty. The French flower-girls did not empty their stalls into the arms of the regiments, as on the first days.

It was an English voice that gave the new-comers the highest praise, because professional.

" A hefty lot ! . . . Wish I were leading them."

The praise and the wish came from a young English officer who was staying in the same hotel with me. For two days I had watched his desperate efforts to avoid death by boredom. He read every line of the *Matin* and *Journal* before luncheon, with tragic sighs, because every line repeated what had been said in the French newspapers since the early days of the war. After luncheon he made a sortie for the English newspapers, which arrived by boats. They kept him quiet until tea-time. After that he searched the cafés for any fellow officers who might be there.

" This is the most awful place in the world ! " he repeated at intervals, even to the hall porter, who agreed with him. When I asked him how long he had been at the base he groaned miserably and confessed to three weeks of purgatory.

" I've been put into the wrong pigeon-hole at the War Office," he said. " I'm lost."

There were many other men at the British base who seemed to have been put into the wrong pigeon-holes. Among them were about two hundred French interpreters who were awaiting orders to proceed with a certain division. But they were not so restless as my friend in the hotel. Was it not enough for them that they had been put into English khaki—supplied from the store-cupboard—and that every morning they had to practise the art of putting on a puttee ? In order to be perfectly English they also practised the art of smoking a briar pipe—it was astoundingly difficult to keep it alight—and indulged in the habit of five o'clock tea (with boiled eggs, ye gods !), and braved all the horrors of indigestion, because they are not used to these things, with heroic fortitude. At any cost they were determined to do honour to *le khaki*, in spite of the arrogance of certain British officers who treated them *de haut en bas*.

The Base Commandant's office was the sorting-house of the Expeditionary Force. The relays of officers who had just come off the boats came here to report themselves. They had sailed as it were under sealed orders and did not know their destination until they were enlightened by the Commandant, who received instructions from the head-quarters in the field. They waited about in groups outside his door, slapping their riding-boots or twisting neat little moustaches, which were the envy of subalterns just out of Sandhurst.

Through another door was the registry office through which all the Army's letters passed inwards and outwards. The military censors were there reading the letters of Private Atkins to his best girl, and to his second best. They shook their heads over military strategy written in the trenches, and laughed quietly at the humour of men who looked on the best side of things, even if they were German shells or French fleas. It was astonishing what a lot of humour passed through this central registry from men who were having a tragic time for England's sake ; but sometimes the military Censor had to blow his nose with violence because Private Atkins lapsed into pathos, and wrote of tragedy with a too poignant truth.

The Base Commandant was here at all hours. Even two hours after midnight he sat in the inner room with tired secretaries who marvelled at the physical and mental strength of a man who at that hour could still dictate letters full of important detail without missing a point or a comma ; though he came down early in the morning. But he was responsible for the guarding of the Army's store-cupboard—that great hangar, half a mile long—and for the discipline of a town full of soldiers who, without discipline, would make a merry hell of it, and for the orderly disposition of all the supplies at the base upon which the army in the field depends for its welfare. It was not what men call a soft job.

Through the hotel where I stayed there was a continual flow of officers who came for one night only. Their kit-bags and sleeping-bags were dumped into the hall, and these young gentlemen, some of whom had been gazetted only a few months ago, crowded into the little drawing-room to write their letters home before going to the front, and to inquire of each other what on earth there was to do in a town where lights are out at ten o'clock, where the theatres were all closed, and where rain was beating down on the pavements outside.

" How about a bath ? " said one of them. " It is about the last chance, I reckon."

They took turns to the bathroom, thinking of the mud and vermin of the trenches which would soon be their home. Among those who stayed in the sitting-room until the patron turned out the lights were several officers who had been on forty-eight hours' leave from the front. They had made a dash to London and back, they had seen the lights of Piccadilly again, and the crowds in the streets of a city which seemed to know nothing of war, they had dined with women in evening-dress who had asked innocent questions about the way of a modern battlefield, and they had said good-bye again to those who clung to them a little too long outside a carriage window.

"Worth it, do you think ? " asked one of them.

"Enormously so. But it's a bit of a pull—going back to that—beastliness. After one knows the meaning of it."

"It's because I know that I want to go back," said another man who had sat very quietly looking at the toe of one of his riding-boots. "I had a good time in town— it seemed too good to be true—but, after all, one has to finish one's job before one can sit around with an easy mind. We've got to finish our job out there in the stinking trenches."

8

I suppose even now after all that has been written it is difficult for the imagination of "the man who stayed at home" to realize the life and conditions of the soldiers abroad. So many phrases which appeared day by day in the newspapers conveyed no more than a vague, uncertain meaning.

"The Front"—how did it look, that place which was drawn in a jagged black line across the map on the wall ? "General Headquarters"—what sort of a place was that in which the Commander-in-Chief lived with his staff, directing the operations in the fighting lines ? "An attack was made yesterday upon the enemy's position at ——. A line of trenches was carried by assault." So ran the official bulletin, but the wife of a soldier abroad could not fill in the picture, the father of a young Territorial could not get enough detail upon which his imagination might build. For all those at home, whose spirits came out to Flanders seeking to get into touch with young men who were fighting for honour's sake, it was difficult to form any kind of mental vision, giving a clear and true picture of this great adventure in "foreign parts."

They would have been surprised at the reality, it was so different from all their previous imaginings. General Headquarters, for instance, was a surprise to those who came to such a place for the first time. It was not, when I went there some months ago, a very long distance from the fighting lines in these days of long-range guns, but it was a place of strange quietude in which it was easy to forget the actuality of war—until one was reminded by sullen far-off rumblings which made the windows tremble, and made men lift their heads a moment to say : " They are busy out there to-day."

There were no great movements of troops in the streets. Most of the soldiers one saw were staff officers, who walked briskly from one building to another with no more than a word and a smile to any friend they met on the way. Sentries stood outside the doorways of big houses.

Here and there at the street corners was a military policeman, scrutinizing any new-comer in civilian clothes with watchful eyes. Church bells tinkled for early morning Mass or Benediction. Through an open window looking out upon a broad courtyard the voices of school children came chanting their A B C in French, as though no war had taken away their fathers. There was an air of profound peace here.

At night, when I stood at an open window listening to the silence of the place it was hard, even though I knew, to think that here in this town was the Headquarters Staff of the greatest army England has ever sent abroad, and that the greatest war in history was being fought out only a few miles away. The raucous horn of a motor-car, the panting of a motor-cycle, the rumble of a convoy of ambulances, the shock of a solitary gun, came as the only reminders of the great horror away there through the darkness. A dispatch rider was coming back from a night ride on a machine which had side-slipped all the way from Ypres. An officer was motoring back to a divisional headquarters after a late interview with the chief. . . The work went on, though it was very quiet in General Headquarters.

But the brains of the Army were not asleep. Behind

those doors, guarded by sentries, men in khaki uniforms, with just a touch of red about the collar, were bending over maps and documents—studying the lines of German trenches as they had been sketched out by aviators flying above German shrapnel, writing out orders for ammunition to be sent in a hurry to a certain point on the fighting line where things were very "busy" in the afternoon, ordering the food-supplies wanted by a division of hungry men whose lorries are waiting at the rail-head for bread and meat and a new day's rations.

"Things are going very well," said one of the officers, with a glance at a piece of flimsy paper which had just come from the Signals Department across the street. But things would not have gone so well unless at General Headquarters every officer had done his duty to the last detail, whatever the fatigue of body or spirit. The place was quiet, because the work was done behind closed doors in these private houses of French and Flemish bourgeoisie whose family portraits hang upon the walls. Outside I could not see the spirit of war unless I searched for it.

It was after I had left "G.H.Q." that I saw something of the human side of war and all its ceaseless traffic. Yet even then, as I travelled nearer and nearer to the front, I was astounded at the silence, the peacefulness of the scenery about me, the absence of all tragic sights. That day, on the way to a place which was very close to the German lines, children were playing on the roadside, and old women in black gowns trudged down the long, straight high roads, with their endless sentinels of trees.

In a furrowed field a peasant was sowing the seed for an autumn harvesting, and I watched his swinging gestures from left to right which seem symbolical of all that peace means and of all nature's life and beauty. The seed is scattered and God does the rest, though men may kill each other and invent new ways of death. . . .

But the roads were encumbered and the traffic of war was surging forward ceaselessly in a muddled, confused, aimless sort of way, as it seemed to me, before I knew the

system and saw the working of the brain behind it all.   A long
train of carts without horses stood, shafts down, on the muddy
side of the road.   Little blue and red flags fluttered above
them.   A group of soldiers were lounging in their neighbourhood, waiting, it seems, for something to turn up.   Perhaps
that something was a distant train which came with a long
trail of smoke across the distant marshlands.

At the railway crossing there was a great park of motor
lorries.   They, too, seemed to be waiting for new loads.
Obviously this was one of the " railheads " about which I
had a lecture that morning from a distinguished officer, who
thinks in railheads and refilling stations and other details of
transport upon which the armies in the field depend for their
food and ammunition.   Without that explanation all these
roadside halts, all these stationary lorries and forage carts
would have seemed like a temporary stagnation in the business of war, with nothing doing.

A thrill comes to every one when he sees bodies of British
troops moving along the roads.   He is glad when his motor-
car gets held up by some old wagons slithering axle-deep in
the quagmire on the side of the paved highway, so that he can
put his head out and shout a " Hullo, boys !   How's it going ?
And who are you ? "   After all the thrill of the recruiting days,
all the excitement of the send-off, all the enthusiasm with
which they sang Tipperary through the streets of their first
port of call in France, they had settled down to the real
business.

Some of them had been into the trenches for the first time
a night or two before.   " How did you like it ? "   Well, it
wasn't amusing to them, it seems, but they " stuck it."   They
were ready to go again.   That was the spirit of it all.   They
" stuck it," gamely, without grousing, without swanking,
without any other thought than suffering all the hardships
and all the thrills of war like men who know the gravity of the
game, and the risks, and the duty to which they have pledged
themselves.

I passed thousands of these men on a long motor journey
on my first day at the British front, and though I could not

speak to very many of them I saw on all their faces the same hard, strong, dogged look of men who were being put through a great ordeal and who would not fail through any moral weakness. They were tired, some of them, after a long march, but they grinned back cheery answers to my greetings, and scrambled merrily for the few packets of cigarettes I tossed to them.

Thousands of these khaki-clad fellows lay along the roadsides looking in the distance as though great masses of russet leaves had fallen from autumn trees. They were having a rest on their way up to the front, and their heads were upon each other's shoulders in a comradely way, while some lay face upwards to the sky with their hands folded behind their heads, in a brown study and careless of everything that passed.

Away across marshy fields, intersected by pools and rivulets, I saw our men billeted in French and Flemish farmhouses, of the old post-and-plaster kind, like those in English villages.

They seemed thoroughly at home, and were chopping wood and drawing water and cooking stews, and arranging straw beds in the barns, and busying themselves with all the domestic side of life as quietly and cheerily as though they were on manœuvres in Devonshire or Surrey, where war is only a game without death in the roar of a gun. Well fed and well clothed, hard as nails, in spite of all their hardships, they gave me a sense of pride as I watched them, for the spirit of the old race was in them, and they would stick it through thick and thin.

I passed that day through the shell-stricken town of Ypres and wandered through the great tragedy of the Cloth Hall—that old splendour in stone which was now a gaunt and ghastly ruin. British soldiers were buying picture postcards at booths in the market-place, and none of them seemed to worry because at any moment another shell might come crashing across the shattered roofs with a new message of destruction.

Yet on all this journey of mine in the war zone of the

British front for at least 100 kilometres or so there was no thrill or shock of war itself. A little way off, on some parts of the road men were in the trenches facing the enemy only a few yards distant from their hiding-places.

The rumble of guns rolled sullenly now and then across the marshlands, and one knew intellectually, but not instinctively, that if one's motor-car took the wrong turning and travelled a mile or two heedlessly, sudden death would call a halt.

And that was the strangeness of it all—the strangeness that startled me as I drove back to the quietude of the General Headquarters, as darkness came down upon this low-lying countryside and put its cloak about the figures of British soldiers moving to their billets, and gave a ghostliness to the tall, tufted trees, which seemed to come striding towards my headlights.

In this siege warfare of the trenches there was a deadly stillness behind the front and a queer absence of war's tumult and turmoil. Yet all the time it was going on slowly, yard by yard, trench by trench, and somewhere along the front men were always fighting and dying.

"Gentlemen," said a staff officer that night, "there has been good work to-day. We have taken several lines of trenches, and the operation is proceeding very well."

We bent over his map, following the line drawn by his finger, listening to details of a grim bit of work, glad that five hundred German prisoners had been taken that day. As he spoke the window rattled, and we heard the boom of another gun. . . . The war was going on, though it had seemed so quiet at the front.

9

For several months there was comparative quietude at the British front after the tremendous attacks upon our lines at Soissons and Venizel and Vic-sur-Aisne, and the still more bloody battles round Ypres in the autumn of the first year of war. Each side settled down for the winter campaign, and killing was done by continual artillery fire with only occasional bayonet charges between trench and trench. That long period of dark wet days was the most tragic ordeal of our men, and a time when depression settled heavily upon their spirits, so that not all their courage could keep any flame of enthusiasm in their hearts for such fine words as honour and glory. In " Plug Street " and other lines of trenches they stood in water with walls of oozy mud about them, until their legs rotted and became black with a false frostbite, until many of them were carried away with bronchitis and pneumonia, and until all of them, however many comforters they tied about their necks, or however many body-belts they used, were shivering, sodden scarecrows, plastered with slime. They crawled with lice, these decent Englishmen from good clean homes, these dandy men who once upon a time had strolled down the sweet shady side of Pall Mall, immaculate, and fragrant as their lavender kid gloves. They were eaten alive by these vermin and suffered the intolerable agony of itch. Strange and terrible diseases attacked some of them, though the poisonous microbes were checked by vigilant men in laboratories behind the front before they could spread an epidemic. For the first time men without science heard the name of cerebro-spinal meningitis and shuddered at it. The war became a hopeless, dreary thing, without a thrill to it, except when men wading in water were smashed by shell-fire and floated about in a bloody mess which ran red through all a trench. That was a thrill of beastliness, but gave no fire to men's hearts. Passion, if it had ever burnt in these British soldiers' hearts, had smouldered out into the white ash of patient misery. Certainly there was no passion of hatred against the enemy, not far away there in the trenches. These Germans were enduring the same hardships, and the same squalor. There was only pity for them and a sense of comradeship, as of men forced by the cruel gods to be tortured by fate.

This sense of comradeship reached strange lengths at Christmas, and on other days. Truces were established and men who had been engaged in trying to kill each other came out of opposite trenches and fraternized. They took photographs of mixed groups of Germans and English, arm-in-arm. They exchanged cigarettes, and patted each other on the shoulder, and cursed the war. . . . The war had become the most tragic farce in the world. The frightful senselessness of it was apparent when the enemies of two nations fighting to the death stood in the grey mist together and liked each other. They did not want to kill each other, these Saxons of the same race and blood, so like each other in physical appearance, and with the same human qualities. They were both under the spell of high, distant Powers which had decreed this warfare, and had so enslaved them that like gladiators in the Roman amphitheatres they killed men so that they should not be put to death by their task-masters. The monstrous absurdity of war, this devil's jest, stood revealed nakedly by those little groups of men standing together in the mists of Flanders. . . . It became so apparent that army orders had to be issued stopping such truces. They were issued but not always obeyed. For months after German and British soldiers in neighbouring trenches fixed up secret treaties by which they fired at fixed targets at stated periods to keep up appearances, and then strolled about in safety, sure of each other's loyalty.

From one trench a German officer signalled to one of our own lieutenants :

" I have six of your men in my trench. What shall I do with them ? "

The lieutenant signalled back.

" I have two of yours. This is ridiculous."

The English officer spoke to the two Germans :

" Look here, you had better clear out. Otherwise I shall have to make you prisoners."

" We want to be prisoners," said the Germans, who spoke English with the accent of the Tottenham Court Road.

It appears that the lieutenant would not oblige them, and begged them to play the game.

So with occasional embarrassments like this to break the deadly monotony of life, and to make men think about the mystery of human nature, coerced to massacre by sovereign powers beyond their ken, the winter passed, in one long wet agony, in one great bog of misery.

10

It was in March, when the roads had begun to dry up, that our troops resumed the offensive at several points of the line. I was at General Headquarters when the first news of the first day's attack at Neuve Chapelle was brought in by dispatch riders.

We crowded again round a table where a staff officer had spread out his map and showed us the general disposition of the troops engaged in the operation. The vague tremor of distant guns gave a grim significance to his words, and on our own journey that day we had seen many signs of organized activity bearing upon this attack.

But we were to see a more impressive demonstration of the day's success, the human counters which had been won by our side in this game of life and death. Nearly a thousand German prisoners had been taken, and were being brought down from the front by rail. If we liked we might have a talk with these men, and see the character of the enemy which lies hidden in the trenches opposite our lines. It was nearly ten o'clock at night when we motored to the railway junction through which they were passing.

Were they glad to be out of the game, away from the shriek of shells and out of the mud ? I framed the question in German as I clambered on to the footboard at a part of the train where the trucks ended and where German officers had been given the luxury of first-class carriages.

Two of them looked up with drowsy eyes, into which there came a look of surprise and then of displeasure as I spoke a few words to them. Opposite me was a fair young man, with soft blond hair and a silky moustache. He looked like a Saxon, but told me afterwards that he came from Cologne. Next to him was a typical young aristocrat of the Bavarian type, in the uniform of a Jaeger regiment In the same carriage were some other officers sleeping heavily. One of them, with a closely-cropped bullet head and the low-browed face of a man who fights according to the philosophy of Bernhardi, without pity, sat up abruptly, swore a fierce word or two, and then fell back and snored again.

The two younger men answered some of my questions, sullenly at first, but afterwards with more friendliness, against which their pride struggled. But they had not much to say. They were tired. They had been taken by surprise. They would have time to learn English as prisoners of war. They had plenty of food and tobacco.

When the next batch of them arrived I was able to get into a closed truck, among the private soldiers. They were quite comfortable in there, and were more cheery than the officers in the other train. I was surprised by their cleanliness, by the good condition of their uniforms, and by their good health and spirits. The life of the trenches had not left its marks upon them, though mentally, perhaps, they had gone to the uttermost limit of endurance. Only one man fired up savagely when I said that they were lucky in being captured. " It is good to fight for the Fatherland," he said. The others made no secret of their satisfaction in being out of it all, and all of them described the attack on Neuve Chapelle as a hellish thing which had caught them by surprise and swept their ranks.

I went back to my billet in General Headquarters wishing that I had seen something of that affair which had netted all these men. It had been a " day out " for the British troops, and we had not yet heard of the blunders or the blood that had spoilt its success. It was hard to have seen nothing of it though so near the front. And then a promise of seeing something of the operations on the morrow came as a prospect for the next day. It would be good to see the real business again and to thrill once more to the awful music of the guns.

Along the road next day it was obvious that "things " were going to happen. As we passed through towns in our motor-cars there were signs of increased activity. Troops were being moved up. Groups of them in goatskin coats, so

Z

that English Tommies looked like their Viking ancestors, halted for a spell by the side of their stacked arms, waiting for orders.   Long lines of motor-lorries, with supplies to feed the men and guns, narrowed the highway for traffic.   Officers approached our cars at every halt, saluted our staff officer, and asked anxious questions : " How are things going ?   Is there any news ? "

In the open country we could see the battle front, the low-lying marshlands with windmills waving their arms on the far horizon, the ridges and woods in which British and German batteries were concealed, and the lines of trenches in which our men lay very close to their enemy.   We left the cars and, slithering in sticky mud, made our way up a hillock on which one of these innumerable windmills stood distinct.   We were among the men who were in the actual fighting lines and who went into the trenches turn and turn about, so that it became the normal routine of their lives.

In the early days of the war these regiments had suffered heavy losses, so that there were new drafts in them now, but there were lads here who had fought at Mons and Charleroi and had seen their comrades fall in heaps round about Le Cateau. They told their tales, with old memories of terror, which had not made cowards of them.   Their chief interest to-day was centred in a football match which was to take place about the same time as the " other business."   It was not their day out in the firing line.   We left them putting on their football boots and hurling chaff at each other in the dim light.   Out of the way of the flying shells they forgot all about the horror of war for a little while.

Forcing our way through the brushwood on the slopes, we reached the crest of the hillock.   Near by stood two generals and several staff officers—men whose names have been written many times in the Chief's dispatches and will be written for all time in the history of this war.   They were at their post of observation, to watch the progress of an attack which was timed to begin shortly.

Presently two other figures came up the hillside.   One of them arrested my attention.   Who was that young officer, a mere boy, who came toiling up through the slime and mud, and who at the crest halted and gave a quick salute to the two generals ? He turned, and I saw that it was Edward, Prince of Wales, and through the afternoon, when I glanced at him now and again as he studied his map and gazed across the fields, I thought of another Edward, Prince of Wales, who six centuries ago stood in another field of France. Out of the past came old ghosts of history, who once as English princes and knights and men-at-arms fought at St. Omer, and Ypres, Bailleul, and Béthune, and all that very ground which lay before me now. . . .

More than an hour before the time at which the attack was to be concentrated upon the enemy's position—a line of trenches on a ridge crowned by a thin wood immediately opposite my observation point—our guns began to speak from many different places. It was a demonstration to puzzle the enemy as to the objective of our attack.

The flashes came like the flicking of heliographs signalling messages by a Morse code of death. After each flash came the thunderous report and a rushing noise as though great birds were in flight behind the veil of mist which lay on the hillsides. Puffs of woolly-white smoke showed where the shrapnel was bursting, and these were wisped away into the heavy clouds. Now and again one heard the high singing note of shells travelling towards us—the German answer to this demonstration—and one saw the puff balls resting on the hill-spur opposite our observation post.

Presently the fire became less scattered, and as the appointed hour approached our batteries aimed only in one direction. It was the ridge to the left of the hill where lines of German trenches had been dug below the fringe of wood. That place must have been a hell for half an hour or more. Through the mist and the drowsy smoke I could see the flashes of the bursting shells like twinkling stars. Those glittering jewels sparkled in constellations, six or more at a time, and there was never a minute without the glint of them. It was not hard to imagine the terror of men crouching in pits below that storm of fire, smashing down upon their trenches, cutting up their barbed wire entanglements, killing any human life that could not hide below the ground. The din of guns was unceasing, and made a great symphony of staccato notes on a thunderous instrument. I could distinguish the sharp crack of the field batteries and the deeper boom of the heavier guns. When one of these spoke there was a trembling of earth, and through the sky a great shell hurtled, with such a rush of air that it seemed like an express train dashing through an endless tunnel. The bursts were like volcanoes above the German lines, vomiting upwards a vast column of black smoke which stood solid on the sky-line for a minute or more before being torn down by the wind. Something within me seemed to quake at these engines of destruction, these masses of explosive power sent for the killing of men, invisible there on the ridge, but cowering in fear or lying in their blood.

How queer are the battlefields of life and the minds of men ! Down below me, in a field, men were playing a game of football while all this business of death was going on. Above and between the guns I heard their shouts and cheers, and the shrill whistle for " half-time," though, there was no half-time in the other game so close to them. Nature, too, was playing, indifferent to this bloody business. All the time, while the batteries were at work, birds were singing the spring song in ecstatic lyrics of joyfulness, and they went on far flights across a pale blue lake which was surrounded by black mountains of cloud.

Another bird came out, but with a man above its wings. It was an English aeroplane on a journey of reconnaissance above the enemy's lines. I heard the loud hum of its engine, and watched how its white wings were made diaphanous by the glint of sun until it passed away into the cloud wrack.

It was invisible to us now, but not to the enemy. They had sighted it, and we saw their shrapnel searching the sky for it. The airman continued his journey on a wide circling flight, and we saw him coming back unscathed.

For a little while our fire slackened. It was time for our infantry attack upon the line of trenches which had sustained such a storm of shells. Owing to the mist and the smoke we could not see our men leave the trenches, nor any sign of that great test of courage when each man depends upon the strength of his own heart, and has no cover behind which to hide any fear that may possess him. What were those cheers ? Still the football players, or our soldiers scaling the ridge ? Was it only a freak of imagination that made us see masses of dark figures moving over that field in the mist ? The guns were firing again continuously, at longer range, to check the enemy's supports.

So the battle went on till darkness began to creep up our hillside, when we made our way down to the valley road and took tea with some of the officers in a house quite close to the zone of fire. Among them were the three remaining officers of a famous regiment—all that were left out of those who had come to France in August of 1914. They were quite cheerful in their manner and made a joke or two when there was any chance. One of them was cutting up a birthday cake, highly emblazoned with sugar-plums and sent out by a pretty sister. It was quite a pleasant little party in the battle zone, and there was a discussion on the subject of temperance, led by an officer who was very keen on total prohibition. The guns did not seem to matter very much as one sat in that cosy room among those cheery men. It was only when we were leaving that one of them took a friend of mine on one side, and said in a kind of whisper, " This war ! . . . It's pretty rough, isn't it ? I'm one of the last men out of the original lot. And, of course, I'm sure to get ' pipped ' in a week or two. On the law of averages, you know."

A few days later I saw the wounded of Neuve Chapelle, which was a victory bought at a fearful price. They were streaming down to Boulogne, and the hospital ships were crowded with them. Among them were thousands of Indians who had taken a big share in that battle.

With an Oriental endurance of pain, beyond the courage of most Western men, these men made no moan. The Sikhs, with their finely chiselled features and dreamy inscrutable eyes—many of them bearded men who have served for twenty years in the Indian army—stared about them in an endless reverie as though puzzling out the meaning of this war among peoples who do not speak their tongue, for some cause they do not understand, and in a climate which makes the whole world different to them. What a strange, bewildering mystery it must have seemed to these men, who had come here in loyalty to the great Raj in whom they had faith and for whom they were glad to die. They seemed to be searching out the soul of the war, to find its secret.

The weeks have passed since then, and the war goes on, and the wounded still stream back, and white men as well as dark men ask God to tell them what all this means ; and can find no answer to the problem of the horror which has engulfed humanity and made a jungle of Europe in which we fight like beasts.

CONCLUSION

In this book I have set down simply the scenes and character of this war as they have come before my own eyes and as I have studied them for nearly a year of history. If there is any purpose in what I have written beyond mere record it is to reveal the soul of war so nakedly that it cannot be glossed over by the glamour of false sentiment and false heroics. More passionate than any other emotion that has stirred me through life, is my conviction that any man who has seen these things must, if he has any gift of expression, and any human pity, dedicate his brain and heart to the sacred duty of preventing another war like this. A man with a pen in his hand, however feeble it may be, must use it to tell the truth about the monstrous horror, to etch its images of cruelty into the brains of his readers, and to tear down the veils by which the leaders of the peoples try to conceal its obscenities. The conscience of Europe must not be lulled to sleep again by the narcotics of old phrases about " the ennobling influence of war " and its " purging fires." It must be shocked by the stark reality of this crime in which all humanity is involved, so that from all the peoples of the civilized world there will be a great cry of rage and horror if the spirit of militarism raises its head again and demands new sacrifices of blood and life's beauty. The Germans have revealed the meaning of war, the devilish soul of it, in a full and complete way, with a most ruthless logic. The chiefs of their great soldier caste have been more honest than ourselves in the business, with the honesty of men who, knowing that war is murder, have adopted the methods of murderers, whole-heartedly, with all the force of their intellect and genius, not weakened by any fear of public

359

opinion, by any prick of conscience, or by any sentiment of compassion. Their logic seems to me flawless, though it is diabolical. If it is permissible to hurl millions of men against each other with machinery which makes a wholesale massacre of life, tearing up trenches, blowing great bodies of men to bits with the single shot of a great gun, strewing battlefields with death, and destroying defended towns so that nothing may live in their ruins, then it is foolish to make distinctions between one way of death and another, or to analyse degrees of horror. Asphyxiating gas is no worse than a storm of shells, or if worse then the more effective.

The lives of non-combatants are not to be respected any more than the lives of men in uniform, for modern war is not a military game between small bodies of professional soldiers, as in the old days, but a struggle to the death between one people and another. The blockading of the enemy's ports, the slow starvation of a besieged city, which is allowed by military purists of the old and sentimental school does not spare the non-combatant. The woman with a baby at her breast is drained of her mother's milk. There is a massacre of innocents by poisonous microbes. So why be illogical and pander to false sentiment ? Why not sink the Lusitania and set the waves afloat with the little corpses of children and the beauty of dead women ? It is but one more incident of horror in a war which is all horror. Its logic is unanswerable in the Euclid of Hell. . . . It is war, and when millions of men set out to kill each other, to strangle the enemy's industries, to ruin, starve, and annihilate him, so that the women may not breed more children, and so that the children shall perish of wide-spread epidemics, then a few laws of chivalry, a little pity here and there, the recognition of a Hague Treaty, are but foolishness, and the weak jugglings of men who try to soothe their conscience with a few drugged tabloids. That at least is the philosophy of the German war lords, and granted the premises that war may be waged by one people against another it seems to me sound and flawless in its abomination.

Germany thrust this thing upon Europe deliberately and after careful preparation. Upon the heads of her diplomats and princes are the blood and the guilt of it, and they stand before the world as murderers with red hands and blood-shot eyes, and souls as black as hell. In this war of self-defence we are justified and need no special pleading to proclaim our cause. We did not want this war, and we went to the extreme limit of patience to avoid it. But if there is to be any hope for humanity we must go deeper into the truth than the mere analysis of White Papers and Yellow Papers with diplomatic correspondence. We must ask ourselves whether in England, France, or Russia, "the defenders of modern civilization," there was any sincerity of belief in the ideals and faith for which civilization stands. Did the leaders of modern thought do anything with their genius or their knowledge to break down old frontiers of hatred, to enlighten the ignorance between one nation and another, or to put such power into the hands of peoples that they might have strength to resist the tyranny of military castes and of military ideals ? Have not our politicians and our teachers, with few exceptions, used all their influence to foster dark old superstitions which lurk in such good words as those of patriotism and honour, to keep the people blind so that they might not see the shining light of liberty, and to adulterate the doctrine of Christ which most of them profess, by a gospel of international jealousy based upon trade interests and commercial greed ? The military castes have been supported in Europe by putting the spell of old traditions upon simple peoples. The Christian Churches have bolstered them up and failed utterly to preach the words of peace because in the heart of the priest there is the patriot, so that every Christian nation claims God as a national asset leading its battalions. There will be no hope of peace until the peoples of the world recognize their brotherhood and refuse to be led to the shambles for mutual massacre. If there is no hope of that, if, as some students of life hold, war will always happen because life itself is a continual warfare, and one man lives only at the expense of another, then there is no hope, and all the ideals of men striving for the progress of mankind, all the dreams of poets and the sacrifice of scientists, are utterly vain and foolish, and pious men should pray God to touch this planet with a star and end the folly of it all.

PRINTED AT
THE COMPLETE PRESS
WEST NORWOOD, LONDON

Milton Keynes UK
Ingram Content Group UK Ltd.
UKHW022031121023
430505UK00004B/61

Reading
My Mother

Kathleen Jones

Dedicated

To my children

David, Peta, Meredith and Michal

For the cousins – who were also there

*Anne, Jean, Joan, Norma, William, Graham,
Susan, Ian and Alison*

In memory of my brother Jon Gordon Slight

What Reviewers say about Kathleen Jones' books.

'*A compelling narrative of a writer's passion for her work.*'
Helen Dunmore [Katherine Mansfield: The Storyteller]

'*. . .reading it becomes a gripping, almost addictive experience.*'
Angela Leighton, TLS [A Passionate Sisterhood]

'*What a wonderful story it is.*'
Margaret Forster [A Passionate Sisterhood]

'*I read it with huge enjoyment – I think it's by far the best biography yet.*'
Dame Jacqueline Wilson [Katherine Mansfield: The Storyteller]

'*I found the Sun's Companion an engrossing read, hard to put down. If you like to "disappear" into the world of a book, you'll find this a satisfying read.*'
Linda Gillard, author of 'Cauldstane' and 'House of Silence'.

'*Kathleen Jones (no relation) is such a good writer and never more so than when she is writing about people engaged in the creative process – sculptors and painters as well as writers.*'
Julia Jones [Three and Other Stories]

'*Utterly gripping and I didn't want it to end.*'
Debbie Bennett [The Sun's Companion]

'*A perceptive, beautiful, and ultimately inspirational novel.*'
Mari Biella [The Centauress]

'*This is such a bravura exercise in biography, I would suggest Kathleen Jones not only wins her case but should be awarded costs.*'
Charlotte Cory, TLS [Catherine Cookson: The Biography]

Books by the same author

Poetry:
Hunger
The Rainmaker's Wife
Mapping Emily
Not Saying Goodbye at Gate 21
Unwritten Lives

Biography:
A Passionate Sisterhood: The Sisters, Wives and Daughters of the Lake Poets
Katherine Mansfield: The Storyteller
Christina Rossetti: Learning Not to be First
Catherine Cookson: The Biography
Finding Alexander
A Glorious Fame: Margaret Cavendish
Norman Nicholson: The Whispering Poet
Margaret Forster: A Life in Books

Travel:
Travelling to the Edge of the World

Fiction:
The Sun's Companion
The Centauress
Mussolini's Hat
As Kate Gordon:
A Practical Guide to Alternative Weddings
A Practical Guide to Alternative Baptism and Baby-Naming
A Practical Guide to Alternative Funerals

When my mother died, I discovered that she had kept a reading diary for sixty years, since the end of the Second World War. I hardly ever saw her without a book – in her hand, or face down on a cushion, or bookmarked on the bedside table. We weren't rich, so all our books were borrowed. One of my earliest memories is of standing with my mother in a travelling library and inhaling the strange, addictive odour of books.

She was a compulsive reader. In remote crofts and farmhouses beyond the reach of electricity, she taught me to read and helped me to discover a whole new world of story and adventure. Part-Italian, a town girl, she'd had a tough life and, as an adult, my relationship with her was often fraught. We had very little in common. Reading was almost the only thing we shared – a place of safety.

'We are what we read,' Jacob Epstein wrote. Books shape us in ways we often don't understand. My mother was altered by the books she read – they made her what she became, just as the books I read shaped me. After her death, reading through the lists in her tiny diaries, absorbing her comments on them, I gradually began to understand the woman who had taught me to love the written word.

Contents

'*Every poem, every book I've ever read has been a friend and a lover, good or bad. They're part of the landscape of me.*'
Clare Shaw

"*Before writers are writers they are readers, living in books, through books, in the lives of others that are also the heads of others, in that act that is so intimate and yet so alone.*"
Rebecca Solnit, 'Flight', *The Faraway Nearby*

'*I feel certain that if I could read my way back, analytically, through the books of my childhood, the clues to everything could be found.*'
Elizabeth Bowen, *Collected Impressions*

1

MOTHER AND DAUGHTER

The day before my mother died, she warned me that I would find my father's love letters, and her own, in the old bureau in the sitting room.

'They're not very exciting,' she said, with a smile that seemed almost regretful, as she leaned back against the pillows in the bed she'd shared with my father. She was as thin as a bird and her skin was almost transparent. 'We didn't write about passion.'

I suspected that, if the letters had contained anything very intimate, she might have already destroyed them. But perhaps I was doing her a disservice. After she died, I discovered that I didn't know my mother as well as I thought I did.

Later that evening, when she'd slipped into a morphine-induced sleep, from which I'd been warned she might never wake, I opened the bureau to look for the certificates and other documents I would shortly need. Overwhelmed by sadness, feeling guilty, as if I was trespassing on a very private life, I opened the crocheted woollen 1940s clutch bag in which she kept important things. It was a hideous shade of khaki. I cringed to think that my mother might once have carried it, but wartime fashion wasn't about beauty or style. Inside the hand-sewn cotton lining, together with ration books and identity cards, there were about a dozen small Basildon Bond envelopes. I recognised my father's looped scrawl and my mother's neat copperplate, in faded blue ink, on fawn-coloured paper that might once have been cream or white. The ink had smudged in places. I didn't open the letters; it would have felt obscene to read such private communications while my mother slept in the next room.

As I sorted through birth certificates and insurance policies, I realised the bag also contained a collection of little notebooks. One or two were a horrible khaki colour, like the clutch bag, with a government logo in the right-hand corner, a legacy of post-war austerity. Others had pretty floral covers. Curious, but also half-reluctant in case I'd stumbled on something not meant for my eyes, I opened one of them. A date was written at the top of the first page: January 1964. That was the year I'd left home for a more exciting life in London, the year my mother had what used to be called 'a nervous breakdown'. But it wasn't a diary.

Ella, Harold and their daughter in 1949

Down the page, neatly divided under monthly headings was a series of book titles and their authors, each one given a star rating from one to four, with the occasional comment from my mother. These were her reading diaries, and they ran from 1948 – two years after she married my father – to the present; almost sixty years of reading history.

I can't remember my mother without a book in her hand; she read with her morning coffee and her afternoon tea. In the evenings in remote farmhouses she and my father sat in front of the fire and read by oil lamps or flickering candle-light. Sometimes it was a guilty pleasure – busy farmers' wives weren't supposed to bury their heads in books when they could have been doing something useful. I remember her jumping up to hide her book under a cushion when a neighbour knocked on the door and the lunch dishes were still in the sink. She put her finger to her lips to warn me not to say anything, and her cheeks flushed with shame.

As a small child, bedtime stories (and sometimes daytime stories) were a regular feature of my life. Beatrix Potter's tales were my favourites, but I loved poetry even when I didn't understand what it meant. My mother could recite huge chunks of Shakespeare and Wordsworth and almost the whole of *The Rubaiyat of Omar Khayyam*. Her rendering of Longfellow's *Hiawatha* was unforgettable, and the tragic saga of the *Forsaken Merman* always reduced me to tears as she reached the mournful conclusion: 'Come away, children, come away'. The idea of a mother leaving her children was beyond my comprehension. Lewis Carroll's *Jabberwocky* and *The Walrus and the Carpenter* were also in her repertoire. It didn't matter how often I heard them, they gave me pleasure – and still do, because I can hear my mother's voice when I read the words. She had a way of reading poetry aloud that caught the imagination. When she recited Omar Khayyam –

They say the Lion and the Lizard keep
The Courts where Jamshyd gloried and drank deep:
And Bahram, that great Hunter – the Wild Ass
Stamps o'er his Head and he lies fast asleep.

– the words took me straight to the Persian palaces of Persepolis and I became part of a fairytale, watching the Sultan's tower 'noosed with light' and the stars outside my bedroom window flung into 'the bowl of night'.

I knew all about Persepolis. On my mother's bookshelves, next to the poetry books and the medical encyclopaedia, was a large, rather boring-looking tome in a plain binding, called *The Wonders of the World*. The photographs and drawings were in black and white, but the splendours of the world's most famous antiquities were bright with colour in my imagination. It was too heavy for me to carry very far, so I read it on the floor. Persepolis, the book told me, had once had gates of gold and ivory before it was sacked by Alexander the Great. I looked at it so often that its carved staircases and pillared porticos were as familiar to me as pictures of my local village.

And only a decade and a half later, when I walked through the ransacked palaces of Persepolis as a young mother with a small child in my arms, I thought of my own mother and the book that had inspired my dreams of travel. The words in my head were the ones she used to recite; as a child I had not understood them but had loved their music. Now, as an adult in this abandoned city in the middle of the Iranian desert, the words made perfect sense:

> One Moment in Annihilation's Waste,
> One Moment, of the Well of Life to taste –
> The Stars are setting and the Caravan
> Starts for the Dawn of Nothing – Oh, make haste!

Apart from our love for Omar Khayyam, there was a gulf between my mother and me. I didn't get on terribly well with her when I was young. I was my father's favourite, a tomboy, closer to him in temperament than to her. Her favourite was the brother who arrived nearly six years after I was born, a gentle, quiet baby who loved being cuddled and wasn't always getting into mischief. 'You were such a handful,' she once told me, 'I waited until you were at school before I had another.'

1948 – The infant bookworm

'Books,' Anthony Powell wrote, 'have odd effects on different people'. Our tastes were fundamentally different. I despised the

5

tacky sentiments of Patience Strong and the morally uplifting epigrams in the *Friendship Books of Francis Gay*. My mother was also very fond of a column called 'the Man Who Sees' in *Woman's Weekly*. It was a series of thoughtful ruminations on various subjects while 'the man' went rambling outdoors in a trilby hat with a pipe in his mouth. My mother loved his cosy philosophies and so, for a while, did I – there were truths there that I could relate to. 'Go into the woods in company and you come back empty – go alone and you come back with more than you can hold' meant something to a girl who roamed the countryside on her own. But by the time I was thirteen or fourteen, I'd outgrown it and was hungry for things that went further into the wild hinterland of the mind. I gave my mother a hard time – once, in an argument, I called her gullible. I suspect there were times when I made her cry after I had ridiculed some precious belief of hers.

After she died, when I was numb with the loss of someone I still hadn't fully appreciated, I took the things she'd left me back home and, for the first time, sat down to look at her reading diaries. The pages were covered with the titles of books I'd never read, by authors I'd never heard of. Some of these unknown books had been given four stars and underlined. I realised how little I had known this woman who had given me my love of literature – perhaps even the compulsion to become a writer myself. But those little diaries also took me back to darker places I was reluctant to revisit.

2

ELLA

When I was in my early teens, my mother ran away. She left the house in the middle of the night, barefoot, in her cotton nightdress, and ran down the fell track towards the main road. My father went after her and eventually brought her back, weeping and shivering, to sit by the fire. He wrapped her in a blanket, put another log on the embers and made her a cup of tea. 'It'll be all right, Tiny,' I heard him say. 'It'll be all right.'

But it wasn't.

Everything I'd believed to be secure crumbled that night. The scaffolding of my childhood collapsed and nothing would ever be the same again.

My father called her Tiny but her name was Ella. When she met my father, her surname was Brown, but on her birth certificate she was Ella Gordon Sutherland. She was born in a rented terraced house in North Shields, a poor suburb of

Newcastle on the banks of the River Tyne, a fishing community that was also very dependent on the ship-building yards and the nearby coal mines for its prosperity. Her father was half-Italian, with a romantic history. His own father, William Sutherland, was the son of a family that owned ships and property. He had fallen in love with a pretty Italian girl on the quayside in Genoa, married her and brought her back to Tyneside after a mere three-

The very Italian-looking Thomas Sutherland

week acquaintance. Francesca Maria Theresa Nagaro spoke no English and did not thrive on the Tyne, but she had two children, my grandfather Thomas and his sister Rosella, sometimes anglicised to Rose-Ella.

My grandfather used to teach us odd words in his Italian mother tongue. He liked his bacon and eggs cooked in olive oil – then only available at the chemist for medicinal purposes – and he could cook a decent macaroni. By the time the First World War broke out, all the family money, sailing ships, pubs and houses had gone – together with my great-grandmother Fanny, the 'Italian Lady', who died of a genetic degenerative heart condition she passed on to my mother. She also passed on her thick black hair (which was never cut) and her Roman nose. My mother was very self-conscious about her nose and so, when I inherited it, was I. If plastic surgery had been available when I was eighteen, it's the one thing about myself I would have changed. But on my mother it somehow matched her dark hair and Latin looks.

Thomas Sutherland married Annie Gordon Young – another Tyneside girl from across the river at South Shields – whose father had been a merchant seaman. She was one of eleven children, eight of whom survived, brought up in one of those 'two-up, two-down' terraced houses with the capacity of a Tardis. Annie adored her father Jack, a fun-loving man who was something of a practical joker, but she hated her mother who apparently hated

her back and was always subjecting her to petty cruelties. Annie told me it was because she didn't have curly hair like her sisters. It left a deep mark.

I had always wondered why everyone in the family had Gordon as a second name – even the girls. My grandmother told me that her own grandfather had been conscripted into the English navy – press-

My grandmother, Annie Gordon Young, standing next to her father, second row

ganged against his will, something that often happened in the 1800s. He had jumped ship in Germany, changed his name to Young (perhaps Jung?) to escape the death penalty for absconding, made his way back home and settled down under his new name. But, true to his Scottish roots, he insisted that all his children and their descendants should also be called Gordon.

There was a lot of Scottish blood in my mother. On her father's side, the Sutherlands had been displaced by the Highland Clearances, though how they got so much money and property wasn't clear. My grandfather thought they'd had illegitimate aristocratic roots, but it was probably more to do with entrepreneurship. They were a kind of Onedin family – owning sailing ships and public houses in a small way. At one time they owned streets of houses in North Shields but it was all gone by the time my grandfather turned ten years old.

Their lack of money was a tragedy for him because Fanny Nagaro had passed on the gifts of art and music – my grandfather taught himself to play the violin well enough to give lessons to others, and he was a spectacularly good painter. His work caught the eye of a Royal Academician living locally and he was given free lessons, but there was no money to send him to art college or educate him in music. By the time he was thirteen he was a bicycle delivery boy for a greengrocer, and at sixteen he was earning a living as a painter and decorator. He specialised in trompe l'oeil and special effects and was good enough to work on restoring stately homes across the north of England. His sister gave operatic recitals, and his son, my mother's brother, became a very talented pianist.

Annie Gordon Sutherland, my grandmother

My mother had a beautiful light soprano voice and music was a big part of my childhood. She belonged to the local choral society and I used to help her learn the parts. I was a natural contralto and we used to sing in harmony: *Messiah* for Christmas, *St Matthew Passion* for Easter, and in between we learned Vaughan Williams' *Towards the Unknown Region*, *Belshazzar's Feast*, Elizabethan madrigals, Elgar's *Dream of Gerontius*. It was through my mother that I grew up in a world of song. We had a wind-up gramophone – a wedding present – and a stack of records, mostly opera. Puccini was her favourite, but we had a lot of Verdi too. My mother knew all the stories – as a girl her father had taken her to operas in Newcastle and she used to sing bits of the arias as bedtime treats. We were always spellbound.

My mother didn't get on with her own mother. They were like sugar and salt. Annie's personality had been marked by her upbringing and what life had done to her. Before my mother's birth, there had been a baby boy, Billy, who caught gastro-enteritis and died at six months old because there was no money for the doctor. This was during the First World War, when working-class people usually just went to the local chemist for medicine. The doctor was an expensive last resort. My grandmother Annie was haunted by the possibility that Billy might have lived if he had been taken to the doctor in the beginning. She talked all her life about the pain of losing him and how she had walked the floor with breasts so engorged that my grandfather had to suck the milk out of them to relieve her.

I wondered sometimes how much that death had affected her relationship with my mother, born in Billy's shadow. Ella was the opposite in temperament – she took after her father, quiet, romantic, sensitive to the point of anxiety. She was serious and worried about everything. Her mother Annie was a good-time girl. She loved socialising, was intensely practical and very courageous; 'game for anything is our Annie' was the family saying. She could deliver babies, lay out the dead, and even knew how to procure abortions with a syringe of soapy water and a rubber tube. Growing up in the back streets of Tyneside had taught her everything she needed to know about being human at the most basic level.

Annie loved gossip and storytelling and rarely read anything other than the tabloids and magazines featuring 1940s celebrities. I loved her completely, without reservation. You knew that whatever you did she would help you without judgement or sermons. But between her and my mother there was a complete lack of understanding – bewilderment in fact. My mother felt that Annie was callous towards her; Annie thought my mother was too soft and romantic and feared what life would do to her. There were also personal betrayals and feelings of revulsion that, as a child, I didn't understand.

My mother did well at school, particularly in English. She won a merit medal for her matriculation results and wanted to stay on to become a teacher or a librarian. The headmistress came to plead with my grandparents to keep her there after her fourteenth birthday – but there was no money to pay the fees and scholarships were few and far between. My mother understood that but couldn't forgive the remark she overheard my grandmother make to the headmistress: 'Besides, she's only a girl and she'll get married in the end and it'll all be wasted.' In Annie's experience, educating girls was a waste of time and money.

Our bookshelves at home contained a lot of books my mother had read as a young girl. They had soft mock-leather covers and titles in goldleaf on the spine. The pages inside were so flimsy you could almost see through them; and they had the distinctive smell of old paper, animal glue and printer's ink that any book-lover will recognise. Once I had firmly connected the idea of black squiggles on a page with words, I began to read my way across the shelf. My mother had been a precocious reader and her parents had given her Charles Dickens' *A Tale of Two Cities* for Christmas when she was only eleven. I tried it but failed to get beyond the first chapter. Dickens was one of the authors we argued about. She adored him, but I found the people in his novels too much like cartoon characters. When I was eight or nine, she told me the story of the *Old Curiosity Shop* with tears in her eyes; but I laughed when she got to the death of Little Nell because I thought it was so melodramatic that it tipped over into farce.

That was a gulf too wide to bridge. But there were other books on her shelves that appealed to me. By the time I was twelve years old, *Little Women*, *Anne of Green Gables*, *Rilla of Ingleside* and *Emily of New Moon* had all been read, and their moral codes absorbed. My mother had all L.M. Montgomery's other 'Anne' books and I loved those too, inhaling their subliminal messages of womanhood and permissible female behaviour, along with the smell of printed paper, wood-smoke and damp sitting rooms. But it was the rebellious Anne I identified with, the girl who challenged her conventional guardians at every turn; not the good wife and mother, the 'Mrs Dr dear', she later became. In *Little Women* I loved Jo best, though my mother preferred Amy and, as a child, I could never see why. Jo is the one who is different, who is always getting into scrapes, who wants to be a writer and often despairs; Amy is the one who achieves the perfect life, secure in love and money.

My mother's favourite was *Rilla of Ingleside*, the story of Anne's youngest daughter. The story is set at the beginning of 1914, when the first rumours of war in Europe begin to arrive in Canada, to shake the peaceful routines of Rainbow Valley. Rilla's eldest brother immediately wants to enlist and most of the young men in the community are in uniform within weeks. Rilla is only fifteen but promises to remain faithful to the boy she is in love with for the duration of the war, expecting it to be over in a few months.

The book is jingoistic – a pacifist sympathiser has his windows smashed in, with the approval of the main characters. Rilla's brother Walter, the poet, receives white feathers in the post. It's full of wartime mythology, apple pie and sewing bees and moral certainties. The women are courageous, holding themselves together when their sons are reported 'missing', making blankets and bandages and running fund-raising events. There's even a dog who won't leave the station platform after seeing his owner get on a train to go to war. The poet enlists and dies a heroic death in France. Self-sacrifice is the main theme. 'Everything,' Rilla discovers, 'has to be purchased by self-sacrifice'. Rilla finds herself looking after an orphaned baby and abandons all thoughts of going to college like her siblings. She decides that she wants nothing more than to be a good wife and mother. When her fiancé returns four years later, she is waiting for him. I can see now that this book resonated with my mother's experience. Her whole life was changed by war and, like the girls of Rainbow Valley, she would wait until the end of the war for a man.

The *Emily of New Moon* stories, also written by L.M. Montgomery, were, for me, the ones that cut deepest, even though they're the most obscure – almost unread now, for very good reasons. Like Anne, Emily is an orphan but she's not such a likeable character and her stuck-up relatives are an unattractive bunch. Emily knows from a very early age that she's going to be a writer; she has 'flashes' when poems and stories start to write themselves in her head. I could relate to that – Emily was me at that age. But there was a disturbing element in the book that called into question the morality of writing. In order to go to college, Emily has to promise her aunt she will only write what is true, because fiction is all lies and therefore immoral. Even when Emily writes things that are true, she mustn't write anything that might be considered cruel, unkind or offensive – which doesn't leave much, other than didactic, saccharine mush designed to uplift and improve. Emily's punishment for being rebellious is to be silenced and forbidden to write at all.

I read the *Emily of New Moon* books at a time when this argument was going on in my own head. My mother had become a Methodist when she married my father; and although my parents were quite liberal, their friends and associates were not. At chapel and Sunday School, I heard fiction denounced as 'falsehood' and 'the work of the devil to corrupt young minds'. There was a list of 'approved' books –Victorian morality tales designed to turn young girls into copy-book wives and mothers. I hated those books and couldn't believe that the ones I loved were in any way sinful. But were they? And was I absolutely free to write anything, regardless of its impact on other people? This made a deep impression on me. It was the first time I realised that writing had a moral dimension or that writers might have a responsibility to society.

Books can be dangerous. They have a tremendous influence on children, going far beyond any information they might impart; books shape a child's character and imagination. According to Russell Kirk, the twentieth-century American political theorist, there are four levels of reading. First there is Fantasy – the stimulus for what he calls the 'moral imagination'.

This first encounter produces a kind of programming, rather like brainwashing, which imbues the child with the cultural, moral and social mores of the society they live in. Victorian children's literature was very didactic and so, in the first half of the twentieth century, was the kind of English literature that was approved of by the Establishment – religious, political and educational.

Only the old fairytales of the Brothers Grimm and Hans Christian Andersen hark back to something darker and deeper, as they mine the harsh truths of human existence – domestic violence, fratricide and matricide, child abuse, inequality, poverty and death. In them lie the realities of a woman's life. Most of the girls in these stories have to rely on someone else to rescue them. Cinderella's own goodness isn't enough to get her an invitation to the ball; she has to be magically transformed in order to be released from oppression. But not everyone has a fairy godmother. Her sisters cut off their toes to make their feet fit the glass slipper, in a perfect demonstration of the way women have, for centuries, been willing to deform themselves to fit the story they long for; in this case, a story that belongs to someone else. As a child I loved the Brothers Grimm tale of the Goose Girl in which the talking horse, Falada, is brutally beheaded in a terrible betrayal. I loved it because its underlying message was that goodness and beauty will always be recognised in the end.

I already knew I wanted to be a writer. I wrote poetry at primary school and one day, when I was about nine, a teacher sent off one of my poems to a magazine and they printed it.

I will always remember the feeling I had when she showed it to me. My parents were very proud. I knew then that this was an experience I wanted to repeat. It was the beginning of an addiction to seeing my name in print, despite the moral barriers erected during my childhood, and the mental wound that Emily of New Moon inflicted. 'You can't make an omelette without breaking eggs,' my grandmother said when I talked to her about it. But then, she read the News of the World. My internal censor was already highly developed, and it would be years before I had the courage to defy it. Feminism took a long time to reach the north of England.

Most of the books on my mother's bookshelf were Christmas or birthday gifts – she never had the money to buy books for herself. The names written neatly on the fly-leaves were mostly those of 'The Aunts', of whom I had a lot. My grandmother came from a big family of brothers and sisters, some of whom were almost grown up when she was born, some much younger than herself. They were all called 'aunts' and 'uncles' alongside my mother's brother and sister. Some of the older 'aunts' had children the same age as my mother – and they also became my aunts. So, too, did my mother's best friends from school.

It was all rather confusing, and I still haven't a clue how some of them were related to me. There was a very wealthy Aunt Lilian who turned up regularly in a big car and a fur coat with Uncle John and Uncle Jim (it was always a threesome). There were two children called Young Lilian and Young John. These privileged, privately educated children were apparently my cousins, but must really have been more distantly related. I had several cousins the same age as me who were really second or even third cousins – it was a huge extended family whose members quarrelled and fought and supported each other, closing ranks against the outside world when necessary. My grandmother's parties, where everyone brought a plate, a bottle and a musical instrument, were legendary. Neighbours invited themselves – sometimes the whole street turned up. Annie Sutherland was very popular.

One of the aunts was never talked about when children were listening: Aunt Margaret, a school friend of my mother's, had married my mother's brother. Margaret was the reason my cousins and I sought out a dictionary in the local library to look up the word 'lesbian'. My uncle's divorce made the *News of the World*, because Margaret had eloped with a woman, which meant that my uncle couldn't claim adultery, only desertion. He tried to get round it by claiming that the 'other woman' was a hermaphrodite, calling her doctor as a witness, which was why it made the tabloid press. It tore the family apart because, as a lesbian and therefore 'morally corrupt', my aunt was separated from her children and not even allowed to see them. The girls were brought up partly by my grandmother and, during the school holidays, by my mother.

It affected her quite badly because she and Margaret had once been inseparable. My mother, who identified as heterosexual and was so naive she once asked me if I knew what homosexuals did in bed, had loved Margaret deeply. At fifteen the girls had exchanged passionate love letters and spent every possible hour in each other's company. My mother told me that she sometimes got up in the night when she couldn't sleep and walked round to Margaret's house and stood under her window. They shared poetry and books. Margaret had even shown my mother an illicit copy of the banned novel *The Well of Loneliness* by Radclyffe Hall.

There's a beautiful notebook with gilt-edged pages and a chinoiserie cover, which my mother used as a commonplace book. Inside the cover, in her schoolgirl copperplate script, she has written the date and: 'This book was given to me, Ella Sutherland, by Margaret, to whom I dedicate it'. The first quote she copied into it, on the facing page, is from *Vanessa* by Hugh Walpole:

> I love you, as I shall always love you; because you are part of me, because you are all that I have in the world; because without you I am always lonely; because I am not alive without you.

The memory of those feelings disturbed my mother, particularly as she now realised the true nature of Margaret's feelings for her. Once, before the divorce, Margaret had told Mum that she had only married her brother so that she could always be close to her.

This wasn't the only instance of secret love in the family. There were also two honorary aunts – girls my mother had met at a church youth club at the age of fifteen – Aunt Nancy and her companion Aunty Jenny, who came to stay and shared the spare bed. Aunty Jenny had had a 'disappointment' in the war; Aunt Nancy wore a tailored suit and had very short hair and a moustache. She was headmistress of a girls' school, and always brought me wonderful books as presents. She seemed to know exactly what I would like. Aunty Jenny gave me frilly petticoats and make-up. Their relationship was never talked about as I grew up; although, as a child of the wild sixties and even wilder seventies, I knew far more than my mother could ever imagine about human sexual desires and their diversity.

Male homosexuality was illegal in Britain until 1967, so most gay men kept their sexual preferences secret and lived in fear of being exposed. I realised after leaving home that several of my uncles were gay. Among the great-uncles there was a Gordon who worked in London, was fond of 'snappy dressing' and shared a flat with a 'friend'. They went everywhere together, including holidays abroad. No one said anything. Although there were muttered comments about 'fairies' and 'batting for the other side', men who stayed single and preferred the company of their own sex were simply known as 'confirmed bachelors'.

Like thousands of other women, my father's aunt, Hilda, who worked at Carr's biscuit factory in Carlisle, thought she'd missed her chance of marriage after the slaughter of young men in the First World War. By the 1940s, she was over thirty-five and found herself in what was considered 'the last chance saloon' for marriage. In desperation, she accepted a proposal from a shy man, the only son of a widow from the same Northern Irish community in Carlisle. Fred was eccentric and rather camp, a hypochondriac who held the record for sick leave in the civil service, de-listed by almost every GP in the city. Hilda had known him since their school days, so she knew what he was like, but she wanted a husband, and children. Fred, like many closeted gay men, felt the pull of respectability. His nerve almost failed on their wedding day, but the bride's male relatives wouldn't allow him to jilt her. He was pushed into a marriage that was desperately unhappy for both of them, and disastrous for Hilda's mental health. Fred's inability to 'manage' the necessary consummation became a family joke.

3

LOVE AND LOSS IN WARTIME

As I got older, I progressed further along the family bookshelf into the Russian section: Dostoevsky's *The Brothers Karamazov*, Tolstoy's *Anna Karenina* and *Resurrection*. I began to dream of Russia. Among the poetry books was a small Everyman edition of the *Collected Works of Milton* that wasn't a present from The Aunts, Mum's parents or her best friend. The name on the fly-leaf was 'David', written in a firm hand, and below it was a Latin tag: *Sola Nobilitus Virtus* – Nobility Only in Virtue. It wasn't a secret that my mother had been married before she met my father, and that her first husband's name was David. I also knew that my mother particularly loved Milton and had committed his poem *Lycidas* to memory, but I didn't know why she wept when she recited:

Bitter constraint and sad occasion dear

Compels me to disturb your season due;

For Lycidas is dead, dead ere his prime . . .

She rarely got past the lines:

He must not float upon his wat'ry bier

Unwept, and welter to the parching wind,

Without the meed of some melodious tear.

As an adolescent I was curious to know more.

When my mother left school at fourteen, she went to work in a department store in North Shields – Walker's, a very respectable family-run enterprise. My grandmother had also worked there, and she had met my grandfather at Walker's when he came to paint the front of the shop. She had been arranging a window display and had played peek-a-boo with him, behind a pair of extra-large ladies' knickers. Apparently he was so embarrassed he fell off his ladder. At least, that was the story we were always told.

When her daughter needed a job, Annie marched down to Walker's to have a word with the supervisor, and my mother was taken on as a trainee. The teenage Ella, in her 'Miss Sutherland' persona, worked her way up from selling handkerchiefs and gloves to evening dresses and fur coats. David was one of the travelling sales reps, an intelligent, serious, very religious man who had always wanted to be an engineer, though his working-class background and the need to support a widowed mother denied him the chance. Like my mother, he loved books, and he sometimes wrote poetry. They had shared interests and ambitions. Acquaintance turned into friendship and then into something more. They started going to church together, attending a youth fellowship. My mother's upbringing, until then, had been completely secular. Her father, Thomas, had been brought up as a Catholic but had no time for priests or the rigmarole of the Roman church. Annie was a natural pagan with a Scottish Calvinist heritage. She had no interest in religion of any kind; so my mother's deepening faith took her further and further from her family.

In the late 1930s it became clear that war was inevitable. Ella and David got engaged, even though Ella was still a teenager and neither of my grandparents approved of the match. Annie told me that he was 'a bit of a dry stick'. My grandfather, a quiet, serious man himself, didn't think David would make my mother happy. 'He was too stuffy and bossy,' he told me. 'Patronising' was the word my grandparents sometimes used when talking about him. Something of this is apparent in one of the books he gave Ella a couple of months after the outbreak of war. He wrote in the front:

Say not, my soul, that life is disappointing,

That youth's fresh visions were but things unreal

For kingship follows God's annointing

And humble service still is God's ideal.

Traditionally, a woman's life was expected to be full of self-sacrifice and disappointment, according to the girls' conduct books found in almost every nineteenth-century home. A woman's ambitions must be put aside, and priority must be given to those of her brothers and her husband. It was God's will, the natural order of things.

Similar sentiments could be found in the books my mother was reading, from *Little Women* to *Rilla of Ingleside*. That David felt it appropriate to repeat them wasn't exactly a guarantee of future happiness. But David was everything my mother had ever dreamed of, and she was too deeply in love to listen to criticism.

David on honeymoon in the
Lake District

When he was 'called up' and joined the Royal Engineers a few months later, Ella was allowed to marry him. In a precious photograph album, at the back of the bookcase, were tiny black and white snaps of a wartime wedding, taken with an old Box Brownie: my mother in a blue woollen suit, David in uniform. They honeymooned in the Lake District; and she later confided that the wedding night wasn't very successful. She was too sore, after the initial consummation, to make love for the remaining precious days of his leave. David, possessor of a strict moral code, regretted their virginity and surprised her by saying, 'I wish we hadn't been so good.'

As a child, I was shocked to realise that my parents had sex. On a farm you can't escape the reality of reproduction. Copulating sheep, hens and cows, horses with erections the length of a cricket bat – it's all around you. But it's still quite a revelation to discover that human beings are animals too. My parents always answered my questions, even the embarrassing ones, and I will always be grateful for their honesty. They were openly loving and passionate with each other, though the

exhaustion of early mornings and long days of ha
byres and fields left little energy for sex. Every now and ,
would have what they called 'an Innings'. My father wou.
the fire in the bedroom, sandwiches and a flask of tea would be
prepared on a tray, the radio placed on the bedside table, candles
on the dressing table, and they would retire to bed as soon as my
brother and I were safely tucked up in ours. It was understood
that they were 'not to be disturbed'.

By the time I was twelve, I'd begun to read my mother's library
books – mostly romances, historical novels and biographies. We
shared our thoughts on Anya Seton's *Katherine*, the story of an
ordinary woman who became a royal mistress and eventually
a wife. We were both fervently anti-apartheid and loved Alan
Paton's classic novel *Cry, the Beloved Country*. When my mother
brought home *The Beautiful Visit*, I discovered Elizabeth Jane
Howard. But the novel that really changed my life and the way
I looked at my mother was a library book called *The Feast of
Lupercal* by an Irish writer called Brian Moore. I'd never read
anything like it. The prose was raw, merciless and sexually
explicit. Was it possible, even permissible, to write like this?

I blushed scarlet as I read, taking the book upstairs to bed
where there was no one to witness the shame I felt when I turned
the pages. As well as guilt, there was shock – my mother read
dirty books! But Brian Moore's novel doesn't appear in her diary,
so perhaps she never did. Challenging contemporary fiction
wasn't to her taste; she had seen too much of 'that sort of thing'
in reality, she told me. She never borrowed any of Brian Moore's
books again, but I went on to read his entire output and his novel

I am Mary Dunne was one of the biggest influences on my own writing and the discovery of my identity as a writer.

My mother was reading more and more non-fiction and naturally, being a precocious reader, I followed her into the history and biography section of the library. This is what Russell Kirk calls Reading Level Two – the development of the intellect to match the imagination. Level Three is Reflective Fiction and Poetry, through which, Kirk asserts, we gain 'distilled wisdom' and 'an understanding of human nature', without having to go through the same painful experiences as the characters. We can learn, in the space of a few hundred pages, what it would take us a lifetime to learn otherwise. Finally, if you read enough, you come to Level Four: Philosophy and Theology. 'Scientific Truth', says Kirk, is ever changing, but 'Poetic and Moral Truth' don't change much from generation to generation. I used to argue about this with my mother, because I believed in scientific truth, and was convinced that moral absolutes were human constructs that changed over time. My mother was firmly on the side of the moral absolutes. What she needed most were certainties.

For Christmas 1940, David gave my mother *The Complete Poems of Rupert Brooke*, with a little note saying the book had been bought from Sidgwick and Jackson, the publishers, at 3 Adam Street, London. Brooke's lavishly embellished poetry and chiming rhymes were just what she loved. She would stand at the kitchen sink, up to her wrists in suds, gazing dreamily out of the window at the rain lashing down outside, chanting lines from 'The Old Vicarage, Grantchester':

Just now the lilac is in bloom,
All before my little room;
And in my flower-beds, I think,
Smile the carnation and the pink…

It didn't matter to her that the poet had written that stanza in Berlin, 'sweating, sick and hot', as an example of an impossible idyll. At the beginning of the Second World War, Rupert Brooke's poetry embodied all the patriotic sentiments she and David held dear: 'England's the one land, I know, / Where men with Splendid Hearts may go'. It was important to believe that somewhere everything was normal, that the church clock stood permanently at ten to three and that there would still be honey for afternoon tea, without any need for a ration book.

For me, reading these poems at the end of the 1950s, with *Saturday Night and Sunday Morning* showing in the cinema, John Osborne and the Angry Young Men in bookshop windows and Kingsley Amis dominating the poetry scene, my mother's Georgian taste was almost fatal. I was seduced by the overblown metaphors and rhyming lines. The poetry I wrote, under Brooke's influence, was terrible. I knew that, but I didn't know what to do about it. There was no modern poetry on our bookshelf at home. I was saved by an English teacher at school, who sent me to the library with a reading list, escaping interminable lessons spent listening to my classmates stumbling through a classical text I'd already read in an afternoon. Little magazines I didn't know existed were on the list, critical essays by F.R. Leavis, poets like Stephen Spender and W.H. Auden. It was overwhelmingly masculine, but it was a start – and it took me further from my mother.

The years 1940–41 were difficult for Ella. She was a married woman, but she still lived at home and still worked at Walker's, and she often didn't know where her husband was. He wrote to her every other day from camps at undisclosed locations in the south of England. David was training to be an engineer and finding the war more fulfilling than being a drapery rep in the north. He was, my mother told me, something to do with radar installation, though it was all top secret and he wasn't supposed to tell her anything.

All too soon he got his first posting, to the Far East, and my mother went to London for his embarkation leave. Although Newcastle and North Shields had already experienced German bombing raids, nothing could have prepared her for London after the Blitz. From the beginning of September 1940, London had been bombed by the Luftwaffe for fifty-seven consecutive nights. My mother was profoundly moved by the sight of St Paul's rising from the smoking ruins. Her parting from David was terrible, she said; 'like losing an arm or a leg'.

Back in North Shields, aware that married women without children were about to be conscripted for the

David in tropical kit

30

war effort, Ella decided to volunteer. She had seen the physical effects of the munitions factories on her friends, the yellow skin and thinning hair, and was determined to avoid that fate. One alternative was the Land Army and my mother, who loved the countryside, signed up as a land girl. Her family doubted she would be able to cope with the heavy physical work. She was tiny, a little over five feet tall, with a size eight figure and beautifully manicured nails. She also had what was then known as a heart murmur. Nobody thought she would last the training.

Ella chose a very unpopular placement, the Lake District. 'It rains a lot and there's no social life,' the baffled recruitment officer told her. 'Are you sure you want to go there?' But the Lake District was one of my mother's favourite places. Before the war, my grandfather had worked on the restoration of a stately home called Dalemain, not far from Ullswater. My mother used to go there at weekends, putting her bicycle on the train to Penrith and then cycling with her father, staying in hostels and bed-and-breakfasts, to walk the fells. She and David had honeymooned there. Photographs show her posing romantically, in unsuitably high-heeled shoes on a rock at Lodore Falls and sitting on top of Helvellyn in a tweed skirt. The thought of being able to live there seemed like heaven to my mother. Her favourite lake was Ullswater. In her commonplace book she copied lines from Vita Sackville-West's 'Orchard and Vineyard':

Dear God! The heart, the very heart of me,
That plays and strays a truant in strange lands,
Always returns and finds its inward peace,
Its swing of truth, its measure of restraint,
Here among meadows, orchards, lanes, and shaws.

In brackets underneath she has written, 'That place, for me, <u>is</u> <u>Ullswater</u>.'

Ella at Lodore Falls

So my mother joined the Land Army and learned to milk cows, lamb sheep and hoe turnips. After a rudimentary training course, she was sent to a family farm just outside the northern city of Carlisle. The lives of land girls could be very hard, but Ella struck lucky – the family she was sent to were caring and friendly[1]. She was well fed and, although expected to work hard, treated kindly. It was the beginning of a friendship that lasted her whole life. There wasn't much time for reading and most nights she fell asleep as soon as her head touched the pillow, physically exhausted. Letters arrived from David at irregular intervals, with a few photographs now and then to give clues to his whereabouts. Sheltered in the Lake District, Ella found it hard to believe in the realities of war. Cumberland (as it v. then) was so far away, a haven of peace and normality. Produce that was rationed elsewhere was freely (though not always legally) available on the farms; a steady supply of eggs, butter, milk, and home-made cheese and bread and meat meant that my mother ate well.

But in the spring she was moved to another farm, the ominously named Foulbridge, owned by an old-fashioned stickler for discipline and hard work called Isaac Milburn. Ella was a little afraid of him, but soon won his respect for her courage and willingness to tackle any task. He liked the way she handled the horses. She was a 'plucky girl', he said, even if she was a 'townee'. Isaac also had a couple of 'hired lads' on the farm, one of them an eighteen-year-old boy called Harold. On her first day at the farm, Ella found herself in a ten-acre field, hoeing turnips beside him. They didn't speak – he was extremely shy – but my father said afterwards that he had fallen in love with her the moment he saw her in that field.

Harold was the son of a dysfunctional Irish family living in Carlisle. His father was the illegitimate child of a Catholic woman and an unknown cattle drover. His mother was the daughter of Protestants from Northern Ireland who had come to Carlisle to work in the cotton mills. It was a terrible, unhappy mismatch. They lived in a terraced millworker's house in crowded rooms. My father's parents slept in one tiny bedroom, and his sister May slept in the other with her aunt Hilda and a grandfather, their beds separated by a curtain. My father slept downstairs, on the settle beside the fire in the living room. Doing well in

and winning a grammar school scholarship, he
's great hope of bettering themselves. But Harold
and he hated living at home in an atmosphere of
misery and conflict. His Irish ancestry, of cattle drovers and small
farmers, was pulling him towards a different life. 'Those genes,'
he wrote, 'seemed to gather in me with a vengeance.' He craved
the outdoors and spent all his spare time on a farm outside the
city, helping with the horses. Horses were his passion.

At fourteen, he ran away with the milkman – quite literally.
He'd been getting up at 4am each day to cycle to a dairy farm
outside Carlisle, to help with the milking and the horse-drawn
delivery, before going to school. One day he simply didn't come
back. The farmer offered him a job and he took it. The Mason
family changed his life forever. They made him a member of
the family, fed him well, valued his contribution to the working
life of the farm, and boosted his confidence. Mary
Mason, in particular, had a special place in his
affections. She mothered him and introduced
him to the Methodist religion. Mary was a
committed Wesleyan and her simple, practical,
compassionate Christianity offered my
father something he badly needed. Her
faith was rooted in a view of all life as
sacred, and the beauty of the natural
world as a manifestation of God.
Harold was quickly converted. He

Harold at 14

joined the sing-songs round the organ in Mary's parlour on Sunday evenings and bowed his head during morning prayers at the breakfast table. This was also the beginning of his long journey as a passionate environmentalist.

By 1941 Harold was a hired lad on a much bigger farm and earning a better wage. He lived in and was 'kept', as they said, so the money he earned was all his own. He spent a lot of it on books. He loved reading and wrote poetry in romantic moments, some of it to my mother. She didn't take him seriously at first; after all, she was a married woman in her twenties. 'He was only a boy,' she said later. 'I thought he'd grow out of it.' But he didn't.

In 1942, Ella received the welcome news that David was on his way home on leave. It was nearly two years since they had seen each other. She was ecstatic and organised time off from the Land Army. Meanwhile, Harold was very troubled. He was in love with a married woman, much older than himself, whose company he was finding increasingly necessary to his happiness. He struggled with his conscience and considered moving farms at the next hiring date. Farm workers were traditionally hired twice a year, at the old feasts of Whitsun and Martinmas. Together with Candlemas and Lammas, these dates were the pegs around which the farming calendar

My mother in her Land Army
uniform with her father

was arranged. They were the old Quarter Days of the Scottish Calendar. In England the Quarter Days were different – Lady Day and Michaelmas were the hiring dates – but Cumberland, which had sometimes been part of Scotland, still looked north.

Just before Christmas, a few weeks before David was expected home, my mother received a telegram – David was missing. His troop ship had been torpedoed and he was among those unaccounted for. To say she was devastated would be an understatement. Her whole world was shattered, and her longed-for future had sunk with David's ship to the bottom of the ocean. Even more cruelly, the telegram and the letter that followed allowed her a gleam of hope. He was missing – not officially dead, not even 'believed dead' – and might yet be found alive among the survivors who had been taken to the Japanese concentration camps.

My mother sank into depression. She went to stay with her parents in North Shields for a short period of compassionate leave. And this was when my father came into his own. He wrote her a beautifully worded letter and she wrote back, saying that it had helped a lot, though 'at a time like this there is just nothing anyone can say or do'. When she came back to the farm, still overwhelmed by sadness, Harold listened to her talk, let her weep on his shoulder and offered comforting words.

Holidays in wartime were difficult affairs and not always affordable, even if the time could be spared. In June 1943 Ella arranged for Harold to spend a week with her parents to get some sea air. He had been over-working – Isaac was a demanding boss – and she felt it would do Harold good. She was also anxious for him to meet her family, though their friendship was still a guilty secret. In North Shields, Harold was happily accommodated in a household already stretched to bursting. Ella, when she was at home, slept with her younger sister in a tiny upstairs room completely filled by a double bed, a wardrobe and a treadle sewing machine. You could only get into the bed if you turned sideways and wriggled between them. My grandparents slept in the main bedroom, which was scarcely any bigger. Ella's brother Gordon, now married to Margaret, had slept in the living room when he was at home, in a put-u-up bed that turned into a bureau during the day. It was now folded out for my father.

Harold wrote a letter of thanks to Ella, saying how much he had enjoyed the company of her relatives. They had made a big fuss of him (Annie Sutherland was no fool) and made him feel quite at home, 'especially your brother and father, whom I felt I had known for years'. Harold went to my mother's favourite beaches at Tynemouth and the fishing village of Cullercoats, which were shrouded in barbed wire and anti-tank placements, but still beautiful. He was a man of mountains and rivers but wrote that 'I can understand now your longing for the sea, in fact I have contracted that longing myself'. His letters are scattered with expressions of love for Ella. Although he might address the letter to 'My dearest friend', or 'Tiny', the pet name he had for her, he tells her he loves her on every page. 'Today, I have realised just how much I love you; it is an agony to be absent from you my darling.' In another he describes himself as 'the linnet deprived of its song'. Harold had been living independently since he was fourteen and he was much more mature than the number of years on his birth certificate suggested.

Ella's affection for this 'boy', now very much a grown man, gradually deepened into love and this only increased her confusion. If David was only missing and still alive in a concentration camp somewhere in the Far East then she was guilty of faithlessness. She was betraying him. Her favourite novel at this time, another gift from David, was *Anna Karenina*. She had seen the 1935 film with Greta Garbo in the title role and been captivated by it. Now, the story echoed her own situation. She was a married woman in love with another man.

Feeling that she was in moral jeopardy, my mother asked for a new placement – living under the same roof as Harold seven days a week was torture. Ill and mentally exhausted, she was sent to what was regarded as a 'light' post in a market garden. Harold was also suffering from the stress of the situation and from the exacting demands of his fiery boss. Isaac Milburn had a famous temper and could rarely keep employees for long. My father's letters to my mother described how Isaac had chased one of the hired lads from the field with a hoe. Another lad had 'bolted' during the night, climbing out of a window with his suitcase.

Harold, who was not a bolter, gave notice, after a bitter and trivial argument with Isaac, and found himself a more congenial hiring. He went to a farm called Ellerton Grange to work for a couple called Henderson. They were, he wrote to my mother, still in love with each other after forty years of marriage. Being by nature open and frank, he soon told them about his personal situation and they offered good advice, telling him to wait and be patient. They also fed him well. 'There is pudding every day – and cream on it,' Harold wrote. 'Bacon and eggs each morning

– and cake – and there is always tea
and cake at bed-time at whatever
time we come in.'

In November 1943 Ella was
in London, on holiday with one
of her uncles, and my father was
bombarding her with love letters.
She wrote back with a slightly
reproving tone. 'I cannot thank
you for missing me, but I can

Ella's Land Army medal

thank you for the love and friendship you have given me. It
has helped me more than I can ever say during these long and
difficult months.' And then she gave him just a glimmer of hope.
'There are lots of things I would like to say which I feel I cannot
say – yet.' She was beginning to heal.

By June 1944 many of those proscribed things had been said.
The dilemma that Ella faced made her ill again. 'Oh, Harold . . .
the stronger I feel our love becoming the more afraid I am. Afraid
because it may all have to end, we don't know how soon, and
it would be so hard now.' She was sent home to her parents for
medical treatment for 'exhaustion'. Ella longed for letters from
Harold but was still anxious to keep their relationship secret. 'I
am fairly wearying for you. Of course, I don't let anyone suspect
this . . . I must ask you to be discreet and not write too many
letters. Much as I hunger for them and love to get them, darling.'
One of her regular chores was to visit David's widowed mother.
She had never got on with the possessive, critical mother-in-law
who always refused to forgive the girl who had taken her only
son away. My mother was always aware of this coolness. She told

Harold the visit 'was a real ordeal and I was glad when it was over. I'm afraid I just don't have any love for her'.

Annie Sutherland was a great believer in spiritualism – known as 'the spooks' in the north-east. One of her party tricks was to get out the Ouija board; she also read palms and claimed to have second sight. She had a good friend who was a clairvoyant. In her turmoil, Ella secretly went round to see this woman, taking an old pullover and some letters – almost all that she had left of David. The clairvoyant surprised my mother by telling her that the man these things belonged to had been bringing her presents ... silver ... jewellery ... 'across water'. David had told her in a letter that he was bringing her a beautiful silver bracelet he'd bought in Sri Lanka.

Then the woman hesitated for a time, and finally told my mother that he was almost certainly dead. 'You love someone else,' the woman said. 'A good man. Don't turn down the chance of happiness.' Afterwards Ella, who was deeply religious, felt ashamed. She didn't tell Harold, or her parents. But, many years later, she told me. 'Of course she was a charlatan,' my mother said. 'Anyone could have guessed the things she told me, but at the time it helped me a lot.' It didn't occur to her that the clairvoyant might have been told the story by her friend Annie.

Ella was enjoying the fuss and loving care her family gave her but sensed that she no longer belonged to their world. When she heard my father's favourite Strauss music played on the radio she almost broke down. 'It will remind me of you, always . . . It's a strange life this, Harold, made up of our love, heartaches and dreams, and our yearning for the unattainable.' There was no one she felt she could talk to, other than Harold. She struggled to sleep. One night she sat on the edge of her bed until 2am, watching the night sky 'filled with planes and searchlights'.

The next morning she wrote to my father: 'I have been thinking over all that you have told me this past week; and I will promise that when this war is over, and if everything is all right, I will become your wife . . . I keep praying that everything will come right for us.' In her commonplace book she copied lines from Dostoevsky's novel, *The Brothers Karamazov* – a present from David before he had gone away: 'It's the great mystery of human life, that old grief passes gradually into quiet, tender joy.'

That June, the Allies had begun to storm the beaches of France and it was once more possible to hope. Ella took off her wedding ring and when she came back to the Lake District she allowed Harold to buy her a beautiful platinum engagement ring with three diamonds diagonally set. But there was still a doubt in both their minds. David was only missing. Ella made my father promise to wait until all the concentration camps had been liberated, though in June 1944 the end of the war still seemed a distant dream.

4

A FARMER'S WIFE

Ella and Harold were married in October 1945. The last shred of doubt had been removed when one of David's shipmates got in touch, after the Japanese camps were liberated, and told her that David had not escaped the sinking ship. She knew for certain that he had not survived but felt permanently grieved that he had never had a proper burial; that there was no place to go to mourn him. When she eventually told me about it, I understood the significance of the *Lycidas* poem and why she shed tears when she got to the lines 'He must not float upon his wat'ry bier/ Unwept . . .'.

She chose to marry my father in his home town rather than hers, and in the Methodist Central Hall. It was a clear statement of her new commitments. Post-war weddings were often bleak affairs, with rationing still in force and many things unavailable, and my mother was a second-time bride so the traditional white was thought to be inappropriate. Through her connections with Walker's department store, she managed to get a beautiful evening outfit suitable for a wedding. The top was in shimmering silver-gold lamé and the short A-line skirt was made from layered silk crêpe in a deep turquoise. In her hair she had a coronet of wax flowers that had been her mother's and a wisp of veil. The black and white photograph, hand-coloured in lurid shades, shows her looking radiant, arm in arm with my father, holding a big bouquet of blue and purple chrysanthemums.

They went to Silloth for their honeymoon – a small seaside town on the Solway Estuary – and stayed in a little bed and breakfast, off the promenade. The owner was an elderly widow, extremely lonely, who didn't know they were newly-weds. She couldn't stop talking about her recently deceased husband and her son who'd been killed at Dunkirk. She kept them up late, showing them her photograph albums, while they were aching, desperate after years of restrained passion, to get into bed with each other, but too polite to extricate themselves.

As a married man, it was impossible to continue as a hired lad. At first my father tried to lease a farm, but he was deemed too young and inexperienced, so he had to be content with a married man's job. This meant that my mother had to do light work on the farm, feeding hens and helping out with haytime and harvest, but at least they had a small rent-free cottage to live in. Harold had no problem with references; he was a workaholic with a lot to prove. 'He was always anxious to get on with the work,' one employer wrote. 'He was always keen to work longer hours at night than I cared to work myself.' Some of his referees described him as 'a servant', which seems incongruous but accurately reflected the nature of his employment. It rankled. My father wasn't servant material; he was proud, intelligent, and very ambitious. He didn't intend to be a servant for long.

His first post as a married man was on a big farm called Beech House at Raughton Head – a small hamlet in the Caldew Valley.

There's a description of it in unfamiliar handwriting among the letters in my mother's bag. 'Its white houses cluster on the hill-top and look over the lovely valley of the River Caldew.' Raughton Head is not exactly on a hilltop, more a slight rise in the undulating countryside, and consists of a handful of farms with their cottages grouped around a meeting of country lanes. The church is small and square, with a few remnants of Jacobean oak panelling. The eighteenth-century Cumbrian poet Susanna Blamire is buried in the graveyard. According to the description, she 'wrote charming poems of country life'. The farm was close to the Bishop's Palace at Rose Castle in a landscape still dominated by feudalism. My father's wages were £4.00 (a pound above the minimum wage) plus three pints of milk a day and as many potatoes as they needed. He was also allowed to keep a pig.

My parents' cottage was one of a terrace of stone-built cottages down a cobbled track. It was my mother's first home and she loved it, despite the cold flagged floors that had to be scrubbed, the earth closet outside, the black kitchen range that was difficult to keep alight in bad weather, the draughty doors and lack of plumbing and electricity. It was furnished with the utility furniture they'd saved up for, all the wedding presents from the extended family, and a wind-up gramophone from Ella's parents. My father's employers at Ellerton Grange gave them a feather bed.

Ella disliked cooking but joined the Women's Institute, in order to learn, and spent the autumn and winter battling with jam that wouldn't set and cakes that wouldn't rise, made with (and sometimes without) ingredients that were still rationed. I have her W.I. post-war cookery book on my shelf, which includes instructions on how to make scouring powder, embrocation, window cleaner and other essentials that hadn't been available in the shops for years.

Among the old standards, such as Apple Crumble, Oat Biscuits and Blackberry Jam, there are recipes for Chinese Chews, Courting Cake, Eggless Fruit Cake (made with lard instead of butter), German Pound Cake, and the improbable 'Mock Crab'. This wartime wonder was made with eggs, vinegar, mustard and a week's ration of cheese, all mixed together and formed into a mound which was presumably supposed to resemble a crab. There's also a recipe for a solution to paint stone cottage walls so that the penetrating damp won't stain the wallpaper, which takes me straight back to my childhood – the unheated rooms, the smell of damp, the mildew at the back of the wardrobe.

W.I Cookery Book

For my mother, it wasn't all work; for the first time in her life there was also time for leisure. Ella joined the local Choral Society, which was rehearsing Handel's *Messiah* for an important Christmas concert in Carlisle Cathedral – the first after the war. Now free to spend time reading, she got herself a library ticket. Once a fortnight she walked to the main road, got on the bus to Carlisle, did some shopping, visited her in-laws and went to the library for her books. It was, she told me, one of the happiest times of her life.

In her reading diary for this period she noted only three books: *There are Four Seasons* by Richmal Crompton (two stars), *The Twain Met* by German author Ruth Feiner and *Royal Flush* by Margaret Irwin (both three stars). The pattern of her interests was already clear. She liked comforting women's fiction and historical romance throughout her life. In subsequent months she read Jane Austen's *Emma* and Hugh Walpole's *The Inquisitor*. But the only book that was given four stars was *Helbeck of Bannisdale* by Mrs Humphry Ward.

This novel had been published in 1898 and was a bestseller. Set in the Lake District, it has a feisty heroine who has been brought up as a free-thinking atheist but falls in love with a man whose Jesuitical religion requires her to give up all her own beliefs and freedoms in order to marry him. She refuses and their relationship ends in tragedy. It's been described by one reviewer as '*Villette* meets *Brideshead Revisited* in the style of Mrs Gaskell with an added dash of *Wuthering Heights*'[2]. Most readers hated the ending, which followed the nineteenth-century tradition that didn't allow unconventional women, who transgressed moral codes, to find happiness. Many nineteenth-century novelists were forced to twist the natural trajectory of a plot so as not to offend Victorian morality. There was never any chance that *Tess of the d'Urbervilles* would be given a happy ending. The message was clear; women were expected to be pure, obedient and faithful. The double moral standard applied to both fiction and real life.

My father was also spending a lot of time reading. He was studying theology in order to become a Methodist Lay Preacher. His parents were bemused. For his Northern Irish mother, church was a social ritual, observed only for respectability. His Southern Irish father's experience of the abuses of the Catholic church, and the horrors of the First World War, had left him with a violent hatred of religion of any kind. Harold's religious beliefs and his desire to become a preacher were incomprehensible. 'Where does he get it from, Ella?' my grandmother is reported to have asked. 'There's nothing like that in our family!' My mother fully supported him, even though her faith was more naturally Anglican. She missed the beautiful words of the liturgy in the plain chapel services. My father said he could never be doing with all that sitting down and standing up and repeating verses that no one really understood. It was one of their most fundamental disagreements, but their mutual faith was solid and they agreed to differ in their ways of expressing it. Ella continued to go to church on Sunday morning and they both walked down to the chapel in the evening.

They didn't intend to have children straight away; they planned to have some time to themselves and establish a more permanent home first. Specialist training was being made available to women like my mother who had been in the services – she had thought, briefly, about becoming a librarian. But my parents were deeply in love and both inexperienced lovers with little knowledge of contraception. Nine months and two weeks after the wedding, I put in an appearance. My mother was twenty-six, with a heart defect and still suffering the physical effects of the heavy work she'd had to do as a land girl. She didn't have an easy pregnancy and was often exhausted, as a result of chronic anaemia. Distanced from her own family, and in the days before NHS mother and baby clinics, she had very few people to give her sound advice. But the little front-room post office in Raughton Head was run by an elderly woman who had been a nurse and Ella found her friendship a great comfort during her pregnancy and the anxious months that followed.

When my father could get a few days off, they made their first visit as a married couple to my grandparents. It was winter, but the rough, stormy sea was what my mother craved. When she had been numb from the loss of David, the sea was the one thing that made her feel some emotion. The rhythm of the waves crashing on the rocks calmed her. But the delight of being at home with her parents, showing her husband all her favourite places, was spoilt by a terrible discovery.

My mother had left all her belongings at her parents' house, to be collected once she was settled in her new home. There were clothes and books and some childhood treasures, as well as a hat box that contained letters and other memories of her relationship with David. 'He wrote such beautiful letters,' she told me. But when she went into the wardrobe to get the box, it wasn't there. Eventually she asked her mother where it was.

'I threw it out,' Annie Sutherland replied.

My mother was devastated. There was an angry scene; she lost her temper – something my mother rarely did. 'You had no right,' she shouted. 'They were mine – they were all I had left of David.'

'You have a new husband now,' Annie said. 'You have to leave the past behind. It's not fair to him to be continually raking it up.'

The atmosphere was frigid for the rest of the visit and even my grandfather's intervention couldn't mend their relationship. My mother, against all her religious principles, never completely forgave Annie.

I was born in the cottage, just before breakfast in 1946 – conveniently between haytime and harvest. My father sent a telegram from the corner post office to my grandparents, announcing the birth of 'Angela'. My Italian grandfather, with an uncharacteristic lack of tact, sent a telegram back saying 'What a B**y awful name'. My father confessed, sheepishly, that he wasn't keen on it either. And then there was the fact that I didn't look like an Angela. I was a big, plain baby with a square face and a mop of straight, strawberry blonde hair. My Irish grandmother suggested gently that Kathleen might be a good name. My parents both loved Kathleen Ferrier's contralto voice and my father was given to singing 'Kathleen Mavourneen' in a light Irish tenor while he shaved. So Kathleen I became, teased thereafter by renderings of 'I'll take you home again Kathleen' and other musical martyr-doms. My father stood firm on the 'Gordon' issue though, so I became the first female in the family not to have it as a middle name, though I've written under 'Gordon' as a pseudonym and have always regretted the ending of the tradition.

The christening photographs show a 'female mafia' in post-war coats and skirts with government regulated hems. The family divisions, religious and political, are present as a sub-text. My father's relatives, the Irish Protestant Blairs are ranged, stiffly formal, on the left; Great-Grandfather Blair monumental in his Sunday suit, even without his Orangeman's regalia. My father's mother, Elizabeth Blair, is dauntingly respectable in a dark wool outfit specially bought for the occasion. Her husband Harry, rather surplus to requirements, stands at the back – not a single member of his own Irish Catholic family in the frame.

Christening

Huddled together on the right, my mother's assorted Scottish and Italian relatives, including quite a few of 'The Aunts', look a rather raffish bunch by comparison: Annie Sutherland with her hat at a tipsy angle, showing more leg than was perhaps appropriate; Thomas with his pipe clenched between his teeth. My grandfather looks glum, as if he would rather be pottering about on his allotment or having a pint at the working men's club. I'm there somewhere, the cause of this awkward social occasion, centre stage in my mother's arms, invisible under a mound of lacy veils and shawls, keeping unusually quiet.

The first winter of my life went down in history. The temperature had been below zero since early December, freezing cattle troughs and water pipes and making it impossible to harvest root crops for fodder. Early in January, my parents killed their pig and distributed the sausages and bacon among their neighbours. Because there were no fridges or freezers, this was the custom – whenever anyone killed a pig it was immediately shared. My grandparents came over from Newcastle on the bus to help with the making of sausages and brawn and went home loaded with unrationed meat for relatives. As they left, the first flakes of snow began to fall out of an iron-grey sky. They were lucky to get home at all.

My father wrote that the blizzard that raged for days was 'a white hell'. 'We got up one morning to find every landmark gone, every road in the British Isles blocked by snow and we had only the strength of men, shovels, and horses and carts to deal with it.' Remote hamlets were cut off for months. Families burned their furniture to keep warm; sheep and cattle died of starvation. In the Lake District hundreds of sheep, which had taken shelter under crags, were snowed in and suffocated. When one valley was eventually dug out, it contained the bodies of more than seven hundred sheep. Farmers on the Pennines shot their own livestock rather than watch them starve to death.

My parents were luckier than most; the water in the tap continued to run, the larder was stocked with pork, and there was always fuel for the fire. Their only concern was their small baby, who developed pneumonia. The roads were blocked, so there was no possibility of a visit from the doctor. The nurse in the corner shop was consulted – no antibiotics in those days – and various bizarre remedies were tried. The kettle was kept boiling on the hearth to help my breathing, my chest was rubbed with goose grease, and I was wrapped in a sheep's fleece to keep me warm. My mother was beside herself with worry, remembering the death of her baby brother Billy in 1917, who had been the same age as me when he died. She didn't sleep for two days until the danger was past and it was clear I was going to live.

One of my mother's favourite poems was 'A Prayer for my Daughter' by W.B. Yeats. She was particularly fond of the line where the poet wished her to be 'rooted in one dear, perpetual place' – something my mother always longed for. But she had married a man who was restless and determined, like his itinerant Irish ancestors, so Ella was destined to become a nomad.

Just before my third birthday, my father took a position as an assistant shepherd and we moved to a remote location in the Cheviot hills, in what were known as 'the Debatable Lands' beyond the Roman Wall. It was a kind of no-man's land between

England and Scotland, fought over for centuries by Romans and Vikings and then by generations of feuding Border Reivers. The shepherd's croft, which has since been swallowed up by Kershope Forest, was called Coldslopes and it was aptly named. A traditional Scottish longhouse, it was perched on the moors below Christenberry Crags. At one end there was a wooden byre, with a hayloft above, and a door into a narrow kitchen that was more like a passageway. This opened into a tiny living room, going through into one bedroom that led into another. There was an earth closet at the back. In those days there were no trees to break the strength of the wind off the Solway Firth; it was totally exposed. There was no road leading to it, only a rough track across the fell; but as we didn't have a car, this didn't seem to matter. There were only two farms within walking distance: the Crew, whose lights could just be seen further up the fell; and, across the beck and down through the woods, the Flatt Lodge where the gamekeeper and his wife lived.

The nearest village, several miles away, was Bewcastle, which had a shop and a small school attached to the church. It had once been an outpost of Roman, Saxon and then Viking civilisation, and the churchyard contained the Bewcastle Cross, carved with Celtic knots and fantastical beasts, possibly dedicated to Alcfrith, son of the seventh-century King Oswiu of Northumberland. My parents both loved history and they passed their enthusiasm on to me in the form of stories and images that fired my imagination. Bewcastle was where I first discovered the fascination of living in a layered landscape, the concept of 'deep place', a location marked by thousands of years of habitation.

On the moor above Bewcastle

Just before we left Raughton Head, my father bought a small Ayrshire cow, called Betty, and eight Sussex hens and arranged to have them delivered. His employers generously gave him a young border collie pup called Flo. On moving day, a local cattle wagon came to take the furniture, while my parents were driven up by a friend who had a car. It wasn't possible to take the lorry to the house, so the furniture was unloaded at the roadside and taken across the moor by horse and cart. It was a bumpy journey and my mother watched, anguished, as her precious post-war austerity furniture bounced around on the cart, and the wardrobe fell off into the heather. But everything was eventually in place, a picnic supper eaten, the cow tied up in the byre, paraffin lamps lit, and a small daughter put to bed in a strange room.

My father later wrote that 'Coldslopes became for Kathleen *Green Gables* and *The Little House on the Prairie* … rolled into one'. The kitchen door opened onto the moor and I roamed free among rushes as tall as I was, curlews' nests, and mattresses of sphagnum moss. The sky seemed to go on forever. I played in the hayloft, searched the rush beds for hens' eggs, and regularly fell into the small beck that ran just below the croft. My mother couldn't keep me in and eventually gave up trying. After all, what could happen to me in such a remote environment? The family called me 'Little Miss Independence'. I came in for tea filthy, wind-blown, tired and brown as a nut.

Mum was not so happy. She missed the sea, and she missed the lakes and the mountains. An entry in her first reading diary records 'March, spring, homesickness'. It was an intensely lonely existence for someone who had been brought up in a city and loved companionship. Even when she did go to community events, she found she had nothing in common with her neighbours. Most of the local farmers' wives had little education and had never been more than a few miles from their homes. The radio became her lifeline during the day. In the afternoons we both enjoyed *Listen with Mother*. But her biggest treat was the mobile library, which visited every three weeks.

Cumbria has a long history of mobile libraries. Back in 1857, a man called John Sanderson became the first person to provide a 'Perambulating Library service'. He walked around isolated Lake District villages every six weeks, pushing a box of books on wheels, come rain or shine. He was once reported to have walked a hundred and fifty miles in two days. Subscribers paid a penny a month to use the service. It was all the idea of a northern philanthropist called George Moore, who was interested in promoting literacy and wanted books to be available in remote communities. By the end of the Second World War, the library was motorised and resembled a removal van on the outside. Inside, you had to climb up steep steps into a dark corridor lined on both sides with books. The librarian sat in a little cubicle behind the driver's seat, ready to stamp your books in and out. My mother always borrowed as many as she was allowed.

The mobile library system also operated at the school in Bewcastle, delivering a box of books every two weeks. As the school covered an age range of five to fourteen, there was quite a variety of reading matter. I discovered a new world of children's literature, from *Thomas the Tank Engine* to *The Children from One End Street*. There were rules that decreed what was 'age appropriate', but I could usually persuade my teacher to bend them. *Milly Molly Mandy* came home with me, as well as *Just William*, which I adored.

What I didn't like were stories about girls in posh boarding schools, leading unrecognisable lives, saying things like 'Jolly hockey sticks', 'Crumbs!', 'Good sport,

John Sanderson in 1857
(Mealsgate.org.uk)

old fellow' and other phrases that were incomprehensible to a Cumbrian child who spoke the local dialect as a second language in and out of school. Cumbrian is unique; a complex mix of Old Norse, Anglo Saxon and Celtic, which didn't begin to change until medieval times when a few new expressions crept in, and even now has its own counting system. It was, and is, as Melvyn Bragg has observed, better understood in Oslo than in London.

My father spoke it at work, in the auction ring, or when mixing with fellow Cumbrians in the community; my mother never. The farms she'd worked on as a land girl were in lowland areas where dialect wasn't generally spoken. She was also regarded as rather posh because she'd had elocution lessons at school to iron out her north-eastern accent, and now spoke a clear middle English. I was expected to speak like that at home, but at school and in the playground I talked the same as the rest of the children. When someone came to the door and asked my mother, 'Ist tha thrang?' I knew that they were asking if she was

Feeding the calves before bed.

busy, though she sometimes couldn't make out what was being said. In the wild lands beyond the wall, a certain amount of Scots had found its way into the dialect too, and the accent was a soft burr. Speaking so 'properly', reading so prolifically, my mother had no chance of being truly accepted by the local women. Her speech clearly marked her out as an offcomer.

But to me, as a small child, we all seemed happy. During the day my mother did her domestic chores and read her books; my father worked among the sheep. If he was going up to the crags in search of strays, he sometimes took me with him, perched on his shoulders when my legs needed a rest. There was a ruined house that had once been a way-station for whisky smugglers, and an old track he said had been a drovers' route across the Scottish Border. He would look at it wistfully, perhaps wondering whether his unknown Irish drover grandfather might once have walked along it.

In the country beyond the Wall, over the White Lyne river, nature still ran unchecked. He showed me adders and grass snakes, identified moss-cheepers, curlews and lapwings. Once, he got me out of bed at dawn to climb up to the crags to see the wild goats. We hid behind rocks to watch them graze, slithering across the scree in search of better fodder. The old billy was enormous, with huge horns that curved up and back, as wide as the span of my arms. The Romans had introduced them, he told me, and they had since gone feral. (Later I learned that he was wrong – the Cheviot goat was introduced by early nomadic tribes in the Neolithic period, moving north after the last ice age.) As the sun rose higher, the mist began to rise from the ground and obscured our view. The goats vanished into the cloud and I've never seen them since.

In the evenings, once I'd been put to bed, my parents read and listened to the radio. As there was only a thin, badly made wooden door between my bedroom and the living room, I listened to the radio too. They weren't fans of the highbrow Third Programme, preferring the light classical music and factual information provided by the Light Programme, which had begun in 1945, and the Home Service – a forerunner of Radio 4. Sunday lunch was always accompanied by the mellow voice of Cliff Michelmore and *Two-Way Family Favourites*. Sometimes on Sundays in summer, we would put sandwiches in a basket and go up the fell for a picnic. My father turned his underpants back to front and went into the river to fish for minnows. Even my mother tucked up her dress and paddled in the freezing water.

Ella had more courage than any woman I've ever known. She had gone through the war fearing that at any moment her family might be bombed out of existence; she had lost her first husband, attempted a man's share of manual farm work, and was now more isolated than she had ever been in her life. 'You make your bed and you lie on it,' she used to say to me. 'I knew what life would be like with your father and I chose it.' She swore that, given the chance, she would have made the same choice again. Later, much later, she changed her mind. She had been brought up, and every book she had read had conditioned her, to believe that a woman followed where a man led. Where it led was not always comfortable, particularly for children. I was not so compliant. For years, I blamed her for some of the decisions that blighted our lives.

5

THE DEBATABLE LANDS

The people who wrenched a living from the land around us could trace their ancestry back into the murk of pre-history; they belonged to that land as we could not. Around Bewcastle, people were not known by their surnames but by the names of their holdings. There was Bobby the Shop who was the blacksmith at Shopford, Dick the Crew who farmed the holding above us with his brothers Watty, Johnny and Ted. Then there was Olive the Row who regularly invited my mother and me to tea. The tradition didn't apply to offcomers like my parents, or to our social superiors.

My father's immediate boss was the land agent for the estate, referred to as 'the Captain', who lived, for some of the time, with his aristocratic wife and little daughter at the big farmhouse near the Flatt Lodge. The Captain was said to have had 'a bad war', and suffered from what we would now call post-traumatic stress disorder. He could be very kind, but had a ferocious, unpredictable temper and sometimes disappeared for weeks on end. His wife was the same age as my mother, but class differences prevented them ever becoming friends.

I was sometimes invited to play with Lady Caroline, who was the same age as me but led a cosseted life; never allowed to go anywhere unless accompanied by a parent or a nanny. I have photographs of us together – she has pretty curly hair, is dressed in children's clothes from Harrods and tiny, buttoned, kid slippers, while I'm in a home-made pinafore and hand-knitted jumper. She had a nursery playroom all to herself, and it was filled with toys, including a rocking horse like the ones in storybooks. I had so few toys I can only remember a beloved teddy bear who went everywhere with me. The rest were kept in a cardboard box in a corner of the living room. On library days, and occasionally if we needed to see the doctor, we would be given a lift to the village in the Captain's vintage Rolls Royce. It was the first time I became aware of class difference and the sense of social hierarchy that pervaded our rural community.

My parents were by nature liberal, in both religion and politics. Brought up in families where there was always conflict between Catholic and Protestant, they had become Methodists. My maternal grandfather was a fervent socialist, a card-carrying member of the Labour party and member of a union – 'somewhere left of Lenin and still travelling,' as he used to say. My paternal grandparents were right-wing Tories. I suppose it was inevitable that my parents should vote for the Liberal Party.

Cumberland was a Tory stronghold, so they were always going to be on the losing side, but they believed in Liberal principles and objectives and voted for them in the face of huge opposition. This caused a dilemma. Living so far from a polling station and not having any transport of their own, they had to rely on lifts from the designated 'election cars'. This meant travelling to the polling station in the Captain's car, driven by his wife. The estate my father worked on was owned by the Lord Lieutenant of the County and it was made quite clear that his employees were expected to vote 'the right way'. It troubled my mother's conscience that she was accepting a lift in the Tory Party car and then voting for someone else. My parents argued about the ethics of it; my father didn't care and he laughed at my mother's anxiety. There were two elections while we lived in Bewcastle. In 1950 the Labour government of Clement Atlee was reduced to a majority of just five seats, despite winning more votes and having a bigger share of the votes than the Conservatives. Another election, called in 1951, brought Churchill to power again and my parents, although they supported his actions during the war, weren't pleased. They were both uneasy with class privilege and saw Churchill as one of its representatives.

The Flatt Lodge was an imposing Georgian building with an elaborate walled garden and had been built for the Lord Lieutenant as a shooting lodge for himself and his friends. The gamekeeper Edmund Bowes lived there with his wife Mary, who was the cook-housekeeper. She kept the lodge clean and cooked for the house parties, which could sometimes number thirty 'guns'. One day I went into the kitchen and there were sixty stuffed sheep's hearts laid out in trays ready to go into the two gigantic Agas that lined the kitchen and kept it warm.

My rambles as a child often took me to the Flatt. Mary's kitchen could always be relied on for home-made biscuits and hot milk sweetened with brown sugar. Mary loved me and encouraged me to come. She had only one child of her own, a grown girl who was at boarding school. Sometimes my mother came too and I listened to conversations I wasn't supposed to understand. Mary said she would have liked to have more children, but she confided that she didn't like 'that sort of thing' and had 'put a stop to it' soon after she married. My parents laughed about it over supper. Apparently Mary never took her clothes off in front of anyone, even the doctor. 'Poor Edmund,' my father said. 'No wonder he's so quiet.' I liked Edmund. He rarely spoke, being better with animals than people, and was always willing to let me see his ferrets and the rabbits he reared in the barn – not as pets but for his wife's ovens.

There was something about Mary that I loved, and I stayed in touch with her even after I'd grown up. She eventually died on the bathroom floor, from a heart attack, unwilling to open the door until she'd put on some clothes, a victim of Victorian morality and a primitive fear of sexuality.

In the walled garden at the Flatt: Mary Bowes and my baby brother, Annie Sutherland, my mother and me.

My mother's social life had contracted to the narrow, isolated community we found ourselves in. It never occurred to me, as a child, that she was lonely, but she was. I was out on the moors, appearing only at mealtimes; my father was up on the fells, looking after sheep; and Mum was at home alone, with only the radio for company. The trite lines she copied into her commonplace book seem to indicate unhappiness, if not depression:

> Somewhere the sun is shining,
> Somewhere the skies are blue
> Then what is the use of repining
> Because they shine not on you.

Mum hated domestic chores but, being dutiful by nature, she swept and scrubbed and dusted conscientiously. There were no electric labour-saving devices to make things easy. Carpets had to be beaten on the washing line, flagged floors had to be scrubbed on hands and knees, using carbolic soap. She often took refuge in religion, trying hard to make the work 'a grace'. She talked to me about Martha and Mary, and how Jesus had excused Mary from domestic chores, justifying it to her sister Martha by saying that she had chosen a more valuable route to salvation. I knew which woman my mother identified with. A poem Mum found in a woman's magazine was quoted often, 'The Kitchen Prayer' by Klara Munkres:

Make me a saint by getting meals and washing up the plates.
Although I must have Martha's hands,
I have a Mary mind
And when I black the boots and shoes,
Thy sandals, Lord, I find . . .
Warm all the kitchen with Thy love
and Light it with Thy peace
Forgive me all my worrying
and make my grumbling cease.

But there were some social occasions to dress up for. The village hall was the venue for any gathering marking birth, marriage or death, as well as all the traditional feast days of the calendar, and the whole community came, whether or not they were invited. So long as you brought a 'plate' of something, you were welcome; and, once seated on the benches at the long trestle tables, people talked across the Victoria sponges, jellies and potted meats. Beyond the reach of electricity and far from any cinema or other forms of entertainment, everyone told stories, while others played folk tunes and jigs on the fiddle or the accordion.

As children we were never excluded. Wherever the parents went, their children went, however late at night. I listened to George the Underwood, born in 1858, describing the lime-burners on the moors, and the drovers who had brought the cattle down from Scotland. I also heard about someone nicknamed 'Pipe Head', a shepherd who lived even further out than we did, who was renowned for his appetite and not particular what he ate. His wife was said to have once removed a dead rat from the butter churn before continuing to churn it. I heard tales about the winter of '47: how Billy the Hope had spent three days floundering through the snow with a horse and sled to fetch supplies for his starving family. His story, as they told it, sounded like a Greek epic. I learned about travelling teachers and dancing masters who boarded at the farms for a few weeks and taught the neighbourhood children for pennies and their keep, though it must have been more than fifty years since these itinerants had stopped coming. It was still an oral culture and events lived on in the minds of those who told the tales.

First Nation people say that when an elder dies, part of their history dies too, because of the stories and memories that are lost. My grandparents had been born at the latter end of the nineteenth century; their parents in the 1850s; and one or two of their grandparents predated Queen Victoria. That's a long memory line. Socrates believed that reading was detrimental to oral culture, because it diminished the capacity to remember; a book could only ever be 'a reminder'. For Socrates, cultural memory had a deeper significance; he claimed that oral literacy preserved the morals and customs of a society in a way the written word could not. In Bewcastle, literary and digital culture had not yet dislodged the ability to remember.

At home, visits from grandparents, uncles and aunts led to nights sitting round the fire talking. It was here that I learned my own family stories as I listened to my parents' parents talking about ancestors who went across the sea on sailing ships to bring back cargoes of bananas and marry exotic women; of others who drove herds of cattle from Ireland to London; how they despaired over errant children, disinherited their offspring and fought bitterly over religion. These were stories they had learned from their own grandparents.

I was aware, even at five or six, that I was listening to an unbroken memory line going back two hundred years – stories passing like heirlooms from one generation to another. The tellers seemed to know exactly what my Irish great-great-grandmother Bridie had said to her daughter Frances Theresa when she came home with a baby she wasn't supposed to have – fathered by a footman in the fine house at Warren Point where she was in service. The fancy rooms, the uniforms, the very porcelain dishes she'd washed in a lead-lined sink were all there in the story, leaping like a hologram in the firelight before my eyes. The account of my great-great-uncle Edward, who had stood preaching the gospel of temperance outside his father's pub on a Tyneside quay, was pure Catherine Cookson. It was hardly surprising that I grew up with a love of history, language and narrative that was somehow woven into the wild, untamed landscape beyond the kitchen door.

For my mother, the relatives who constantly came to stay were welcome company but also a worry. She worried about everything: how to feed so many people on a very low wage; where they could all sleep in three small rooms. Guests were always given my parents' bedroom at the end, which had windows on two walls, with views towards the Solway. My parents slept with me in the middle room, in a double bed that almost filled it. I was ignominiously put into the cot wedged between the wall and the bed. Any other surplus relatives slept on 'shake-downs' on the living-room floor. Trips to the closet in the night meant waking the whole household, so we all had chamber pots under the bed.

One visitor came regularly. Aunt May, my father's younger sister, a beautiful, sophisticated woman who was a ward sister at the Cumberland Infirmary in Carlisle. Unlike my father, who was a blue-eyed, Irish Viking with a shock of corn-coloured hair, May had the traditional black hair, white skin and grey eyes of the 'Irish colleen'. As soon as she was old enough, she had escaped the claustrophobic two-up-two-down near the cotton mills to qualify as a nurse; and when she was on duty she lived in a sister's bedsit at the nurses' home. On her days off, rather than go to her parents', she preferred to make the long bus journey up to Bewcastle to stay with us. She would arrive in a wave of French perfume, bringing her silk underwear and a welcome lightness to my mother's life.

May was always laughing. She loved music and dancing, jewellery and expensive clothes. She had rich boyfriends who drove fast cars. The austere Northern Irish Protestantism that had shaped May's childhood had been abandoned. My mother inherited her cast-offs and was horrified by how often she gave things away before they were worn out. For someone who wore the same clothes year in year out, the idea of throwing something away simply because you were tired of it was shocking. May also brought glossy magazines, like *Vogue* and *House beautiful*. I loved looking at them, but they seemed quite foreign, removed from our own daily lives. They reflected the clothes May wanted to wear and the houses she wanted to live in.

The books my mother was reading at this time show her escaping into history and travel. According to her notebooks, she loved *Anson's Voyage Around the World*, Patrick O'Brian's recently published novel *Journey to Samarkand*, H.V. Morton's *In Search of Ireland* and Dana and Ginger Lamb's *The Quest for the Lost City*, a search for the lost empire of the Mayans. She read, and wept over, biographies of ill-fated women such as Mary

May on the hospital tennis courts.

Tudor, Marie Antoinette and Katherine Howard. In fiction she recorded books by Marie Corelli, Pearl S. Buck and Thomas Hardy (only three stars). Her top read was Shirley Seifert's aptly titled *Waters of the Wilderness* which has a lurid cover with Indian canoes and a swashbuckling hero in deerskins (complete with buffalo rifle) looming above the shrinking heroine.

When she was reading, my mother entered another world, oblivious to what was going on around her, unless we called her back. It was something I didn't yet understand. She moved back and forth between the worlds of imagination and reality. For me, as a child, there was no division between the two. What happened in my head was as real as anything that went on outside it. I inhabited a world of ghosts, created imaginary kingdoms in the ruined houses on the fell, and filled them with imaginary characters whose existence was concrete. I was often punished for telling lies. This felt like a terrible injustice because the stories I told about the things that had happened, or the people I had talked to, were true, *for me*.

Having no division in their brains between imagination and reality makes children very creative. In his Nobel Prize acceptance speech, Mario Vargas Llosa said that, as a child, 'reading changed dreams into life and life into dreams'[4]. But our educational system doesn't encourage this kind of creativity once a child leaves primary school. In secondary education, facts and data are prioritised over the creative arts. Generating a love of language and the ability to analyse abstract concepts is seen as less important than scientific learning. John S. Dunne (a professor at the University of Notre Dame) wrote, in an essay on the contemplative life, that 'The way of words, of knowing and loving words, is a way to the essence of things, and to the essence of knowing'.[5]

In 1952 my mother's flowing list of books slowed to a trickle. This was the year I acquired a baby brother, christened John Gordon, but always called Gordon. I remember it clearly because I had to stay with my father's parents in Carlisle for two very boring weeks. Because we lived so far from a hospital, without transport, my mother had to stay near the maternity home when she reached her due date. The doctors had also discovered her heart condition and identified her as 'a mother at risk' so she wasn't allowed the home birth she had had with me.

When she went into hospital for a ten-day stay, I wasn't allowed to see her at all. The regime was draconian. Children weren't welcome on the wards – and husbands were tolerated only in the visiting hour. I was taken to George Street to stand on the pavement outside, while my mother held the baby up at the window and waved. When I finally got to hold him, wrapped in the lacy shawl my mother had been knitting for months, he gazed up at me with unblinking eyes of Viking blue – a perfect replica of my own. Gordon was a chubby, happy baby with a lot of blond curls and was a delight for my mother. She finally had a baby who would wear frilly hats without tearing them off and throwing them out of the pram; a baby who would sit where he was put and play quietly for hours on end. He was placid and good-natured and didn't wriggle away when cuddled. I don't remember ever being jealous. He kept my mother company while I went to school or wandered off with my father.

Getting to school was quite a journey. At five I had to walk across the moors to the road on my own, in sunshine or rain, before being picked up by a taxi to take me to the village. I did the reverse journey in the evening, and it was often dark when I got home in winter. It was a very small school – fewer than thirty children aged between five and fourteen. In those remote communities, unless a child passed the 'merit exam' for the grammar school, they stayed at the local school until they were old enough to leave.

Most were farmers' children, and the boys weren't in school a great deal during the summer months because they were helping their fathers with ploughing, or haymaking, or sheep shearing, or some other agricultural chore. They brought the cows in for milking before they came to school, and fed calves and chickens when they went home. Too tired to learn much when they were there, some of them left without being able to read or write fluently. The older girls were conspicuously absent on wash days and baking days.

Happy kids! I'm on the left with the pigtails.

I loved school. I could already read, so I romped through the elementary syllabus. I was hungry for information. At the end of the day, the teacher made us all sit around the fire while she read a story, and this became my favourite part of the day. Reading to children is very important. Neuroscientists have evidence that:

> Children who never have a story read to them, who never hear words that rhyme, who never imagine fighting with dragons or marrying a prince, have the odds overwhelmingly against them.[6]

All that reading and listening to stories gave me a head start. I was also encouraged to write my own stories and poems. Classmates, decades later, remembered that I'd written a poem about red shoes and read it to the class, so it must have made an impression. I was too young to have read the savage Grimm's tale, so it can only have come from my mother telling me the story of *The Wizard of Oz* – a film she loved. Nobody ridiculed me for being bookish or writing poetry. I made friends, coming out of what had been a very isolated childhood into company. There were more boys than girls in the school and, being a tomboy, I naturally gravitated towards them. I didn't play with dolls, so I didn't have much in common with most of the girls. But there was one girl I played with more than the others. She also came from one of the outlying homesteads and was quite a lively character. She was the reason why, at the age of six, I ran away from home.

One day my school friend gave me an invitation from her mother to come and spend the weekend on their farm. I was very keen to go because they lived across the river in the valley, in a big farmhouse that could only be reached by shuffling along a wire, suspended over the water, holding onto another wire at chest height. When I went home and told my mother about the invitation, she said I couldn't go because my father's parents were coming up from Carlisle for the weekend. She wasn't looking forward to their visit. My mother had never felt quite comfortable with her in-laws. It was an era when it was usual to call in-laws 'mam' and 'dad', just like your own parents, but my Carlisle grandparents were always referred to as 'Harold's mam' and 'Harold's dad'. Face to face, she was careful not to call them anything.

I disliked my father's parents, particularly my grandfather, though at that age I couldn't put the reasons into words. My father's mother, Elizabeth Blair, was a cold woman, who cared very much about material possessions and outward appearances. The phrase, 'What would people think?' featured in her conversation regularly. She bought a new 'costume' every Easter and a new coat every winter. Her house was immaculate. There were crocheted doilies under everything. Sugar-starched crocheted dolls covered the toilet rolls in the bathroom. A new sofa stayed in its wrapping for years, only uncovered for visits from the minister, or the doctor, or any other suitably important person.

Harry Slight, my grandfather, who was also known as Henry Hugh Cunningham, was an injured First World War hero. Before the war he'd been a champion boxer, but the almost fatal injuries he'd sustained at Ypres had ended his sporting as well as his military career. He had four paralysed fingers on one hand and much of the muscle and flesh missing from his arm. Sometimes he would roll up his shirt sleeve and ask my brother and me to feel the shrapnel still buried under the skin. My brother loved it and used to giggle as he located the pieces of metal; I avoided touching him.

Before the war, Harry had survived a difficult childhood as an illegitimate boy living with his mother and four siblings in extreme poverty. After his military service, he worked for the post office, in a job reserved for disabled war heroes, and wrote a weekly column for the local paper. In his free time, he ran a small amateur theatre company which toured village halls performing the sketches he wrote. There was also poetry, which made my mother blush and my father cringe whenever it was produced. He was estranged from his own family, supposedly because he had married a Protestant, but there may have been other reasons. His sister didn't speak to him and there was an unexplained feud with his older brother James that lasted a lifetime.

I had no intention of staying at home to see my Carlisle grandparents, but I knew that argument would be useless. So I went back to school the next day and told my friend that my mother had given permission and I would be coming home with her on Friday. There were no telephones, so no one could check. In the morning I pushed my nightdress and a toothbrush into my school satchel without my mother, who was busy giving my baby brother his breakfast, noticing anything. After school, instead of getting into the waiting taxi, I went home with my friend and her mother.

The farm was everything I'd hoped for. The thrill of shuffling across the wire bridge, the lovely warm house with mullioned windows, an oak staircase, a grandfather clock in the hall, and that musty smell all old houses have. We ate supper with her family around a big pine table in the kitchen with a Tilly lamp hung from the beams, then we were bathed together in the deep Belfast sink. It was such fun. We were put to bed and took a long time to go to sleep because we were chattering and giggling under the covers. I was woken in the middle of the night by a torch shining in my face and several people standing round the bed having a conversation. Then I went back to sleep.

I had no notion of the anguish I'd caused when I failed to come home from school and the taxi driver reported that he hadn't seen me. My mother feared the worst. The Captain was the only person who had a telephone and my parents had gone down to his house to ring for the police. A young geologist called Angus, who was lodging with Mary and Edmund at the Flatt, volunteered to go looking for me on his motorbike. He and my father had toured the neighbourhood asking people if they'd seen me; the policeman had gone door to door in the village, getting the headmaster out of bed to answer questions. No one knew where I'd gone after I left the school.

It was quite late before my mother remembered the invitation I'd been so keen to accept earlier in the week. So Angus, my father and the policeman had gone to the farm and found me. They had all decided that, as I was safe and well, it was better to leave me there until the morning. Angus came after breakfast on the motorbike to take me home, where I faced an inquest. My mother looked as if she'd been crying all night. I was given a stern 'talking to' and forced to apologise to her for all the trouble I had caused. I said 'sorry', though I didn't feel in the least bit repentant. I had no idea of the grief I'd caused until I was much older, when, as a mother myself, the full impact of what she must have felt finally sank in.

6

LOW LING

Angus had come into our lives when my mother discovered, on one of her fortnightly visits to the travelling grocery shop in the Flatt Lodge yard, that Edmund and Mary had a lodger. He was a post-graduate student doing research into fossil formations for a PhD in palaeontology. He was regarded as rather 'posh' but had a lively, curious mind and was bored stiff at the Flatt. So my mother invited him over to the croft and he was delighted to find two like-minded people of a similar age to himself. Soon he was coming over every evening to listen to records on the wind-up gramophone and argue about books and politics with my parents.

He and my father shared the same sense of humour. Once, he helped my father to move the sideboard so that they could paint the wall behind it and an ornament, a wedding present from one of the aunts, fell and broke. My mother was in tears, but Angus said, 'Ella, we've done you a favour, it was hideous,' and my father said, 'I've always hated it, Tiny, but I didn't like to say.' They both began to laugh uncontrollably, while my mother cried. Eventually she too saw the funny side and agreed that she had never liked it either but felt obliged to display it in case the aunt came to visit. That was my mother – a person who would never hurt anyone's feelings if she could avoid it.

Angus was an incredibly romantic figure, roaring up on his second-hand BSA motorbike, curly hair blowing in the wind. He talked to me like an adult and took me for rides. Through him, I discovered that the layers of landscape went even deeper than I knew. If you followed the beck up the fell, eventually you came to a waterfall, where the water poured over a crag in one long, powerful plunge. Rowan trees had sprouted in cracks in the rock and a pair of ravens had made their nest in one of them. On my scrambles up the beck, I had never noticed anything more than the nest and the peat-brown water of the pool underneath. Angus showed me where the water had worn away the rock to reveal a fossilised tree fern. Beneath it, where the rocks had sheared along a plane, there were fossils of sea creatures, trilobites and ammonites that had once scuttled across an ancient sea floor. The idea that the fellside could once have been a tropical seashore was breathtaking. Angus explained how the rock had been heaved upwards over millions of years, transforming the sea floor into part of a mountain. 'It's as old as the stars,' he told me. I often went there, to touch something that was so old it was almost beyond imagination.

Angus was there the next time May came to stay and the results were entirely predictable. Handsome, intelligent man meets beautiful, intelligent woman. Soon the BSA was burning the rubber between the Flatt and Carlisle in the evenings. He bought her the record of Mario Lanza's 'Be My Love' and apparently went down on his knees to propose. Within a year I was a bridesmaid and Angus had become my uncle, living in a caravan with May in one of the fields below the house. They had a new baby and no money but a lot of ambition. Once Angus had his doctorate, he planned to move abroad, to work as a geologist for an oil company.

My father was also becoming restless. He and the Captain had started having arguments about stock management. When he came home in the evenings, my father would often throw his cap on the floor and start ranting about rich idiots who knew nothing about farming. Our departure was only a matter of time. A job was advertised in my parents' old neighbourhood, a farm manager's post at a much better salary with a large house to live in. My father applied and was accepted. So we began the move to Rosley, a village not far from where I'd been born and about seven miles from Caldbeck, which was to be the focus of the rest of my childhood. Our belongings were taken back across the fell on a cart and loaded into the cattle wagon.

It wasn't easy to find a replacement shepherd to live in such a remote location. The Captain was not pleased that my father was leaving and made it very difficult. I got caught up in the war between the two men. A year or so earlier, the Captain had given me a pet lamb to rear and the much-loved Jennifer was now a fully-grown sheep. She was part of the family and used to follow me around like a dog. She had given birth to triplets that spring, so I now had four sheep. Naturally, she and her lambs were moved, with the rest of my father's livestock, to our new home. The Captain asked for her back, implying that she'd been removed 'improperly'. Angry letters were exchanged. But the legal position was that she (and her issue) belonged to me, except that, in reality, they were my father's.

Low Ling was a big farm – two hundred acres of fertile arable land. The farmhouse was an imposing Georgian building, as unlike the property we had left as anything you could imagine. Even the Captain didn't live in anything so big. It was approached by a long driveway, through impressive stone gateposts, and inside it was

Me cuddling Jennifer, with my cousin Joan.

enormous. A door from the farmyard opened into a big 'back kitchen' where all the wellington boots and coats were kept and the weekly wash was done. There were bells on the wall that had once rung for servants. A butler's pantry housed an incubator the size of a billiard table for hatching chicks. There was another huge kitchen, which immediately became our living room. It had a new Raeburn, a smaller version of the Aga that kept the kitchen perpetually warm.

These three rooms alone were bigger than the entire croft, but they were only the beginning. At the front there was a drawing room with a tiled Victorian fireplace and long graceful windows, giving a view out onto the driveway, and a door into a big conservatory. The dining room next to it became a spare bedroom for guests. Then there were the larders, stone-flagged and cold, an apple store, and one that had deep stone sinks for curing hams. In the kitchens and the bathroom, hot water poured out of the taps, heated by the Raeburn. Even more magical, there was electricity. For the first time, I discovered what it was to click a switch and make the lights come on. No more cleaning paraffin lamps and fiddling about with delicate mantles that disintegrated at a touch. No more candles, spilling wax everywhere.

Upstairs there was a proper bathroom, a separate flush toilet and a sewing room, which became a repository for junk. There were four big bedrooms on this floor; and up another flight of stairs, two more that had formerly been occupied by servants. My brother and I made these our playrooms on rainy days. Outside there was an orchard and a small lake – a flooded quarry over a hundred feet deep – surrounded by trees. The country lanes we

The family at Low Ling, with Prince the horse and Flo the collie.

walked down were shoulder high with cow parsley, ragged robin and ladies bedstraw. It should have been paradise, but the well-ordered, prosperous fields were not what my heart ached for. I was homesick for the moors, the open land and the sky.

My mother loved being back in civilisation. On Saturdays she could take the bus and go into Carlisle to do her shopping and visit the library. The village had a school, a church and a small shop. The church hall was a short walk down the road for WI meetings, and she rejoined the Choral Society. She began to go to morning service again, reciting the beautiful words of the creed, which she loved, and the psalms she knew by heart. The vicar was very strange. He refused to see his parishioners, communicating with them only via the letterbox. Parish work was mainly done by a young curate and soon after we arrived the vicar retired. The school at Rosley was a church school, so for the first time I went to Sunday School while my mother was at Matins. There we coloured in pictures, learned Bible stories and were given glossy cards printed with a religious image and a text to take home. There was one called 'The Light of the World', by William Holman Hunt, which I was particularly fond of.

Every weekday morning my mother brushed and plaited my hair and I walked down the lanes to the village school. When my brother was four years old, I was given the job of taking him too. I had never been a reliable baby-sitter. Shortly after we moved to Low Ling, my mother asked me to look after him while she did the big weekly wash. I had friends round to play and wasn't very pleased, but I took him out into the field with us. The boys decided that we were going to build a treehouse beside the lake, and I knew I wasn't allowed to take Gordon anywhere near the water, so I tied his reins to a small rowan tree growing in the field and went off to play with my friends. I forgot all about him until my mother called us in for tea. He was still sitting under the tree, crying quietly. It was one of the few times I was spanked. My parents didn't believe in physical punishment for a child, but there were times when I drove them beyond reason.

At the school there were only four children in my age group, and they were all boys. We were farm children, and an unattractive bunch. We had impetigo and ringworm from the cattle, or from the pet lambs that nibbled our ears, cat fleas and dog fleas and chicken fleas. My mother waged a constant battle with hygiene and pest control around the house. It didn't bother me at all – I was too busy having a good time. I climbed trees, was dared to do forbidden things, wandered around the woods like a little savage and watched, incredulous, when the boys had peeing contests. I was the girl with the torn dress, grubby socks and skinned knees. I didn't enjoy girlie things and I was beginning to rebel against what we'd now call gender stereotyping.

In 1953, the school gave out prayer books to celebrate the Queen's coronation. There were blue ones for the boys and a light shade of pinkish red for the girls. I absolutely refused to have a girl's prayer book and it caused consternation. The solution was to give me the blue one intended for my little brother – who was too young to care – while he had the one destined for a girl. When my Carlisle grandmother gave me a baby doll and a pram for Christmas, I gave them away to a girl from school. Her mother came to the house and asked Mum whether she shouldn't give them back. She was obviously worried by the extravagant gift. My mother was very angry with me – what was she going to say to Nana when she next came to visit? – but she agreed that, as I had given it away, in all fairness the gift should stand. My friend's mother thought I was mad, but her daughter was delighted. Later Mum said that she had hoped it would teach me a lesson. But I never regretted parting with it.

At school I was encouraged to write, and the headmistress sent one of my poems to a teachers' magazine. Mum had been telling me the story of Shakespeare's *The Tempest* and I'd been captivated by the fate of the sprite, Ariel, who had been shut up in a tree trunk by a witch. The poem, called 'Ariel's Lament', was written from Ariel's point of view, recording how it felt to be imprisoned. I had also begun to create stories, which I told my brother when we went to bed in the evening. There was a creature with eighty legs who had all sorts of adventures, as well as ghosts, witches and fantastic beasts. When my cousins came to stay, I told them the same stories and was told off because one of them became frightened and had nightmares.

My parents didn't know what to do with a daughter who lived so completely in her imagination. I sometimes told tall stories about things that hadn't actually happened. They weren't lies; in my mind these events had really taken place. The school was coaching me for the eleven plus, even though I was too young. Because my birthday fell in the second half of August, I could go to the grammar school a year early if I passed; and if I didn't, I had the option of taking it again the following year. It all went over my head. If I was precocious (and apparently I was), I was never made aware of it. My parents tried to keep my feet firmly on the ground. I wasn't allowed to 'get ideas'.

There was something about the house at Rosley that reminded my mother of Manderley. *Rebecca* was one of her all-time favourite books. She often told us the story, reciting the first lines from memory: 'Last night I dreamt I went to Manderley again'. It was possible at Low Ling to imagine Mrs Danvers walking down the stairs, summoned by the servants' bell. I was mesmerised by the story, empathising with the naive girl who became the second Mrs de Winter, though too young to understand the sexual politics. The idea that romantic fiction was 'a form of oppressive ideology, which works to keep women in their socially and sexually subordinate place' hadn't yet reached the north of England.[7] For me, it was simply a tale of love and jealousy, natural justice and loyalty. It was one of the books we both liked.

I had also begun on the classics. Woolworths was selling abridged classic texts in a cheap uniform edition, and I began to spend my pocket money on them. I bought *Black Beauty*, *Treasure Island*, the *Scarlet Pimpernel*, *Arthurian Myths*, and others now forgotten. Books were my friends, my daily companions. In *A Saint in Swindon*, a dystopian, futuristic story about the power of books, Alice Jolly writes that:

> the simple act of reading is a truly amazing process. It is both intensely solitary and amazingly sociable. The reader not only encounters the writer, he or she also meets all the characters who inhabit the story. Beyond that, the reader also engages with all the other people who have read the story – or who might read it in the future. The writing is remade again and again as it is considered.[8]

Each time we read a book, we read ourselves into it. *Rebecca*, which I read as a teenager and again in my twenties, was a huge influence; and it meant something different to me each time I read it. Brought up half-wild, firmly working class, as a young woman I was never confident in social situations; I was an outsider, who sat on the sidelines and watched, afraid to open my mouth in case I said the wrong thing, afraid to eat in company in case I picked up the wrong fork. I empathised with the second Mrs de Winter and her search for identity. After my mother's death I wondered whether she, too, had felt like that. For her it was a seminal novel. We used to argue about the message it contained: how no one can escape their past, however far they travel.

I was destined to have relationships with two men who carried torches for other women considered more sophisticated and beautiful than me. The second Mrs de Winter became my alter-ego. I was what the wild moors of Coldslopes had made me; and the thought that your past can never be conquered haunted me. My mother was also the product of her upbringing between the wars: a town girl who loved the country, a girl whose life and youthful promise had been blighted by prejudice and then by a world war. She had lost her first love and her future; and was in the process of remaking her life differently.

One of the disadvantages of living in civilisation again was that my Carlisle grandparents became frequent visitors. They used to come every Thursday on the bus, arriving in time for lunch and leaving in the evening after tea. In the afternoon, my grandfather used to go down to the school to walk us home. I grew to dread it. Sometimes I would climb over the school wall at the back, pushing my brother through a gap in the fence, and walk home through the fields rather than go home with him. And then I would face an inquisition from my mother and grandmother as to why I hadn't come home with Grandad.

How could I tell them the whole story? His idea of walking us home was to ramble back through the woods, where he would strip me naked and ask me to touch his erect penis. He did this with my four-year-old brother watching. My brother and I were told we mustn't tell anyone about our little walks. But I had no words to describe what was happening. I was used to trusting grown-ups, particularly my close relatives. Brought up to respect my elders, I was used to doing what I was told, more or less. Obedience was drummed into my brother and I. Were the strange things my grandfather did to me, however horrible, some kind of grown-up ritual I had to get used to?

I was saved by my brother. Too young to really understand, or be bound by my grandfather's strictures about secrecy, he made a remark to my mother one day about my grandfather's willy and asked why he'd come into the bedroom with his trousers undone. He was questioned and what he said horrified my mother. When she brushed my hair the following morning before I went to school, she began to ask me about my grandfather and I answered her as truthfully as I could. It was a relief to tell someone, though I feared I wouldn't be believed. I was a child who told tall stories; who would believe my word against the word of a grown-up? When I asked my mother years later, she said that I could never have made up the details I revealed unless it had actually happened. But I hadn't told her everything; that was too difficult. And there were things I simply didn't remember. I had terrible nightmares about something sharp that came up out of the mattress and hurt me. My mother was always losing the kitchen scissors and mystified to find them under my pillow.

My parents were very innocent. They knew nothing of paedophilia and had never thought that someone so perverted could exist in their own family. My father wanted to call the police; my mother didn't want a fuss. She could already imagine the newspaper headlines. There was a family conference. One of the aunts revealed that Harry had 'interfered' with her young daughter; an uncle said that it was known in the Post Office that he had pornographic pictures of children in his coat pocket. Another uncle went home and questioned his children and the answers he got led a group of men to waylay my grandfather after work and give him a beating. He was told to stay away from his grandchildren. We were never allowed to be alone with him again. He was a bad man, my cousins and I were told, but we would be protected from him.

My father didn't speak to his own father for years. It grieved Mum that my grandmother kept on asking what was wrong and she couldn't tell her; they had all agreed that she mustn't be told. 'It would kill her,' I heard one of the uncles say. Later they admitted they had been wrong. My grandmother did know the kind of man he was. There had been an 'incident' with a neighbour's daughter when my father was young, and they'd been forced to move house. But despite this, she had made no attempt to protect any of us. The respectable, public, face had to be preserved. She loathed her husband – wouldn't even share a bed with him. Knowing for certain what he'd done, and knowing that other people knew, might have given her the impetus to leave him.

At first I blamed my parents for not having my grandfather arrested. I felt angry that he'd been left unpunished. But as a grown woman I became

Harry as a young boy, with Lord Lonsdale and his flyweight boxing trophy

glad that they hadn't involved the police. When I studied law and saw how children were treated in the justice system, I realised that I was too sensitive a child to have survived the brutal, adversarial, cross-examination process. My predilection for fantasy meant that I would never have been believed. Then I felt guilt because, in being saved from that, I had condemned other children to be abused. My grandfather haunted children's playgrounds, so there must have been other victims. But there was one casualty of his sexual predation no one thought about, and the damage he had done wouldn't become obvious for years.

My mother's reading trebled at Low Ling. Her reading diary was now divided into monthly sections, rather than yearly. Not only was the physical work of keeping house there less time-consuming, but she also had regular access to the county library in Carlisle. It was a graceful Georgian building with classical pillars at the entrance. Inside there were rooms and rooms full of books. I got a children's ticket and, while my mother roamed the adult library, I scoured the children's shelves. I read everything, and some books I read twice.

Living in rural locations, we didn't often get newspapers. My parents would bring one home on Saturdays, usually the *Carlisle Journal* or the *Cumberland News*, sometimes the *Manchester Guardian*. My grandparents bought *Reveille*, which they insisted on giving to my parents after they'd finished with it. It was trash, my mother said, and my father wouldn't read it, commenting that it was only fit to light the fire with. I was fascinated by the almost naked ladies on the cover, posing in their underwear with improbably large breasts and small waists. I lapped up the stories about the Queen and her children, illustrated by copious photographs. I envied Princess Anne her fitted wool coat with a velvet collar. There were romantic stories and gossip about film stars such as Marilyn Monroe, Doris Day and James Dean, evidence of an unknown glamorous world beyond the farm.

My mother bought *Women's Weekly*, mainly for the knitting patterns and the quiet, inoffensive fiction it contained. My grandmother passed on *People's Friend* but Mum considered that magazine rather 'lowbrow'. Elsie, the girl who occasionally babysat for my brother and me, read little picture book stories, set out like black and white cartoon strips. In them, women broke their hearts over deceitful lovers, and agonised over which man to marry. Sometimes they 'went too far' and were thrown out by their parents, only to be rescued by their lovers from a fate worse than death. These stories had titles like 'Lust', 'The Doctor's Daughter', 'Will she ever see him again?' and 'She didn't know it was wrong'. My mother called them Penny Dreadfuls and refused to let me read them. I hid the box of books that Elsie had given me in the attic; and I began to realise that the world of literature contained a whole new hierarchy of snobbery.

My father had now qualified as a Methodist lay preacher and took services at various local chapels within cycling distance every Sunday evening. He soon became popular. He had a lovely speaking voice, with a soft northern burr, and a way of preaching that sounded as if he was just talking to you over the fence. Because we had no car, the rest of us were forced to stay at home unless we could get a lift from someone. It wasn't much fun for my mother.

My parents rarely went out together and holidays were even rarer. On a farm, animals need feeding every day of the year; any holiday for a farmer means paying someone to do the work for them. But on their tenth wedding anniversary, my father took a few days off and they went to London. Apart from a couple of long weekends spent with my mother's parents in North Shields, this was their only holiday since they'd married. Mum talked about it for years. There are one or two photos of my mother – very smart in a new summer dress – and my father looking uncomfortable in his Sunday suit. Towns were not his natural habitat and he wasn't used to walking on pavements. He came back with blisters on his feet.

THE ROAD TO ROUGH CLOSE

Rosley was the most normal part of my childhood. We lived in a house that was like other people's houses, and we had electricity and running water. There were abundant Christmas and birthday presents because my parents could now afford things. As a farm manager, Dad was paid a very good wage. There were new clothes in the wardrobe, a modern three-piece suite in the drawing room and a carpet. They were buying Mozart's *Eine Kleine Nachtmusik* in instalments, one 78 record at a time, at the end of every month. But most of the money was put into a savings account to go towards a deposit on a farm of their own. My father was a man in a hurry – he had no intention of spending his life working for someone else. He didn't have the temperament for it. There was constant friction. My mother would sigh and say, 'He won't let anyone be the boss of him,' and it was true.

It was through the chapel that we met the Routledges, four elderly brothers and a sister who lived on a neighbouring farm. They were never seen except on Sundays; neighbours said they were very reclusive and if you met them they rarely spoke to you. I was fascinated by their farmhouse, which was a sturdy, black and white, traditional Lake District house set in a beautiful cottage garden. Tom was one of the younger brothers, a lean, craggy man with a face creased and brown from the weather. When he smiled, which was often, you could see that he had a mouthful of rotten teeth. To sweeten his breath, he sucked extra-strong mints, and kept several packets in his coat pocket which were liberally offered to everyone he met.

He came to the local chapel and became my father's biggest fan, cycling to wherever he was preaching. Soon he was coming down to Low Ling in the evenings for a 'bit of crack', bringing a bunch of flowers from the garden for my mother. It became obvious that he had, in my parents' words, 'taken a shine to her'. No one mentioned the word 'love'. I remember those evenings, sitting by the fire in awkward silence, once the initial pleasantries had been exhausted. Tom was no conversationalist. Every now and then the stillness would be punctuated by an indrawn breath and an 'Aye', that could have meant anything. My parents dreaded his visits, because they couldn't read books or listen to the radio while he was there, and attempts at talking were strained. Eventually, after a couple of hours and the consumption of tea and cake, Tom would get up and say, 'Better be off', put on his overcoat – a brown dog-tooth wool affair that he wore winter and summer – slip on his bicycle clips and step out into the night.

We were honoured to be invited to the Routledge house for tea. It was a journey into a previous century – nothing had changed since the Routledge parents had furnished it when they had married decades earlier. There were flagged floors with rag rugs and a gigantic grandfather clock in the hallway. The interior was dark because there was no electricity, and there were candle sconces on all the walls. The rooms were papered in old-fashioned floral prints in greens and reds, darkened by decades of paraffin fumes and candle smoke. There were heavy velvet curtains in medieval red, and the furniture was Victorian mahogany the colour and sheen of chestnuts. It had a patina that only decades of polish can produce. There were table covers of chenille, and glass lamps in blues and greens with painted glass shades. Above the fireplace a text embroidered in cross-stitch announced: 'Christ is the Head of this House, the Unseen Guest at Every Meal'.

We were introduced by Tom to his sister Ginny, a thin, stooped woman in an overall, with grey wispy hair drawn back into a bun. She avoided our eyes, whispered hello in a voice that could barely be heard and beckoned my mother and me towards the sitting room door. Inside, the curtains were drawn and it was as dark as a cave, lit only by a fire in the grate, although it was August. Beside the fire, in an upholstered, spindle-back rocking chair, was a woman so ancient I wondered if she was real. Mrs Routledge was dressed as I'd seen pictures of old Queen Victoria, in a full-length black gown trimmed with buttons and frills. The room was full of the scent of decay, as she held out a shaking hand to greet us. We were given tea round the kitchen table with the brothers. It was a silent affair, apart from my parents' attempts at conversation. Ginny didn't sit down with us, but ran round slicing home-made bread, putting out home-cured ham with beetroot jelly, scones and cakes, making tea in an antique silver service. She looked at me nervously as she put down a slice of apple cake and smiled a quick shy smile that almost seemed to escape from her mouth against her will.

Gradually, as Tom gained confidence in us, their story began to emerge. Their parents had been extreme non-conformists in some small sect. Methodism was deemed to be too liberal. The only book they had been allowed to read was the Bible. Once, when Ginny won *Alice in Wonderland* as a school prize, her father put it on the fire as the work of the devil. The only time they were allowed to go anywhere was to worship. When she was in her thirties, Ginny had a boyfriend she'd met when she went to the market to buy groceries. She used to sneak out of the house to meet him on the main road, where they walked up and down for half an hour before she ran back home. When her father found out what was happening, it was stopped. It broke her heart, Tom said. Only their eldest brother had escaped. He had thumbed a lift on a wagon and gone south. He'd sent a letter to say he was in Oxfordshire, working on a farm and wouldn't be coming back. Although their father had been dead ten years, nothing had changed. They still had no electricity or telephone, or any other modern conveniences. His stern influence was as thick as woodsmoke within those four walls and their mother, slowly fading in the sitting room, was still feared and respected, like a spider at the centre of a web.

I often wandered up to the farm on fine days and Ginny would pat my head and give me tea and cake and let me chatter. Tom would take me out into the garden, which I quickly realised was his special place. He grew sweet peas, lupins, sweet william and enormous dahlias. It was a traditional cottage garden with white lilac and purple lilac by the gate, peonies and Alchemilla on either side of the path and, against the wall, roses as big as mop heads, buzzing with bees. He would go into the greenhouse and give me strawberries, or raspberries – whatever was in season – to take home to my mother.

My Aunt Nancy had just given me *The Secret Garden* to read, and Tom's garden was everything I imagined a garden should be. Neither of my parents did any gardening; they had neither the time nor the energy. In our garden at Low Ling the unmown grass was waist high. The conservatory remained unused, the gardening equivalent of Miss Havisham's sitting room, with stacks of cracked pots, a few weeds struggling up through the floorboards, rusting tools, and shawls of cobweb everywhere. It smelt rank, the scent of a rogue shrub that had shouldered its way between the wall and the frame.

One of the good things about Low Ling was that my mother's parents came more often, making the trip from North Shields to Carlisle by bus. I called them Nana and Grandpa. Mum didn't look forward to their visits with the same enthusiasm. Annie Sutherland was becoming very deaf and talked incessantly and loudly about anything and everything. After a day or so, my mother would begin to look persecuted. At mealtimes Nana talked about operations, on which she was an authority, and the illnesses and deaths of her many friends. I saw my father, who was squeamish, turn pale and push his plate away during a particularly gruesome episode. My brother and I were fascinated.

Nana sometimes let us watch her getting ready for bed at night. Her hearing aid, a gift from the recently introduced

'National Health', was a cumbersome porcelain device attached by wires to the heavy battery that powered it. She clipped the wires into her hair to conceal them, and ran them down through her clothes to the battery which swung between her legs, in a cloth bag she had made herself. It must have been annoying, but she rarely complained about the inconvenience and it didn't stop her doing anything. These trials were meant to be borne, she told me.

Two years earlier, she had discovered a lump in her breast, but, because she was struggling at the time to mother her grandchildren, my cousins Jean and Anne, Aunt Margaret's two abandoned daughters aged five and three, she hadn't gone to the doctors until it was obvious that it was cancer. It had spread to her other breast and into the glands in her armpits. The surgeon she saw, at the Royal Victoria Infirmary in Newcastle, told her it was inoperable, but a newly qualified registrar said he would like to try operating if she was willing to take the risk. It was a die/die situation. Nana had always been a gambler. She put all her chips down on young Dr Mawson.

He did one of the most radical mastectomies in the textbook, taking away both her breasts, the lymph glands and a lot of muscle tissue in her upper arms. He then prescribed six months of radiotherapy. Nana survived. For about a year she was unable to do even simple household tasks, but she exercised every morning with a hairbrush, trying to lift it above her head, first with one hand and then the other until, eventually, she succeeded. Dr (soon to be Mr) Mawson became a miracle maker, the hero of her story, which she told endlessly to anyone who would listen.

I used to watch, riveted, as she took off her bra before bed and laid the two false breasts on the dressing table, beside her hearing aid. You could see her ribs through the skin, and her chest was criss-crossed by scars. She would turn to me and say, 'All I need is a wooden leg, pet', and laugh in the strange, tonal voice of the very deaf.

Grandpa Sutherland was his wife's opposite; a quiet man who spoke only when necessary. He loved fishing and I would sit beside him on summer evenings, in silent companionship, while he smoked his pipe and cast his line in the lake, aiming for the places where the flies hung low over the water. The fish in the lake were mostly perch that flipped and flapped in the grass on the end of the line. Taking them off the hook required skill to avoid their spines. The smallest were thrown back, the biggest fried until they were crisp for supper. Eating them was something of a penance because they were so bony and tasteless. Grandpa lived in hope of catching a pike – a lake with so many fish in it was sure to have some, he reasoned. But he never caught any. One year, when it rained torrentially for days, the lake flooded and a river of eels wriggled across the farmyard, miraculously appearing out of the lake and making their way across land in a mysterious journey that I was told would end in the Sargasso Sea.

My mother was never allowed to settle. No sooner had she acquired curtains for the big windows and enough linoleum for the bedroom floors than my father was talking about moving. Mum was reading Walpole at the time. He was one of the older generation of English novelists, having published his first book in 1909. Born in New Zealand, the son of an Anglican minister, he'd been sent to England to be educated at boarding school, where he was profoundly miserable:

> I grew up ... discontented, ugly, abnormally sensitive, and excessively conceited. No one liked me ... I believed that I was profoundly misunderstood, that people took my pale and pimpled countenance for the mirror of my soul, that I had marvellous things of interest in me that would one day be discovered.[9]

It was the perfect training for a novelist. Walpole became one of my mother's favourite authors, though she remained blissfully ignorant that he had been both an atheist and gay. He had lived in the Lake District until his death in 1941, not far from where we lived, in a house called Brackenburn, overlooking Derwentwater. The surrounding countryside provided the setting for his *Herries Chronicles* which Mum had read as a girl in North Shields but now began to read again in their proper setting. She also read *The Dark Forest*, a story about a Red Cross ambulance driver in Poland during the First World War, and *Katherine Christian*, which was a prequel to the Rogue Herries novels. Katherine was another of Walpole's feisty women, forging a path for herself in the English Civil War. It was left unfinished when the author died but this didn't seem to matter to my mother, who gave it four stars. Grevel Lindop, writing in the *Times Literary Supplement*, explains why Walpole's novels, sneered at by Virginia Woolf, were so popular:

> the books are well worth reading for their drama, their incredible visual imagination, their narrative drive, and notably for Walpole's amazing imagination for the

grotesque and terrifying. He's a superb Gothic writer: death, witchcraft, hallucinations, madness, violence and terror bring out the very best in him.[10]

Walpole used actual locations for his novels and one of them was a house not far from us, just outside the village of Mosedale, in the shadow of Carrock Fell. We were unaware of this until one evening my father said that a friend was going to give us a lift to look at a farm for sale. Stone Ends Farm was a traditional Lake District farmhouse with a long history. The interior was low-ceilinged, but it had a lot of rooms; it wasn't as big as Low Ling, but bigger than the croft. There was even a 'back staircase' which would originally have been used by servants. Mum instantly recognised Stone Ends as the licentious Squire Gauntry's house in Walpole's *Judith Paris*. This appealed to her romantic spirit. But the rooms seemed dark and gloomy and there was an atmosphere about the house, a sadness that seemed to have settled around it. Added to that, there was a structural crack in the end wall and, although there was a 'fell right' for keeping stock on the hill, there were less than forty acres of what was called 'in-bye' land, reclaimed land enclosed by stone walls. I was very glad – and so was my mother – when Dad did his calculations and decided that it was too expensive and too small to be viable.

My mother was incurably romantic and it made her vulnerable. Looking at her commonplace book, which she filled in alongside her reading diaries, the entries have an almost Gothic sentimentality. She liked John Buchan and copied out a series of quotes from *The Dancing Floor* which capture how she felt about poetry and nature. Looking at something beautiful, or reading something she thought sublime, she could enter a kind of ecstasy, which we often observed as children. When she copied out 'I felt a sort of poet's rapture as I looked at those shining spaces, and at the sky above, flooded with the amber moon', that was what she felt. What she yearned for in life were 'revelations of loveliness'. But her interests were wide. At the same time as reading Walpole and Buchan, she was binge-reading Joseph Conrad, Mary Webb and Arthur Koestler.

She talked all the time about the books she'd read. Sometimes, even now, I'm not always sure whether I read some of those books myself, or simply know them from my mother's account of them. I knew the stories of Shakespeare's plays long before I was old enough to read the originals. She would quote all the best bits for my brother and me and act them out in the kitchen using a wooden spoon and a tea towel for dramatic gestures. I liked the death of Desdemona and Prospero's renunciation of his powers, but was equally moved by her rendering of Henry V's rousing speech before Agincourt and the pathos of Cymbeline's 'Golden lads and girls all must, / As chimney-sweepers, come to dust'. Her talent for literary performance meant that she was often in demand for special occasions at the village hall.

Mum and I were now part of a gospel singing group that toured the small chapels of the northern lakes. It had been formed by two of my parents' friends who lived near us and who quickly became an honorary aunt and uncle. An elderly lady in a cardigan, called Eva, played the organ, and her son Noel belted out rousing choruses on an accordion. Aunt Florrie, who had a clear, flute-like soprano voice, sang duets with her sister Kathy and sometimes with my mother. Uncle Alf sang tenor and a young man called Geoff Walby underpinned it all with his magnificent, resonant bass. Aunt Florrie had a daughter the same age as me, called Tina, and we were paired to sing songs we'd learned at Sunday school. My mother gave recitations, showing off her elocution-trained voice, reading poems and pieces of prose with a spiritual theme. Soon I was being coopted to read verses deemed suitable for a child – poems such as Blake's 'The Tyger' and Christina Rossetti's 'Birthday'. Dressed in frilled, smocked, hand-me-downs, I was wheeled out like a performing seal to delight the rows of elderly people in the chapels we were invited to.

At home I became aware of a new atmosphere; tense conversations in the kitchen, my mother frowning all the time, my father cajoling her in his most persuasive voice. 'Tiny,' he used to say, 'Come on, Tine.' Once I heard her say 'Oh, Harold! No!' A couple of times I saw her weeping. They had been to see another farm, Rough Close, this time without us. Dad was planning to borrow money from his parents and from one of my mother's uncles to put down the deposit and get an agricultural mortgage for the rest. Owing money to anyone was one of Mum's nightmares. She couldn't bear the thought of it. They were taking such a risk with other people's money. It wasn't a risk, Dad argued. The land was the guarantee, and after all, what could go wrong? They were young, they knew about farming. Why work for someone else when you could be putting all that effort into a place of your own? And there was my brother Gordon to consider. Round and round the arguments went. Round and round, but the final decision was never in doubt.

The house needed decorating, my mother said; it hadn't been lived in for a long time. My grandfather, newly retired, came over from North Shields to help. He and I hitched a ride on the milk-collecting lorry, sitting high above the wheels, among the engine fumes, in a cab shaken by vibrations, as it struggled up hill after hill until it reached the top and you could see the whole of the northern fells: Skiddaw, Overwater lake, Bassenthwaite, mile after mile of hill and dale. 'That's where you're going to live,' Grandpa said, pointing to the first line of fells, 'Up there.'

The milk lorry dropped us off at a road end and we had to walk across a footbridge over a ford and then up a narrow road, through wild land with deep ravines on either side and fells rising steeply on the left, carrying bags of wallpaper, tins of paint and brushes and a rucksack with flasks of tea and sandwiches. It was a long walk, almost a mile, and the road, which was tarmacked for the first few hundred yards, degenerated into a rough track long before we reached the farm.

The buildings, once whitewashed but now weathered almost grey, were built in a square around a cobbled yard. The house faced inwards, towards the barns, with a long sloping roof at the back, against the prevailing wind from the Solway. There was a small garth of trees, mainly sycamore, ash and horse chestnut. Grandpa took a key from under a stone and opened the peeling red front door. The smell of damp, abandoned places met us, and moisture condensed on our skins in a cold mist. The stone-floored central passageway opened on the right into the living room and on the left into a parlour. In both rooms jackdaws' nests sprawled across the floor in stinking heaps of twig and feathers where they had come down the chimneys. Wallpaper moulted from the walls in strips. I was horrified. 'We can't live here!' I said to my grandfather, bursting into tears.

He laughed and said, 'Better get those nests cleared up, pet, because at the end of the month you will be!' But it was the first time he had seen the house – and he looked almost as shocked as I did.

8

A PLACE OF OUR OWN

Rough Close meant everything to us. For the first time we had somewhere to belong. This land was ours; we owned it. For my brother and me, it became a place of magical enchantment; for my mother it was the 'dear perpetual place' where she could make long-term plans; it was my father's lifelong dream – a farm of his own, with no one to tell him what to do. He was thirty-two, my mother four years older.

We arrived on a cloudy northern day in two cattle wagons that lumbered and lurched their way over the ford and up the rough track.

Rough Close

Our possessions were in one, the animals in another. The front door was open and a fire had been lit in the grate of the black range. A woman in an overall was on her knees scrubbing the stone flags. She got to her feet shyly and introduced herself as Nellie, one of our new neighbours. A kettle was hanging from the hook over the fire and soon we all had mugs of hot tea. She had brought an apple cake to eat and, as soon as we were finished, she slipped away before my mother had time to thank her properly. It was our first experience of the kindness of people from the northern fells. After a couple of hours, the furniture was all in the right rooms, if not the right places, and the beds had been screwed together so we could sleep in them as night fell.

While my mother unpacked sheets and towels and wrestled pillows into their cases, my father was out in the barns and byres settling the stock he had brought with him from Low Ling: Prince the horse; Jennifer the sheep and her flock of daughters and grand-daughters; two cows with their calves; and Flo the collie. It was a small beginning. Dad intended to use the money he had saved to buy more sheep and cattle at auction in the coming weeks.

While they were busy, my brother and I explored our new home. I'd been there once with my grandfather, but it was the first time Gordon had seen the house he was going to live in. At the end of the passage that led from the front door to the back of the house, there was a stone staircase that had once been outside but had gained a roof at some point. To the left of it was the dairy, with sandstone slabs to keep food cold, and a very small window covered in mesh to keep out the flies and let a cooling draught of air filter through. To the right of the staircase, another door led into the 'back kitchen', which had a sloping ceiling lined with slatted wood and a door that opened out into the garth. This was where the wellington boots and outdoor clothing lived. Another black range was built into one wall, with a wash copper beside it. There was a larder with shelves for dry goods and a deep Belfast sink and wooden draining board. Here, my mother put the pine table she used for food preparation and baking and, against the wall, a gigantic mangle she'd bought at a farm sale.

That first evening, going upstairs, my parents learned that you had to duck your head to avoid the beams under the low ceiling. There was a dark loft at the top of the stairs, still full of the previous owner's junk. My brother and I decided that it was the perfect place for a bogle (Cumbrian ghost) and walked past it as quickly as we could. There were three other bedrooms. A handsome, square room with a Victorian fireplace that was quickly claimed by my parents; my brother was put to sleep in the middle room, just big enough for a double bed; and I was given the end bedroom above the living room, warmed by the chimney breast that went through it. This was the first time I'd had a room of my own – I'd been adamant that I no longer wanted to sleep with my brother. I was ten years old, growing up and needed my own space. The window looked out over the yard. Beyond the barn roof, I could see the treetops, the fells and above them the stars. I opened my window a few inches and lay awake listening to the night sounds – cattle chinking their neck chains as they lay down in the straw, the screech of a barn owl that lived in the rafters, the faint baa of sheep. I was home.

Dad took me to the Carlisle auction with him and I listened to the incomprehensible patter of the auctioneers, which he seemed to understand, above the noise of anxious cattle, sheep calling lost lambs and men shouting over the din. On that first day, Dad bought fifty 'cast' ewes. These were sheep that had already had several lambs and were now past their best.

Horse and cart with my father and cousin Jean.

They were usually sold for pet food, but Dad knew the farmer who had kept these particular ewes. He looked at their teeth and their feet and reckoned that they were likely to have another two or three lambs apiece – and their offspring would give him the flock he needed at a fraction of the price. Even after he'd paid the obligatory 'luck money' to the vendor, he thought they were a bargain. Other farmers thought he was mad.

In the pens at the back of the mart were the horses. Although some milkmen, breweries and delivery firms still used horses, most businesses were modernising. Milk carts were going electric, the railways had converted to three-wheeled Scammell flatbed trucks. Petrol-driven lorries were taking over everywhere. Farming had also mechanised during the war and tractors were now doing the hard work that horses had done before.

But my father had never learned to drive. He was happier with four legs than four wheels. Horses, he said, were kinder to the land than tractors; they were also environmentally friendly and had the great advantage of being able to reproduce themselves. It broke his heart to see so many healthy animals being sold, either for export to the Continent or to the pet food factory. He was committed to cultivating the farm with horses. Over that first year, the stack yard at Rough Close began to fill up with horse-drawn machinery museum pieces. At farm sales no one, except my father, wanted them anymore. Everything went for a song, including the harness. Cleaning it was one of my jobs and I loved sitting in the quiet stable, breathing in the smell of horses mingled with harness oil.

Prince was our only Shire horse, a favourite of my father's since he had worked on the farm at Raughton Head. He'd taken Prince with him to Coldslopes and then to Low Ling. Man and horse were so close, Dad said Prince could read his thoughts. The horse was so tame he would try to come into the house if the front door was left open. Once he had to be backed the whole length of the passageway, after he tried to follow my father into the kitchen. Now Dad had his eye out for another horse. Ploughing needed a team and there were fifty acres of neglected land at Rough Close that had to be turned over. Peter was rescued from the slaughter-house – a young Shire horse in a very neglected state. He limped because the horn of his hooves had overgrown his shoes, one of which was missing, and his coat was rough and full of snags. Properly groomed and shod, my father decided that he would make a good team with Prince. So we came home in the cattle wagon with fifty elderly sheep and a lame horse.

Peter was the first of many. Every time Dad went to an auction, he would break his heart over some fine young Shire or Clydesdale going to slaughter and inevitably bring it home. My favourite was Dolly, a gentle mare who let me ride on her back. Unfortunately, she'd belonged to a milkman and he had trained her, when in harness, to walk along the street a few steps at a time, pause and then take a few more steps. We could never break her of the habit. So Dolly became my horse and I was allowed to harrow a field with her, and at hay time turn the hay with the spider rake. After the hay was turned and dried, I used to lead it back to the barn with the cart. There was never any chance that Dolly would bolt.

This was not the case with Tom, the next young Shire my father bought and quickly regretted. He turned out to be what Dad called a 'reister' – a northern term for a horse with a vicious streak. Tom could be quite normal but would suddenly turn and roll up his eyes and then he would kick and bite. Only my father was allowed to work with him. Once he chased me at a gallop across a field and I could only escape his thundering hooves by jumping into the beck, where I sprained my ankle.

Dad became very attached to his animals. After we had been at Rough Close for about five years, Prince's health began to decline. One day Dad went into the field to collect him and he was standing head down in a corner, sweating, his stomach distended. The vet came straight away and said there was nothing he could do. Prince's kidneys had failed and he was in severe pain. My father couldn't bear to hold Prince's head while the vet put an end to his life. Nor could my mother. So it was me who had to hold Prince's bridle and soothe him while the vet put the bell-gun to his forehead and pressed the button. A ton of Shire horse fell onto the cobbles behind me.

Death is as common an occurrence on a farm as birth. Sheep die in lambing, of bad weather, or parasites; calves develop pneumonia or scour; chickens are eaten by foxes. I was used

Dad ploughing the big field with Prince and Peter

111

to dead animals being disposed of. The knacker man would arrive with his stinking lorry and his winch and take them away. And so it was with Prince. My father cried, and I knew I would remember the sound of Prince's body hitting the ground for the rest of my life.

Rough Close was marginal land. The in-bye fields had been reclaimed from the fell and it took a lot of work to keep them from sliding back into rush and gorse and bog. The fields were enclosed by stone walls that had been allowed to tumble. During that first year, my father was fully employed ploughing and re-seeding, digging drains and building walls. Byres and barns needed cleaning and whitewashing. Doors needed mending where they had rotted with neglect and were repainted in the traditional red. The lime men came to cover the land in white dust to sweeten it and keep the rushes at bay. When I took them their 'bait' in metal cans, they were covered in lime, only their red-rimmed eyes visible under their caps.

In the house my mother was doing similar reclamation work. Although she was no needlewoman, she sewed curtains and cushions, and even began to make a traditional Cumbrian floor rug out of rags. Her parents came to help: Annie lined shelves with oiled paper, while Grandpa put up wallpaper and painted the doors and windowsills. When we'd arrived, everything had been painted in a dark, depressing shade of lettuce green. Now it was cream gloss that reflected the light. The kitchen was distempered in pale yellow. I was allowed to choose the wallpaper for my bedroom. We could afford only the cheapest, so I pointed to the best of the worst – a floral chintz overprinted with a silver leaf.

Between trying to make the house habitable, cooking and baking, looking after my brother, feeding chickens and calves, my mother had very little time to herself. She was also a long way from civilisation again and, as we had no car, had no means of getting there. I have never been able to fathom why only my father had a bicycle. My mother had cycled everywhere before she got married. I would have loved a bike and so would my brother. But they were never bought, and we walked everywhere.

The nearest village, Caldbeck, was five miles away; the nearest big town, Carlisle, was an hour-long bus ride from the village. It might as well have been on the moon. Sometimes it was possible to get a lift with neighbours – who all had cars – but Mum was too proud to ask. She hated having to beg favours from other people. She would agonise over it for days. The loss of her independence hurt. Sometimes she could get to the village in the school taxi, but only if there was room, and she would have to walk back. All her cherished pastimes had to be abandoned. The WI, the Choral Society, church, her weekly trips to the market and the library. Only the gospel singing group continued, so long as there was someone to give us a lift. It was Coldslopes all over again, but she was willing to do it because it was my father's dream.

Her reading diaries reveal the lack of leisure time. Whereas in January, before we moved, she had read eight books, in May she managed only three, in August two and by October it was down to one. Fortunately, the mobile library came as far as the ford once every three weeks, so she could still borrow books without having to make the long journey to Carlisle. But there wasn't a lot of choice and sometimes the borrowed books turned out to be unreadable. Her reading list over the summer months was an eclectic mixture that included a life of Paul Gauguin, Graham Greene's *The Power and the Glory*, three novels by Pearl S. Buck, D.H. Lawrence's *The White Peacock*, and – a name I didn't recognise – *Paloma*, by Mrs Robert Henrey.

When I found this author in her diary, I'd never heard of her, though I knew my mother had enjoyed her books. Who was the real person behind the distinctly old-fashioned name 'Mrs Robert Henrey'? And what kind of woman still hid behind her husband's name in the second half of the twentieth century? A little research revealed a French writer, Madeleine Gal, who was born in one of the industrial areas on the fringes of Paris. She apparently came to London as a young girl in the 1920s after her father, who was a miner, died. Her mother was a dressmaker and settled in Soho, where Madeleine grew up. She married an Englishman, Robert Henrey, who she met while she was working as a manicurist at the Savoy Hotel. He was an old Etonian, a journalist who introduced her to a life she had never imagined – in literary circles and high society.

In the 1930s, Robert bought a farm in Normandy at Villers-sur-Mer and they had several very happy years there before the outbreak of war. Madeleine began to write books about her experiences, calling herself either Robert Henrey or Mrs Robert Henrey. They were bestsellers almost from the beginning: a memoir called *A Farm in Normandy*; and a first novel set in

London called *An Attic in Jermyn Street*, featuring a female reporter during the war. Madeleine was very prolific, publishing three novels and more than thirty non-fiction books, mainly memoirs. Most were gentle stories about life on the family farm in Villers-sur-Mer, members of her wider family, or people she met. It seems strange that all these popular books could have slipped out of sight so completely. She was still writing in 1979 and died on the family farm in France, aged 97, in 2004.

Having researched the author, I found it curious that she chose to write as Robert Henrey, rather than Madeleine Gal. Was Madeleine trying to avoid being identified because she was writing about her village, her friends and her family? Or did she think that she had more chance of being published if she used her husband's name? The answer may have been simpler. Friends said that some of the books were collaborations with her husband Robert, with him either acting as editor or having given her the original idea, though they emphasised that the writing, the characteristic French phrasing of the prose, was entirely her own. If she had written under her own name, perhaps her books would have been revived in the seventies and eighties by one of the feminist presses? Which titles survive from the literature of the past sometimes seems accidental.

Caldbeck was my third primary school in four years. I was only going to be there for a term, so no one bothered to teach me anything. It was loud and rowdy, the headmaster shouted a lot, and he was very free with the cane. My brother was bullied in the playground, and I was quite glad when it was time to leave. Aged ten, I had passed the eleven-plus exam to go to grammar school. I don't remember any particular fuss being made about this, but I was one of only two children ever to pass in several years from any of my primary schools. This wasn't surprising, since they were so small and catered for up to thirty children between the ages of four and fifteen. Since the introduction of the eleven-plus, older children were being phased out, but when I started there were still boys and girls of thirteen or fourteen there. The teaching wasn't very comprehensive because of the age range a single teacher had to cover, and there was a distinct lack of ambition.

There was a sense that we were farm children, and we didn't need much of an education for the lives we were going to lead. This attitude spilled over into the teaching. Although my reading age was years ahead of my actual age, in maths the class hadn't got beyond long division and simple fractions by the time I left. I wasn't exactly prepared for the academic machine I was going into. My parents were very proud of me, but they never showed it, in case I began to think of myself as a 'clever clogs'. There was thought to be nothing worse in a girl than being clever and knowing it. The eighteenth-century writer Lady Mary Wortley Montagu told her daughter in a letter that she must hide her education as completely as she would a deformity of her limbs. Wordsworth's five-year-old daughter Dora was sent away to boarding school because she outshone her brother. By the twentieth century, three hundred years later, things hadn't changed much. Girls were still supposed to be modest and self-deprecating.

When the uniform list arrived, a catalogue of clothes and equipment that had to be bought from special shops, it caused consternation. A hockey stick, school satchel, PE bag, blazer, skirts and shirts, berets and ties and special shoes. Hand-me-down coats wouldn't do; it had to be a green gabardine, school issue. Where was the money to come from? I had begun to understand, dimly, that we were very short of money. On a farm your income comes from selling animals and their produce, but in your first year, you have to buy animals and there is nothing to sell until they have offspring, which then take several more months to grow big enough to take to market. My parents had quickly run through their savings and were now living off something called an 'overdraft'.

There were various plans to make money until the sheep had lambs that could be sold, and the suckler cattle my father had bought, to put out on the fell, had big beefy calves to go to auction. A West Cumberland Farmers' delivery lorry struggled up the track with several cardboard boxes with yellow fluff poking from the air holes. They were opened to reveal day-old chicks. Dad had cleaned out the loft above the stable and hung lamps from the beams above some makeshift pens to keep them warm. My parents were going to rear chickens and go into the egg business. The cockerels would be fattened up and sold for Christmas.

Dad had also decided, despite opposition from my mother, to borrow some more money and go into milk production. It was a lot of work, but it would give them a regular income. The milking shed was cleaned out and smartened up, and the old milking machine in a lean-to at the back was given an overhaul by a friend who was handy with motors. One of the calf sheds was turned into a sterile dairy. Every inch of wall and floor was coated with cement and a false ceiling put up. There mustn't be any dust or surfaces where bacteria could collect, and it all had to be hosed down with disinfectant. An impressive collection of stainless-steel sinks and trays arrived in another delivery lorry and a white coat for my mother to wear when she was scrubbing and sterilising the milk churns. Dad went to auction three weeks in a row and came back with an assortment of cows. One had a broken tail, another a bad leg. Some had horns, others were polled. Most of them were middle-aged, but they had all recently calved and had very promising udders.

Every morning my father was up at five to fetch the cows from the field, and by six the milking machine had started up in the shed. Then he would come into the house, wake my brother and me for school, light the fire and take my mother a cup of tea. In the evening, it was my job to bring in the cows to be milked again. I put cow cake and a little hay in the stalls so they would go in quietly and then I would slip in beside them to hook up the chains, careful not to get squashed or impaled on their horns.

I also had to wash the mud-splattered udders so they were clean for the rubber cups. I knew which cows were prone to kick and which ones would let you do almost anything. Dad taught me to milk by hand, which was very useful when the milking machine failed to start – which happened quite often. I loved sitting quietly beside a cow, my head against her warm, rumbling flank, squeezing the milk down into the bucket. This was my

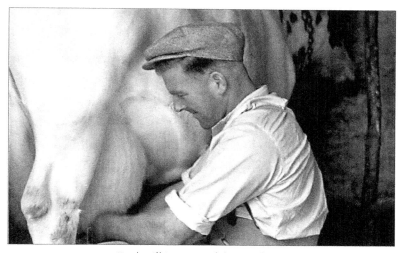

Dad milking one of the Ayrshires

other life, one that made me feel safe and comfortable; it was very different from the life I was being pitched into.

The grammar school was in a town on the Solway plain. This meant that every morning I had to walk down the track, across the ford, to the main road, where the school taxi picked me up and took me to the village. There I waited for a bus to take me to the town. The journey took over an hour; and in the evening, I did it all again in reverse. On winter mornings and nights, I had to do it in the dark and sometimes in bad weather. If it was snowing, my father would walk down to meet me, and I kept my wellington boots and waterproofs in a milk churn near the road. On that first morning, a fortnight after my eleventh birthday, when most children were being taken to school by their parents, I had to do the trip by myself and rely on someone to show me where to go and what to do when I got off the bus at the other end. But I felt very smart in my new uniform which had been purchased, eventually, by my Carlisle grandmother.

The Nelson Thomlinson was a school in two parts – the Nelson had a long history as a boys' grammar school, established in 1714; and the Thomlinson, on the other side of the high street, had been a private girls' school. They'd been amalgamated as a state school only five years earlier. It was small by modern standards, having only three hundred or so students. The buildings were old, with panelled walls and low beams. It was very intimidating. There were more children in my class than there had been in the entire school at Bewcastle or Rosley.

I was surprised to find myself in the top stream, even though I was almost a year younger than the oldest student, and the academic pressure was evident from the first day. In the panelled assembly hall where we were lined up to be told which classes we would be in, there were polished mahogany boards with the names of former pupils who had won bursaries to Oxford and Cambridge painted in gold leaf. They made my heart beat very fast. Was it possible that I could become one of them? A whole world beyond the farm briefly opened up, but my hopes were quickly dashed by reality. Most of the other students in my class had come from town schools and had already covered large parts of the syllabus, particularly in maths. Some had even been learning French, although the modal verbs of Latin were new to all of us. They were all at least a year ahead of me and it was daunting, particularly as it was drummed into us that we were, as 'Miss Jean Brodie' put it in her prime, 'la crème de la crème'.

Education was strictly graded. There was the top stream, where Latin and Greek could be studied by those who were going to be entered for Oxbridge bursaries. Below that were students who learned modern languages and were expected to get O-levels and A-levels, destined for red-brick universities, the professions and white-collar jobs. Below them were those who hadn't passed the eleven-plus and went to the new secondary modern, known to grammar-school children as the 'whitewashed cowshed', up the road. There they learned useful career-orientated skills, like cake baking, confectionery, hairdressing, graphic design, plumbing and light engineering. Snobbery was rife. Grammar-school kids were in the minority on the school bus. Our uniforms gave us away and we came in for a certain amount of bullying. There was name calling, including words I'd never heard before, and some pushing and shoving; berets were thrown out of the window, satchels used for rugby practice in the aisle. I learned to stuff my beret and tie into my pocket as soon as I was out of sight of the school gates. On the bus I kept my head down and read a book. They called me a swot, but it was better than some of the names they called the others.

I remember that first year as a kind of agony. For maths we were taught by a man with an Oxford PhD who wrote mathematical textbooks. He made assumptions about our level of knowledge and began with algebra. I didn't even know what the word meant. My wide reading made up for much that I'd missed in other subjects, and an interest in language kept me afloat in French and even Latin, but in physics, chemistry and maths I was at the bottom of the class. I was lost in a foreign country where I didn't understand the language, without a clue how to find my way back, so I spent the lessons gazing out of the window. 'She refuses to concentrate,' the teacher wrote in my report, 'and produces far too little homework.'

Homework was a big problem. There was no library just down the road where I could look things up. Both my parents had left school at fourteen and everything they'd learned was from the books they'd read. My mother's knowledge of history came from novels and biographies; she read Jean Plaidy, Anya Seton and Nancy Mitford. The information she had was patchy and not always accurate. Ancient Egyptian history came from books about Tutankhamun's tomb and H.V. Morton's travelogues. She knew nothing of Greek history, which we were required to learn in the first year.

Maths was also unknown territory. Neither of my parents could do anything more complex than multiplication and long division. There was no one to explain a square root or define an isosceles triangle. I was often miserable, and my school reports made dismal reading. 'Not good enough for a girl of Kathleen's ability', 'Very disappointing' (underlined twice). In maths, I remained stubbornly twenty-eighth out of twenty-eight. 'This is a disgraceful result,' my maths teacher stormed, underlining the remark in red ink. When I was put into the remedial maths class, my shame was complete. The confident lively child quickly became a shy, hypersensitive and self-conscious adolescent.

My lack of confidence in my numerical ability spilled over into other subjects. In the autumn term I had come first in my year in English; by the end of the summer term I was only tenth in my class. For everything else, I slipped into the lower half. My parents didn't say anything but I knew they were disappointed, particularly my mother. I was being given the chance she'd never had – and I appeared to be wasting it.

At the end of the first year, the headmaster, who happened to know my parents through the Methodist chapel, sent for me. L.I. Stowe, B.Litt, M.A., Oxon, was a small man with sharp eyes and a Charlie Chaplin moustache, quick on his feet, who would appear out of nowhere at unexpected moments. I often saw him striding down the corridor, his black gown blowing out behind him like the wings of a bat. Everyone was afraid of him. This was the first time I'd been summoned to his office and I was shaking. Unexpectedly, he seemed to understand what I was going through and spoke kindly. I was capable of doing good work, he said, but I wasn't doing my best. That would have to change, or I'd be demoted. For a girl who'd always had approval, who had effortlessly achieved top marks, it was a big shock.

9

A HAUNTED LANDSCAPE

Every day began with the weather forecast. We had an old radio that had glass batteries filled with acid, and a Bakelite dial that had to be carefully tuned. Lying half asleep in my bed above the living room in the shadowy light before dawn, I could hear the solemn voice of the shipping forecaster intoning words that suggested far-away places and stormy seas. I rolled their names round and round in my head like a found poem: Cromarty, Forth, Tyne . . . Dogger, Fisher, German Bight . . . But the names my father listened for were Rockall, Malin and Irish Sea. On a subsistence farm the weather affects everything and can make the difference between profit and ruin. Dad, whose sense of humour rarely failed him, faced hardship with a rendering of Carson Jay Robison's country blues, the Cumbrian accent softened into a southern drawl: 'There's a mouse a-chawin' on the pantry door. / He's been at it for at least a month or more, / When he gets through there he's sure goin' to be sore. / There ain't a durn thing in there.'[11] Our pantry was never empty, but it was sometimes dangerously low.

Mum was reading *The Grapes of Wrath*, Steinbeck's novel about the struggles of small farmers at the time of the Dust Bowl disaster in the American Midwest. She joked about needing a bit of drought now and again, though it was difficult to imagine a place so dry that the soil blew away. Here, it rained constantly. The fells faced west, towards the Irish sea. You could watch the storms rolling in from the Atlantic, ready to empty themselves on the first obstacle they met, which was exactly where we lived. Occasionally we had flash floods that made the ford at the bottom of the track impassable and we were trapped. You could hear the boulders grinding down the beck behind the farm.

Mondays were wash days, come rain or shine. Dad lit the fire under the copper boiler in the back kitchen when he went out to milk the cows. After breakfast, my mother would begin sorting the washing. White things first, sheets, cotton shirts and towels, while the water was boiling; then, after it was allowed to cool, ordinary clothes; and finally – when the water couldn't get any dirtier – my father's work clothes. Everything was rinsed in a zinc tub, which was filled from the kitchen tap, and then put through the mangle. Sheets took two people and, if I was at home, that was one of my jobs. If I was at school, Mum had to enlist my father's help. The leading edge had to be fed between the rollers, trying to keep your fingers clear, while someone turned the big handle. It was difficult to avoid any part of the sheet touching the floor while you did it. If it became soiled again, it had to go back into the boiler. Pegging the washing out on the line in the garth was an art form and almost impossible in a gale. There were times my mother and I sat and cried at the kitchen table after sheets had blown off into the mud.

It's difficult to imagine, in these days of connectivity, just how isolated we were. There was no telephone, no electricity, no television, no public – or private – transport. If you needed the doctor, you walked the five miles to the village and five miles back. If you were too ill to walk, you had to beg a lift from one of the neighbours. If you needed to make a telephone call, there was a public phone box a couple of miles away. The post girl, Margaret, cycled up the track every morning to bring the letters and collect any mail that needed posting. She was the source of most local news, going from farm to farm and chatting with all the neighbours. My mother often made her a cup of tea on cold mornings, and Margaret and my mother became good friends.

The world ticked like a clock – every week the same. Washing on Monday, ironing on Tuesday, cleaning the living rooms on Wednesday, bedrooms on Thursday, baking on Friday. As for shopping, we relied on travelling shops for everything. The butcher's van came on Friday and my mother had to buy enough to see us through into the following week, fresh meat carefully wrapped in greaseproof paper and put into a mesh box in the larder to keep off the flies. On Monday it was the baker, with bread and cakes. The grocer came on Tuesday and Mum bought all her dry goods, flour, sugar, tinned fruit, Fray Bentos steak pies, tins of tuna and salmon for sandwiches. He also sold cheese, sliced ham fringed with yellow breadcrumbs, cold tongue and corned beef. Everything came wrapped in paper or in jars or tins. We had very little waste. Anything combustible was used to light the fire, jars were kept for home-made jam or storing goose grease for frying, the Fray Bentos pie dishes made feeding bowls for cats and dogs, the tins went into the tool shed for nuts and bolts or to mix paraffin wax, cattle drench and paint.

Once every couple of months, we had a visit from a Mr Pergavie from Scotland, whose van was full of clothes and soft furnishings. You could get a jumper, a hearthrug, some work overalls and a couple of tea towels, pay a deposit and tip up the rest the next time he came. I loved his visits, the smell of new clothing spread out in our living room to tempt my mother into buying something. Most of the time I was at school when he came, so I wasn't there when he asked Mum if she'd like to go upstairs with him. She was shocked. But, he told her, there were a surprising number of women on these isolated farms who were glad to see him.

During the Suez crisis, anyone was allowed to drive without having passed a test. My father bought a car for £50 from someone he knew at the auction mart and taught himself to drive by lurching up and down the track, though he never managed to pass a test. The car was an old Austin Ruby Seven and it was a wreck. One of the door catches had gone and Dad tied it shut with a length of baler twine. The engine smoked when going uphill, filling the car with fumes. But having a car meant that, for a short time, my mother could go down to Carlisle on a Saturday and sell butter, eggs and chickens at the market.

My Friday nights were spent scrubbing the dirt off the eggs and eviscerating the chickens. Dad wrung their necks on Friday mornings and hung them upside down in the barn, out of reach of the cats and rats, ready to scald and pluck. I was also paid sixpence a time to turn the butter churn. We had two churns, a small glass one that made the butter for the house, and a big one that looked like a barrel on a stand, that churned large quantities of cream. Every morning, my mother would put some of the milk through the separator to get cream for the butter. She had to be careful not to skim off too much cream because the Milk Marketing Board required a certain percentage of butter fat in the milk, and nasty letters would arrive if it dropped below a certain level. My mother dreaded getting them.

Having a car also meant that we could go, as a family, to chapel on Sundays wherever my father was preaching. We didn't always arrive. The car sometimes died of exhaustion before we reached our destination. Friends who knew about cars used to come and help my father repair whichever part had worn out, but the Austin Ruby was the joke of the neighbourhood, spending more time parked up on grass verges than it did on the road. One Saturday, Dad agreed to take me to a nearby village to stay the weekend with a school friend, but, as we drove through the fell gate towards the main road, there was a tremendous bang and clouds of smoke and steam billowed out from under the bonnet. Below, a pool of oil and water was forming on the track. It was obvious we weren't going anywhere. I cried with disappointment, but my father was enraged. He kicked the bodywork, threw his cap on the ground and then, in a final spasm of temper, gave the car an enormous push and let go. He had intended just to push it onto the verge, but he put so much energy into it that the car shot off the road and trundled over the edge of the ravine, ending nose-down in the stream below, where the wreckage remained for years.

The fell gate.

There was always a fell gate in my childhood. At Coldslopes it was the gate that separated the road from the moor where the croft was built. At Rough Close we had two. One was the entrance to the cart track, which was kept closed to keep the animals from straying onto the road. The other was the gate between the walled in-bye fields and the unfenced fell. It seemed to symbolise a boundary in my life, a threshold between the wild land of the imagination and the ordered reality of daily life. It was the ultimate liminal space and I escaped through it whenever I could, wandering the fells pretending to be Emily Brontë, making up stories in my head and talking to imaginary friends. There were places to explore, including some abandoned silver mines not far away, dating back to the twelfth century. You could go a little way in before the passages were blocked by roof falls. And there were long-abandoned ruined houses, stony memorials to places where making a living from the land had ceased to be possible. It was easy to believe that the ghosts of the people remained there.

We lived in a haunted landscape, where every rock, tree, lake and hill already had someone's name on it. William Wordsworth was a towering presence, followed by John Ruskin, Hugh Walpole and Arthur Ransome. It was hard, as a young woman beginning to write poetry, to escape their shadow. Like Elizabeth Barrett Browning, I looked everywhere for role models 'and found none'. There were very few well-known female authors' names; Beatrix Potter was the only one I'd heard of, and she wrote children's books. I didn't yet know about Dorothy Wordsworth, William's overshadowed sister; or Harriet Martineau, who had lived at Ambleside and smoked a pipe like a man. Most of the writers I knew about were in the past.

The only contemporary writer whose name I occasionally heard mentioned was a man: Norman Nicholson. My English teacher showed me a poem by him, written in a rhythm that rang true to my ear, using familiar, colloquial words – Cumbrian phonetics that, Seamus Heaney commented, 'cracked like a plaited whip'. Here was a poet who wrote, not about a beautiful, romantic landscape, but about Cumbria's industrial fringe, the coal mines and factories, the nuclear power station. When he wrote about the lakes and dales, it was as a working, not a tourist, landscape – and I recognised the same hard, unforgiving land that we, as a family, struggled with every day:

Wet bracken kindles slowly and the brown, charred hills
Hang from the sky like canvas, swaying through the mist.[12]

The community of little fellside farms we lived in was very close knit. The same families had lived there for generations. Everywhere you went, you encountered certain names:

Braithwaite, Fell, Graham, Hetherington, Armstrong. I went to school with Pattinsons and Birkbecks, Teesdales and Sowerbys. They had all intermarried at some point and everyone was related to everyone else. As in Bewcastle, some of the older people had never been more than thirty miles away from home, but things were beginning to change and among the younger generations were a couple of Alpine climbers, a champion fellrunner and a TV personality. Two of the nearest farms had daughters around my age – one older, one younger – but we didn't go to the same schools and had little in common. They both seemed happily domestic, interested in learning how to run a house and be good farmers' wives. They made me ashamed that I wasn't. I liked them and we were always friendly, in and out of each other's houses, but never close friends. I suspected they thought I was rather strange. I'd already worked out that normal girls didn't write poetry.

I found it difficult to make friends at school. Most of the conversation was about television programmes I had no way of watching, or the evenings they'd spent in coffee bars with boys. I couldn't join any of the after-school clubs because I had no way of getting home after the school bus had left. I had once asked another girl to stay for the weekend and I will never forget the look of horror on her face when confronted with the earth closet round the back of the farmhouse. The lack of a bathroom, the idea of brushing her teeth and washing in the kitchen sink with people coming in and out, revolted her. She must have said something at school because I began to be called names by some of the bully boys on the bus. It struck home because I often felt dirty. We didn't have a proper bath but I had a sponge-down almost every day in a big plastic bowl in my room and spent all my pocket money on deodorant and scented soap. At least our neighbours shared the same problem. None of the local farms had a bathroom or a flush toilet.

On the other side of the hill, across a muddy track, was High Intack, where Mary and Jack lived. They were both very sociable, and in the evenings they would walk across the fields to visit their neighbours. Jack was tall and thin and smoked a particularly vicious brand of tobacco called Black Dagger Twist. Mary was short and plump; 'Wide as a barn door, tough as an otter,' Jack used to joke. He counted himself a lucky man. At night, in bed, he told us, it was 'grand'. When he went to sleep, he was as snug as 'a yow ahint a dyke'.

Mary was curious about people and asked all kinds of personal questions, which made my mother blush but were somehow impossible to dodge. Consequently, Mary knew everything about everyone and was a kind of local news agency. People joked that she could read bills and correspondence through the envelopes as they sat on the mantelpiece. She claimed to be able to tell immediately if someone was pregnant. When one of the local girls had a hastily arranged wedding, Mary said, 'I could see it in her eyes, Ella. You know – there's a *look*.' But her deductions were probably based on more practical observations, as she also said, 'And that lad comin' up't lonnin' in that big car. It were askin' for trouble.'

Their families had lived in the area for ever and they knew quite a lot of local history. As children, we were fascinated by one particular ruined farmstead which had a grim, rather desperate atmosphere. Mary and Jack told us the story of the farmer who had lived there. It was a tale of domestic violence that ended in tragedy. Believing that his wife was dead after he'd struck her one evening, the man had pushed her unconscious body down the well. The cold water had revived her and she'd climbed out, asked a neighbour for help and gone to live with her sister in Carlisle. Meanwhile the farmer, full of remorse, had hanged himself from a beam in the barn. My cousins, my brother and I spent hours peering down the well into the darkness below, to see how far she'd had to climb, and trying to work out which beam of the ruined barn he'd attached the rope to. The house was obviously haunted.

Another story Mary told was about the ghost of Overwater Hall. Overwater was a small lake not far from the farm. The Hall was very grand, with views out across the valley towards Skiddaw. It was part of the darker history of the Lake District, a story of prosperity built on slavery. I grew up in Cumbria without ever seeing a person of colour. There was no ethnic diversity at all. But the local delicacy was rum butter, which my mother regularly made, and she explained that it was a legacy of our connection with the West Indies.

Whitehaven, a town on the west coast, had once been at the centre of the slave trade. Ships had sailed out of the harbour, bound for the African Gold Coast, to pick up slaves and take them to the West Indies to sell to the plantation owners, before coming back with sugar and rum. Ship owners also occasionally brought slaves back to England with them to work on their own estates. This explained why several pubs in the area were called 'The Black Boy', with signs depicting people who were still called 'darkies' at that time.

Mary told the story of a black servant, kept by the owner of Overwater Hall, who had escaped one night in the pelting rain and had been tracked down by the hounds he kept for the foxhunt. The man's ghost was supposed to haunt the road that led to the Hall. Jack claimed to have seen it on one of his peregrinations to the Snooty Fox pub in Uldale on a Saturday night. Later I heard the story of a black woman, believed to have been the Jamaican mistress of the owner, who had followed her husband to Cumbria and been drowned in the lake when he took her out in a boat and pushed her overboard, chopping her hands off to stop her clinging to the side. Her ghost is supposed to haunt the Hall and many claim to have seen it. According to owner and journalist Charles de Courcy-Parry, writing in the *Horse and Hound*, she has 'terrified a great many people'. He claimed to have seen her gliding up the stairs.[13]

In the absence of television, books were the medium that brought the outside world to our remote farm. I'd read about slavery in *Uncle Tom's Cabin*, which I'd been given a couple of years earlier, a book that Mum had read as a child, which had changed the way she looked at people whose skins were not perfectly white. In North Shields, where she was brought up, there was considerable prejudice. My grandfather had endured his share of abuse as an 'Eye-Tye' and he'd once been called a 'wog'. 'Wogs' apparently began at the English Channel. But my grandfather was a left-wing socialist who believed that everyone was born equal under the sun, and this was drummed into my mother as she was growing up. My father had similar beliefs, rooted in the manifesto of John Wesley. Wesleyan Methodism was extremely political, with its aims of educating and elevating the working class. Slavery of any kind, according to Wesley, was an abomination. In my ignorance I assumed that trading in human beings was something that had happened far away on the other side of the Atlantic. I found it almost impossible to believe that the landscape I loved had been touched by this brutal trade, or that there was long-established racism among my friends and neighbours.

Mary Benn was a kind woman, and I was always welcome in her kitchen where she made delicious cakes and pies. She had a teenage son called Billy – always referred to by my father as 'that daft lad' – who had a van and offered his neighbours' daughters lifts to the Young Farmers' Club dances down at the village hall. He was very free with his hands, so we were careful to go in a group. I was managing to find a teenage social life, despite our isolation on the farm. There were dances in the village hall, as well as events organised by the Methodist Youth movement.

Sometimes I stayed overnight with friends from school and went to the cinema. I saw Elvis Presley's *Love Me Tender* three times and fell in love with 'Elvis the Pelvis'. One of my uncles gave me a small battery-powered record turntable that played the new 'singles' and I was allowed to listen to Radio Luxembourg for an hour on our precious radio, while my parents did the evening chores and I did my homework on the dining table. For my birthday, Dad bought me membership of the official Elvis Fan

Club, sending the money all the way to the USA. I waited eagerly for the magazines to cross the Atlantic in the other direction and papered my bedroom wall with posters.

We had a telephone now. Because we lived in the Lake District National Park, the utility companies hadn't been allowed to erect visible telegraph poles or pylons. Putting the cables underground was very expensive, so we went without electricity and telecommunications until the problem could be resolved. The wealthier farms had diesel generators, but there was no question of us being able to afford such a luxury. The telephone was the first modern appliance to arrive – it would be years before we got electricity. The phone was black, with a white porcelain dial, and it looked very important sitting on a table in the hallway. Our number was Low Ireby 610. My brother and I had strict instructions that it had to be incoming calls. We could dial out only in emergencies – but it was thrilling to know that we were at last connected to the outside world. For my father, it meant no more cycling to the public phone box in the rain to make essential calls. But, as Mum pointed out, it was just one more bill to pay.

Money was in very short supply and my hand-me-down wardrobe was often embarrassing. I was growing quickly, 'filling out' as my mother called it, and clothes that still had a lot of wear in them simply didn't fit any more. Aunt May was now in America and sent me a party dress from a Sears catalogue. It wasn't a very flattering design, and it was lavender, a colour that didn't go with my hair, but it was new and very smart. One of the aunts bought me a bra and nylon stockings and a pair of kitten heels for Christmas. For once I could go out without feeling ashamed of how I looked.

Usually, apart from school uniform, I had to rely on cast-offs from my cousins, who were different shapes and sizes. Their mothers also had very different tastes. I was a tomboy and allergic to anything with frills. Mum picked up things in jumble sales, but I loathed wearing other people's clothes. My Carlisle grandmother could be relied on to buy me one new outfit every Easter, but I knew I couldn't ask my parents for anything else. Apart from a couple of winter jumpers from Mr Pergavie, my mother hadn't had anything new since we moved to Rough Close. When I read the chapter in *Good Wives*, where Meg gives up the pretty dress she'd wanted to make for herself in order to buy a new overcoat for her husband, I immediately thought of my mother. She always put her husband and her children first.

Much of our social life revolved around the chapel: the gospel singing group, where I was now relied on to provide the alto line in the close harmonies; and the youth groups, prayer meetings and my father's Sunday sermons. My soul had even been saved by Billy Graham. So it was difficult to tell anyone that I'd begun to have doubts about many things I'd been brought up to believe. My education in science and history was presenting me with facts that were inconsistent with belief in a Supreme Being or a literal interpretation of the Bible.

Education was also teaching me to question everything and evaluate propositions with logical arguments. I was always wanting to know 'why'. It began in small ways. When I was awarded a school prize, I was told to choose a book. There were two piles, one for boys and one for girls. Why? I asked. The book I liked was in the boys' pile. I wanted to read a maritime adventure called *No Time for Tankers*; I wasn't in the least bit interested in reading about *Anne: Air Hostess*, or Enid Blyton's *Malory Towers*; and the *Chalet School* series bored me rigid. I wanted stories that explored the world, and showed girls in more daring roles, like the *Nancy Drew* novels. The school gave in, and I was allowed my choice. I was beginning to get a reputation as a rebel. In the debating society I won a debate with an argument against the existence of God.

The House of Faith that had provided a sense of security during my childhood had started to crumble. There was so much that didn't make sense. How could this omniscient God allow such suffering in the world? If he really cared for every sparrow that fell out of the sky, how could he not be aware of people being sent to concentration camps? And if he was all-powerful, why hadn't he done anything about it? In the chapel congregation there were some people who believed that the Holocaust was God's punishment of the Jews for crucifying his son. What kind of sadistic, vengeful god was that? And what did it say about the people who could believe in such a god? Then there was the unanswerable conundrum about the people who had lived before Jesus was born. Did they have to spend eternity in purgatory because they hadn't been 'saved by the blood of Christ' or did they just go straight to hell? The theological gymnastics and tergiversations these questions initiated made my head spin. If I brought up such issues in Bible class, I was always told the same thing: I wasn't old enough to ask questions like that.

My mother didn't have any answers when I confessed my doubts; she just said, 'You have to make a leap of faith.' She had a small copy of *The Imitation of Christ,* a fifteenth-century devotional book written by Thomas à Kempis, and she read it often when she was feeling low. I tried to read it but couldn't. I admired the beautiful medieval language, but when I came to the chapter on the necessity of subjecting Reason to Faith I gave up because I was so troubled by what I read. The Voice of the Beloved declared that 'A dutiful and humble enquiry after the Truth, is allowable, provided we be always ready to be taught, and that we study to walk according to the sound opinions of the Fathers'. There was no mention of Mothers having sound opinions. The good Christian was supposed to leave 'the difficult ways of questions and disputings' and accept what they were being told by the scripture. It was not for us to enquire into the 'depth of the mysteries'; doubts were the voice of the devil. But what did this ancient, misogynistic, Augustinian monk know about anything? And why was it relevant in the twentieth century? I was now being pulled in two directions, by my mind and my heart. Which could I trust to tell me the truth?

This crisis of faith was one of the reasons why my mother and I became more distant, but there were others. There are very few photographs that include my mother from those years at Rough Close. It's as though she was gradually fading into the background. I have only one photo, a grainy black and white I took on the Box Brownie my grandfather had given me for Christmas, complete with a developing kit for the negatives. The homemade print shows Mum in her milking clothes, standing

Mum at Rough Close

outside the byre. She's smiling but her eyes look sad. The smart, pretty woman in earlier photographs has vanished. Mum hasn't been to a hairdresser in years, and her figure shows the result of living on the cakes and pies she cooked for us all. Carbohydrates were cheap, but they weren't healthy.

She must have felt very lonely sometimes and no doubt wanted companionship from her daughter. I had reached an age when I was expected to help in the house, but I hated housework of any kind. The only thing I enjoyed was baking, so I could be relied on to make cakes and buns when needed. I loathed sweeping and dusting and, most of all, washing up. I did it with bad grace and often broke things. I avoided housework by being out on the farm with my father. That was where I wanted to be. My brother, whose place it was, preferred playing with one of the boys at a local farm. He was excused because he was still young. I was the one who milked cows, heaved hay bales, mucked out byres, hoed turnips and went out with Dad, shepherding sheep, helping with clipping and lambing. When I wasn't with my father, I was up on the fells, inhabiting my own imaginary landscape, and when I eventually came home, hot and tired, my mother would be wearing the face of a martyr, slamming the dishes down on the table – a table I should have set – but rarely telling me off. The life she lived was not the life I wanted for myself. The only enduring point of contact we had left was books.

One day, after a trip to the mobile library, my mother brought home Elizabeth Jane Howard's *The Beautiful Visit*. Alan Bennett, in a talk I once heard him give, said: 'The most that a reader can expect from a writer is to be able to say "This is what it feels like to be me".' One of the great things about reading books was finding myself in them. It made me feel normal and not alone in the world. I didn't know at the time that *The Beautiful Visit* was the author's first novel; the teenage girl at the heart of the book, and her secluded, lonely childhood, were so perfectly drawn. When she goes to stay with wealthy friends, the odd one out, only invited to make up the numbers, her embarrassment and sense of being alien were my own. How could the author possibly know what it felt like to be different and socially awkward? My mother gave the novel four stars, so perhaps, unknown to me, she understood.

'Mothers and daughters – it is the most difficult relationship, is it not?' says a character in a novel.[14] It is also one of the most important because it affects how you see yourself and the kind of woman you eventually become. As a child it's easy; everyone has an idea of how the child/parent relationship works. But how do you relate to your mother as a woman? Some girls seem to slide effortlessly from that simple childhood dependency into an adult interaction between two women. I didn't. My mother and

I were too different, in temperament and ambition. I thought I knew the kind of daughter she wanted.

For years, during the school holidays, my cousins Jean and Anne, Aunt Margaret's children, had been coming to stay with us to give my grandmother a break. Being motherless girls, they looked on mine as a replacement. By the time we moved to Rough Close, Anne was already a precocious teenager, preoccupied with clothes and make-up, confiding her 'crushes' on various boys to my mother. Her younger sister Jean, eighteen months older than me, loved my mother completely. They were very close. They had the same dark Italian hair and Mediterranean skin. They were introverted, shy, dutiful, and both inclined to worry about everything. Jean helped Mum around the house without having to be asked, and even the more frivolous Anne could be relied on to do the dusting.

When their parents' divorce hit the tabloids, it was my mother who explained the situation to them, though none of us understood what the word 'lesbian' meant. 'Having Sapphic tendencies' was the nearest definition we found, though we didn't know who Sappho was either. All we knew was that Margaret had run off with a woman called Miss Barmer who ran a market garden, and that Margaret had been a very talented painter who had confided to my mother that she hated sex.

In the Easter holidays, as well as the long summer break, the house was full of cousins. My grandmother's younger brother ran a fishmonger's business, buying fish on the quays of North Shields to sell it, gutted and filleted, from a shop in Wallsend. Alf Young had a great sense of humour and painted a slogan on the side of his van that read 'Eat the Fish that keeps Alf Young'. He was one of the relatives who had lent my father money for the farm. My Aunt Dora, really a great-aunt, was the same age as my mother, and she worked in the shop alongside her husband, which meant juggling childcare in the holidays. They had three children, Joan, Norma and William, who loved to come and stay on the farm and help with the haymaking. Norma and William were closer to my brother's age, but Joan was only a year younger than me. With Jean we formed a trio of girls, slept in the same double bed and talked far into the night, sharing secrets.

One of the many subjects we talked about was mothers. I was the only one of us who knew my real mother. Joan's parents had been unable to have children and had chosen her, as a newborn, from a cot in a mother and baby home in Newcastle. In those days the pressure on unmarried mothers to give up their babies was immense. Small tragedies were being enacted every day somewhere in the United Kingdom, because it was considered immoral to have a child if you didn't have a ring on your finger. Some of the mothers were only children themselves. All Joan knew about hers was that she came from 'a good family who lived down south' and that she had given up her baby unwillingly. Joan was very happy in her adopted family and much loved; Jean was struggling with a new and unsympathetic stepmother after her father had remarried. Both shared their longing to know more about their birth mothers.

We had a lot of fun together. It was just as I'd imagined it might be to have sisters. We sneaked out into the fields on moonlit nights and had illicit picnics beside the river. We sang songs we'd learned in school music lessons in two-part harmony. Joan and I concocted stories and wrote little plays, while Jean sketched. She had not only inherited her mother's talent, but also our grandfather, Tom Sutherland's, gift for painting and drawing. Other cousins came for the holidays too. Uncle Angus, married to my father's sister May, was now working for oil companies in the Middle East and his eldest daughter, Susan, was at boarding school. Her younger brother, Ian, was only slightly younger than my brother. When Angus and May were on leave, they also came to stay on the farm. May wept on my mother's shoulder about how unhappy she was as an expatriate wife. There were other, more disturbing, revelations. She claimed to have seen the Hand of Fatima (a potent symbol in the Middle East) on the wall of their house in Tripoli and also admitted that she had a spirit guide who came to her in dreams. Angus, without telling either May or my mother, lent my father money.

Dad was very popular with the cousins. He was at his best with children and had a great sense of humour, laughing so much at his own jokes that he never got to the punchline. Sometimes there were four children to a bed, as well as various relatives sleeping on 'shake-downs' in the parlour. My mother found herself running a hotel, cooking vast numbers of eggs on toast for breakfast and marshalling half a dozen children of various ages as well as her own. For us it was wonderful. Joan and I came up with the idea of performing our little plays in the barn, using one of the lofts as a stage. We called it the Barn Theatre. Jean designed the scenery, which we painted on old sheets and hung from the beams. We sang madrigals and songs from the shows, performed comedy sketches, recited poetry and scenes from Shakespeare. When the parents came to collect their offspring at the end of the summer, they sat on hay bales in the barn, paid two pence for programmes we'd coloured in by hand, and were entertained with a show.

One of the Barn Theatre Programmes

As teenage girls together, Anne, Jean, Joan and I talked about our hopes and dreams. Anne had just got an apprenticeship as a tracer in an engineering factory and Jean hoped to go to art college. Joan wanted to be an actress. Perhaps it was because of my cousins' encouragement, sharing their own ambitions, that I began to believe in myself again. In my second school year, I discovered just how competitive I was; no one was going to put me down, particularly not myself. I read books all through the holidays and at weekends. Going with my mother to Carlisle on Saturdays, I went to the library and looked for titles that might be useful, while she sold eggs in the market. I learned my French and Latin verbs in bed at night before I went to sleep; I pored over maps, memorising countries and capital cities. My mother taught me a useful rhyme for the names of English kings and queens.

Back at school, I began to crawl up the rankings, though nothing could be done about maths, which remained an impenetrable mystery. But my new teacher, a patient young woman just out of university, who wore elegant dresses and high heels, was encouraging. 'Still very weak,' she wrote, after I managed to come twenty-sixth out of twenty-eight, 'but Kathleen is making an effort to overcome her difficulties'. By the end of the year, I'd worked my way up to twenty-fifth, and I was top of the class again in the humanities. In the autumn term of the following year, I managed to come seventh in (remedial) maths but was top of the class overall and won the English prize. It began to seem as though the golden lettering on the board might be within reach. The next two years would be critical. I was signed up for ten O-level subjects and expected to pass them all, including 'maths for dumbos' as the practical and applied maths I was studying was jokingly called.

10

THE YEAR OF THE MONEYLENDERS

Dad was a very good farmer, but a terrible businessman. Mum was much better with money, but he would never listen to her. Her anxiety got in the way of everything, he said, and he brushed her worries aside. It was true that my mother was very cautious, but that wasn't a bad thing. Dad was an incorrigible optimist and needed a pinch of pessimism to balance it out.

'He should have waited until we had more money behind us,' Mum told me later. 'And he should have taken a part-time job at the beginning and started off slowly, buying things when we could afford them. Instead, he tried to run before he could walk and we all paid the price.' What I remember is the constant arguing. There was no more dancing the Gay Gordons with my mother round the kitchen to Jimmy Shand and his Band on a Sunday morning, no more singing the Kentucky blues. Dad looked grim and Mum was red-eyed from lack of sleep. Once I came downstairs in the middle of the night to get a glass of water and saw the faint glow of candle-light in the living room. My mother was sitting in the armchair staring into the embers of the fire.

The West Cumberland Farmers' bills for cattle and chicken feed, calf-milk and other necessary supplies came in brown window envelopes. They were supposed to be paid within thirty days, but there was another period of thirty days' grace. After that, a reminder came with a little picture of an elephant in the top right corner and the caption: 'An elephant never forgets, but perhaps you have?' The next one had a clock with wings that said 'Time Flies: Time to Pay Up'. After that came the solicitor's letter. Dad often asked me to do errands for him in my lunch break when I was at school. Sometimes it was a trip to the hardware shop, sometimes a message for the auctioneers, and now and again I'd be given a cheque to cash at the bank in the high street. I dreaded it. The cashier would look at the name and go off to talk to someone in a cubicle at the back. Often he would say, 'I'm sorry but there isn't enough money in the account'. I would grow hot with humiliation. Even now I find it difficult to walk into a bank.

Sometimes creditors would come to the door, asking to be paid. My mother would hide upstairs and, if I was at home, I would be sent to the door to tell them that my parents weren't there. That year, Dad was hardly home at all. He had taken full-time employment in an attempt to shore up the family finances and pay the mortgage. He worked at the nearby Barytes mine for a while. This was a job he hated, but it paid good money, and sometimes he worked at one of the nearby farms that was too big to be farmed by one man, but not big enough to support permanent labour. Dad was up at 4am to do the chores at Rough Close, off to work by 8 and not back until the evening, when he would have a quick cup of tea and a sandwich before going out for what was called the 'doing up' every night. By 9 o'clock he was in bed.

During the day, my mother ran the farm, with help from me when I came home from school. Outlying cattle and sheep needed to be fed, calves and chickens managed. There were byres to muck out and there was milking equipment to sterilise. Mum had never been strong – and the heavy work took its toll on her physically. She was peri-menopausal and suffered from what the doctors called menorrhagia. She swallowed iron tablets every morning but was still permanently anaemic from the heavy bleeding. I remember going into the back kitchen once and seeing her standing on newspapers changing her sanitary pads in a pool of blood. She was also taking painkillers for painful joints. My father used to rub her back with horse liniment which, he said, was better than the stuff you could buy at the chemists.

My North Shields grandparents came for their annual visit, joyfully anticipated by my brother and I, who looked forward to evenings playing cards with Nana Sutherland. My mother was always co-opted to make a four, Grandpa would be smoking his pipe beside the fire and my worn-out father asleep in an armchair opposite. Nana liked playing Newmarket, which involved gambling for pennies and a great deal of raucous laughter. When we ran out of pennies, we used buttons. She cheated relentlessly and always won. We knew, but somehow it added to the fun.

During the day, I helped Grandpa whitewash the farm buildings, while Nana embarked on spring-cleaning the house. Carpets were beaten, windows cleaned with vinegar, mattresses turned, and quilts hung on the line for a good airing. All the

Helping Grandpa

jobs that my parents hadn't had time for were gradually ticked off the list. But on this visit, there was a strange, tense atmosphere. One Saturday, my mother and I were in the kitchen making tea when we heard my grandparents talking outside.

'I'm very worried about Ella,' Grandpa said. I could hear the click of his pipe stem on his teeth as he took it out and put it back in again. 'She shouldn't be doing all that heavy work.'

'It's all *that man's fault*,' Nana said, stressing the words with considerable venom. 'Dragging the girl up here to the middle of nowhere. Working like a slave. It'll be the death of her.' Her voice carried clearly, in the ultra-loud tones of the very deaf.

There were more remarks about my father; his recklessness when it came to money, his irresponsible attitude to his wife and family. My mother looked stricken. Her hands froze on the pastry she'd been moulding in a pie dish. She put her head down. 'Oh, Kathie,' she said. 'How can they say such things about Harold?' I was old enough to recognise that some of the criticisms had substance, but my mother put family loyalty before everything.

Her parents had no right to criticise the man she loved. The thought that they believed him to be in the wrong was hurtful.

The bank refused to lend my father any more money. Mum suggested renting out some of the fields to pay the mortgage while Dad worked until they'd paid off the outstanding debts. But that wasn't good enough for my father. He saw an advert in the paper for loans secured against assets and, ignoring my mother's pleas, wrote to enquire. Mum was so against it that, for once, she stood up to him. They had a massive row in the back kitchen and didn't speak for two days. But a week later, on Sunday, a large black Bentley bumped up the track and parked in the stack yard.

Mr Goldstein was a cheerful middle-aged man, rather plump, dressed for the city rather than the farm. His polished black shoes weren't made for inspecting barns or byres. His wife was, to my teenage eyes, incredibly glamorous. Her dark hair had been styled by a hairdresser, her face beautifully made up. She wore the kind of clothes you couldn't buy in Carlisle and on her fingers she had several gold rings set with precious stones. I was fascinated by a sapphire the size of a hazelnut set in diamonds. In contrast to my mother's five-year-old Gor-ray skirt and mended blouse, Mrs Goldstein was dressed like the Queen. She was also very gracious.

My mother took her into the parlour, where the fire had been lit for the first time in months, and she sat in an aura of woodsmoke and moth balls, drinking tea without milk, refusing the cakes and biscuits my mother had made, and making polite conversation. She noticed the piano, a recent present from my

Carlisle grandmother, and asked if I could play. She talked of her own children and a recent holiday in Israel. She and my mother talked about 'the Holy Land'. Mum had recently read H.V. Morton's *Through Lands of the Bible* and had lots of questions, which she hoped were politically correct. It was all very awkward. Eventually Mr Goldstein returned, told us what a lovely farm we had, and how he'd be happy to help two deserving young people like my parents. Some documents were produced from a briefcase and my parents were asked to sign on the dotted line. Dad was smiling; Mum looked terrified. From that moment, effectively, the farm belonged to our wealthy visitors, who climbed back into their Bentley and drove cautiously back down the track.

My mother's reading diary records the ironically titled novel *Profit and Loss* by Jacobine Hichens, a writer whose name and reputation have since dropped out of view. Increasingly, Mum was taking refuge in historical novels. *Here Lies our Sovereign Lord*, *The Poisoned Crown*, *The Devil and King John*, *The Iron King*, *The She Wolf of France*, are just some of the titles listed on those cramped pages. The past was a safer place than the present; at least you knew how things had turned out. But there were also several books about self-healing. *And I Shall be Healed*, by Edeltraud Fulda, got four stars, as did Isabel Kuhn's *By Searching* and a book called *Lovingly in the Hands of the Father* by Evelyn Whitell. Aunt May was now a follower of Harry Edwards, a famous faith healer, and sent my mother his address, which she wrote in her reading diary: 'The Sanctuary, Burrows Lea'. She read one of his books, but there's no evidence that she ever contacted him.

A fortnight after the Goldsteins' visit, I came home from school one afternoon to find Mum packing a suitcase, white-faced, tears running down her cheeks. 'Your Dad's had an accident,' she said. My uncle and aunt were coming with the car to take her to the hospital. The next-door neighbour's son, Alan, was going to do the evening milking if I could help him. I changed out of my uniform, called the dogs and went to get the cows.

It was late when Mum phoned to say that Dad was in intensive care, and she would be staying overnight in Carlisle. Could I look after my brother and make sure he got to school? She'd arranged for Alan to do the morning milking as well. Mum came back the next day and told me the whole story. My father had been working on another farm, leading hay to the fell sheep. He'd been on top of the bales on the trailer, while his boss was driving the tractor. Going over a pothole in the road, Dad had fallen off the trailer and his boot had caught in one of the bale strings. His head had bumped along the road behind the trailer until a passing car had alerted the tractor driver. Dad had a fractured skull and had lost a great deal of blood. He was still unconscious – and it was touch and go.

Sitting beside his hospital bed, my mother made a decision. The money from the Goldsteins was still sitting in their bank account. Dad intended to spend it on some good cows, settle some of the urgent debts and add to the pedigree Aberdeen Angus herd he was beginning to breed out on the fell. There was some regret at the hasty signature. Reading the small print of the agreement after the Goldsteins left, my parents had discovered that the interest rate on the loan was more than 30%, that a single default on a repayment would mean the farm was forfeited, and there was a steep penalty clause if you wanted to pay off the loan early. All this had caused some consternation. My innocent parents didn't know that these terms were quite usual. Moneylenders were the lenders of last resort; their loans were high risk and they charged accordingly.

Mum picked up the phone and rang Mr Goldstein's office, to ask him to take the money back. He was initially quite frosty, but he could hear my mother's genuine distress. Her husband, she told him, was in hospital critically ill and they didn't know whether he would survive. 'Please,' I heard her say, 'please'. She sounded desperate. He told her he would think about it and ring her back. There was an interval and we both suspected that he was ringing the hospital to confirm her story. Then the phone rang and Mr Goldstein, charming and regretful, told my mother that in this instance, he would cancel the loan and take the money back. There would be no penalty. Mum's relief was so great that she collapsed onto the sofa, shaking so much she could barely hold the cup of tea I'd made her. The following morning, while in Carlisle to see my father, she went to the bank and arranged to transfer the money straight away.

During the time it took Dad to recover, my mother and I ran the farm, doing the milking and the shepherding, while my nine-year-old brother took on feeding the calves and chickens. Three weeks later, fresh out of hospital and intensive care, my father was staggering about the farm, grey with fatigue. There was no more talk of borrowing. Dad sold one of the fields to a neighbouring farmer for a good price and we were safe again. But the farm was less viable.

At school everything was going well. I usually managed to get into one of the top three places in the class, and in English I was well out in front. We were studying T.S. Eliot's *The Waste Land*, much of which I didn't understand. But the best poetry works in the underground channels of the mind, tugging at emotions like deep ocean currents. The first line needed no interpretation: 'April is the cruellest month'. April was lambing time, when all the fell sheep had been rounded up and brought into the twenty-acre field where they could be fed and closely watched. April was staggering across the field with a Tilly lamp, in icy rain or powdered snow, at 3am. April was starved lambs in the bread oven, bottles of milk on the kitchen drainer. April was digging sheep and lambs out of drifts behind the walls. I learned how to lamb a ewe that was in trouble, kneeling on the frozen ground with my arm covered in shit and blood. I watched my father push back wombs that had been prolapsed by a bad birth. I watched him bury dead lambs.

At the end of the spring term, I suddenly fainted in assembly. I'd had a vague stomach-ache for days, but no one seemed to think there was anything wrong with me. In the staff room, the teacher who knew about first aid thought differently. I was taken to hospital and diagnosed with acute appendicitis – and operated on that evening. It was all quite exciting. I'd never been to a hospital before, not even to visit my father – children weren't allowed. The female Nightingale ward was parallel to the men's ward. I began waving to a boy at one of the windows, and then a nurse, trying not to laugh, brought me a note he'd written 'to the girl in the blue pyjamas'. Sometimes we met in the corridor and talked. He was sixteen, also having his appendix out. We wrote letters to each other after I was discharged and talked on the telephone a couple of times, but it was difficult to have any kind of relationship so many miles apart, without any means of transport.

Back home I felt fine and had the Easter holidays to recover. But then I got up one morning, feeling wretched, and found that I was covered in red spots. I had caught measles in the hospital and spent a week in bed and then another month convalescing. I missed a great deal of school. But when I took my end-of-year report home, I was ecstatic to discover that my English teacher had written: 'When she was here, she outshone all the others.' I had a head the size of Roald Dahl's Giant Peach.

Gill, Doreen and Kathie. Best Friends Forever,
Nelson Thomlinson School, 1961.

I went to my grandparents in North Shields for a fortnight's holiday in the second half of August. My parents thought fresh sea air was just what I needed to get completely well. But it was a wet, cold summer. It was great to spend more time with the cousins, but swimming in an outdoor saltwater pool in the rain wasn't much fun. I caught a chill, and then began to run a high fever and feel really ill. It was hard to explain to anyone, but I felt worse than I'd ever felt in my life. I thought I was going to die. My grandmother said I had a bad case of influenza and my uncle drove me home in his car. I went to bed, feeling relieved. I was home and safe and my mother was there to look after me. But when I was well enough to get up again, I found that I was rather wobbly on my legs, and sometimes one of them would give way and I would fall over. My hands felt numb and prickly and I kept dropping things. When I collapsed in the kitchen one afternoon, my mother asked a neighbour to take us down to the doctor's surgery in his car.

He asked me a lot of questions, particularly about where I'd been staying for my holiday, prodded and pulled me, and then told my mother that he was sending me to the Cumberland Infirmary straight away in a hospital car. Once the emergency doctor read the letter that had been sent with me, I was admitted to the isolation unit, to be barrier nursed, with no visitors allowed. It was only afterwards they told me that they suspected I'd been in contact with polio. I was there for several weeks while they did a lot of tests. My blood was showing abnormal results. A virus was in my system, but they didn't know what it was. After a while, when I didn't get any worse, I was sent home and ordered to rest. It would have been hard to do anything else; I felt so exhausted that even getting dressed was sometimes more than I could manage.

The beginning of a new term came and went while I was in hospital and, after I was discharged, for weeks afterwards I was too tired to make the long trip to school and back. It was my O-level year, and my chances of an academic career were slipping away. Everyone tried to help. A local councillor organised a taxi to come up the track to the farm so that I wouldn't have to walk to the road. I was allowed to go to school for three days a week and could go into the rest room and lie down at lunchtime. But it all seemed pointless when my fingers were too weak to hold a pen for long enough to write an essay.

It was February before I felt normal again. Too late to catch up on all the work I'd missed. I wasn't top of the form anymore; I wasn't the golden girl everyone expected me to be. It was as though an earthquake had upturned the landscape so that nothing was where it had been. The headmaster confidently expected me to return to school in September to repeat the year. But being away had changed me. I couldn't face going down a year, being among strangers, having to make new friends. I knew, too, that if I wanted to go to Oxford or Cambridge, I'd have to do an extra year in the sixth form. That meant another four years of school. During the time I'd been sick, I'd begun to imagine another future.

I'd been writing prolifically for years, scribbling in notebooks after I went to bed; and the school magazine, *Operis*, published some of my earliest poetry. I'd also begun to send pieces off to various other publications in the hope of being noticed. I had no idea how to go about it and didn't know there was such a thing as the *Writers' and Artists' Yearbook*. But somehow I muddled through and learned from my mistakes. One of the first things I had accepted was a funny piece on kissing men with beards, which was published in a teenage magazine called *Marty*. I was thirteen and hadn't kissed anyone. Then there was a series of 'letters from the farm' in the *Farmer's Weekly* on being a teenage girl on a hill farm, milking cows in stiletto heels and other crazy scenarios.

Cumbria magazine published something I wrote about a visit to Carlisle Castle, imagining Mary Queen of Scots riding through the gate to imprisonment, and I received a letter from California that took me completely by surprise. Someone had read my piece in the magazine and felt 'compelled' to tell me how much they liked it. 'You have written in such a way that you take the reader by the hand and let him live with you in the past as he travels the present,' she wrote. 'This is more than clever. It is an acquired art of creative writing.' If I kept my 'lively imagination' working, she predicted, I would find 'a reader-participation to bring you great satisfaction in the future'. This meant a great deal to me. It was one thing for friends and family to say they liked my writing; they were only going to tell me what they thought I wanted to hear. But for a reader to write from halfway across the world, to tell me I could write in a way that moved them, was amazing. Self-belief is the hardest thing for a writer to acquire. When I read that letter, I began to believe that one day I could be a writer.

Lying in bed, I decided to put my medical experience to good use and wrote a series of articles for the *Carlisle Journal*, intended to amuse. The first was called 'How to Antagonise Your Doctor in Six Easy Lessons'. My father bought me a correspondence course on journalism, which I really enjoyed, and on one of his trips to the auction he brought back an old Remington typewriter with a long carriage. It was almost too heavy to carry and echoed through the wooden floorboards like thunder when you thumped the keys.

One of my first acceptance letters.

I decided I wanted to become a journalist. This brought instant disapproval from my parents' friends. 'You can't let her do that, Ella,' I overheard my Aunt Florrie say. 'Just think of the company she'd have to keep!'

My parents, though not as strict as their friends, felt the same. Journalists on local papers haunted the law courts, the police station, the scenes of accidents and crimes. They hung around in pubs and smoked cigarettes.

They probably had extra-marital sex. It was no place for the well-brought-up Christian girl I was supposed to be. Love can become a kind of tyranny, and I found it impossible to hurt my parents. But I knew that if I wanted to become the person who was struggling to survive inside me, I'd have to leave. There were other factors too. I was tired of walking around in other people's clothes, tired of not having any money for make-up, or records (things my friends took for granted), tired of not being able to go out in the evening and have fun like other teenagers.

The idea of leaving Rough Close almost broke my heart. It meant to me what I imagined Haworth must have meant to the Brontës. But I comforted myself that it would always be there to return to, whenever I needed it. Places are constants – more reliable than people. So, against all advice from teachers and relatives, I left school three weeks before my sixteenth birthday; and three weeks after that I left home. The writer Yiyun Li, observes in her autobiography that 'one always knows best how to sabotage one's own life'.[15]

11

INDEPENDENCE

If I couldn't be a journalist, I decided that I would do something useful. Being in hospital so much had given me an interest in nursing. While I was ill, I'd been given *Sue Barton, Student Nurse* and loved it. I sought out all the other *Sue Barton* books in the library. They were American, but beautifully written and painted a romantic picture of life as a hospital nurse. Sue marries a doctor in the end, which was an added attraction. Hormones were beginning to swamp feminism. After all, what were girls bred for except marriage? That was what you did if you were born female. Nothing I'd read so far gave me any other blueprint for a woman's life.

Even in the books where girls went out and had adventures, they always met some amazing bloke and came back with a ring on their finger. And as far as I could see, the life of a career woman wasn't exactly a bundle of fun. In the 1950s, there were still a lot of unmarried, middle-aged women who had lost the chance of marriage in the carnage of the First World War. Villages and towns were full of single women who taught children in schools, nursed the sick, ran the civil service, provided charitable relief and delivered meals for the Women's Voluntary Organisation. They were invaluable to society, but they didn't seem to be enjoying much personal fulfilment. They had an air of desiccation, something faded, an aura of regret. I didn't want to be like them. At sixteen I wanted everything – an interesting life *and* a husband and family.

Nursing was quite hard to get into; you needed university entrance qualifications – O levels and A levels. But I discovered that it was possible to begin training by a different route. I could become a pre-nursing student at the hospital, do my exams at evening class and on day release at a local college, and, a year later, go into an accelerated four-year nursing programme. This sounded much more fun than school. I was accepted, providing I passed my medical. Given my history, there was a possibility that I wouldn't be fit enough, but the doctor who examined me said I was as strong as a horse and he didn't anticipate any problems. I moved into the nurses' home at the beginning of September, with a new cohort of cadets, all wearing horrible yellow uniforms.

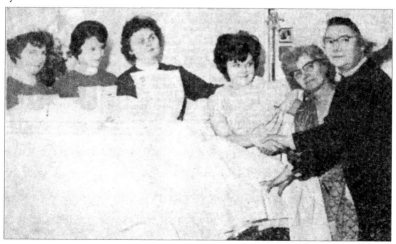

Nurse Slight, far left. Matron, far right.

I loved hospital life from the very beginning. There was always something exciting going on, always someone with a story to tell. We lived in the nurses' home and ate in the canteen. We were a group of girls from diverse backgrounds, but we all got on. I made friends with Jenny from Scotland who had worked in a convent, washing the nuns' habits and starching their white shovel-shaped coifs. Nunneries, she said, were like catteries, full of hissing and spitting. She had been brought up a Catholic, but after a year in the convent laundry she was completely disillusioned with religion.

The nurses' home was very strict because almost every one of us, even the senior student nurses, was under twenty-one and Matron took her role as substitute parent very seriously. My bedroom was at the end of the wing on the top floor, next to the fire escape. So it was my lot to be woken in the middle of the night by girls who had no exit pass and were desperate to get back in without being reported. Some of the older girls found the rules very restrictive, but for me the limited freedom was exciting. I could go to the cinema, coffee bars (pubs were out of bounds at sixteen), wander round the shops, the museums and libraries. One day a week, I went to college and prepared to take some of the O-levels I'd missed. I was paid a small amount at the end of every month, after my keep had been taken out. I bought clothes and shoes and make-up. I bought Roy Orbison records, had my hair properly cut and began to feel like a teenage girl.

My first posting was in A & E with two other cadets. We were definitely thrown in at the deep end. We took down patients' details, fetched x-rays and records, sterilised instruments and helped to run the out-patient clinics. We felt very important when patients called us 'Nurse'. In between, we ate cakes in the linen cupboard and talked about our boyfriends. I now had a boyfriend for the first time. There had been one or two near misses. I'd been madly in love with Jim Stobart (of the haulage dynasty) at fourteen, only to discover that all the attention I was getting was because he was in love with my best friend.

I met my new boyfriend at a Christmas party. He was six years older than me, a farmer, and his name was William. His mother insisted that it mustn't be shortened to Willy, which, as his surname was Little, was inevitable. I also had a surname, Slight, that could be made into a joke, so that was an immediate bond. He owned a van, which he used around the farm, and it wasn't unknown for him to turn up for a date with a calf in a straw box in the back. He bought me a driving licence for my seventeenth birthday and I got to drive the van.

Once a month, I got a bus to Caldbeck and begged a lift back to Rough Close for the weekend. The silence would always hit me as I walked up the track on a winter's evening; the way the wind made a particular sound as it came over the brow of the hill, combing its way through the tussock grass. And the stars – after the streetlights of the city, the sky seemed full of planets and constellations. The Milky Way, that cloudy river of stars that cartwheels over our heads every night unnoticed, glowed brightly against the darkness of space. I could see the seven sister stars of the Pleiades, and Cassiopeia, Orion, and the bent handle of the Plough, among the millions and millions of stars I had no name for. Sometimes you could even see the northern lights flickering faintly over the distant Cheviots.

My parents were always glad to see me. 'The house is so quiet without you, Kathie,' my mother would say. Dad just smiled and gave me a bear hug. On Saturday morning I would wake up in my own bed with the sound of the milking machine, buckets clanking in the byre, calves mooing for their milk. I was where I belonged.

Things seemed more settled, at least on the surface. Now that there was only my little brother at home, the financial burden on my parents had eased. Although he was more than five years younger than me, I had always loved Gordon and was very protective towards him. He was a quiet boy, who was often bullied by the bigger, cruder farm boys. He was very musical and could hold a tune long before he could talk. He had been given a guitar for his ninth birthday and taught himself to play. He was less keen on being out on the farm, and it wasn't because I was already out there in my wellies helping Dad with the chores. My leaving home had made no difference. Gordon had little interest and my father despaired. Mum was constantly having to intervene in his defence. He was too young; give him time, she kept saying. My father thought he was just lazy. The farm was to be my brother's future, not mine. But I'd begun to suspect that it was a future my brother might not want. The Irish farming genes seemed to have passed him by.

On one of my first visits back home, I asked my brother if things were any better on the financial front, but he just pulled a face. He was now at secondary school and, according to Mum, seemed to be enjoying himself. 'It's not the Nelson, though,' he said, quite aggressively, when I asked. In the middle of the family's economic crisis, Gordon had failed his eleven-plus exam for the grammar school. This was a great disappointment for my

Kathleen (aged 9) and Gordon (4)

parents but not a surprise. My brother didn't like school, didn't do the work, skipped off classes and sometimes got into trouble with a group of lively local boys.

'It was all right for you,' he added bitterly.

What was all right? I wanted to ask. A failed academic career hardly felt like a suitable subject for envy. 'You shouldn't have been messing about,' I told him. 'If you'd worked a bit harder . . .' He was furious.

But it was true. Gordon had only failed the exam by a few marks. His grievance was that my parents could have appealed, on the grounds of family circumstances, and asked for a resit, but, although they discussed it, they didn't. By their own moral code, it would have seemed as though they considered themselves 'above' everyone else, that they thought their son was too good for the secondary school. There could be no special pleading. If Gordon had failed, perhaps it was because he deserved it. My brother went, with the rest of his class, to the local secondary modern, and he resented their decision for the rest of his life.

Living in Carlisle I was confronted every day by the other half of my family history. This bleak border city was where my Irish relatives had settled when they migrated across the water. The chimney of Dixon's Mill, where my Northern Irish great-grandfather had worked as a Jacquard pattern-maker, dominated the skyline, rearing above the narrow streets of mill-workers' houses where many of the family still lived. Robert Blair had been the leader of the Orange Order in Carlisle, heading the annual procession, in full regalia, mounted on a cart horse. By the time I knew him, he was coughing up his lungs in the bedroom of my grandmother's house, a victim of the lint from the machines which he'd been breathing in from the age of twelve.

The centre of the town was criss-crossed by alleyways known as Lanes, with old, derelict buildings crumbling on either side. This was where my grandfather's Catholic mother had brought up four illegitimate children in cold, rodent-infested rooms on scarcely any money at all. My grandfather, her youngest child, said that his earliest memory was of the mice chasing each other round the skirting boards. Most people liked Annie Cunningham and went out of their way to help her. She bought, or was given, clothing too poor to be sold by the 'rag man', Joe Longthorne, who owned the second-hand shop in the market. She was a skilled dressmaker and cut the old-fashioned clothes down to make items to sell. A Victorian crinoline would make several blouses and silk petticoats. She hooked the worst of them into rag rugs which she sold on the street in an area called 'Paddy's Market' where the Irish diaspora lived.

In the evenings, people told me, she had sung Irish airs round the pubs. She liked a drink, they said. This was not the romantic story my father had told me. He loved his grandmother and mourned her death when she'd been found in the coal house during the war, having died from a stroke. He wanted to believe the best of her and accepted what he had been told as a child. He didn't even know that the man he presumed to be his grandfather, Robert Slight, had been a soldier. Annie had told him his grandfather was an Irish drover, but neglected to add that his name wasn't Robert Slight.

There was so much illegitimacy on that side of the family, and so many cover-up stories, that it was difficult to believe anything anyone said. But the facts on public record show that Annie Cunningham, who had recently given birth to her first child, had been widowed when her husband, Robert Slight, was one of three men drowned in the River Caldew during a

Annie Cunningham (standing) with her mother Frances Theresa.

169

regimental exercise. She was evicted from the Border Regiment's military quarters they'd occupied at Carlisle Castle with the two other wives, causing great hardship. There was a public campaign to raise money for the victims.

Annie never remarried. Her other children were, according to her older son, fathered by an Irish drover who passed through Carlisle regularly. But no one knew for certain. She took lodgers. One of them, an Irish market porter, was living with her at the time my grandfather was born. And Annie herself was illegitimate. Her mother, Frances Theresa, had only been fifteen when she became pregnant, in service at Warren Point, and was lucky that her parents decided to bring the baby up as one of their own, rather than handing her over to the Magdalene sisters who ran the infamous laundries. Annie was only a couple of years younger than her uncle.

Frances later made a respectable marriage to a farmer who never knew about her child. She came over to Carlisle to stay with Annie once, but she never told her who her father had been. Some members of the family joked about a footman; others speculated that Frances might have been 'taken advantage of' by one of the gentlemen she worked for. My grandfather never admitted that he was illegitimate and deliberately 'lost' his birth certificate. Because of the uncertainty surrounding his real name, it was only discovered years after his death. Two generations of illegitimacy didn't bother my father at all and he didn't care whether he was descended from a footman or a lord. He just laughed and quoted John Wesley: 'Love, like death, makes all distinctions vain'. Between the sheets, in the coffin, we're all the same.

The city was a landscape of stories. My grandfather's childhood had been full of characters. I liked hearing about them, but struggled with my feelings of revulsion for the storyteller and came into contact with him as seldom as I could. In Carlisle, this was more often than I was comfortable with. I took my washing to my grandmother once a week and he would sometimes be there. He used to push himself up against me in the kitchen or the living room when my grandmother wasn't looking. He obviously thought he had 'got away' with his abuse of me and lost no opportunity to make physical contact in the most blatant way, sometimes having his flies open so that his penis brushed my clothes.

Why I never challenged him I will never know. There was some subconscious taboo about disturbing the family status quo. I'd been brought up not to make a fuss. I talked to no one. Where sexual abuse is concerned, a code of silence often descends on a family. No one says anything. But when my Aunt May, on leave from Libya, stood in my grandmother's kitchen one summer afternoon, with her hands in the pockets of her fashionable slacks, and said, 'Oh, how I *loathe* that man,' I knew exactly what she meant. I also loathed the grandfather I was supposed to love – and my hatred was so deep and so powerful, it frightened me.

Sometimes I would get him to talk about his childhood as a distraction or a way of making conversation. He was writing his memoirs and told me about having to cut up rags to help his mother make rugs, sleeping on the floor while the lodgers slept on the sofa, about begging wooden boxes from shops to use as firewood, and picking coal out of the gutter near the depot. All the children had to work. His eldest sister was put into the mills as a 'machine cleaner' by the time she was thirteen. He himself was apprenticed as a boxer at one of Lord Lonsdale's gymnasiums by the time he was twelve and also played football for Brampton and in the Carlisle United reserve team.

But there was a gap in his history. He claimed to have been under-age when he joined the Border Regiment at the beginning of the First World War. He was vague about his age. But when I eventually found his birth certificate, long after his death, it was clear that he had been twenty-one when he signed up to go to the Front in 1914. Where had he been in the years between thirteen and twenty-one? There's a photograph of him, a young teenager, standing beside the seated figure of Lord Lonsdale (of the famous Lonsdale Belt), with a trophy on a stand in front of him. But it couldn't have all been boxing and football. These were amateur sports. He must have had some kind of job. And why had he been ostracised by his brother and his sister, even his mother? That lifelong feud was surely not just because he'd married a Protestant girl? By the time

My paternal grandfather in 1914
Private Henry Hugh 'Harry'
Cunningham Slight, Border Regiment

I found the certificate there were so many questions he was no longer there to answer. Carlisle was full of Irish relatives I didn't know – great-aunts and uncles, cousins I wouldn't recognise if I passed them in the street.

My grandfather wrote a column in the local papers under a pseudonym. When he talked, or wrote, about the past, he opened a window onto a different world from the streets I walked every day. I was always fascinated by the story of Old Brewer, the tramp, who lived in a tree on the Zero Path beside the River Eden, who wore four overcoats to keep out the cold, but still froze to death in his nest of straw and flour sacks one exceptionally cold winter. My grandfather had once seen a dancing bear chasing its injured Italian trainer, Dambrosio, down English Street, pursued by three policemen.

He also talked of being taken by his mother to see Monkey Green, the barrel organ man, who played Irish jigs for Annie and let him stroke the monkey. Street entertainers and musicians were a regular feature of city life at the beginning of the twentieth century. In the city centre now, there's a bronze statue of Jimmy Dyer, the fiddler – another of Annie Cunningham's acquaintances. I had heard about him from my grandfather and my father, who used to quote one of his songs regularly. Its popular sentiments would not have pleased the gentry at the hiring fairs where he played:

> Servant men, stick up for your wages,
> When to the hirings you do go,
> For you have to face the long winter,
> In the rain, hard frost and snow.

I found the city very bleak after the fells. The nurses' home was centrally heated, so we were always warm, but the weather in December 1962 and early 1963 was unusually cold. This was the winter of the great storm that gave us the longest, coldest winter of the twentieth century. There was no warning. I was at home for Christmas and New Year. We all went to a Boxing Day party in the village and, when we came out after midnight, it was snowing hard, blowing the flurries along the road to decorate fences and hedgerows and already drawing the outlines of drifts along the walls. The person giving us a lift home abandoned the drive after only a mile and offered to take us back to the village for the night. But my father said he had to be home for the morning milking and he would walk. My mother said he would get lost in the drifts on his own, so she would go with him. My brother and I flatly refused to go back in the car. If there was going to be an adventure, we were going to be part of it.

We walked the four and a half miles, arm in arm, across the moors in a raging blizzard that turned everything, even the air, white. We stumbled along, snow blind, only knowing we were on the road because I was wearing metal-tipped heels that pierced the snow and clinked against the tarmac. After a while we could no longer feel our feet. I couldn't see for the snow frozen to my eyelashes and my fringe. We were dressed for a party, not an expedition to the North Pole. I think that was when my father realised we'd done something very foolish. This wasn't a normal winter snowstorm. I heard him begin to pray under his breath.

Afterwards, none of us remembered the last mile up the track, floundering through drifts that were now above our knees. It was a grim exercise in survival. In the warmth of the house, the pain began and the shivering that was uncontrollable and exhausting. Dad had banked up the fire with ash before we went out, to 'keep it in'; he quickly raked it through and threw on some coal and logs so it was soon roaring up the chimney. The pain in our feet and hands was agonising. I remember the phone ringing and it was the concerned friend who'd given us a lift, desperate to know that we were safe.

In the morning, the road to the farm was impassable and it was still snowing – big flakes, like someone crumbling bread over our heads. Every now and then, a huge wind would come roaring down out of the north and pile the snow in drifts up to the eaves, filling in the roads that had been dug out, burying parked vehicles and snowploughs. I was unable to get back to the hospital, but Matron gave me an extra week's grace.

The road across the moor in 1963.[16]

The most pressing worry was the livestock. We had two hundred and fifty sheep out on the open fell, exposed to the storm. In the face of the blizzard, they would take shelter and that meant they risked being buried by the snow. During lulls in the weather, Dad, my brother and I went up onto the fell to try to find sheep and drive them down into the big field. We found fewer than a hundred, some behind the fell wall, covered by drifts. The dogs hunted them out and we poked the drifts with sticks to locate the air pockets before we dug them out. The Aberdeen Angus herd, already in the fields, was brought into a big shed my father had only just finished building out of old railway carriages as a winter shelter.

Our biggest problem was water. The ghyll where the beck ran at the back of the farm had filled in with frozen snow and Dad had to hack out a flight of steps down to the river. It was impossible to carry enough water for all the cattle and the milk cows – each animal drinks about five gallons twice a day. So the cattle had to be taken down to the river individually to drink, sliding down the icy steps, which had to be dug out again almost every day as the overnight wind filled them in. It was exhausting, desperate work, as the blizzards continued, and the cattle grew visibly weaker.

By this time, the drifts were over the roof of the house and my father had to dig tunnels from the front door to the byres. I could walk from my bedroom window to the barn roof on frozen snow. I made it back to Carlisle during a break in the weather, when the snowploughs cleared the road across the moor temporarily. I walked the two miles to the crossroads and my boyfriend picked me up to go back to the hospital. In frequent phone calls and the local news, I heard about the situation that was developing at home. Food began to run out on outlying farms, after weeks of isolation. My father made a sledge out of one of the hay carts, and the old milk horse – Dolly – dragged it over the drifts to Caldbeck, with three of our neighbours on board. Supplies of flour and butter and meat and cattle feed were loaded up for the return journey.

No one was laughing at my father's eccentricity now. The horse could go where no tractor or wheeled vehicle could. The roads to the farms were blocked by several feet of snow and it was impossible to break through without a bulldozer; four-wheel-drives simply fell through the frozen crust if they attempted to go over the drifts. Ironically, my father had finally bought an old 'Ford Fergie' tractor a couple of years before. He hated driving it, but it saved him the time he normally spent harnessing the horse to take milk churns down to the ford in the morning before he left for work. Now the tractor stood in the stack yard, frozen-solid and irreparable. RAF helicopters began dropping hay and cattle feed for the outlying farms. But the biggest problem was still water. Every pipe was frozen – and the beck was the only source, at the bottom of the ravine, flowing like an underground stream beneath the frozen snow.

That January was the coldest month of the century. From 26th January to 3rd March there wasn't a single day when the temperature lifted above freezing in the north of England. Up on the fells it lingered into spring. In the city, apart from the news reports, we noticed nothing. The pavements were icy, but the traffic flowed normally in the streets. A few miles further out, in the Lake District, the lakes were all frozen solid for the first time in decades and my boyfriend took me to Derwentwater on my day off to explore. We walked out across the lake to the islands in a surreal landscape. Someone had even driven a car out onto the ice.

Weeks turned into months and the frozen snow was still there, six feet high in the gateways and as solid

Kathleen (16) with William.

as concrete. But as the blizzards stopped and the temperature began to rise, Dad went up onto the fell again, in search of his sheep. It was the smell that drew him to them. Charleton Wath, the deep ravine where the mountain stream ran between one fell and another at the border of our fell-right, was level with crisp, white snow. It was May before it thawed out – and gave up the carcasses of over a hundred of my father's flock and a similar number belonging to our neighbour.

As the pipes unfroze and the spring grass began to push up through the last ice crystals in the fields, animals that had survived the long winter also began to die. Too many of the surviving sheep, all pregnant at the beginning of winter, either aborted or gave birth to stillborn lambs. That was when Jennifer died. She had been head sheep for ten years, grandmother to half the flock. Now she was just another carcass. The pedigree Aberdeen Angus herd that Dad had been breeding over the last five years began to stagger and fall, one by one. I found him one weekend, weeping in the corner of a field by the carcass of one of his prize heifers. It was a cruel blow, just as my parents thought they were emerging from all the struggles of the previous years.

Dad went back to work in the Barytes mine. I went to Durham to start a four-year nursing course, two years in the orthopaedic hospital and two more years in general nursing. The work was challenging because the hospital was the major intake for accidents, which often occurred at high speed, on the major A1 route from London to the north. It was also in the middle of the coal fields and there were a lot of mining accidents. I saw young men lose both legs in motorbike crashes, healthy working men in their prime with broken backs after a rock fall, as well as men and women with tubercular bones in complete body casts. I loved orthopaedics – it was the practical challenge of putting bodies together again with a spanner and a drill, like carpentry or engineering.

It was at Durham that I first witnessed the death of a human being. I was working on the female geriatric ward, full of old women with broken hips and fading minds who had spent months in bed. Pneumonia was so common, some of the nurses called it 'the old people's friend'. One day the ward sister asked me to go and sit with an elderly lady who wasn't expected to recover and had no relatives to sit with her. 'No one should have to die alone,' the sister said. I was quite afraid, sitting behind the drawn curtains, hearing the normal activity of the ward going on outside the cubicle. I held the patient's hand, which was curiously cool, and listened to her laboured breathing. I sat there for a long time, drifting off into my own thoughts, and suddenly realised that I was holding my breath. I had unconsciously synchronised my breathing with hers. I crossed her hands over her chest and pulled the sheet up over her head, before going to tell the ward sister that she had 'passed'.

'Right,' she said. 'You'd better help Nurse McGurk get her ready for the morgue.' And so I began to learn the rituals for the laying out of the dead, which women have performed since human beings first prepared members of their tribe for the after-life.

Orthopaedic nursing was heavy work. Many of the patients had their limbs in leather-and-iron splints with metal weights dangling from pullies at the end of the bed. Others were in plaster casts. Most were bed-bound. I was only five feet tall and I weighed seven and a half stones. We weren't supposed to lift patients on our own, but during a winter flu epidemic we often found ourselves working alone. I hurt my back lifting a patient and woke up, doped with morphine, in a bed on my own ward. Matron eyed me up and down and said, 'We can't have nurses with bad backs, now, can we?' She glanced down at some paperwork. 'Who did your medical?' Then she suggested I might like to try a job that was less physical. It was the end of another career. It was also the end of my romance. William wrote me a letter explaining that a farmer's wife with a dodgy back wasn't a good thing.

I was just seventeen and back at home, all my hopes and dreams shattered. I felt like a total failure and became very depressed. What was going to become of me? I was rescued by the Caldbeck village doctor, Michael Cox, who was a legend among his patients. He didn't just care for our ailments; he took a real interest in our lives, recognising that sometimes illnesses had their roots in social problems. He made me an offer. He would pay for me to go to secretarial college in Carlisle if I would be a receptionist for his evening and Saturday morning surgeries. It would mean long days, getting the school bus to the city in the morning, back in the afternoon, then working until 7.30pm, sometimes later. But it would give me a qualification and I would be able to get a job almost anywhere. I accepted his offer and enrolled at the Gregg College of Shorthand and Typing.

My father used to collect me from the surgery when I'd finished in the evening. He'd bought an old Lambretta scooter from a local farmer's son, with the idea that I could take myself backwards and forwards from work more easily. But it was a big, powerful machine and proved too heavy for me to learn to ride. I'd never learned to ride a bike, so I found it difficult to balance and, because my legs were too short to put both down on either side of the scooter at the same time, I tended to fall over when I stopped. It was a big humiliation. But my father rode it with no problem at all and passed his motorbike test. At last, he and my mother could go out together without having to ask for lifts.

At college I learned fast. I could already type, after a fashion, and I could play the piano, so touch-typing came easily. Shorthand, too, was just a matter of memorising squiggles on a page and practising until they became automatic. I realised that if I was going to become a writer (still my most secret, constant ambition), I would need to be able to type and journalists had to have shorthand. Three of the other students, two boys and a girl, were trainee reporters on the local papers. But it soon became apparent that I had made a bad choice. Gregg shorthand was easy to learn, compared to Pitman, but very few colleges taught it. I had been taken on under false pretences. The owner of the college planned to retire at the end of term. No one had been found to take it over, so it would be closed. Students who had just begun would have to transfer to a Pitman's college and start again.

That option wasn't open to me. Dr Cox's offer was time-limited, and there was no way my parents could pay the fees. At that moment, it seemed that every avenue I tried to go down was being closed off. I became so depressed, I thought seriously about taking some of the morphine from the locked cabinets I had access to and simply going to sleep for ever. It was only the thought of the distress I would cause my parents that kept me from doing it. My parents, wrapped up in their own worries, failed to notice my misery. I couldn't confide in them because I knew I would be adding to theirs.

I met my headmaster again at a chapel event. He had heard about my predicament. Why didn't I come back to school? he asked. I was still only seventeen. They would be delighted to have me back. I would have to work hard but could easily do my A-levels in one year instead of two. Oxford and Cambridge were out of the question now, but I could get a place at another university. This offer seemed like salvation. My Carlisle grandmother offered to pay my pocket money if I went back. I put on a second-hand green uniform, got out my exercise books and went back to English, Human Biology and French.

The school, reckoning that I wouldn't need anything more than a little revision, threw in O-levels in Music and Religious Instruction as well. I set my heart on getting a place at Newcastle University to study Social Work and was accepted. I worked like a demon. As soon as I got home from school, I tackled daunting quantities of homework and fell into bed every night exhausted. On Saturdays and Sundays, I read piles of books and made notes for essays. My form teacher wrote on my report, 'In returning after two years, she faced a difficult challenge, which she is meeting sensibly and steadily.' But by the time he had written those words on my report, my life had changed utterly.

12

THE SHAME OF FAILURE

My mother ran away. One person's dear place may be another person's nightmare. In the middle of the night, she got out of bed and left the house in her nightdress, running barefoot down the track, like a white ghost. She reached the fell gate before my father caught up with her. The next day she stayed in bed. The following morning her hand shook so much, holding the teapot, that she had to put it down.

That evening my Uncle Alf and Aunt Florrie arrived in their car. My mother was wrapped in a rug in the chair by the fire, weeping. I remember Florrie reaching into her handbag and bringing out a roll of banknotes held in an elastic band. 'Alf and I have talked about this and prayed about it,' she said. 'This is my egg money, and I want you to have it.' Florrie sold eggs and chickens in the Carlisle market every Saturday, so it was a considerable amount. There were protests from my parents, but eventually the money was in my mother's lap. 'You'll get it back,' I heard my father say. 'As soon as we're on our feet again.'

My mother never talked about this period in her life, and I wondered whether there would be clues to her state of mind in her reading diaries. I found that she was reading an increasing amount of non-fiction, much of it religious, as she sought spiritual consolation. On the pages that cover this year of her life, there are books with titles such as *His Touch Has Still its Ancient Power*, *Life After Death*, *Bridge to God*, *Mind in Life and Death, With Might We Banish Sorrow* and the life of St Thérèse of Lisieux. Books were her refuge and support. Even the few novels that she read had affirmative titles: *The Heaven Tree*, *A Favourite of the Gods* and Olivia Manning's *The Doves of Venus*.

Among the non-fiction titles was one that made me smile – *How Not to Kill Your Husband*. Did she ever blame my father for all he had put her through? Or did she remain totally loyal to him? There are two published books with this arresting title: one, a contemporary Australian self-help book for women with hormonal problems who might, just possibly, resort to violence; the other, written by 'a family doctor' and published in 1957, is really a guide to keeping a woman's spouse alive by looking at 'the stresses, strains and illnesses that can put your husband in an early grave'. It seems that my mother may have been worrying more about my father's health than her own. She feared he would kill himself through overwork.

The books I was reading couldn't have been more different. My parents had bought me a subscription to the World Book Club for Christmas. Every month, throughout the year, a new book was delivered by the post-girl and I had the option of keeping it or returning it. One of the first novels to arrive was *Wide Sargasso Sea* by Jean Rhys, a retelling of the story of Bertha, the first Mrs Rochester, from *Jane Eyre*, the 'mad woman in the attic'. Graham Greene wrote that 'perhaps it is only in childhood that books have any deep influence on our lives'. [17] For me, nothing could have been further from the truth. This was the first book I read as an adult that altered my life. Later there would be others, but Jean Rhys made a very deep impression. It wasn't just that her novel explored colonialism and gender politics; it also showed me what was possible for a writer. This was a new way of writing, abandoning old notions of narrative, moving from mind to mind, seeing everything through the eyes of the characters, without explanation, and all in prose that was as lyrical and vivid as poetry. I read it again and again. This, I decided, was how I wanted to write. I still have that book, with its tattered cover and thumbed pages. My mother, who had loved *Jane Eyre*, tried to read it but gave up after the first chapter. She didn't care for modern literary fiction.

This was also the first book I read in the harsh glare of electric lighting. The electricity grid had finally arrived, with cables laid in underground trenches. It caused some trauma for Mum and Dad, who didn't have the money for the wiring of the farm and no possibility of borrowing any. But it was obvious that this was something that couldn't be refused. The atmosphere was tense for weeks. My parents were totally preoccupied. There were conversations my brother and I weren't allowed to listen to and a sense of hopelessness that excluded us. In the end Dad sold all the milk cows. It made sense in one way, because it was difficult to cope with the morning and evening milking while he was working in the mine. His working days were too long, and my mother wasn't fit enough to do it herself; I wasn't there to help and my brother didn't want to. But in another, very important, way it was disastrous because it deprived my parents of the regular income that was paying the mortgage. They were running out of options.

The wiring wasn't easy. Parts of the farmhouse were fifteenth-century or even older and built out of local stone, cobbles and chunks of granite, held together with a very old form of cement that was as hard as concrete. Getting a drill into the walls was almost impossible. But in the end it was finished and the evening came when my father could flick a switch to put on the lights. It was dazzling. The light from the naked bulbs was also harsh; it illuminated dark and dusty corners, revealed every crack in the ceiling, and the damp stains on the wallpaper. Candle-light and lamp-light had thrown shadows and left dusky voids to be filled with imagination. Electric light was stark and unforgiving. Dad ordered a television and for the first time we could sit around the fire at tea-time and watch the programmes that others had been talking about for years. We had a small celebration.

One evening before Christmas, Dad came home and said he'd sold the farm to a neighbour. I couldn't even begin to take it in. The effect was shattering. The places we call home give us 'continuity, something to return to . . . a familiarity that allows some portion of our own lives to remain connected and coherent'.[18] Our connections were torn apart in a few seconds. Nothing made sense anymore. Worse, he announced that he had taken a job down south, almost as far as he could go from the Lake District, in Lincolnshire.

I remember asking, 'And what am I to do?' There was a silence. This was my one chance, my year of A-levels to get into university. All I needed was six more months to pass my exams.

Couldn't my father stay at least that long? The neighbour really only wanted the land, and was going to let the house, so it would have been possible to arrange to keep on renting it for a short time; but Mum said afterwards that my father couldn't bear to stay in Cumbria, living with the shame of failure.

At the time, my mother stared at me as if this was something she hadn't thought of. She looked utterly exhausted. 'You'll just have to go and stay with your grandparents in Carlisle,' she said in a flat, listless voice. I was so upset I couldn't speak. Did she not remember? Did she realise what she was asking me to do? There was no way I could stay in that house, sleep in that place, in close proximity to that monster, to be abused over and over again. The dream was over. That night I cried myself to sleep. Through the partition wall, I could hear my brother doing the same.

My parents started packing for the move to Lincolnshire, to a big estate just outside Grimsby. Dad was going to work for the Earl of Yarborough, looking after his pedigree herd of cattle. I wasn't asked to go with them. Somehow it was just assumed that I wouldn't. The farm cottage they were moving to had only two small bedrooms. Most of the furniture would be left behind, including the piano my brother had just begun to learn, which wouldn't fit in the tiny cottage. There was no room for me either. But I no longer cared where I went, so long as it was far away.

My mother was a very sick woman. Apart from the breakdown, she was suffering from arthritis, massive monthly bleeding and extreme fatigue. She looked gaunt. The doctors could find very little wrong with her, physically, to make her feel so ill. As with so many middle-aged women, assumptions

were made. The inference was that her problems ᴡ
with the menopause and were largely in her own min
herself put a lot of it down to stress. She was borrowing   ᴀs
from the library on mental health. There's a series of self-help
books in her diary. *Nerves and Their Cure* got three stars, as did
a Christian guide to *Psychology for Pastor and People,* before she
widened her reading into eastern mysticism and spirituality,
with *Life Ahead: On Learning and the Search for Meaning*, by J.
Krishnamurti. In between, she read a lot of C.S. Lewis and even
a book on spiritualism, in her search for emotional equilibrium.

I left it all behind. I was tired of living with depressed people
in an atmosphere of grief. I wanted bright lights, optimism, the
sense of a future worth having. I abandoned my mother at a time
when she desperately needed someone to be there for her. I was
angry with both my parents for depriving me of my chance to
succeed, for not considering my brother or me at all. At least I
was old enough to be independent. Gordon was being wrenched
away from his friends, and everything he knew, at a difficult
age. He was thirteen, just finding his feet at school, learning to
play music, getting a band together, discovering who he was. In
my father's blind desire to get as far away from the shame of his
bankruptcy as he could, he had broken up the family. I found it
difficult to forgive my parents; my brother never did.

It's hard to know where to go, when you can go anywhere. But
London was apparently where you went to become a writer, so I
decided I would go there. I found an advert in the back pages of
The Lady for an au pair in Kensington, and my headmaster wrote
me a better reference than I deserved. 'She has been tempered

by adversity,' it ended, 'and I have a great deal of time for her.'
A fortnight after Christmas I was standing on the platform at
Carlisle Station, with a cheap cardboard suitcase containing my
whole life, waiting for the train to London. I couldn't imagine
what the future would be like.

13

'The Wizard, London.'

Katherine Mansfield

In *The Faraway Nearby*, Rebecca Solnit writes that stories are the very fabric of our lives: 'We tell ourselves stories that save us and stories that are the quicksand in which we thrash and the well in which we drown.'[19] London was a blank page on which I could rewrite my life. The day Rough Close was sold and my parents moved to Lincolnshire was the day my past vanished. It was as though Cumbria had never existed. I couldn't go back home because there was no home to go back to. There was only a void I could fill with stories.

I arrived in Farm Place, Kensington, with my cheap suitcase and no money for the taxi I'd been instructed to take from Euston. For several awful moments I thought no one was at home, as I stood on the doorstep like Orphan Annie. The taxi driver was becoming unpleasant by the time someone answered my frantic knocking. I'd gone to the wrong door. It wasn't a good start.

My employers were an odd couple. He was a middle-aged ex-naval officer who'd gone into the city; she was the daughter of wealthy aristocrats with a house in the country, racehorses, and an elegant apartment in Eton Square. Her income, from investments and Daddy's allowance, was bigger than her husband's salary. Their eighteen-month-old daughter Claire Louise was very sweet. I was amazed at their confidence in handing over such a precious infant to a teenage girl they'd never met. I knew nothing about babies and my track record in looking after my little brother wasn't exactly a recommendation. But on paper a farmer's daughter from the north, with nursing experience, probably looked ideal.

I made every mistake in the Norland Nanny's handbook as well as committing a long list of social solecisms. When sent to Dickins & Jones to buy the baby some shoes, I bought the wrong kind and they had to be sent back. I risked choking her by giving her muesli for breakfast. I gave my employers kippers on toast with fish knives and forks. I'd never used a washing machine before, so I put the baby's clothes in on the wrong cycle and shrank her little Harrods' cashmere cardigans. My child-caring skills certainly didn't come up to the standards of 'Old Nanny', the elderly woman who had brought up Mrs C-H and her siblings. Old Nanny lived in a 'grace and favour' apartment and was sometimes invited to tea. She looked me up and down and did not approve.

Every afternoon I had to walk the baby in her pram in Kensington Gardens with all the other au pairs and nannies. The snobbery was astonishing – I hadn't anticipated uniform and pram envy. But nannies also had a lively social life that ran in parallel with that of their employers. We had play-days and away-days and invited each other and our charges round to tea. I made friends with two other au pairs. Anne, from Devon, who intended to spend a year in London while she decided what to do with her life, working for a merchant banker in Holland Park, and Liz, from Norfolk, who worked for a TV scriptwriter and his actress wife and wanted to be a career nanny. We were invited to smart houses and television studios. Seeing 'how the other half lived' opened our eyes very wide indeed. I met one Scottish girl who was desperately homesick. She was working for a husband and wife who were both doctors with three children under five. She rarely managed a night's sleep and her employer had just announced that she was having another baby. Sheila hadn't felt courageous enough to tell them she wanted to leave, so she had put an entry on the family calendar: 'Sheila is leaving on the 30th'.

At first I loved the cosmopolitan feel of London. I went to art galleries and museums, and looked longingly at clothes I couldn't afford in shops like Biba and Mary Quant. I joined the young Socialists, read *Paris Match* to keep up my French, and bought a new publication called *Nova*, which was flagged as 'a politically radical, beautifully designed, intellectual women's magazine'. When I stood on the pavement to watch Churchill's funeral cortège go past, I thought I was at the centre of things that mattered. But I felt nothing. Emotionally, I was in some kind of limbo.

I went out clubbing with Anne on our evenings off, staggering back along the deserted streets in various stages of inebriation, ignoring the kerb crawlers. I fed the baby breakfast through hangovers as thick as black fog. I lost my virginity to some newly arrived South African I met at the International Club in Earl's Court. I went back to his hotel room for a coffee and was too embarrassed to admit that I hadn't realised that coffee was a euphemism for sex. I risked pregnancy, rather than admit I was a green girl from the country and not the sophisticated, cool young woman I'd been posing as. He gave me a five-pound note to get a taxi home but didn't bother to get out of bed to see me out. It felt like prostitution. I put the fiver in the first bin I came to, and walked. I got away with it, but it was a dangerous game.

After a couple of months, I was given a weekend off and went to Lincolnshire to visit my parents for the first time. The landscape didn't attract me. The flat lands of East Anglia spread out to the far horizon on either side of the train; they were featureless prairies that did nothing for my spirits. My father collected me from the station and took me out to the Yarborough Estate. I was shocked at the small, terraced cottage they were living in, part of a complex of estate workers' houses. There was one living room, barely big enough for the three-piece suite, a narrow, cold kitchen, downstairs bathroom and two tiny bedrooms above. I slept on a put-u-up bed wedged behind the sofa in the living room.

When my parents were in bed, my brother and I sat up talking. He told me how much he hated the comprehensive school he'd been sent to. It was twice the size of the Cumbrian school he'd left and best described as rough. I guessed he was being bullied again. One of the things the boys tormented him about was the family's new mode of transport. The Lambretta had only been able to hold two people, which meant that they could never go out as a family. Exposure to the cold winds of East Anglia was also proving difficult for my mother's arthritis, so

Dad had sold the scooter. He couldn't drive a car, but because he had a motorcycle licence he could drive a three-wheeler and he'd bought a new Reliant Robin. Gordon was mortified. He was still bitter about all the other things that had been left behind – the piano, his friends, and particularly the farm. 'Dad didn't need to sell it,' he said. 'He could've rented out the land and carried on working.'

I thought much the same, but neither of us was thinking about our mother and what it had done to her. She still looked ill. She told me the doctor at the hospital in Boston thought she had rheumatoid arthritis and they were going to send her to a spa for treatment. She was in so much pain she'd had to give up knitting, and even holding a book was difficult. Apparently the agent for Lord Yarborough wasn't impressed, because my mother was supposed to feed all the poultry as one of her responsibilities (husbands and wives were a job lot), but her wrists were too painful to carry the buckets. She was finding my brother moody and uncooperative and difficult to understand. In her reading diary she borrowed *Journey Through Adolescence* by Consultant Psychiatrist Doris Odlum, which received three stars.

Dad didn't seem particularly happy either. Tugging his forelock wasn't something he did naturally. But he said he was learning a lot about pedigree breeding and took me to see the prize-winning Hereford herd he was looking after. He was very proud of them, but they weren't his own. Every payday was a reminder of his status; his payslips said 'stockman' at the top, a big step down from land-owning farmer. On the Sunday of my visit, we went to Grimsby for the day. It was a town that felt as if

195

Dad and a prize-winning Hereford

it was dying, though it had obviously once been a thriving fishing port. We stood together on the dock, eating fish and chips, and watching the mud-coloured sea rolling in and out with the tide in a mood of collective dejection. We were a family in exile.

Whatever the distance between us, Mum and I always managed to find something to talk about. Almost the first thing we would say to each other was 'What are you reading?' Mum's writing during those years, in her little diary, was strangely unlike her usual elegant copperplate, as her crippled fingers struggled to find new ways to shape the letters. Non-fiction titles outnumbered fiction by four to one. She had become very fond of memoirs, but I was intrigued to find that *Surprised by*

Joy, written by one of her favourite authors, C.S. Lewis, was only given three stars. There were a few books related to East Anglia, and there were the usual self-help titles, including *Healing and Wilderness* and *Women and Fatigue*. My mother's underlying medical conditions were still undiagnosed, and she was very far from the wilderness landscapes she loved. When I asked her what she thought of Lincolnshire, she replied cryptically, 'It's very flat.'

Much of her reading was now centred around the growing debate on apartheid in South Africa. She read novels about the Boer War, factual books about the Boer settlement of southern Africa and then found *Naught for Your Comfort* by Father Trevor Huddleston, which became a seminal book for her, and for me when she passed it on. 'You have to read this book,' she said, and went on to read everything he wrote and quote him regularly in her letters and conversation. He became one of her heroes.

Trevor Huddleston was born in Britain but sent out to South Africa as a priest. He was appalled by the inequality and brutality of conditions there for black people, and became a friend of Nelson Mandela and a partner in the fight against apartheid. He founded the Anti-Apartheid Movement and threw himself into youth work. He set up a jazz band and is credited with giving Hugh Masekela his first trumpet. The young Desmond Tutu, later to become South Africa's first black bishop, was one of his protégés. Huddleston worked so tirelessly for the anti-apartheid cause that his life was endangered. Eventually the Church recalled him to England, where his stark, moving account of the struggle was responsible, together with Alan Paton's *Cry, the Beloved*

Country, for drawing international attention to conditions in South Africa. Books are powerful.

I was too busy enjoying myself to be reading much, but I was writing my first novel, a Gothic horror set on the wild northern moors, somewhere between *Wuthering Heights* and *Cold Comfort Farm*. In a magazine I had found a photograph of a girl sitting with her knees drawn up and her back to the camera, on a chair in front of a window. She was gazing out, but it wasn't clear what

she was looking at. There was something about that girl that made me want to write about her. What was she dreaming of, as she looked out of the window? I began to write about a girl whose parents are divorcing, whose mother goes to London. She feels torn between town and country. I threw in some sexual abuse, a few family secrets and a haunted ruin.

Mary in Short Street, from my first novel

Meanwhile Mum, clinging on to sanity by her fingernails, separated from her family and friends, was still reading self-help books and consoling herself with poetry. Wordsworth was her favourite – and she had a small anthology that she'd bought on a visit to Keswick when she was eighteen and had fallen in love with the Lake District. One of her favourite poems was 'Lines Composed a Few Miles above Tintern Abbey'. For my mother, as well as the poet, the 'tall rock, / The mountain, and the deep and gloomy wood' were 'Felt in the blood, and felt along the heart'. Despite all the hardships and isolation, she still longed to return to the north. Loyalty to my father kept her from complaining, but it was being tested to the limit. She was also reading Thomas Moore, another, lesser-known, early nineteenth-century poet, and she copied a revealing verse from one of his most famous poems, 'Farewell! – But Whenever You Welcome the Hour' into her commonplace book:

> Let Fate do her worst, there are relics of joy,
> Bright dreams of the past, which she cannot destroy;
> Which come in the night-time of sorrow and care,
> And bring back the features which joy used to wear.
> Long, long be my heart with such memories filled!
> Like the vase in which roses have once been distilled—
> You may break, you may shatter the vase, if you will,
> But the scent of the roses will hang round it still.

I was writing my own poetry by now–bleak, homesick, teenage verses. I desperately wanted to be a published writer but didn't know how to make it happen, where to go or who to talk to. I was too shy to speak to the intimidating TV scriptwriter who lived round the corner from my employers in London. A few years earlier, a friend had recommended that I send my work to a poet who was the cousin of historian A.J.P. Taylor. She wrote me a nice letter, telling me that if I wanted to be a writer I had to 'practise, practise, practise', which was exactly what I was doing. There were no creative writing courses in those days and 'being a

199

writer' was never mentioned as an option in career counselling at school. I didn't even know about the Poetry Society in London. If I'd found it, I would have been able to listen to contemporary poetry and meet other young writers starting out.

Instead, a boyfriend took me to the Troubadour and I started singing folk songs. I also discovered the shops selling second-hand books in the Charing Cross Road, where I bought tattered copies of poetry collections and novels. It was there that I bought the second book that would change my life: a French edition of the *Journal of Katherine Mansfield*. It had been owned by a Madeleine Kupfer in 1933 and she had scribbled all over it, as I was about to do.

Mansfield had been christened Kathleen, like me, and her father was also called Harold. She had come from New Zealand to London as a teenager and lost her way in a 'strange country'. Later I found out that she had been cast off by her family because she'd had an illegitimate child. She had made an impulsive marriage to a man she didn't love, to try to cover her mistake, and left him on their wedding night. The baby died and she contracted tuberculosis. Her life was short and tragic and magnificent. I fell in love. Here was someone who thought and felt as I did, who had struggled, as I was doing, with the longing to write something of quality. Someone who wanted to experience life without all the restrictions placed on women. 'Risk!' she wrote. 'Risk anything! Care no more for the opinions of others, for those voices. Do the hardest thing on earth for you. Act for yourself. Face the truth.'[20] That last instruction was something I wasn't very good at. No one knew me or my family in London, so I constructed a different narrative about my life for almost everyone I met. Sometimes I killed my parents off in a car crash. Sometimes I was running away from a violent home life. Once I told a man on a train that I was a widow with a small boy I'd left for my parents to bring up. Being just plain me was very boring.

Back in London, I wasn't very good at keeping in touch with my parents. When I'd been in Durham, living at the nurses' home, Dad had taken to phoning my boyfriend William to find out what I was doing and whether I was all right. In London, my mother telephoned every fortnight. They no longer had a phone in the house, so she had to walk up to the phone booth in the village to call me. Even if I was in when she called, I couldn't tell her anything that was going on in my life – I hadn't even been able to confess that I smoked and drank – but there was always family news to catch up on.

The mysterious Aunt Lilian was back in England, newly widowed. She had been on a ship coming back from Karachi, where Uncle John was a government official, and he had died suddenly from a seizure. In the blazing heat of the Indian Ocean, he had immediately been buried at sea. After years of suffering his violent temper, she had thrown her gigantic opal and diamond engagement ring into the sea after him. The ring was a symbol of everything Uncle John had stood for. Everything had to be big – cars, houses, jewellery, salaries. Mum told me about the rows they'd had when they came to stay. I remembered being taken out of the house to stand in the yard in hushed silence while they shouted at each other. Mum said that it wasn't just words;

Lilian had shown her the bruises. John had flown Spitfires and Lancasters during the war, surviving against all the odds and rising to the rank of Group Captain – another man who'd had a 'bad war'. No one talked about PTSD then.

At least Lilian was there to comfort my North Shields grandmother. They had always been close, and she needed support now more than ever. Recently my grandfather, Thomas Sutherland, had been diagnosed with cancer, even though he had only been retired for a little while. The tumour had started in his mouth, a legacy of pipe smoking the doctors said, and spread to his brain. It hurt my mother to be living so far away and unable to help. I could hardly believe that I might never see him again. Cousin Jean, who was training to be a nurse, moved in to help our grandmother care for him. I planned to go up to stay during the Easter holidays, but he died while Mum was in the spa receiving treatment for her arthritis.

A fortnight later I lost my job. Dissatisfaction had been growing on both sides. Several times I forgot to put the toys away in the nursery before I went out for the evening. I grew tired of trying to fit my own social life round that of my employers. They often changed their minds at the last moment. 'I hope you don't mind,' Mrs C-H would drawl, 'but we've been invited out to drinks with John and Laura. You didn't have any important plans, did you?' I'd have to cancel any date I had or stand them up. I also hated having to peel vegetables and wash up for their frequent, lavish, dinner parties. At weekends I had to take them breakfast in bed and had only one day off a week, which was sometimes shortened to half a day if 'something came up'.

They also disapproved of my social life, which was wild by Cumbrian standards. I was like a child loose in a sweet shop, exploring the world of men. I even dated the man who came to fix the gas meter. He was a cockney, very entertaining, with old-fashioned ideas of how to treat a lady. He took me round to meet his mother and afterwards I got my friend Anne to ring him up and tell him I didn't want to see him again. I lost count of the men I went out with. One night, one of them rang my employer's number at about 1am, clearly inebriated, asking for Kathie. Mr C-H came down to my room to 'blast me out of the water' (in naval terminology), and was even more furious to discover that I wasn't in.

The final straw came on a wet Sunday night when I'd arranged to go out with a young Sri Lankan air force pilot. Sunday was his only free day. My employers were late back from their weekend away and I didn't feel I could leave him standing out in the rain. So I invited him into the small sitting room they allowed me to use. It was all very innocent. He was an intelligent, respectful man whose company I liked very much. I didn't think anything of it – the baby was in bed and the sitting room was mine to entertain my friends when they came round. However, when my employers finally arrived it was obvious that they were livid. Doors were banged. I was told that they would 'see me in the morning'.

They were waiting for me in the breakfast room the next day when I brought the baby down. They were not happy with my behaviour, I was told. They felt their child was 'in moral danger' and they were going to write to my parents. I was given a week's notice and Mr C-H said that he felt I should go home and grow up a little.

The upper classes, I'd discovered, had a very old-fashioned moral code. My employer's youngest sister, the same age as me, was a debutante, doing 'the season'. One night, she and a girlfriend had invited two or three university students back to her parent's Eton Square flat for drinks after a party. This ranked as a potential scandal, a family emergency. Mrs C-H went round to read the riot act and her parents arrived from the country. Susannah was gated. The students weren't part of 'society' and didn't know its rules. She and her friend weren't allowed to be alone with men without a chaperone. Dating a person of colour would have been a crime so terrible there would have been no rehabilitation. By inviting my Sri Lankan pilot in, I had apparently tainted their sitting room forever.

I'd been expecting to be sacked ever since I arrived, almost courting it, but I was still stunned when it happened. Mrs C-H wrote a patronising letter to my father. She made the mistake of telling him my crime; I had invited a coloured man into the house without their permission. Two days later she showed me his reply. It didn't surprise me at all, though it obviously shocked her. My father's dignified letter stated that he had absolute confidence in his daughter and was sure that she would make her own way in the world. They trusted me completely, and I felt a flush of shame because I knew I was not to be trusted at all. I was letting them down every day in some way or other. I felt permanently guilty.

I couldn't go home. There was no home to go to. Even if I'd wanted to go back to my parents, the Lincolnshire cottage had no room for me. I went down to the Labour Exchange and asked for a job. They took my details and seemed very interested in my O-levels, my nursing experience and my shorthand and typing (which I prayed I could still remember). They sent me to the Ministry of Health, Staff Welfare Department, to be interviewed for the position of personal assistant to the Chief Welfare Officer.

Gerry Asquith was an ex-Welsh Guards Officer. He was compassionate, extremely knowledgeable about human nature and had a marked twinkle in his eye. We liked each other straight away. Within twenty-four hours of being sacked, I had another job. Staff Welfare also held the civil service list of approved lodgings. Two days later, I had a bedsit in the attic of an opera singer's house in South London. I was free to be my own person, whoever that was. I was still trying to create a self that I could bear to live with, inhabiting an alternative reality. 'Elaborate are . . . the labyrinths in which we hide the minotaurs who have our faces,' writes Rebecca Solnit.[21] I was the Minotaur's daughter, lost in the dark corridors of my own intricate labyrinth.

I wrote to my parents, telling them my new address and saying how sorry I was that I hadn't made a success of the job. My father replied, saying that neither of them had expected the nannying to last, and wishing me all the best in my new position. He added that he was writing because my mother's hands were too painful to hold a pen. I didn't know it, but they must have been worrying themselves sick over me.

On my first day, I signed the Official Secrets Act. The Staff Welfare filing cabinet held personal files on everyone, up to the Top Job. I would be prosecuted if I disclosed information. Some of it was very sensitive. Senior female civil servants were not allowed to marry and were forced to resign their positions if they did. I was surprised by the number of very high-ranking women who were secretly married and had even managed to conceal the births of children. Gerry Asquith knew everything about everyone.

My life settled into a routine. Every morning I woke to the sound of scales being sung two floors below. Up and down, up and down, in ever increasing tonal increments, until my landlady reached the limits of her range. The last few notes were always excruciating. Sometimes a male voice would accompany her. There were late-night parties in the garden below. It made me feel very lonely.

Every morning I walked, part of an anonymous human herd going in the same direction, to Brixton Station, where I caught a train to the Elephant and Castle and the featureless 1960s glass and concrete building I worked in. During the day I typed letters, filed papers, and ate my lunch in the canteen. I came home every evening to my attic room, with its single bed under the eaves, a stale bottle of milk, and enforced solitude. The dormer window looked out onto a bleak London landscape of soot-stained trees and rooftops. I had my garret, but it wasn't creative.

I was an exile, in mourning for a familiar farm, the sound of crows in the garth, a line of hills. There are some places that seep into your bones, become so part of you that separation feels like an amputation. I wrote poems and stories in an attempt to make myself whole again. When I read the New Zealand author Janet Frame's autobiography, I understood exactly what she meant when she wrote, 'All writers are exiles wherever they live and their work is a lifelong journey towards the lost land'. [22]I was trying to write myself back.

On sunny days my future seemed to be opening up, but I still didn't know what direction I would take. There were so many choices. I had a place at Newcastle University if I passed my A-level exams. But that meant studying at evening classes for another year. I went to a couple of sessions in a cold school hall with a bored and disillusioned Further Education teacher and gave up.

I was still going to the Troubadour and other folk clubs in London. My friend Anne and I went to Sidmouth Folk Festival. Music had always been a big part of my identity. Could it be all of it? I'd had some rudimentary training from the school choir and the gospel singing group, but I wanted to be able to sing properly. I'd started taking singing lessons when I arrived in London. Answering an advert in a shop window in Kensington, I'd signed up with an Australian who'd written books on vocal training and who seemed to know what he was doing. It was all muscle control, apparently. I had a lot of chest muscles from heaving hay bales around, so that seemed like good preparation. But when I lost my job, I didn't have the money to pay for lessons.

However, Gerry Asquith could fix anything. Very soon, I was being auditioned by an Irish tenor with the English National Opera who did some tutoring at the Royal Academy. John agreed to coach me for free. He told me there was a scholarship, named after Kathleen Ferrier, for young singers who came from Cumbria. I liked him, and the evening lessons, with three or four other hopefuls, always ended in the pub. I learned to sing songs by Mahler and Elgar; I sang Handel, Gluck and Saint-Saëns. I felt alive and happy. And I was still writing. I finished the novel, typed it up on a borrowed typewriter and sent it off to a publisher whose address I copied from the inside of a book in the library. Writing or music? It seemed there was a choice, but I couldn't do both. Singing required absolute dedication, John told me. The three or four other people he taught were very committed, with tunnel vision. I could see that there would be no room in my life for anything else if I carried on with my vocal training.

If ever there was a time when I needed good advice, this was it. But during this period of my life I wasn't in touch with my mother. I felt that my parents had abandoned me and it was Mum's fault. She could have persuaded my father to stay in the Lake District if she'd tried. There was no need to move so far away and dislocate all our lives. On top of all that, I had discovered on my first visit to Lincolnshire that Mum had thrown away all my childhood belongings during the removal. My diaries had gone, my notebooks, and many of the books I had assumed were safe. Had my mother learned nothing from her own mother's destruction of Mum's belongings after the war? It made me very angry and I stopped writing to my parents. Dad wrote to me every few weeks – rather formal letters that lacked Mum's chatty style. She had been to the spa for mud baths, massage and physiotherapy, he reported. She felt better after three weeks of total rest, but was still having difficulty writing. Her fingers had twisted until they resembled swans' necks. I didn't go to Lincolnshire to see her, partly out of a sense of hopelessness and partly because I didn't have the money for the train fare.

In London, things changed for the worse. My friend Anne went home to Devon. She'd had enough of being an au pair. Liz moved further away to another job as a proper nanny. An intense relationship with a pharmacist ended badly when his supposedly ex girlfriend and I discovered that he was seeing both of us at the same time. The people I worked with were all much older than me. I knew no one my own age and wasn't confident enough to go out to clubs alone. If I went out in the evening, I didn't feel safe walking back through Brixton on my own late at night. I was desperately homesick, chronically lonely, but too proud to admit that I might have made a mistake in coming to London. It was too big. There were too many people, too many houses, in too many noisy streets stinking of exhaust fumes and garbage. I was used to solitude, actually longed for it at times, but this was a different kind of isolation. I missed open spaces, trees, the sound of a beck falling over rocks, curlews. I read the nineteenth-century mystic and naturalist Richard Jefferies, having stumbled on his work in the library. One of the books he wrote, a collection of field notes and observations, was *Nature Near London* and in it he put into words what I felt about life in the city: 'There is a dust that chokes the spirit . . .'[23]

At exactly this moment, I met the man whose life I would share for the next twenty years.

14

FOR BETTER OR FOR WORSE

One Sunday evening, depressed and homesick, I crept into the back of the church on the other side of the street from my lodgings. It had a comforting familiarity: the stained glass, the lit candles, the smell of musty hassocks, the chanted repetitions of the liturgy my mother loved, the organ music throbbing from the pipes overhead. Even though I had given up on religion, I still felt its pull; the attraction of certainty and the illusion of security. What was that chorus we had sung at the back of the bus on the way to our gospel gigs? 'Safe in the arms of Jesus, Safe in the arms of Love'.

Part of me still longed for that feeling of being cared for. But the congregation was small and elderly. I was disappointed to discover that there would be no youth groups here, no chance to meet other people my own age. Afterwards, as we filed out, the vicar drew me to one side. He was an elderly man, only a few inches taller than me, plump, balding, but with kind eyes behind his wire-rimmed glasses. He welcomed me to the church, asked where I lived, and where I'd come from. 'Oh, the Lake District!' he said. 'I go there every year for my annual holiday. You must come to tea!' and then, looking down at someone who had come up to stand at his elbow, added 'Mustn't she, mother?' The tiny lady standing beside us, swathed in fox furs, looked fragile, but had a kind of fierce energy, as she said, 'Of course!' The fine-lined, heart-shaped face, almost invisible under the veil of her dark blue hat, was a caricature of what it must once have been. 'Come!' she said to me over her shoulder as she stomped off. It was impossible to refuse. This was my first meeting with Hilda Glover Jones, always known as Gran, the indomitable force at the centre of the family.

The vicarage behind the church was like a Victorian Gothic movie set. The front door opened into a vast hallway with a wide mahogany staircase on two sides leading up to a gallery. Above my head was a glass lantern to let in the light. Some of the panes were cracked and there was a bucket in the middle of the floor to catch the leaks. I was ushered into a freezing sitting room with floor-to-ceiling windows, through which the wind easily found its way. Around the empty marble fireplace was an assortment of shabby antique furniture and a threadbare oriental carpet. My offers of help with tea were refused by Gran as though I had committed an offence, so I perched on the edge of one of the chairs and waited.

The vicar arrived without his robes and chatted politely, standing with his back to the non-existent fire. He had a daughter about my age, he said, who had just gone up to Newcastle University to study modern languages. We made stilted conversation until the door opened and two young men came in, one pushing a trolley. They were introduced as his sons, presumably the owners of the sports cars parked outside the door. Paul, the eldest, already balding like his father, barely spoke. Christopher, slim and bearded, shook hands in a friendly manner. He ordered Gran to sit down, which seemed to be a familiar joke between them, positioned the trolley next to her while he poured her a cup of tea, and then brought one to me. A cake stand, holding rather dry fruit buns, scorched at the edges, was passed around. These were, I was told, Gran's famous cakes. To refuse was not an option.

I was aware of a strange dynamic. All three men deferred to the frail bundle of energy in the smallest chair. And there was a distinct feeling of antagonism between the sons and their father. There was no mention of a mother. I felt that I had walked on stage in the middle of a Chekhov play. As the conversation went on, more details were revealed. They were from Wales originally, an alliance of two families, the Joneses and the Glovers.

Gran was a Glover. She talked of having brothers who were six feet tall. One of them owned a castle. Her family had not approved of her marrying a Jones, so her name had been added to his. She talked of being in Algiers before and during the First World War. Her husband had been sent there originally by the family business to sell coal to the ships going in and out of the Mediterranean. She had entertained all the ships' captains and even ridden on a camel. The vicar had been born there, in 1909, and I realised that he was more than ten years older than my mother. I was shown photographs of Gran and a friend, in front of a huge villa, posing as statues, in long dresses, twirling parasols. The sons were very quiet, and, after the vicar got out the photographs of his Lake District holidays, they disappeared.

After tea I walked back across the road to my bedsit. 'Do come again,' the vicar said, as he shook my hand warmly at the door. I murmured some kind of pleasantry, but I had no intention of doing so; I'd already begun to think of moving. Naively, I thought that changing location might lift my spirits, not having learned that when you move you take your problems with you. I only knew that living on the fringes of Brixton restricted my social life.

Staff Welfare was always given a block of tickets for theatre, opera and West End shows when audiences were thin. Gerry Asquith made sure that some of them came to me. I saw Wagner's *Ring Cycle* from so far up in the gods that you needed a telescope to see the stage, but still came out stunned. I went to the Royal Court to see plays by Joe Orton, Samuel Beckett and John Osborne. There were tickets for the Old Vic, where I saw Oscar Wilde and Bernard Shaw for the first time. I went to revues on Shaftesbury Avenue, and laughed at *Camelot*, *Oh, What a Lovely War* and *Wait a Minim*. I saw all the classics, as well as terrible shows in empty theatres and newly opened try-outs. It was great fun but always spoiled by the thought of that long scary walk back through dark streets.

I looked at the civil service accommodation list and went to see a bedsit in a house just off the Finchley Road in Hampstead. It wasn't far from a tube station that went straight to the Elephant. The owner of the house was an elderly spinster with a whiskery chin who told me that she earned a living as a private nurse. I imagined glamorous locations and rich clients, but it was mainly, she said, giving enemas to gentlemen who didn't, medically, need them. It all sounded very peculiar. But the room was comfortable, with a south-facing window and the location was buzzing with activity.

I didn't realise it would be just as difficult to meet people there as it had been in South London, and it was much more expensive. Out of my wage of seven pounds eight shillings a week, I had to spend three pounds ten shillings on rent. Sometimes I had to choose between eating and the tube fare to work. I ate as much as I could in the canteen, using my luncheon vouchers, and smuggled the odd bread roll home in my bag. The people I worked with were aware of my situation and I had several weekend invitations to lunch. They were all very kind, but it somehow made me feel worse. Their happy, settled lives were a million miles away from mine.

One Sunday I fell asleep on the tube going home and woke up at one of the stops near Camberwell. On impulse, instead of changing stations and getting another train, I got out and walked back to my old lodgings. As I stood looking up at the house, wondering if my old landlady was in, the church bells began to ring. The Rev Jones was standing outside to welcome parishioners to Evensong. He waved to me and I went over to say hello. He seemed to assume that I was coming to church, so I did. I found the building even colder and more depressing than the first time. When I came out, Gran was waiting for me. It seemed that I was going to the vicarage for tea again.

There was only one sports car outside the door this time. Inside I heard the sound of laughter and a young female voice from the sitting room. 'This is Yvette,' Gran said, as she introduced me to the tall, dark girl who came forward to meet us. 'She's our new French teaching assistant at the school.' Yvette's personality was impulsive, warm and lively and everyone seemed to respond to her. The two young men were in the sitting room and Paul, the older of the two, was actually smiling. Over tea and the inevitable buns, Yvette teased the vicar, flirted with his sons, and bossed Gran around in a scandalous manner.

It was now dark outside and I was invited to supper. Cold meat and fried potatoes left over from Sunday lunch were laid out on the table. Yvette said that she couldn't eat any of it because of her delicate digestion and helped herself to a bowl of Cornflakes. Gran looked disapproving but said nothing. Afterwards as I got up to go, the vicar suddenly said, 'Oh, it's much too late to walk to the station on your own.' He turned to his sons. 'Christopher, can you give her a lift in my car?'

As he opened the door of the rather battered Rover in the driveway, Christopher explained that he'd 'pranged' his own car on the way back from Brands Hatch and it was still being repaired. Although very quiet in the house, once we got into the car he began to talk, asking me questions about my parents, my childhood, what I was doing in London. He seemed genuinely interested in the answers. 'I might as well take you up to Hampstead,' he said. Soon we were talking animatedly about everything and anything. We discovered that we both felt 'different', slightly apart from the life that was going on around us. We both had the sense that we didn't fit in.

He asked me to call him Chris and told me he'd been brought up in a vicarage in Derby, in a house he'd loved with a big copper beech in the garden. His mother had died suddenly when he was eleven and they'd all come to London so that Gran could look after them. He'd been at boarding school since he was six years old. The few details he shared were bleak. He was now twenty-six, a civil engineer working for a consulting firm in West London. He'd been engaged to marry a girl he'd known since she was sixteen and he was twenty, but she'd jilted him at the last moment to marry someone else. 'She was pregnant,' he said. 'But it wasn't mine.'

When we reached Lithos Road we sat outside in the car for over an hour, just talking to each other. He didn't make any attempt to touch me, which was surprising. My previous experience of men had been very different. As I gathered my belongings to leave, he suddenly asked if I would like to go out to dinner one evening the following week, once he'd got his own car back. I said yes and gave him my phone number. I hoped he meant it.

He took me out to a very expensive restaurant on the riverfront at Henley and drove me down the M4 in his newly repaired sports car, with the top off. Unfortunately, he'd left the top at home and there was a sudden thunderstorm on the way there. I'd taken a lot of trouble to dress and do my hair for this date, but by the time we got to Henley we both looked as if we'd been fished out of the river. I thought the head waiter was going to refuse us entry, but he led us to a table in an obscure corner at the back of the restaurant where we sat, dripping quietly onto the carpet and laughing into our wine. I wasn't used to restaurants of any kind, but my time in Kensington had given me a knowledge of tableware and etiquette that came in very useful.

We drove home, still soaked, and still laughing at the ridiculous situation. When we called in at the vicarage to retrieve the top of the car, there was considerable surprise, not altogether approving, on the faces of both the vicar and Gran. Chris was going off to Germany with his sister Jenny at the weekend, so this was the last time I would see him for a while. Back in my bedsit, I wondered if I would ever hear from him again. What did he see in me? He was one of the public-school-educated, young professional sports-car set, hanging out in classy clubs, doing the rounds of Twickenham, Wimbledon, Henley, Brands Hatch, and other places people went to be seen. He even had a season ticket for the Proms. I was a gauche teenager from the north, in cheap clothes, with a Cumbrian accent, a big nose and no glamour. Worse still, I had no social conversation and only wanted to talk about politics and books. Most men I met said I was 'too intense'.

But letters began arriving from Germany. Jenny said afterwards that he had told her he had met the most amazing girl, a girl he wanted to spend his life with. When he came back, he rang me straight away to invite me out, but I was going to a Foreign Office party with my boss, as his PA. Chris arranged to pick me up afterwards. It was a very sophisticated party, with drinks and canapés circulating freely. Having grown up in a teetotal household, I was inexperienced where alcohol was concerned. I knew about beer and wine, but no one had told me not to mix my drinks. I didn't understand that cocktails were a lethal combination of spirits. They may have tasted of orange juice or lemonade, but they were deceptively strong.

When Chris arrived to collect me, I could barely walk. He didn't feel he could take me back to my lodgings in the state I was in, so he took me to the vicarage, where Gran and the vicar had gone away for a long weekend in Wales. He put me to bed in the spare room and I spent the night throwing up in the bathroom and everywhere else. Chris's father and grandmother returned unexpectedly in the night and were very shocked to find me there, but it was obvious that nothing immoral was going on, as I could barely lift my head out of the toilet long enough to say hello. They plied me with black coffee in the morning, but I was still too ill to go to work. How our relationship survived this unpromising beginning, I have no idea. My in-laws never forgot their first impressions.

Our relationship became serious very quickly. It was the first deep love affair I'd ever had. I was lost. He took me to places I'd only ever dreamed of. A friend owned a racing car so we went to race tracks; he took me to Annie's Room, the new jazz club everyone wanted to go to. I met his friends and their girlfriends, who were all terrifying. The girls had long hair and long legs, clothes by Mary Quant, and had been educated at St Paul's and Cheltenham Ladies College. I wore the same jumpers and skirts I wore to work, mostly bought in chain stores. Patent leather was in fashion at the time and I had a new imitation patent handbag I thought was quite acceptable by my parents' standards. But when he brought me home that night, Chris said he didn't want to see me with it again. It was cheap and shoddy and let him down. He would buy me a decent one for Christmas. It hurt, but I knew he was right. To be with him and his friends, I needed some decent clothes. I spent most of my time with them feeling inferior.

A few weeks after we met, Chris was sent down to Plymouth as an engineer working on a new cement factory. It was part of his career path, he said, that he would have to travel and go anywhere the company had a contract. I was alone in London again and, apart from Yvette, without friends. I was also afraid that Chris would meet someone prettier, more confident, altogether more suitable, and I would lose him. I spent a lot of time at the vicarage with Yvette, curled up in her big double bed to escape the freezing cold of a huge Victorian house the family couldn't afford to heat. She had come from a warmer climate and wasn't used to it. She, like me, found the atmosphere in the house depressing. Chris's brother Paul never appeared except, briefly, for meals, and rarely spoke or made eye contact. He was an enigma.

As soon as they were aware that we were seeing each other seriously, the attitude of Chris's family changed. Gran became my enemy. Chris was her favourite grandson and I simply wasn't good enough. I was a 'silly girl' with no background. The vicar changed from being a genial clergyman to a cold, critical figure who questioned my suitability as a partner for his son. I found him austere and distant. My thin veneer of self-esteem dissolved in the atmosphere of hostility, and Chris wasn't there to defend me.

I became suicidal, crying all the time; so depressed I couldn't even go to work. Gerry Asquith came to my lodgings and arranged for me to see a doctor, who then referred me to a psychiatrist at a London hospital, where I talked and cried through several interviews. To make things even worse, the publishers returned my novel. I read the letter very quickly and all I saw was the refusal. I barely read the paragraph that told me the writing had promise and if I rewrote sections of the book they would look at it again. I was too inexperienced to know that this was encouragement. I threw the manuscript into the bottom of the wardrobe and vowed to stop writing. I also gave up singing abruptly. I didn't go to a concert where I was supposed to sing, and went Christmas shopping with my future sister-in-law instead. Afterwards I was thoroughly ashamed of myself, but I never went back, not even to apologise and thank John for what he'd done for me.

I was prescribed pills that made me look at the world as if through cloudy glass. There was nothing wrong with my mind, the psychiatrist said. I was sad, homesick, lonely and coping with family animosity on my own. Then he said something that turned my world around. 'If my son brought you home and said he wanted to marry you,' he told me, 'I would be immensely proud to have you as my daughter-in-law.' It wasn't me, it was them.

On his next weekend in London, Chris decided the situation was impossible and we should get married straight away. We got officially engaged sitting on the stairs at a rather wild party in Islington. In those days it wasn't possible for us to live together out of wedlock; the son of a vicar and the daughter of a Methodist preacher couldn't share a bed without causing a scandal. Marriage meant that I could move to Plymouth and we could rent a flat together. I would get some kind of job while we saved money. This whirlwind relationship raised eyebrows. Chris's father called his son into the study and asked whether there were 'any pressing reasons' for such a hasty marriage. But I wasn't pregnant – more by luck than by good behaviour. Chris didn't care about the disapproval. His father disapproved of him anyway, he said; and his elder brother Paul didn't even speak to him, though he never explained why. The brothers always referred to their father as 'the old man'.

Chris didn't buy me an engagement ring, which upset me at first. He was superstitious because he'd bought his previous fiancée an enormous sapphire and diamond ring before she jilted him. He was also short of money, as he was still paying for the fence he'd demolished on the way back from Brands Hatch, which hadn't been covered by the insurance. We drove up to Lincolnshire, where my parents gave Chris their approval. From their point of view, he was a lovely, polite young man with a secure career and he was a vicar's son. There was nothing to object to, apart from my age. They signed the consent forms and didn't try to talk me out of it.

Perhaps they were relieved to have me safely off their hands. But they had never stopped me doing anything, however foolish, and I sometimes wished, later on, that they had. Didn't they care what happened to me? It was only later that I realised how tolerant they had been, with such a headstrong, stubborn daughter. My mother would look at me with hurt, bewildered eyes, while I tore up all her hopes and dreams for me, but there were never any recriminations. I asked her once, when things had gone badly wrong in my life, 'Why didn't you stop me?'

'Oh, Kathie,' she said wearily, 'I could never stop you doing anything once you'd decided to do it.'

I couldn't have a church wedding in London. That had been planned with the previous fiancée and Chris was adamant that he didn't want to go through it again. I was disappointed not to be 'princess for the day', but I knew my parents couldn't afford a church wedding with all the trimmings. They were still paying off their own debts. The sale of the farm had repaid the mortgage and the bank loans, but not the money they had borrowed from family and friends.

I would have loved to have been married in Caldbeck village, in the chapel, with all my friends and family around me, but it wasn't possible under the archaic laws of the time, because I no longer lived in the parish. That was a big blow. It would have to be the register office near Chris's family in London. Brixton was still one of the most impoverished areas of London – gentrification was far into the future – but Brixton it would have to be. My mother sent me a hundred pounds to buy my wedding dress, shoes and a going-away outfit. It wasn't much, but it would be just enough if I was careful.

What did one wear for a register office wedding? I was determined not to let my new husband down in front of his family and friends. I chose a short, white, Swiss lace cocktail dress with a matching coat, bought in the wedding department of John Lewis. One of the women in the office suggested I should have a hairband of flowers in place of a veil, rather than a hat. It was all very sixties; a rebellious, anti-traditional affair, with a do-it-yourself reception in the church hall. The only exception was the cake. Gran was going to make me a present of a three-tier fairytale confection and Princess Margaret's cook was going to make it. It added a touch of class to what was, in his family's view as well as mine, a shabby wedding.

Two weeks before the wedding, a parcel arrived at my lodgings. Inside, wrapped in layers of damp newspaper, were some twigs with enormous, brown buds just beginning to feather into green. There was a letter with them from a woman called Gill Curwen. She and her husband had bought the farmhouse at Rough Close as a holiday home. She said she knew how special the place had been for me, neighbours had given her my address and she thought I would like the sticky buds from the chestnut tree in the garth. 'Spring is so beautiful here,' she wrote. Just holding them and remembering made my heart ache. I put them in a jam jar on the windowsill and watched them unfurl in the warmth.

There was a Highgate address on the letter and I was invited to visit for an evening meal when they came back to London. The Curwen household was one of the happiest and most chaotic I had ever been in. There were children and cats (at least four of each) everywhere. The plates and cutlery didn't match, some of them weren't very clean, and the cats walked up and down the table while we ate. My mother would have been horrified, but I thought it was wonderfully eccentric. Gill seemed completely unfazed by anything. She was a painter, she explained; her husband, Michael, was a hospital administrator. They would only be at Rough Close during school holidays. Would I like to go and stay sometime? Had we booked a honeymoon anywhere?

We had arranged to go to Derbyshire so that Chris could show me his old home, but it would be no effort to drive a hundred and fifty miles or so further north so that I could show him mine. I wanted to be back at Rough Close more than anything and I felt it wouldn't be possible for anyone to understand who I was until they had seen where I came from.

On the weekend of the wedding, my grandparents came down from the north and we all stayed in student rooms at King's College. It was bleak, cold weather. The rooms had shilling meters for the gas fires, and we soon ran out of coins. The day before the wedding, we were all invited to lunch at the vicarage. It was an ordeal for everyone. My future father-in-law put on his heartiest 'meet the parishioners' manner. My parents quailed before the array of family silver and cutlery set out by Gran on the antique lace tablecloth she'd chosen for the occasion.

My Carlisle grandparents became suddenly very 'working-class posh', and Annie Sutherland talked loudly across the table in her broad Tyneside accent to anyone who would listen, giving excruciating details of her husband's final moments. At least she could be relied on to be herself. Aware, as I now was, of the middle-class protocols to be observed on these occasions, I found myself, to my own mortification, both ashamed of my family and angry at my in-laws for forcing the people I loved into this false situation. Afterwards, Dad said that he'd felt patronised.

'It was as though I had straw in my hair,' he said. It was the only time my in-laws and my parents ever met.

On the day, I was up very early, unable to sleep, soaking in a hot bath in the student bathroom before going to get my hair done. Was I doing the right thing? Marriage was such a big step. I crushed any doubts far down inside. I wasn't going to jilt him, whatever last-minute wobbles I felt. So I dressed in my lace outfit with a headdress made of hyacinth blossoms, individually wired onto a satin band, and went, with my parents and grandparents, to the register office in Brixton, which was in a building that was due to be demolished. The wrecking ball stood outside in

Wedding day with my parents and father-in-law

the street, ready to begin and, although we laughed, it did feel rather ominous. But I didn't care. Everything was going to be all right. This was how it ended in fairytales, wasn't it? I wasn't a girl anymore, but on the threshold of becoming a woman, and I was married, no longer alone; I was stepping out into a shared future. It was a new adventure, a new chapter in the book of my life, though I had no idea where the plot was taking me. Jeannette Winterson wrote that every book is an adventure. 'Adventures are about the unknown. . . The situation can take us anywhere — across time and space, the globe, through the lives of people who can never be like us — into the heart of anguish we have never felt. . . Books read us back to ourselves.'[24] And that was where I desperately needed to go, back to my real self, if only I could discover who that was.

Caught up in the excitement of my new life, I failed to see that my mother was going through the same crisis. In the tangle of financial troubles, being loyal to my father, bringing up children, coping with chronic illness, she had lost sight of herself. Books with titles such as *The Radiant Life* and *The Secret of Happiness* appear in her diaries the year I was married, as well as a book that promised to show the reader how to *Be Your Real Self*, by Dr David Fink, which received three stars. In her commonplace book she copied out two inspirational passages from an anthology called *The Human Spirit*. The first is by the French philosopher priest, Teilhard De Chardin.

'I stepped down into the most hidden depths of my being, lamp in hand and ears alert, to discover whether in the deepest recesses of the blackness within me I might not see the glint of the waters of the current that flows on . . . I realised that my poor trifling existence was one with the immensity of all that is and all that is in the process of becoming.'

My mother added a line from Simone Weil; 'If we go down into ourselves we find that we possess exactly what we desire'.

On my wedding day, unaware of her mental and emotional turmoil, I changed into my going-away outfit and climbed into my husband's car. An item in the local paper showed a smiling couple under the headline 'Vicar's son marries budding authoress'. I didn't just want to be a woman; I wanted to be a woman and a writer. The manuscript of my first novel and its rejection letter were lying at the bottom of the wardrobe, hidden by clutter, but a new notebook and pen had been packed optimistically into the battered cardboard suitcase I'd brought from Rough Close, which still held all I possessed. I couldn't wait to begin again.

Postscript

Why does anyone write an autobiography? That's a question I kept asking myself over the five years it's taken me to write this one. Firstly, it's been an attempt to understand my mother. Secondly, to try to understand my own childhood and the ways it marked me and my brother – him, in particular. He became estranged from the family, causing a great deal of grief, and died before he became an old man, as a homeless alcoholic. So, I suppose that was a strong motivation. Lastly, I wrote this for my children and his children, so they could know and understand their heritage.

Writing it has been hard, forcing me to revisit painful episodes from childhood. I was helped by diaries, notebooks, scrapbooks and letters that I've kept from my teenage years, so I didn't have to rely on memory alone. I've tried to be as accurate as possible – I've tinkered with timelines occasionally to avoid repetition, and sometimes names have been altered to protect identities. It's as near the truth as I could make it. Everyone has a 'truth'.

This is mine.

With thanks to Angela Locke, friend and colleague, who read the first draft of the manuscript and my editor Kelly Davis, who's done a wonderful job with the original. Also, to Russell Holden of Pixel Tweaks for designing the cover and the interior.

I'm grateful to all the friends out there who've encouraged me to write this and for so many conversations with fellow writers about the problems of autobiographical writing. You all helped me to get it over the line.

Enjoyed reading this book? Want to know what happened next? *Reading My Mother, Pt 2: Writing My Way Home*, will be available soon. Advance publication details at: **www.kathleenjones.co.uk**

Bibliography

A Saint in Swindon, Alice Jolly, Fairlight Books, Oxford, 2020.

In Praise of Reading and Fiction, Mario Vargas Llosa, Farrar, Straus & Giroux, New York, 2011.

Bookworm, Lucy Mangan, Vintage, London, 2018.

On Reading, Marcel Proust, Souvenir Press, London 1972.

The Faraway Nearby, Rebecca Solnit, Granta, London, 2014.

The Child that Books Made, Francis Spufford, Faber, London, 2002.

The Prose Factory, D.J. Taylor, Vintage, London, 2016.

Proust and the Squid, Maryanne Wolf, Faber, London, 2007.

End Notes

1   The Weightman family, Wreay.

2   Goodreads, *Griselda*, www.goodreads.com/user/show/5752834-griselda accessed 03/06/20.

3   www.andthenweallhadtea.blogspot.com/2017/11/the-kitchen-prayer.html

4   Mario Vargas Llosa, '*In Praise of Reading and Fiction*', Nobel Acceptance Speech, Farrar Straus Giroux, New York, 2011.

5   John S. Dunne, *Love's Mind: An Essay on Contemplative Life*, University of Notre Dame Press, Indiana, p. 72.

6   Maryanne Wolf, *Proust and the Squid: The Story and Science of the Reading Brain*, Icon Books Ltd, London, 2008.

7   Alison Light, '*Returning to Manderley*', Feminist Literary Theory, ed. Mary Eagleton, Blackwell, Oxford, 1986.

8   Alice Jolly, *A Saint in Swindon*, Fairlight Books, Oxford, 2020.

9   Hugh Walpole, '*Childhood*', The Bookman: A Literary Journal, Volume 56, 1924, p. 294.

10 grevel.co.uk/lakedistrict/watendlath-a-wet-wednesday-with-walpole/ accessed 24/04/2024.

11 Carson Jay Robison, '*Life Gets Teejus, Don't It*', 1948.

12 Norman Nicholson, '*Grass of Parnassus*', Rock Face, Faber & Faber, London, 1948. With the kind permission of Irvine Hunt.

13 www.overwaterhall.co.uk/about/history/

14 *The Centauress*, Kathleen Jones, The Book Mill.

15 Yiyun Li, *Dear Friend, from My Life I Write to You in Your Life*, Penguin Random House, London, 2017, p. 25.

16 *Shepherd's wife* Irene Rutherford in 1963, photographed by her husband. Shutterstock.

17 Graham Greene, *The Lost Childhood and Other Essays*, Viking, New York, 1969, p. 13.

18 Rebecca Solnit, *The Faraway Nearby*, 'Mirrors', Granta, 2014, p. 30.

19 Rebecca Solnit, *The Faraway Nearby*, 'Apricots', Granta, 2014, p. 3.

20 Katherine Mansfield, *The Notebooks*, edited by Margaret Scott, Vol. II, p. 286.

21 Rebecca Solnit, *The Faraway Nearby*, 'Ice', Granta, 2014, pp. 52/53.

22 Janet Frame, *The Envoy from Mirror City*, The Women's Press, London, 1985, p. 166.

23 Richard Jefferies, *Nature Near London*, Chatto & Windus, London, 1883, p. 171.

24 www.themarginalian.org/2021/01/31/jeanette-winterson-reading-oranges-audible-introduction/ accessed 28/04/2024.

Printed in Great Britain
by Amazon